The West Bank of Greater New Orleans

The West Bank of

Greater New Orleans

A HISTORICAL GEOGRAPHY

Richard Campanella

Louisiana State University Press   Baton Rouge

Published with the support of a Carol Lavin Bernick Faculty Grant from Tulane University.

Published by Louisiana State University Press

Manufactured in the United States of America
First printing

Designer: Barbara Neely Bourgoyne
Typeface: Whitman
Printer and binder: Sheridan Books

Title page image: Spring storm over Algiers Point, 2018. Photo by Richard Campanella.

Library of Congress Cataloging-in-Publication Data
Names: Campanella, Richard, author.
Title: The West Bank of greater New Orleans : a historical geography / Richard Campanella.
Description: Baton Rouge : Louisiana State University Press, 2020. | "Published with the support
    of a Carol Lavin Bernick Faculty Grant from Tulane University"—T.p. verso.
Identifiers: LCCN 2019044180 (print) | LCCN 2019044181 (ebook) | ISBN 978-0-8071-7297-1
    (Cloth) | ISBN 978-0-8071-7366-4 (pdf) | ISBN 978-0-8071-7367-1 (epub)
Subjects: LCSH: West Bank (New Orleans, La.)—History. | New Orleans (La.)—Social conditions. |
    Neighborhoods—Louisiana—New Orleans.
Classification: LCC F379.N56 W473 2020 (print) | LCC F379.N56 (ebook) | DDC 976.3/35—dc23
LC record available at https://lccn.loc.gov/2019044180
LC ebook record available at https://lccn.loc.gov/2019044181

For Marina and Jason

and to the memory of

S. Stewart Farnet Sr. (1933–2018),
Harvey Canal Limited Partnership

New Orleans looks strange, very strange, from the opposite shore. . . . Its general aspect seemed wondrously changed[,] very different from what I had expected, and I may add totally different from the general view of any city I had ever seen or imagined.

—Thomas K. Wharton, upon visiting the West Bank, 1855

Contents

Part III: Landscape Suburbanization, 1950s to Present

Illustrations follow page 176.

Preface

French explorers called it the "left bank," because it was *gauche* as they ascended the Mississippi. Mariners later called it the "right bank," and still do—more properly the "right descending bank." New Orleanians in the 1800s also called it the "right bank," as Parisians do of the Seine, else "across the river," "over the river," or "opposite the city." Not until the 1900s did the vernacular converge on "West Side" and "West Bank," the latter finally prevailing. Federal highway signs fused the words into "Westbank" so as not to imply a cardinal direction—for, as New Orleanians love to point out, the West Bank lies *east* of downtown, beneath the rising sun.[1]

The West Bank has been a vital part of greater New Orleans since the city's inception. It has been the Kansas, the Birmingham, the Norfolk, Atlanta, Pullman, and Fort Worth of the metropolis—that is, its breadbasket, foundry, shipbuilder, railroad terminal, train manufacturer, and livestock hub. At one time it was the Gulf South's St. Louis, in that it had a diversified industrial sector as well as a riverine, mercantilist, and agricultural economy. It served as a jumping-off point to the western frontier, and a Cannery Row for the "great thalassic littoral" to the south.[2] The West Bank has also been the Queens and Oakland of New Orleans: an affordable if rather plain purlieu, proud but not pretentious, pleasant if not prominent, comfortable in its own skin—even if at times thin-skinned vis-à-vis the grandiloquence of its cross-river counterpart. A majority-black subregion of a majority-white metropolitan area, the West Bank is home to some of the most diverse demographics in the region, including many immigrants.[3] Yet it also has substantial populations of deep-rooted locals, folks who speak with New

Orleans accents, who practice old cultural traits with a minimum of pomp and self-awareness, and who, in some cases, retain family ownership of lands held since antebellum times. The West Bank makes up 30 percent of the metro population, and a commensurate amount of its urbanized footprint. It is, in short, integral to greater New Orleans in every way.

Yet the story of the West Bank has never been told holistically, on its own terms. Most books about New Orleans—and there are thousands—treat it as a sideshow or an afterthought, if at all. The limited literature on the West Bank has been at the community level, and published only locally. Various dissertations and government reports have been written on certain West Bank topics. But a full-length, in-depth book about the whole subregion? You'll find plenty about that *other* West Bank, in the eastern Mediterranean, but none about the one on the lower Mississippi.

This book positions the West Bank front and center, viewing it as a genuine subregion unto itself, with more holding it together as a social and economic space than dividing it by various jurisdictions. It understands West Bankers to have had agency in their own place-making, and challenges the notion that their story is subsidiary to a more important narrative across the river.

The West Bank of Greater New Orleans is not a traditional history of mayoral administrations and prominent political figures such as Martin Behrman and John Alario. Nor is it a cultural history, paying homage to beloved natives like Mel Ott and Frankie Ford, or notable restaurants such as Mosca's. (I am fascinated by the regularity with which East Bankers mention Mosca's whenever the West Bank comes up in conversation.) Rather, it is a historical geography—that is, a spatial explanation of how the West Bank's landscape formed: its terrain, environment, peoples, land use, jurisdictions, waterways, industries, infrastructure, systems, neighborhoods, and settlement patterns, past and present. It explores the players, power structures, and decisions behind those landscape transformations, and their contexts, contingencies, and consequences. *The West Bank of Greater New Orleans* explains how the map of this subregion came into shape, and how this *place* came to be.

I did not employ fixed boundaries of what was inside or outside my study area; as a geographer, I tend to resist such artificial lines. I instead used a core/periphery approach, in which the emphasis is on the Algiers-Gretna-Harvey-Marrero-Westwego core of the urbanized West Bank, but not to the exclusion of important places on the periphery, such as Belle Chasse, Avondale and Waggaman, the Nine Mile Point and English Turn promontories, Lafitte, and even Grand Isle. There are times when the regionality of the West Bank becomes one and the same with the Barataria Basin, or extends out to the German and Acadian coasts, even to Texas. If the evidence took me to the periphery, I went there—but never to the point of losing sight of the core.

To avoid anachronism, I originally intended to use language contemporary to the era—"Left Bank" in the early 1700s, "Right Bank" for the 1800s, "West Bank" for the 1900s, and so on. But it proved unwieldy, so I decided to use "West Bank" throughout, except in quoted material. Contrary to the style sheets of some local publishers, I capitalize both West Bank and East Bank as proper nouns, treating them as genuine subregions.

I came to this topic after nearly twenty-five years studying the geography of New Orleans, having authored ten books and over two hundred articles with mostly an East Bank focus. In June 2017 I received an out-of-the-blue email from Stewart Farnet, an architect, former board member of the Harvey Canal Limited Partnership, and descendant of the Destrehan and Harvey families, who asked if I might be interested in writing a history of his illustrious ancestors.

Meeting with Stewart and his son Clay in an uptown coffee shop, I explained that while I was probably not the right person to scribe a genealogy, I was well suited to write about place and the people who made it—in other words, a geography. Perhaps I could research the Destrehan land that became Gretna and the Harvey Canal? Or a history of the Gulf Intracoastal Waterway, which the Harvey Canal became? I soon came to realize that neither story could be told without also telling all the antecedent and adjacent stories—and so perhaps the book ought to be about the entire West Bank. Stewart agreed heartily.

I got to work in the summer of 2017, and over the next two years found myself chagrined at how much I did not know about the West Bank, thrilled at how much I was learning, and fascinated by how much I had to "unlearn" about East Bank trends and patterns because they simply did not apply to the West Bank. I came to understand that the area had its own set of drivers and conditions, which further evidenced to me that the West Bank represented a subregion unto itself. In completing this volume, I now realize how incomplete my knowledge of the metropolis had been previously, for there is no "greater New Orleans" without its cross-river component, and the whole metropolis is greater than the sum of its two banks.

Sadly, Stewart Farnet passed away at age 85 two weeks before I completed the first draft. It is to Stewart, as well as my wife Marina and our son Jason, that this book is dedicated.

I wish to thank the Harvey Canal Limited Partnership, including Clay Farnet, the late Stewart Farnet, and their family members and colleagues, for their interest in and support of this project. I am appreciative to Dean Iñaki Alday, Associate Dean Kentaro Tsubaki, and the Tulane School of Architecture, where I hold a faculty position and serve as associate dean for research. Appreciation also goes to Tulane's New Orleans Center for the Gulf South, where I am a Monroe Fellow, and to the Carol Lavin Bernick Faculty Grant Program of the Tulane Office of Academic Affairs, which provided key subvention funds for the graphical section of this book. I thank Editor-in-Chief Rand Dotson, Managing Editor Catherine L. Kadair, freelance copyeditor Gary Von Euer, and the staff of Louisiana State University Press for their continued support of my work.

I acknowledge the following institutions for access to data, archival documents, and source materials referenced in this volume (in alphabetical order): the Algiers Historical Society, Howard-Tilton Library at Tulane University, Jefferson Parish Assessor's Office, Jefferson Parish Historical Society, Jefferson Parish Library and Archives, Louisiana Collection and Special Collections of the Earl K. Long Library at the University of New Orleans, Louisiana Division of the New Orleans Public Library, Louisiana Endowment for the Humanities, Louisiana Research Collection–Tulane University, Louisiana State Land Office, Louisiana State Museum, New Orleans Advocate, New Orleans Notarial Archives, NOLA. com | The Times-Picayune and its predecessors, Orleans Parish Assessor's Office, Preservation Resource Center of New Orleans, Plaquemines Parish Library, The Historic New Orleans Collection and Williams Research Center, Tulane University Biodiversity Research Institute, Tulane University School of Architecture, Tulane University Southeastern Architectural Archive, US Army Corps of Engineers, US Census Bureau, US Library of Congress, and the Westwego Historical Society and Museum, as well as all cited sources.

Appreciation also goes to the many West Bankers and other New Orleanians who shared their perspectives and stories with me. I am indebted to historians such as the late Samuel Wilson Jr., Jefferson Parish experts Betsy Swanson and Sally K. Reeves, Lawrence N. Powell for his insights and papers, and to William D.

Reeves, whose studies of the Destrehan and Harvey clans were provided to me by family descendants. I am particularly grateful to Marco Rasi, a retired engineer and photographer extraordinaire who captured and generously donated drone images and other photos to help illustrate this book.

Deepest appreciation goes to my wife, Marina Campanella, for her love and support, and to our young son Jason Campanella, who enjoys the West Bank for, among other things, our crabbing trips to Lafitte.

I

LANDSCAPE FORMATION, PREHISTORIC TO 1860S

1

Sediment upon the Sea, People upon the Land

At around the time when the Pyramids arose by the Nile, at a locale one-third of a planet to the west and at the same latitude, the mouth of North America's greatest river, the Mississippi, lunged in an entirely new direction as it disembogued into the Gulf of Mexico.[1]

This channel jump (avulsion) would have tremendous implications for the region. But at the time, around four thousand years ago, it was not unusual. This river—"Balbancha" to the natives of its lower banks, "Meschacebe" to those upriver[2]—had been swelling for millennia, as warming temperatures melted ice sheets and sent a writhing flow southward to the sea. So great was its sediment load that the water appeared "exceedingly muddy and very white."[3] So great was the deposition that it filled an indentation in the Earth's crust known as the Mississippi Embayment, today's lower Mississippi Valley. So great was the accumulation at the mouth that mud flats prograded far into the sea, despite the level of the sea itself rising.

It was the accretion of those silty plains, in present-day south-central Louisiana, that nudged the Mississippi to shift courses. Impeded water seeks ways around its blockages, seizing whatever shorter steeper paths to the sea it can find. All it needs is a weak spot on the bank—and it found one downriver of present-day Natchez, Mississippi. Water escaped, and more followed, at first forming a distributary, then a fork, and then finally the main channel. The flow made its way around the terraces of present-day Baton Rouge and wended eastward along North America's southern bight.

Once again, alluvium spewed from the river's mouth. Sediment particles with ever-greater viscosity accumulated until they broke the sea surface, creating saline marsh, then freshwater swamp, and finally bona fide land, in the form of a natural levee (levée, "raised") with an "east" and a "west" bank. Gravity caused the river's channel to meander in yawning crescents, eroding on the convex side (cutbanks), accreting on its concave side (point bars), and at times splaying like fingers in an unclenching fist. Each distributary would form its own natural levee commensurate to its water volume and sediment load. So rose lower Louisiana from the sea.

One of those channel splits was prominent enough for French explorers to name it "the fork," today's Bayou Lafourche. Further downriver, two lesser forks flowed at today's Marrero and Gretna, building up the land starting around three thousand years ago. The first would become known as Bayou des Familles and Bayou Barataria; the other was too meager to earn a name, but nevertheless left behind a relict natural levee underlying today's Gretna.[4]

More avulsions would follow. In the past millennium, the river's main flow abandoned its eastward thrust for a southeastward path, forming the English Turn point bar and pushing a new deltaic lobe farther out into the sea. This would become the Mississippi's current channel, flowing through Plaquemines Parish and out a three-toed splay known as the "bird's foot delta."[5]

All this channel-shifting and land-building created a western bank comprising two long cutbanks and three point bars (promontories) set within five river meanders, among them some of the most acute river bends in the entire region.[6] One promontory, today's Algiers Point, would become both a blessing and a curse to future settlers, as powerful river currents would scour soils, cause cave-ins along the bank, and churn the water column. That force would bend the thalweg—that is, the trench at the bottom of the river, which here formed the deepest spot in the entire Mississippi River—and at times bring that 200-foot-deep "hole" dangerously close to Algiers.[7]

But that sharp meander would also redirect the momentum of the water over to the East Bank after it passed Algiers Point, giving lower Algiers more of a placid and shallow riverfront with a batture (probably from battre, meaning to beat against, as by the current) during low water. The channel geography of the Mississippi thus gave this part of the West Bank a deepwater harbor on one flank—useful for ships, but also erosive—and a shallow riverfront on the other, not particularly good for vessels, but convenient for industry and protected from scouring.

To the south of this dynamic ribbon of water lay the main West Bank landmass, if it could be called that: a low, swampy basin of soft, wet alluvium intersected by two distributary ridges, its entire elevational range spanning at most 15 or so feet, with the lowest spots barely above sea level. Dark, fertile, and loamy were the West Bank's soils, without a single pebble or stone. Instead, only sand, silt, and clay particles survived the long riverine journey. In general, sand and silt particles settled in the largest quantities soonest, closest to the overtopping river, on account of their heavier weight. They formed the higher-elevation natural levees that, because of their coarser texture, contained more air cavities. These allowed water to filtrate through, and enabled organic matter to decompose and integrate into the soil body. What resulted were rich, loamy fertile soils—ideal, as it would turn out, for plantation agriculture. This was true on both sides of the Mississippi, but because the West Bank had more cutbank conditions than point bars, making it vulnerable to fast-moving erosive currents, its natural levees tended to be substantially narrower than those on the East Bank.

Warm and wet was the West Bank's climate, being only six and a half degrees north of the Tropic of Cancer, more prone to humid maritime tropical air masses than dry continental fronts. Just as Lake Pontchartrain took the edge off cold fronts as the air moved southeastwardly across New Orleans, making both the East and West [right] banks balmier than the North Shore, the Mississippi River seemed to have had a similar effect, at least historically. "It is generally admitted that in lower Louisiana the right [West] bank of the river is warmer than the left," reported a French prefect in 1803, "and that the winds coming from the northwest become balmier as they pass over the Mississippi."[8]

With up to 300 days between freezes and fully 63 inches of annual rainfall, vegetation here grew thick and verdant, arranged in contour-like patterns according to topographic elevation. Along the sandy shoals by the river grew dense canebrake and willows—"reeds, brambles, and extremely tall grass" strewn with "an abundance of driftwood," in the words of one early French explorer.[9] Upon the crest and backslope of the natural levee flourished broadleaf hardwood forests dominated by live oak, hickory, sweetgum, and pecan, their branches strewn with mossy epiphytes and thorny briars. As the ground tapered down and the soil texture grew finer, water content and organic matter increased, as did palmettos and tupelo. Finally the water became generally impounded in the form of swamps (forested wetlands), and vast stands of bald cypress prevailed—valuable timber to build structures and vessels, as it turned out.[10]

All around were bayous interconnected with "lakes" (bays, or tidal lagoons) of varying salinities, which were surrounded by marshes (grassy wetlands, or *prairie tremblante*), all of which widened into estuarine bays and finally opened to the Gulf of Mexico. This was the Barataria Basin, the great watershed of which the future West Bank would form the upper edge, defined by the Mississippi River and its natural levee to the north and east, and the distributary of Bayou Lafourche to the west. Throughout the basin, resources from the sea flowed inland with the daily tidal cycle and the occasional storm, while resources from the Mississippi River and Bayou Lafourche flowed outward via distributaries and occasional over-bank flooding.

There were exceptions to the general rule of sand, silt, and clay settling out in the sequence of bank, backslope, backswamp, and marsh. During times when the Mississippi ejected particularly high and powerful waters, it would jettison heavy sand particles to the farthest perimeter of the deltaic lobe, creating barrier islands with white sand dunes along the Gulf of Mexico. A series of such islands formed at the Gulf of Mexico's interface of the Barataria Basin, each nudged westward with longshore currents and marked by ridgetop oak groves (*chênière*). They would be called Chênière Caminada, Grand Isle, and Grande Terre Island, and all three would play the role of backdoor entrepôts, as well as trading partners and recreational destinations, for the future West Bank.[11]

The ebb and flow of water—salty from the sea, fresh from the river—sent a web of rivulets across the West Bank. The largest was the abandoned distributary called Bayou des Familles; others included Bayou Verret, Bayou Segnette, and Bayou Villars, which wended through swamp basins and into lagoons like Lake Cataouatche and Lake Salvador. There were also other, more anomalous features, among them salt domes (buried salt deposits that evaporate water and form low-density extrusive columns) and relict shoals (swept westward by longshore currents and buried by later deposits), mud lumps, and barrier islands. In all, the West Bank and Barataria delta-scape formed a flat, silty, fluid, and protean environment, rigorous and youthful, amassed at the edge of the North American lithosphere, beneath a subtropical sun.

≋≋≋

In 1844, two scientists involved with excavations for a coal-gas tank made an interesting discovery, roughly where the Superdome now stands. "At first, they encountered soil and soft river mud," read an 1853 account. "Then [came] harder laminated blue alluvion; then deep black mould [*sic*], resting on wet bluish quicksand," along with two thin layers of "burnt-wood." Throughout each stratum were the "stumps of no less than four successive growths of trees, apparently cypress," some with diameters of six to twelve feet. Then, digging to "the depth of sixteen feet, the skeleton of a man was found. The cranium lay between the roots of a tree, and was in a tolerable preservation. . . . A small *os ilium* [hip bone part] indicated the male sex. A low and narrow forehead, moderate facial angle, and prominent, widely separated cheek-bones, seemed to prove it of the same race with our present Indians." The scientists learned of similar findings elsewhere, including along the Lake Pontchartrain shore in 1828, when "thirty feet below the surface, fragments of Indian pottery were brought up, and part of a deer's horn, recent shells, and bones of land animals, were occasionally raised."[12]

Setting aside the particulars of these findings, and recognizing that artifacts often sink into muck outside their geological context, the reports make clear that, even in its earliest formative years, the Mississippi Delta was habitat for humanity. Geographical accessibility and ecological productivity attracted people here, and they would develop societies and cultures attuned to both geography and ecology. Whereas indigenous societies would form hunting-gathering economies in Louisiana's piney woods and hill country, those along rivers would establish maize-based agricultural settlements, and those near the coast would dwell upon inter-basin ridges or relict beaches. "In some respects the coastal marshes are hostile to man," wrote geographer Fred B. Kniffen, but for the fact that they "offered . . . vast food supplies," including "freshwater mussels (*unio*), brackish water clams (*rangia*), and saltwater species including oysters (*ostrea*)."[13] Shells from these mollusks could be rendered into arrow heads and other implements, as a critical substitute for stone, of which there is none on the delta. And when discarded in great heaps, called middens, shells shored up local topography and created dry living space. "The shellfish is so abundant," wrote a colonial observer in 1803, "that the different tribes that inhabit these lakes make it their principal diet [and] pile them up [around] their villages, [creating] pyramidal forms that still grow. . . . They were not formed in a single period. We ought then to infer that the tribes which piled them up were innumerable."[14] Two of the largest

7

middens were Little Temple and Big (Grand) Temple, which rose dozens of feet above the western shore of Lake Salvador and would serve as an island refuge for natives, colonials, and freebooters. The coastal marshes also produced abundant finfish, crabs and shrimp, reptiles like turtles and alligators, fur-bearing mammals, and waterfowl.

By the time the deltaic plain took its current shape over the last millennium, the present-day urbanized West Bank would form something of a nexus between two indigenous economies, one of farming societies along the river, the other of coastal peoples toward the sea. More generally, southeastern Louisiana would become home to two major indigenous linguistic groups: Muskogean (Choctaw) languages having been spoken along the lower Mississippi and northward into the present-day state of Mississippi, and Chitimachan from Bayou Lafourche westward. In all, up to eight tongues were spoken in the region, so many that the Choctaw dubbed the future New Orleans area "Bulbancha," which has been translated as "land of many languages"—diverse from the start. Natives used a pidgin known as Mobilian Jargon to communicate across tribal lines.[15]

How many were these peoples, and how did they live? "There is substantial evidence," wrote geographer William M. Denevan, that "the Native American landscape of the early sixteenth century was a humanized landscape almost everywhere. Populations were large[;] forest composition had been modified, grasslands had been created, wildlife disrupted, and erosion was severe in places."[16] Native peoples in Louisiana, like elsewhere, manipulated their environment to the extent of their technology, clearing forests, burning fields, shoring up land, diverting water, and trading far and wide. The West Bank around the year 1500 constituted a patchwork of cornfields and semipermanent villages along the river and its distributaries, and transient encampments in the marsh, with hunters and traders moving about on ridge-top footpaths or paddling in dugout pirogues.

Much of what we believe we know of prehistoric peoples in this region comes through the agents of their demise. Probably the first Europeans in the vicinity were the Spanish explorer Alonso Álvarez de Pineda and his men, who sailed the Gulf Coast in 1519 and reported a "very large and very deep" river, at the mouth of which was "an extensive town," where "natives treated our men in a friendly manner."[17] Nine years later, Pánfilo de Narváez's voyage struggled around the mouth of the Mississippi and past Barataria Bay, eventually getting stranded along the Texas Bend. Surviving crew members under Álvar Núñez

Cabéza de Vaca then set off on an epic trek that, incredibly, landed them at a Spanish outpost near the Pacific Coast in 1536.[18] Accounts of Cabéza de Vaca's remarkable journey inspired one Hernando De Soto, previously a soldier under Francisco Pizarro, to seek riches in those lands. In 1539 De Soto arrived with six hundred men at present-day Tampa, Florida, and proceeded to explore four thousand circuitous miles throughout the interior. The expedition, which was to lose nearly half its men plus its leader over the next four years, would involve the West Bank in two ways. For one, survivors under the command of Luis de Moscoso, under constant Indian attack, made their way down the Mississippi and past the West Bank in July 1543—the first Europeans to do so (unless, as some evidence suggests, they went down the Atchafalaya).[19] Secondly, and more significantly, De Soto's men would unwittingly serve as epidemiological vectors in the spreading of Old World diseases, helping trigger a massive demographic die-off over the next century, including on the West Bank.

Thus, by the late 1600s, when the next wave of Europeans arrived at the delta, they would record indigenous populations massively reduced from generations earlier and continuing to decline. Pierre Le Moyne, sieur d'Iberville, visiting a seemingly robust Indian encampment near present-day White Castle in 1699, reported that "the smallpox . . . had killed one-fourth of the people," and recoiled at the stench of decaying corpses on ceremonial platforms.[20] His younger brother Jean-Baptiste Le Moyne, sieur de Bienville, later described Louisiana as "formerly the most densely populated with Indians but at present [1725] of these prodigious quantities of different nations one sees pitiful remnants," attributing the decline to war and disease.[21] French colonist Chevalier Guy de Soniat du Fossat, writing in 1791 of Louisiana in the 1750s, lamented that Indian "villages and . . . population have decreased about two-thirds in number since the advent of the Europeans, who introduced and brought among them diseases, desires, dissensions and all other abuses of civilization."[22] Fewer Indians meant fewer encampments, fewer clearings, fewer croplands, less hunting pressure, less use of natural resources, and more resources for other species. "[T]he Indian landscape of 1492," recapitulated Denevan, "had largely vanished by the mid-eighteenth century, [and] the landscape of 1750 was more 'pristine' (less humanized) than that of 1492."[23]

Yet even when we read colonial descriptions with this in mind, a picture emerges not of a wilderness but of a populated, altered landscape. A member of the La Salle expedition described in 1682 "fine corn fields and . . . beautiful prairies" along the river in Natchez Indian territory.[24] Iberville, who would later found the Louisiana colony, spotted in 1699 "several fires ashore" along the coast and deemed them to be "prairies which the Indians burn . . . for the buffalo hunt," whereby a grassy strip would be left green to lure the grazing beasts into an ambush.[25]

After penetrating the mouth of the Mississippi, Iberville first approached the present-day West Bank (to him the "left" bank) on March 6, 1699, and over the next three days recorded the first detailed descriptions of its place and people. "The woods and meadows," he wrote of the natural levees, "rise and fall from eight to ten inches in elevation," with "dense foliage [and] vines" in the forests and banks "so densely lined with cane, [up to] six inches in circumference, that it is impossible to walk along the riverside." In the thicket, crew members spotted three alligators, "one of which was a monster," and killed a bison, possibly with an onboard swivel gun, giving the men much-needed protein that evening.[26] With hardly any landmarks in sight, Iberville recorded his progress from a riverine perspective, planting bankside crosses and marking trees as they ascended. He described the future New Orleans area as forming "two or three oxbows [over] two leagues distance"—a reasonably accurate description of three crescents over six miles, the first of which would one day become Algiers.

It was in this vicinity that Iberville spotted six reed canoes "filled with Indians" who landed and fled—except for one, who summoned the rest to come forth after Iberville "saluted [them] in the customary manner." They were members of the Annochy tribe, whom Iberville had first met near Biloxi, and they were allied with Bayougoula farther upriver on the West Bank. Before setting out to find that tribe, Iberville observed "ten huts covered with palmetto fronds [within] a small redoubt," built by the Annochy in response to recent attacks from the Chickasaw region. "Its walls are as tall as a man," Iberville wrote of the ramparts, "and are made of canes in the form of an oval, twenty-five paces wide and fifty-five long." The tiny fortified enclave, probably across from Algiers, gives a general idea of what the native-built environment looked like throughout the delta.

Farther upriver near today's White Castle, Iberville finally found that Bayougoula Indian encampment. He described it as "107 huts and 2 temples, [with] possibly about 200 to 250 men and few women and children,"[27] who tended "cocks and hens," likely introduced by Spaniards. Another crewmember observed "fields where [Indians] cultivate their millet, [which] they break up . . . with buffalo bones."[28] Above Baton Rouge, Iberville visited an Indian village, probably Choctaw-speaking Houma, consisting of 140 huts "on the slope of a hill [covered with] corn fields," with up to 350 warriors among their population.[29] Back downriver were the Mugulasha, who, after various skirmishes, got absorbed into other groups, such that there are various accounts of the Quinapisa-Mugulasha and of the Mugulasha-Bayougoula. There were also the Tangipahoa, a Choctaw word meaning "corn people," and the Acolapissa, both of which lived in the piney woods by the Pearl River but later united and moved to the New Orleans area.[30]

More predominant on the West Bank were speakers of dialects of the Chitimachan language. They are estimated to have numbered around four thousand prior to the French arrival, and lived in three tribes across a dozen or so villages in the Bayou Lafourche-Bayou Teche region. Their neighbors to the east were the Washa tribe, who spoke the Choctaw dialect of the Muskogean language family and hunted in the Lake Salvador region and the coastal marshes to the south, though they also farmed in the present-day Thibodaux area. In his memoir of 1725, New Orleans founder Bienville wrote that ten years earlier he had ordered the Oachas [Washa] to settle across from New Orleans and two leagues upriver (five or six river miles, by Westwego or Bridge City), and described them as allies of the linguistically and culturally similar Chaouachas [Chawasha]: "nomadic," he called them, "wandering here and there in the woods and along the lakes, without law and . . . so-called chiefs," their numbers down to only fifty or so men "fit to bear arms"—clearly a people in demise.[31] Along with the Houma and the Bayougoula farther upstream, the Washa, the culturally similar Chawasha, and the Chimitacha comprised much of the indigenous population of the present-day urbanized West Bank, the remainder being Annochy, Quinapisa, Tangipahoa, and Acolapissa. Trading routes would bring them in economic and cultural interactions with the Atakapan and Opelousas groups to the west, the Tunica upriver, and the Biloxi to the east.[32] Delta natives were highly transitory and ever-shifting in their intertribal relations, at times befriending and collaborating, or raiding and warring, while all along farming, hunting, gathering, settling, and resettling. Louisiana was no pristine wilderness, no forest primeval, no prelapsarian utopia, and neither was the West Bank. This was a human society, and it had humanized the delta landscape.

At first, French colonials viewed indigenous societies opportunistically, as *petites nations* who had valuable local knowledge, could serve as allies against common enemies, and would supply them with vital foodstuffs and supplies.[33]

Population size also favored the natives: into the 1720s, according to historian Kathleen DuVal, "Louisiana Indians numbered well over 35,000," compared to "some 2,500 French, plus 1,500 slaves."[34] This deferential relationship soon shifted to one bent on subjugation and enslavement, for want of labor ("I dare to flatter myself," wrote one French colonial in 1699, "that the savages will do blindly everything we want"[35]), else one of displacement and eradication, for want of land. Colonialism endeavored to extract raw materials and grow crops for export to the metropole for profit and power, a project that would require commitment, expertise, capital, equipment, labor, and above all, land: controlled, cleared, productive land. The replacement of native occupants with colonials bearing land titles would, quite literally, lay the groundwork for wealth production.

2

The Colonial Imperative

How exactly to manage this land? One option was a form of feudalism, in which noblemen were granted estates in exchange for service and taxes to the monarch, and serfs bound to the estates would produce crops in exchange for the noblemen's support and protection. France had held on to feudalism longer than other European kingdoms, and saw an opportunity for the fading system to be "transplanted," according to historian Edward Coleman writing in 1927, "to the virgin soil of Canada, where perhaps, it might regain the vigor of its youth."[1]

Toward this end, French authorities along the St. Lawrence granted land parcels (seigniories) to favored colonists (seigniors, or lords), who in turn assigned plots to *censitaires* (tenants). Both seigniors and censitaires were obliged to live upon and develop the land; the seignior would enjoy his status and possibly enrich himself in exchange for his service and revenue sent to the crown, while the censitaires would garner sustenance and security in exchange for their labor.

Such a system faltered in French Canada for a number of reasons, chief among them the abundance of land, which gave tenants little reason to stay put and endure their overbearing lords. That was also the case in the Illinois territory, where French colonials had attempted to establish medieval-like central villages surrounded by a commons and long-lot ploughlands.[2] The Louisiana colony, meanwhile, was even less suited to revived feudalism, given its distant governing authority, scarcity of settlers, abundant riparian land, and subtropical environs unsuited for grain crops.

These conditions would eventually lead Louisiana administrators to largely discard the idea of tenant labor in favor of an enslaved workforce raising export commodities. What survived from the feudal model, however, was the concept of conceding land, fee simple, to nobles: empowered colonials known as *concessionaires* who would have permanent and absolute control over the land. Demarcation and distribution of the terrain started out in a rather ad hoc manner: concessions in the early 1700s were erratically distributed, inconsistently sized, frequently not surveyed, and oftentimes not formally titled. They were, however, consistently oriented perpendicularly to the Mississippi River or other waterways, extending backward toward the *ciprières* (cypress swamps) in a proportion that was deeper than it was wide.[3]

The desultory nature of the early concession "system" displeased the Crown. Authorities learned some concessionaires had been using their huge grants not for agriculture but for timber and real estate sales, "entirely contrary to the establishment of the colony."[4] The Crown responded with the Edict of October 12, 1716, which called for the return of certain lands for distribution to inhabitants "in the proportion of two to four arpents front by forty to sixty in depth."[5] While the edict's redistribution clause was only partially enforced, its stipulation "that the concessions [have] the same pattern of long, narrow fields that prevailed [along] the St. Lawrence River [and] Cape Breton Island," according to historian Marcel Giraud, "would henceforth be the rule for all lands in the colony."[6]

Thus formally began the French long-lot system in Louisiana, whereby narrow parcels would be surveyed perpendicularly to the river or bayou, imparting transportation and irrigation access along with a slice of the fertile, slender natural levee. This cadastral system, measured by the unit *arpent* (the equivalent of 192 English feet, and used for both linear and area measurement) and laid out by an *arpenteur* (surveyor), would undergird the future urban morphology of the West Bank. It's not just the modern streets and infrastructure that conform to the old surveying pattern; the colonial system is also embedded into our present-day legalese. The official American Public Lands Survey (PLS), invoked in countless real estate transactions as townships, ranges, and sections, usually uses a neat checkerboard of 36 squares to demarcation its sections. But for greater New Orleans, the PLS uses the flailing lines of the old French long lots in lieu of orthogonal sections, and their shapes are far better preserved on the West Bank than on the East Bank.

~~~

Around the time of the 1716 edict, circumstances would change radically for Louisiana. King Louis XIV had died the year before, leaving the throne to five-year-old Louis XV, for whom Prince Philippe II, the Duke of Orleans, would act as the Regent of France. Philippe inherited a kingdom deeply in debt, the result of years of borrowing gold to fund costly wars and lavish palaces. Desperate for fiscal salvation, Prince Philippe lay prone to solutions that were more provocative than prudent.

Enter a Scottish financier by the name of John Law, a recklessly brilliant sophisticate with a forte in macroeconomics and a foible for gambling. Law had been hobnobbing his way across European palaces, peddling various investment schemes to royals, and arrived at Paris to bend the ear of Philippe. He posited to the prince that paper currency could be issued to represent deposits of real wealth—that is, gold, which was all too scarce—and circulate in the economy with greater rigor. Intrigued, Philippe in 1716 permitted Law to establish the Banque Générale in Paris. Law's policies seemed to work, though largely because the paper bills were overprinted.

The apparent success delighted Philippe and emboldened Law to seek another lucrative testbed for his theories. What caught his attention was an exotic-sounding but floundering possession known as "Louisiana" or "Mississippi." An investor named Antoine Crozat had since 1712 held a charter to develop that mysterious land, until sheer frustration drove him to relinquish it. Law's confidence in his own genius—or chicanery—led him to see boundless riches where Crozat met with failure. And riches were exactly what Philippe needed: he couldn't borrow any more gold, nor could he issue promissory notes, and he hesitated to print any more unbacked paper money.

Law's audacious proposal was to issue paper money and back it not with real wealth (gold), but with the promise of commercial wealth, in the form of a company that would extract treasure from a vast wilderness. A debonair city slicker if ever there was one, Law knew nothing of establishing plantations and mines in the American subtropics, yet that is exactly the mercantilist model he envisaged for Louisiana: to grow tobacco and other export commodities, as well as extract valuable metals and raw materials, for shipment to France in exchange for the mother country's support. The colony's financing would come from the sale of stock; its peopling would come from recruited or forced emigration of at least six thousand settlers; and its labor would come from three thousand enslaved people from West Africa. The ensuing profits would enrich all share-holders, including Law and Philippe, while equity in the company would help pay off the national debt.

Better yet, Louisiana-grown tobacco would wean French smokers off Chesapeake leaves, which only sent money to the hated English, while thousands of French subjects along the lower Mississippi would help defend Louisiana from both the English and the Spanish. "The beguiling inclusiveness of Law's plan," wrote historian Lawrence N. Powell, ". . . its promise to retire the national debt, revive the French domestic and overseas economy, and establish an autarkic source of tobacco—is what drew [Philippe] to Law's theories."

On September 6, 1717, shortly after Antoine Crozat formally relinquished Louisiana, John Law's enterprise, the Company of the West, received a twenty-five-year monopoly charter to develop the colony as a private enterprise. A sophisticated continent-wide marketing campaign, featuring fliers depicting Eden-like mountains and friendly natives, ensued to recruit investors and settlers. Stock sold so well that buyers rioted in the streets of European cities, prices rose, more shares were issued, investors gobbled them up, and the "Mississippi Bubble" inflated.

Such a scheme could only be as good as the wealth eventually produced by the colony, and such a colony, so remote and wild, would only be as good as its headquarters. To that end, a clerk on September 9, 1717, scribed into the company's register, "Resolved to establish, thirty leagues up the river, a burg which should be called La Nouvelle Orléans, where landing would be possible from either the river or Lake Pontchartrain."[7] The directive arrived in Bienville's hands by year's end, at which point he assembled men and materials for an expedition to a particular site he had been eyeing since 1699 with his older brother Iberville, now deceased. Sometime between mid-March and mid-April 1718, Bienville's expedition landed at what is now upper Decatur Street in the French Quarter and began clearing cane and trees.

Why the name "Nouvelle Orléans?" To flatter the project's royal sponsor Philippe, the Duke of Orleans, a suggestion that seems to have originated from Bienville himself.[8] Why the specified location? "Thirty leagues up the river" translated to roughly the ninety-five-mile mark from the mouth. "Where landing would be possible from either the river or Lake Pontchartrain" iterated the importance of alternative access, and pointed to the sluggish rivulet which Colapissa natives called Bayou Choupic and the colonials would name Bayou St.

John.[9] Together with a two-mile-long, slightly elevated path (today's Bayou Road and Esplanade Ridge), Bayou St. John would form a convenient portage to the banks of the Mississippi, thus circumventing nearly one hundred miles of difficult river travel.

It behooves this study to contemplate whether New Orleans, as company headquarters or colony capital, could have been located on the West Bank. The answer is no, in both concept and actuality. As vital as the Mississippi was, authorities on both sides of the Atlantic recognized that the treacherous shoals and sand bars around the river's mouth, not to mention inopportune calming of the winds needed to sail against the current, could stifle a bankside city unless it had alternative access to the sea. The East Bank had at least three such "back doors": the aforementioned Bayou St. John; Bayou Trepagnier about twenty miles to the west, which could gain access to the river at present-day Norco; and Bayou Manchac, which wended west through Lakes Pontchartrain and Maurepas and could get coastwise feluccas nearly to Baton Rouge without using the Mississippi. The West Bank also offered backdoor access: one could navigate up Bayou Barataria and Bayou des Familles into the present-day Marrero area, or take Bayou des Allemands to today's Edgard or Vacherie.

But sailing into the West Bank meant a two-hundred-mile journey from the colony's existing establishments at Mobile and Biloxi or Ship Island, and the critical leg into the Barataria Bay would have meant a northward tack unaided by the predominantly westward longshore currents. Getting into Lake Pontchartrain, on the other hand, was far shorter, faster and easier. Bayou St. John also ranked as the shortest and most consistently navigable of the key backswamp bayous; the others required high-water conditions on the Mississippi.

Thus, if the river's mouth was impeded, it was more expedient to circumvent the problem by getting to the East Bank, and for this reason, no serious proposals ever arose to situate New Orleans on the West Bank. There *were*, however, suggestions to locate the company headquarters, or relocate New Orleans wholesale, with or without its name and capital-city status, as far east as Mobile and Biloxi and as far west as Manchac, Natchez, and Natchitoches. Not all suggested sites were on the Mississippi River, but those that were all sat on its East Bank.[10] Circumstances of geography, in the face of the colonial imperative, thus fated the West Bank to play an ancillary role to bigger investments across the river, and echoes of that asymmetrical relationship may still be heard in cross-river relations today.

～～～

Critical to the Company of the West's undertaking was its ability to distribute land, and Bienville took it upon himself to get the process started. With the concurrence of colonial *ordonnateur* Marc Antoine Hubert, Bienville on March 27, 1719, granted himself most of the New Orleans crescent on the East Bank, up to today's Carrollton, plus land on the West Bank encompassing the present-day neighborhoods of Algiers, Behrman, and Aurora.[11] It was the first major official transfer of New Orleans–area land from the collective indigenous domain to private European ownership. But because its sheer size flew against the spirit of the Edict of 1716, Bienville's self-grant ended up triggering a second edict in November 1719 that forbade colonial governors from becoming major concessionaires, allowing them instead smaller parcels for raising vegetables. Bienville reluctantly complied by subdividing some of his holdings and renting them out as "habitations." But the issue would be a flashpoint between Bienville and his bosses for the next twenty years, the former determined to lord over what he felt was his rightful domain, the latter wanting a broader distribution of a larger number of smaller parcels.

Bienville's boss, John Law, also wanted a stick in the Louisiana mud—three, in fact—and pressed his own Company of the West to grant him personal title to land in the Arkansas country, at English Turn near New Orleans, and in Biloxi. Around the same time, Law had gleaned an idea to send German and Swiss *engagés* to Louisiana, which the French Crown disliked for fear of foreigners in its colony. But Law, himself a Protestant foreigner, pressed the idea, needing all the workforce he could get, and aimed to settle the reputedly industrious Germans on his own Arkansas concession. Recruiters advertised in places like Leipzig, and throughout 1720, vessels departed Lorient for Louisiana with hundreds of Germanic people among thousands of Gauls.[12]

These were heady times for the Company of the West, as rumors circulated among shareholders of insufficient capital, grueling travel, and forbidding conditions. Extracting wealth from the swamps, it became clear, would take far more toil than John Law had anticipated, and migrants were proving hard to recruit. Some investors quietly divested, then others, then more—until late 1720, when hundreds rushed to dump their shares. The Mississippi Bubble burst, and riots raged in European cities, this time for the opposite reason than three years earlier. Worse, hundreds of settlers and slaves en route to Louisiana ended up stranded in Biloxi, all but abandoned on account of the chaos in Paris. Many perished, including Germans, and Bienville was "held to blame for the debacle."[13] One desperate cohort from the Alsatian-Rhine Valley region made it up to Law's Arkansas concession, only to suffer equal hardships in that remote wilderness; they returned downriver to try again at Law's English Turn parcel.

News of Law's downfall reached New Orleans in May of 1721, by which time the Company of the West was undergoing a frantic restructuring in Paris. The three concessions granted to the now-disgraced Law transferred to company ownership, putting the surviving German settlers in limbo, since their contract had been with Law personally. They planned to return home, but Bienville, determined to retain a workforce, convinced them to stay by granting them Company land "on the right bank of the Mississippi between . . . Bustard Bend and the Lac des Ouaches," meaning between today's Edgard and Hahnville near Lac des Allemands.[14] By some accounts, this amounted to marginalization, as the French founders considered this area to be useless swampland, and reserved the New Orleans side of the river for their own. In the summer of 1721 settlement began of what would become known as the Côte des Allemands. As the first substantial permanent European community on the west side of the lower Mississippi, "habitants of the German . . . village of Hoffen . . . ten leagues above New Orleans" would play a major role in the demography and development of the future West Bank, as well as a breadbasket feeding the larger colony.[15]

After a two-year period during which the Crown took over colony supervision from the scandal-plagued Company of the West, putting an end to the "old régie," the enterprise reemerged as the Company of the Indies (the "new régie") and resumed its hobbled Louisiana project.[16] It was during this pro-tempore phase that Bienville got some good news for his New Orleans project. On December 23, 1721, his superiors decided to designate Bienville's selected site, today's French Quarter, as colonial capital. "His Royal Highness having thought it advisable to make the principal establishment of the colony at New Orleans on the Mississippi River," he beamed, "we have accordingly transported here all the goods that were at Biloxi," the previous capital. "It appears to me that a better decision could not have been made, in view of the good quality of the soil along the river [and the] considerable advantage for . . . the unloading of the vessels."[17] The status upgrade would give momentum to nascent New Orleans, which in turn would affect the point bar across the river, future Algiers, known at the time as Pointe St. Antoine and later as Pointe Marigny.[18]

Yet the matter of his sprawling self-concession kept Bienville at odds with the new *régie*. One challenge came from a forthright subordinate named Adrien de Pauger, the colony's assistant engineer, best known today as the surveyor of French Quarter streets. Pauger petitioned the Superior Council that in fact *he* and not Bienville had laid claim to "nine or ten arpents" in what is now Algiers Point, and had paid dearly to have it cleared. Pauger was further irritated to learn that Bienville conspired to evict him and cede the parcel to the Company of the Indies, a move that would simultaneously put Bienville in the good graces of his superiors while rebuking his subordinate's insolence.

Rather unsurprisingly, on February 9, 1724, the Superior Council ruled that "Mr. de Pauger be declared in non-possession" of the land and Bienville's claim "be maintained."[19] Thus, Pauger, despite having overseen some of the earliest colonial-era land-clearing and construction on today's West Bank, ignominiously returned to his duties at New Orleans, while his former claim fell into the control of the Company of the Indies.[20] Bienville, meanwhile, retained control of his lower-coast claims, while Barbizan de Pailloux gained control of land upriver toward today's Gretna, and Monseigneur Le Blanc began developing his *Petit Desert* plantation (1720) in present-day Westwego with settlers from L'Orient.[21] Through concessions like these the transformation of the West Bank began, from a dense forest into a permanently settled landscape devoted to the extraction of natural resources and the raising of crops. As for Pauger, the engineer died in June 1726 of "the fever and dysentery," never fully compensated for his land loss, and lies today beneath St. Louis Cathedral—on the East Bank.[22]

Starting in 1719, the Company used its West Bank land at present-day Algiers Point as a multipurpose depot, workshop, lumber mill, and farm in service of the larger colony and the principal settlement across the river. Known as the Company Plantation, the holding served primarily as a depository for Africans recently arrived in chains. During the 1720s, over thirty cabins were built to shelter the enslaved, either temporarily until they were sold, or permanently if owned by the Company itself (as were 154 people at one point, making present-day Algiers Point "the largest single group of enslaved men, women, and children living in Louisiana").[23]

Arrival at the Company Plantation marked the last and most grueling leg of a months-long journey that typically began at the French ports of Saint-Malo or L'Orient, proceeded to West Africa to trade for captives, and sailed westward for two months—the infamous Middle Passage—to the mouth of the Mississippi.

At the transshipment outpost known as Balize, crew and captives switched to feluccas or other shallow-draft vessels to avoid the shoals and sandbars around the embouchure. In the case of the slave ship *Vénus,* as documented by Company clerk Marc-Antoine Caillot and interpreted by historian Erin Greenwald, the initial group of 450 numbered only 320 by the time the vessel docked at Balize—at which point the suffering only intensified. Caillot, deputized to guide a pirogue full of sickly captives on the ninety-five-mile journey up to the Company Plantation, wrote that within hours "four Negroes died of scurvy, which ordinarily strikes most of them when they . . . go on land." Two more would perish en route, while survivors suffered "so many [gnats and mosquitoes] that we smashed them on our faces by the fistful."[24] Under these wretched conditions, over six thousand Africans would be forcibly shipped to Louisiana under French dominion, of whom over two-thirds came from the Senegambia ports of Saint-Louis and Gorée Island where the Company had trading arrangements. Another 27 percent came from Ouidah along the Bight of Benin fifteen hundred miles to the east, and the remaining 5 percent came twelve hundred miles farther south, from Cabinda in the Congo region.[25] The victims represented over fifteen different ethnic groups, spoke various languages, and practiced cultures shaped by environments ranging from savannah to rainforest. Those who survived would eventually be "sold to the Inhabitants at the price of six hundred sixty livres, *pièce d'Inde,*" payable in three installments of rice or tobacco, the latter being the key cash crop driving John Law's Louisiana dream.[26] For those shackled in the depot of the Company Plantation, Louisiana would be a nightmare for generations to come, and it all began on the Algiers riverfront.

By 1726, the Company Plantation comprised sixty arpents of croplands worked by twenty-five slaves, plus a menagerie of livestock imported and sold quite like the human chattel. That same year, Governor Étienne de Périer, who had recently replaced Bienville as colony commander, contracted three Englishmen from Carolina for their expertise in tobacco cultivation, one of whom would be stationed at the Company Plantation, likely the West Bank's first Anglophone. The tobacco project called for more slave importations, and the Company Plantation grew, so much so that Périer recruited Natchez colonist Le Page du Pratz, best known today for his *History of Louisiana* (1758), to manage the operation.

With the West Bank on the rise, Governor Périer, like his predecessor, wanted in on the real estate action. He got the Company of the Indies to grant him ten arpents immediately upriver from the Company land, and supplemented it by acquiring ten adjacent arpents from Barbizan de Pailloux. In this piecemeal manner, control of West Bank lands would steadily shift into the hands of planter aristocracy overseeing slave-wrought wealth-production.[27] By 1727 there were 111 separately owned land parcels on the West Bank up to the German Coast, on which lived 297 members of white master families, 29 white servants, 460 black slaves, and 5 Indian slaves. Over half of this total population, and three-quarters of the enslaved portion, lived within the footprint of today's urbanized West Bank.[28]

The Company Plantation in 1731 spanned over 18 arpents along the riverfront with up to 26 arpents of depth. The entire operation covered 250 arpents in today's Algiers/Gretna area, of which 60 percent was cleared for rice, tobacco, and indigo. Total value: four thousand *livres,* or the equivalent of six able-bodied bondsmen—a remarkable metric on the abundance of land versus the scarcity and criticality of labor. The Company buildings and other materials, valued at 50,255 *livres,* included a rice plant, brick works and forge, numerous slave cabins and hospital, and dwellings for the manager and employees. Rice, though not profitable as an export commodity, was an important local food crop, and the rice mill and warehouse were among the most prominent buildings on the West Bank.

The mill abutted a sluice flume with water diverted from the river during high stage, which turned a millstone to rub off the bran and leave behind the edible grain, surpluses of which were stored in the two-story warehouse. Le Page du Pratz and Alexandre de Batz, both trained as architects, designed most of these early West Bank structures. Each rested on a foundation of brick piers to get the building above soggy soils; walls were made of cross-timber frames filled with *bousillage* (mud mixed with Spanish moss) or brick; and roofs were hipped, steep, double-pitched, and covered with cypress bark or shake shingles. Architectural historian Samuel Wilson Jr. described such early French colonial buildings as looking somewhat "medieval."[29]

In 1731 a census was taken of early West Bankers, counting among the population Le Page, two hired hands, and 221 enslaved men, women, and children. At times the black population would swell to over four hundred, as enslaved visitors from New Orleans would, during Sunday off-days, arrive on pirogues to assemble with brethren, a sort of antecedent of the Congo Square gatherings of the 1800s. Company slaves, meanwhile, were said to cross in the opposite direction "to rob all the inhabitants on the other side." In response to this and other clashes, Le Page developed a callous expertise in what he described as "governing the Negroes." He had the pirogues destroyed and the Sunday assemblies abolished. In his book on the history of Louisiana he advised readers on how to treat, feed, and dress slaves, and, drawing from crude anthropological theories, opined on everything from slave-cabin architecture to plantation geography. "Prudence requires that your negroes be lodged at a proper distance," instructed Le Page, "to prevent them from being troublesome or offensive; but at the same time near enough for your conveniently observing what passes among them."[30]

That spatial proximity between master and slave, which would later appear in residential settlement patterns in New Orleans, once put Le Page in the midst of an early Louisiana slave-insurrection conspiracy. The incident came to his attention when, sometime in 1730 or 1731, an enslaved woman who refused to obey a soldier defiantly retorted, "the French should not long insult negroes," as he beat her violently. Governor Périer had the woman imprisoned for insubordination, but otherwise did not take the remark seriously. Le Page, however, sensing that "a man in liquor, and a woman in passion, generally speak the truth," decided to investigate exactly what she meant. "There must be some conspiracy ready to break out," he reasoned, and if so, it "cannot be formed without many negroes of the King's plantation being accomplices." That night, Le Page, accompanied by an allied slave who spoke African dialects, prowled around the Company's slave cabins and drew close to one with a flickering light. "In this hut I heard them talking together of their scheme. One of them was my first commander and my confidant, which surprised me greatly; his name was Samba. I speedily retired for fear of being discovered." Samba, it turned out, was a Bambara warrior who had previously attacked the French on the Senegambia coast, only to be caught and banished to enslavement in Louisiana. En route, he plotted a mutiny on the slave ship, and once landed he learned of the 1729 Natchez Uprising and imagined his own people joining forces with natives to kill their oppressors. This was the plan discussed furtively in that candlelit cabin somewhere in today's Algiers Point—and discovered by the prowling Le Page. Arrests were made, and each conspirator was "put to the torture of burning matches" to elicit confessions and the names of coconspirators. "The woman [was] hanged before [the] eyes" of the men, who were subsequently "broke alive on the wheel." This, Le Page wrote, "prevented the conspiracy from taking place."[31]

Yet even amidst this violent enforcement of the racial hierarchy, at least two black men in this era managed to not only attain freedom, but buy their own land. They appear in a 1732 list of landowners and their means of acquisition: "SIMON, a mulatto, by possession [working the land] and purchased from a free negro named SCIPION." Adjacent names indicate this parcel was in present-day Marrero.[32]

By this time, 1731, the Company of the Indies finally went bankrupt in Paris, putting an end to the venture of John Law (who died penniless in 1729) and shifting Louisiana oversight back to the Crown. Stigmatized by failure and cut loose from the profit motive, the colony as a whole found itself downgraded as a French priority, and the Company Plantation, now known as the King's Plantation, felt the effects. The tobacco crop, despite the counsel of the Englishman from Carolina, fell short of expectations, and rumors circulated that the West Bank operation was costing the Crown ten thousand livres per year, despite which Le Page thought it "saved at least fifty [thousand]." Worse, the Crown in 1733 replaced Governor Périer, an advocate and neighbor of the Company Plantation, with its old warhorse Bienville, who was the original claimant of said land and felt rather lukewarm about reinvesting in it. "The Plantation of the King was reduced as an economy," lamented Le Page of this transitional period. "My post was reduced; I was also." By late June 1734, the West Bank's first major colonial figure—capable architect and engineer, diligent manager, observant naturalist, ruthless slave-driver—was back on French soil, never to return to Louisiana.[33] Over the next few years, the buildings Le Page designed fell into ruin; the economic operation sputtered, in part because slave imports plummeted after 1731; and people began to refer to the King's Plantation simply as "the King's Domain."[34]

It was not the only parcel in flux. Louisiana colonists in this era acquired, de-acquired, and reacquired West Bank land at a dizzying tempo, as might be expected when a coveted resource is suddenly thrown open for takers. Four mechanisms drove early land transfers: by grants (concessions) from the Company or Superior Council; by purchase from a prior grantee or concessionaire; by marrying the widow of a prior owner, or by "possession," which meant "working the land . . . in lieu of their passage back to France—the equivalent of squatter's rights."[35] As of 1732, of the ninety-five claimed parcels from present-day Gretna up to the German Coast, 23 percent had come into the owners' hands by grants; 12 percent by purchases from previous owners (themselves mostly grantees); 3 percent by marrying landed widows; and 62 percent by possession, most of which were in the German Coast area.[36]

Amid all the real estate wheeling and dealing, Governor Bienville wanted back in on the action, pressing to regain as much of his vast 1719 land grant as possible. His superiors at the Company never liked that act of self-appropriation, and neither did the Crown—so much so that while Bienville was in Paris, France's highest court in 1728 issued a stunning edict annulling all Louisiana land grants from Bayou Manchac downriver. "The decree never mentioned [Bienville] by name," noted historian Lawrence Powell. "It didn't have to. . . . But the overriding purpose was to strip Bienville of his land," so that smaller parcels might be distributed to more settlers, including soldiers needed for defense.[37] Once back in the governorship at New Orleans, Bienville doggedly worked again to reclaim his estate. While he failed to gain back the land fee simple, records indicate he did secure certain rights to the holdings in a manner evocative of the Canadian *seigneur-censitaire* system. A 1737 survey by François Saucier records Bienville as "*Seigneur et proprietaire*" of lands on both banks, worked by tenants who would pay him money, produce, and *corvée*—forced labor, which in the days of feudalism practically enslaved tenants to lords.[38] That 1737 survey shows, along with twenty-two East Bank holdings, fourteen long-lot plantations on the West Bank, starting at present-day Verret Street in Algiers and proceeding down to English Turn. Most spanned six to eight arpents in frontage and forty to sixty arpents in depth, and were rented out to Bienville's nephew Gilles Augustin Payen de Noyan, Lallemand, Dommaine, Cardinal, Provanché, Augustin Langlois, Lasonde, Fleuriet, Estienne Langlois, Louis Langlois, Raguet, Chenier, Francois, and Viel.[39] Bienville granted Gilles de Noyan power of attorney to handle the elder's real estate affairs in his absence. It is unclear how Bienville's relationship to these lands eventually played out; certainly the seigneural system would have been hard to sustain in the Louisiana colony, given its enslaved labor and abundant land.

Bienville by now was growing old and jaded, no longer prime planter stock. He may have been given some form of compensatory relief, and managed to retain full title on one substantial parcel. It measured forty to forty-nine arpents in width and eighty arpents in depth, and on it Bienville had built a country home which he named Bel Air and used for light farming and pasture. His periodic presence there was recorded in the 1727 Census in affiliation with de Noyan, who himself recalled in the 1740s the "old main house [once] enjoyed by . . . Sieur de Bienville." Today, the former site of Bel Air falls near Savage Street, behind the still-standing circa-1840 LeBeuf Plantation House in Federal City.[40]

As the West Bank began to develop an agricultural economy with a resident society, the King's Domain began to see some reinvestment. The change may have had something to do with Bienville's retirement in 1743. Never much of an advocate of the operation, Bienville as recently as 1739 sought to close the place for lack of productivity. But the ordonnateur Salmon argued that the King's Domain served as a vital base camp from which slaves could be dispatched far and wide on various critical work projects for a fraction of the cost of white labor.[41] Three years into his retirement in Paris, the aging Bienville had his nephew de Noyan sell his Bel Air tract to military officer Joseph Desdemème Hugon for fifteen thousand livres. This 1746 sale would mark the end of Bienville's direct relationship with the West Bank, and lay the groundwork for the next generation of land holders.[42]

Bienville's final *adieu* to Louisiana brought in a new leader, Governor Pierre Rigaud de Vaudreuil, who seemed to recognize the value of the King's Domain. Houses, warehouses, and the powder magazine were rebuilt starting in 1749, at which point the operation served as "a sort of receiving station and storage place," according to architectural historian Samuel Wilson Jr. This second generation of buildings embodied important design adaptations not seen in the original, rather austere and medieval-like edifices. The new manager's house, for example, looked very much like what would later become "a typical . . . Louisiana plantation house," wrote Wilson, "illustrat[ing] the evolution of a regional style required by the exigencies of climate."[43] Modifications included an abundance of doors, windows and dormers for ventilation on steamy days, and the addition of an airy gallery to shade the sun's rays, protect the brick-between-post walls from rain, and host an outdoor staircase, thus saving scarce indoor space. Such houses came to dominate both banks of the lower Mississippi to such a degree that a visitor in 1834 wrote they "appear to have been built, all of them, after the same model," with double-pitched hipped roofs, raised, with "no cellars[,] surrounded by galleries[,] with rows of china and orange trees in front [and] quarters of the negroes" in the rear.[44] Greater New Orleans today retains about a dozen of these graceful French Creole–West Indian–style houses, mostly dating to the late 1700s and early 1800s.

Perhaps the largest reconstruction project on the King's Domain came in 1760, when a contract was let to build twenty to twenty-five new "cabins [for] the King's negroes," who worked in the warehouses and on other colony projects, including constructing fortifications around New Orleans.[45] Defenses were needed because France at this time was engaged in a transatlantic struggle with England over colonial possessions. The North American theater of the Seven Years' War came to be known as the French and Indian War, and by the early 1760s it was not going well for France. Foreseeing defeat, and not wanting his vast territory west of the Mississippi River to become British, King Louis XV in 1762 secretly ceded Louisiana to his Spanish cousin, King Carlos III. The Treaty of Fontainebleau would make the West Bank Spanish, but Louis XV was not about to abandon the colony's main city to the enemy. So, rather cleverly, he deemed New Orleans to be an "isle" on account of the Bayou Manchac distributary, thus making it cartographically detachable from the east-of-the-Mississippi mainland.

Spain would therefore get all of Louisiana west of the Mississippi plus New Orleans across the river. It was perhaps the only time in history in which New Orleans on the East Bank would be subsidiary to the West Bank, attached as an afterthought. Had it not, the Union Jack would have risen above the Place d'Armes. Instead, Spain accepted the cession in late 1762, and the war ended in 1763. Yet the actual administrative transfer dragged on for years, allowing animosity to fester among Francophile New Orleanians who were none too pleased to learn *ex post facto* that they were now subjects of a foreign king.

The bureaucracy called for an inventory (1767) of everything France was about to pass to Spain, conducted by Commissary Denis Nicholas Foucault for his Spanish counterpart Jean Joseph de Loyola. The inventory, which appraised the King's Domain at 57,219 *livres,* was sent to the new Spanish governor, Don Antonio de Ulloa. A brilliant if aloof scientist and explorer, Ulloa earned the ire of locals with what they perceived to be half-hearted, ham-fisted attempts at governance. In 1768, the same Denis Nicholas Foucault who oversaw the inventory helped organize a rebellion to evict Ulloa and send him and his family back to Cuba, an incident described by some as an opening salvo of the Age of Revolution.

The effrontery enraged Spanish officials in Havana, who dispatched General Alejandro O'Reilly and over two thousand seasoned troops to crack down on the rogue colonists—and crack down O'Reilly did, executing the conspirators and imposing Spanish authority in no uncertain terms. The general would be remembers as "Bloody O'Reilly" by French Creoles, but other segments of the population would view him more favorably. Among them were the soon-to-increase Spanish-speaking cohort; native peoples, whom he banned from becoming enslaved if they were currently free; and Africans in bondage, for whom he permitted *coartación*—the right to purchase one's freedom using moneys earned on Sundays and holidays. This would give rise to a population of free people of color, whose ranks would grow sixteen-fold over the course of the Spanish regime.[46]

As for matters across the river, O'Reilly rejected the appraisal of the King's Dominion and ordered it redone. Piecemeal archival documents suggest O'Reilly had a different vision in mind for the West Bank land: to sell it off in sections, unburdening the government of its management while letting private settlers put the land to work. A colony, after all, is only as good as the wealth it produces, and Spain found in Louisiana a surplus of land and a deficiency of *pobladores* (settlers). It also worriedly watched its enemy working to increase English-speaking populations in British West Florida, which sat just across Bayou Manchac and Lake Pontchartrain. Starting with Gov. Ulloa, Spanish officials would adopt policies to open the immigration spigot, thus initiating the land-development/wealth-production/taxation cycle, and also creating a Spanish-defended *barrera* (barrier) between British foes to the east and the Spanish Main to the west.[47]

What better place to start than the dormant government land directly across from New Orleans? On February 3, 1770, after half a century of official control, Governor O'Reilly sold most of the holding and its dozen or so buildings to Don Luis de Beaurepos, except for a 346-by-270-foot riverside triangle for a powder magazine, which would become Rue de la Poudriere, today's Powder Street. Within the year, Beaurepos sold the land to Jacques Rixner, who in 1777 sold it to Pierre Burgand, who willed it to his nephew Martial LeBeuf (LeBoeuf) in 1786.[48]

By this time, the West Bank hosted over two dozen long-lot plantations arranged in a fan-like morphology from English Turn to Avondale, double the number from early French days and far more extensive in their arpentage devoted to indigo, rice, sugarcane, some cotton and tobacco, and various food crops (maize in particular), as well as timber. Populations were increasing on this side of the river largely because of generous Spanish land-granting policies.

Among the targeted groups were French Canadians whom the British had harshly exiled from Acadie (Nova Scotia) during the war, sending over ten thousand Acadiens on a years-long diaspora. Starting in 1766, some deportees began making their way to the Louisiana bayous and prairies west of the German Coast, drawn by Spain's permission and the area's Francophone society. Lands granted to them would become known as the Côte des Acadiens, and as brethren continued to arrive into the 1780s and thrive thereafter, their region of influence would become modern Louisiana's "Acadian Triangle." Mostly rural until the mid-1900s, "Cajun" (an anglicized corruption of *'Cadien*) culture remained generally separate and distinct from that of Creole New Orleans. Yet many people of the Acadian Coast, like those of the nearby German Coast, would intermingle with West Bank communities; to this day, places such as Avondale, Bridge City, Marrero, and Westwego, which abut the easternmost corner of the Acadian Triangle, are home to a larger percentage of people of Acadian ancestry than New Orleans as a whole.

The West Bank region, which the Spanish broadly referred to as La Concepción, might also have had a "Spanish Coast" had not nature intervened.[49] Finding themselves overseeing a mostly French-speaking society with questionable devotion to the Spanish king, colonial authorities endeavored to change those demographics. In 1777, they recruited families from Málaga and Granada to immigrate, backing them up with material support and land west of the Acadian Coast. There, the Málagueños and Granadinos would eventually found New Iberia, so named because they were from the Iberian peninsula as opposed to islanders. In subsequent years the Spanish governor, Bernarndo de Gálvez, needing soldiers to keep the British at bay, worked to settle islanders from the Canary Islands at strategic ingresses around New Orleans: at Valenzuela on Bayou Lafourche; at Galveztown along the British West Florida frontier; along Bayou Terre-aux-Boeufs in the eastern San Bernardo region; and on Bayou Barataria to guard against an incursion from the south. This last group included 150 *Isleños* led by Commandant Andrés Jung, who settled near the present-day town of Lafitte in 1779—an inopportune place and time, as it turned out, because two major hurricanes and multiple river floods would pummel this low-lying area.[50] "They moved in the fall of 1782," wrote historian Gilbert C. Din of the weary survivors, joining brethren on Bayou Terre-aux-Boeufs, where descendants live today and where an Isleño cultural revival has recently blossomed in eastern St. Bernard Parish. "Only a handful of Isleños remained behind" in Barataria, Din wrote, "living on their own and caring for their livestock on the terrain's 'trembling prairie.'"[51] Their descendants, plus those of Valenzuela and other Spanish peoples, would add yet another ethnic element to the creolizing Franco-German-Acadian-Afro-Indian society forming on today's West Bank.

Spanish Louisiana has struck latter-day observers as ambivalent and paradoxical, such that the historiography of Spain's 34-year tenure ranges from assessments of diligence and benevolence, to accusations of detachment and ruthlessness. Most historians concur that Spain did not prioritize for the colony, but rather maintained it as a buffer zone protecting its prized assets to the west. Yet most also agree Spain did more for urbanizing New Orleans and populating Louisiana than France had done previously in twice the amount of time. Demographically, Spanish administrators wanted to hispanicize the colony, even as they rather eagerly married into French Creole aristocracy, some having French blood themselves. Linguistically, French prevailed overwhelmingly in everyday parlance, but official business and documents, including surveys, maps, and place names, were pointedly in Spanish (for example, *Pointe St. Antoine*, today's Algiers Point, became *Punta San Antonio*).[52] Spain also softened France's harsh *Code Noir* for the handling of slaves, allowing for manumissions and military service. But it also revived slave imports, this time from the African Congo and Spanish Caribbean regions, and cracked down mercilessly on *cimarróns* (maroons), escaped slaves who ensconced themselves in the swamps and marshes.

One figure who, from his extensive West Bank plantation, embodied Spain's complicated brand of colonialism, was a half-French bilingual Spaniard named Francisco Bouligny. A wearer of both diplomatic and martial hats, Bouligny helped establish Spanish rule in 1769, oversaw Indian affairs and immigration policies, founded New Iberia, fought the British, and personally hunted down desperate maroons while also wheeling-and-dealing in slaves—"a favorite pastime of many of the better-off residents of Louisiana," noted historian Gilbert C. Din. In 1772, Bouligny purchased the Villars family's Barataria Plantation, sixteen arpents along the river in today's Westwego and extending forty arpents deep. Worth 2,080 pesos and including "a house, a sawmill, a warehouse, carpentry and blacksmith shops, 24 slave cabins, 2 furnaces," plus livestock, Bouligny's operation placed among the largest on the colonial West Bank.[53] His 22 slaves, purchased for over twice the price of the plantation, toiled not in agriculture but in timber and lumber production. In the early days, when forest stretched clear up to the river, oxen were used to haul the logs along roads; now, because the big trees were further back in the swamp, cutters felled timber during low-water conditions and waited until high water to float them out, an effort that increasingly called for canals to be cleared. The bondsmen utilized a canal starting two arpents back from the river and connecting with Bayou Fatma (also known as the *Ouatchas River*) and into Bayou Barataria, where the cypress were felled and floated to be milled into staves for crates and barrels. Marked as "Boulini's Bayou" on a 1778 British map of the region, this waterway dates back to 1736–1740, when Claude Joseph Villars Dubreuil Sr., directed his slaves to dig the channel for timber, game, and shell extraction. First of its type and size (twenty-five feet wide) in the region, Dubreuil's canal formed the most prominent man-made adjustment to date of local topography and hydrology. It enabled Dubreuil, a shipbuilder, to construct and deliver twenty vessels to New Orleans to send troops to fight the Chickasaw Indians, which may be viewed as the beginning of the West Bank's shipbuilding industry.[54] During Spanish times, timber extracted from this and other backswamp canals was also exported, as ship lumber, masts, planks, stave wood, box boards, and other products, to places like Havana and the United States.[55] Many years later, Dubreuil's canal came into the possession of Antoine Foucher and then François Gardère, by which time it was known as the Gardère Canal. As a landscape feature, the old colonial channel is gone today, but hydrologically it lives on in the form of the Gardere Drainage Canal in modern Gretna and Harvey.[56]

Neighboring plantations had smaller canals, and while they were always perpendicular to the river, their purposes varied: to drain or irrigate croplands, to flood rice fields, to drain sugarcane fields, to power sawmills with diverted river water, to facilitate the making and movement of bricks, and to access the Barataria Bay's natural resources, including wood, midden shells to make lime for mortar and paint, clay for bricks, and fish, shellfish, and game. The wider canals, such as those of Dubreuil and Bouligny, as well as natural outlets, were also convenient for running contraband around tax collectors at New Orleans—and plenty were willing to try.

3

Entrepôt for Contraband

Economic geography made the West Bank a smuggler's paradise, with supply on the one side, demand on the other, and an unpoliced labyrinth of bayous and bays in between. The same could be said for colonial New Orleans and Louisiana generally, given its strategic emplacement yet thinly spread authority. "When it came to obeying the rules of mercantilism," wrote historian Lawrence Powell, "Louisiana ranked among the New World's worst scofflaw. The entire economy was steeped in smuggling[;] it thrived on contraband trade."[1] Much of the trafficking took the form of an informal retail economy among ordinary folks: off-the-books sales and under-the-table swaps of the needs and wants of everyday life, like pelts, game, produce, grains, and lumber, plus tobacco, rum, wine, and whiskey. The wholesale end of the trade involved corsairs and brigands of every stripe, including French, Spanish, British, natives, transnationals, and later Americans. During the Spanish era, illicit imports would come from Havana, Tampico, Veracruz, and various Caribbean ports, through Balize at the mouth of the Mississippi, and onward to New Orleans, with exports flowing in reverse. If those well-traveled routes proved too risky, pirates shifted to back bays and bayous, particularly Grande Terre Isle, Barataria Bay, and Lake Salvador. "The eighteenth century knew of three routes from New Orleans southward into the Barataria swamps," wrote historian William D. Reeves. "One route employed the Gardere canal to Bayou Fatma which connected with Bayou Barataria. Another route went to Bayou des Familles [via present-day] Marrero. The third tied into Bayou Segnette . . . near Westwego."[2] This positioned the West Bank as a sort of illegal version of New Orleans, an entrepôt for contraband. Smuggling became so quotidian that one observer, tabulating the colony's economic activity for 1801, casually mentioned that because "the contraband [here] is more considerable than on the products of the colony, this sum [of annual legal imports of 5.48 million *livres*] may fairly be doubled." *Fairly doubled:* he was being conservative. "The contraband commerce with Mexico," he added, "is also a considerable advantage to New Orleans."[3]

The West Bank's historical association with piracy explains one of its most colorful toponyms. First appearing on maps in the early 1730s, "Barataria" comes from the farcical island over which Sancho Panza is given dubious reign in *Don Quixote*. But the term was not Cervantes's coinage; it stems from "a Provençal equivalent to the 15th-century French words *baraterie,* meaning deception, and *barater,* meaning to deceive, to exchange, to barter," explained historian Betsy Swanson. "The English equivalent . . . is barratry, one meaning of which is fraudulence or illegality at sea."[4] The name probably originated as a winking allusion to rampant illegal shipping in early French colonial times. The reputation would only intensify over the next century, and by the early 1800s, the toponym became the demonymn "Baratarians." "Barataria was arguably the largest smuggling depot and irregular naval base in North America," assessed historian Robert C. Vogel, "and the presence of so many armed adventurers [Baratarians] on Louisiana soil had become a national scandal."[5]

〜〜〜

Had Baratarians and other denizens assembled at the West Bank riverfront on the sunny warm midday of December 20, 1803, they would have heard the rumblings of a throng across the river, and perhaps discerned a ceremony at the Place d'Armes. "The French colors were lowered and the American flag was raised," recalled French colonial prefect Pierre Clément de Laussat, who had just "handed over the keys to the city" after signing the Louisiana Purchase. "When they reached the same level, both banners paused for a moment, [as] a cannon shot" rang out, to audible cheers and more than a little silent ambivalence.[6] The formalities marked the official transfer of the Louisiana territory from France, which had secretly regained control from Spain in 1800, to the United States, which had pounced on Napoleon's astonishingly generous offer. The December ceremony officially finalized the Louisiana Purchase.

Soon New Orleans would undergo a gradual but dramatic transformation.

A sophisticated yet provincial Franco-Hispanic Afro-Caribbean orphan of two distracted Old World regimes—Catholic in faith, French in tongue, and monarchical in governance—would suddenly find itself administered, then infiltrated, and finally overwhelmed by a capitalistic, democratic, expanding New World nation. The newcomers did just about *everything* differently from the local Creoles: language and law, government and economics, religion and customs, architecture and surveying—even burying the dead. Algiers and the West Bank would have a somewhat removed vantage point from which to observe the contentious cross-cultural collusions that would play out in the streets of New Orleans in the decades ahead, and that distance that would serve to preserve certain aspects of the *ancienne regime* longer than across the river. But Americanization would affect and eventually subsume the West Bank as well, and one of the first upshots involved Barataria smuggling.

Illicit trade intensified in the early American years for reasons related to the political turnover. For one, many expected New Orleans to burgeon under its new dominion, destined to become the premier commercial emporium of the West. All boats would rise with the economic tide, including those of privateers and smugglers. Secondly, starting in 1807, imports from England and France began disappearing from shelves in port cities, on account of the warring nations' practice of seizing American vessels and impressing sailors into service in the Napoleonic Wars (indirectly financed, ironically, by revenues from the Louisiana Purchase). Outraged over the insolence, American congressmen passed the Embargo Act of 1807 banning British and French imports, even as local demand increased—creating the perfect opportunity for smugglers to fill the supply niche.

The highest profits were on slaves, and in that regard the bandits got a double boost: an early territorial act had prohibited the foreign slave trade in the lands of the Louisiana Purchase, which a few years later Congress expanded nationally. The Act Prohibiting Importation of Slaves, which went into effect in 1808, had little effect on those states that had substantial resident slave populations, or that had barred bondage altogether. But Louisiana and the lower Mississippi Valley had an insatiable demand for labor on ever-growing sugarcane and cotton plantations, the former abetted by the 1795 refinement of sugar crystallization techniques, the latter by the 1793 invention of the cotton gin. "In due time," wrote historian Joe G. Taylor, "the interstate slave trade provided an adequate supply of [slave labor] for the Louisiana market, but that was in the future."[7]

Meanwhile, from 1804 to around 1820, illegal foreign slave importation into Louisiana became common and lucrative.

Typically, transnational privateers sailing the Caribbean and Gulf of Mexico would acquire slaves from Spanish colonies as far as Havana and Cartagena or as close as Mexico (Texas) and Spanish West Florida, where foreign slave trading remained legal. Otherwise they would turn to piracy, commandeering slave ships and guiding them into Louisiana waters. At Grande Terre Island and other atolls at the mouth of the Barataria Bay, these "wholesalers" would rendezvous with a loose coalition of backswamp buccaneers known as the Baratarians, coordinated by the brothers Jean and Pierre Lafitte.

There, under a subtropical sun, the scene was furtive, the pace fast, the currency specie-only (no paper bills), and the pricing set at a brutally simple dollar-per-pound. From there, the Lafitte gang would play the role of ferrying middlemen, although at times Jean or Pierre would do their own importing from nearby Baton Rouge or Pensacola, both still under Spanish rule. "From the end of 1809 through the first half of 1812, the Laffites sold an estimated 142 slaves for a sum close to $50,000," wrote historian David Head. "In January 1814, the Laffites sold 415 slaves at once, their largest single auction."[8] As the human cargo made its way to city-based dealers or plantation owners, prices could rise three-, seven-, sometimes ten-fold.

Routes from Grand Terre Island to New Orleans were surreptitiously fluid. One pathway went up Bayou St. Denis and Bayou Perot into Lake Salvador, and proceeded up Bayou Segnette to present-day Westwego; another took Bayou Rigolets into Bayou Barataria and up the man-made canal known variously as Dubreuil's, Bouligny's, and Gardere's. Else the brigands would sail up Bayou Lafourche into the Mississippi and down to Lac and Bayou des Allemands to a transshipment depot known as Little Temple, which sat on an astonishing fifty-foot-high midden in lower Lake Salvador.[9]

By the time the contraband arrived at the West Bank and the metropolis, most of the negotiations had already taken place, and the brazen crime melded into the legal universe of Louisiana slavery. Most whites winked at the practice, and those directly involved—and there were many—either profited handsomely or saved substantially toward the production of additional wealth. "From all parts of Lower Louisiana people resorted to Barataria, without being at all solicitous to conceal the object of their journey," decried Arsène Lacarrière Latour in 1816.

"In the streets of New Orleans it was usual for traders to give and receive orders for purchasing goods at Barataria, with as little secrecy as . . . for Philadelphia or New-York. The most respectable inhabitants of the state, especially those living in the country . . . purchas[ed] smuggled goods coming from Barataria." As for the government, Latour was suspicious: "It cannot be pretended that the country was destitute of the means necessary to repress these outrages. . . . The species of impunity with which [the Baratarians] were apparently indulged . . . made the contraband trade . . . tacitly tolerated."[10] One can only imagine the crushing experience of the trafficking upon the enslaved, considered at once chattel and contraband, torn from kin, sold by the pound, conveyed clandestinely into an environment and culture they did not know, in a language they did not understand.[11]

The West Bank's smuggling economy waned as American authority waxed, as Spanish West Florida became part of the United States (1819), and as the legal domestic slave trade filled the niche created by the international ban. As for the Lafitte band, it was the culminating battle of the War of 1812 that changed their destiny, both as an enterprise and in the eyes of history.

Sparked over continued British impressment of American sailors, the war broke out in the Great Lakes region and shifted to the Eastern Seaboard, namely Washington and Baltimore. Making little headway in either theater, British generals next targeted the soft underbelly of the young nation. American military planners sensed as much, and in 1814 dispatched defensive forces to the Gulf Coast and New Orleans. One wild card was the Lafitte brothers and the Baratarians: these "hellish banditti," as Maj. Gen. Andrew Jackson described them, numbered many, knew the terrain, had arms, and could spell the difference if they "went filibuster" and invited the British onto Grande Terre Island. American forces thus had to quash the outlaws before they allied with the enemy.

Pierre Lafitte was arrested in the summer of 1814, and Master Commandant Daniel Todd Patterson organized a joint expeditionary force to bring order to the rogue region. The "Patterson Raid" at Grande Terre was a success: the Baratarians were caught by surprise; ships and booty were seized and warehouses torched, all with nary a shot fired. Both Lafittes had managed to slip away, but this proved fortuitous, as it enabled Jean to establish communications with Gov. William C. C. Claiborne and Maj. Gen. Andrew Jackson. The pirate boldly offered the services of his guerilla army to the Americans in exchange for pardons for their crimes. Reluctant at first, the Americans, knowing the British were on the horizon and needing all the men they could muster, acquiesced. The Lafitte brothers, their captains, and up to four hundred Baratarians joined the American cause.[12]

Denied a Barataria incursion onto New Orleans from the West Bank, the British instead battled their way from Bay St. Louis to Lake Borgne and approached the city up Bayou Bienvenue on the East Bank. Americans by late December had erected a sequence of earthen ramparts down along both natural levees, including at the Jourdan Plantation around present-day Sullen Place and Ernest Street in lower Algiers.

As British gunners emerged from the swamps and made their way to the East Bank riverfront, the same Master Commandant ("Commodore") Daniel Todd Patterson of the Grande Terre raid rushed to fortify the Jourdan battery, and from the *Louisiana* docked nearby, lobbed shells across the river at the intruding foe. "So constant and vigilant were Patterson's gunners," recounted one narrative, "that the British found it impossible to make any reconnaissance along the river."[13] This gave Maj. Gen. Andrew Jackson and his multiethnic troops precious time to extend their Chalmette fortification further into the swamp and prepare for a climactic battle. Jackson "has now from 15,000 to 18,000 men all burning with eagerness to cross swords with the English," scribed one Frenchman on January 6, 1815. "Nationalities no longer count; we are all Americans."[14]

British planners had rejected using the Mississippi River as a primary ingress on account of Fort St. Philip near the mouth and Fort St. Leon at English Turn. But some British units managed to slip across the river above those bastions, opening up a new front on the West Bank. Only four meager earthworks stood between the enemy and Algiers Point, itself within shooting range of New Orleans. Reinforcements poured in to this weak spot, including every local man available except Englishmen. "A perfect Babel indeed, was that famous marine battery of Patterson."[15]

On the cool foggy morning of January 8, the long-awaited clash exploded on the East Bank fields of Chalmette, pitting raw amateurs against seasoned professionals, and guerrilla warfare against drilled decorum. With Patterson firing from across the river, Jackson's line poured murderous led into the red phalanxes. When the smoke settled, an epic American victory became apparent. Word raced back to New Orleans, and celebrations ensued.

Alas, the hoopla was premature. Confusion had broken out between Patterson's positions on the West Bank and those of Gen. David Morgan, emplaced downriver around present-day Stanton Road plus other undermanned positions. The English exploited the confusion, and despite suffering greater losses, penetrated all four riverside defenses up to today's Leboeuf Street.

These were American defeats by any measure, except that they had been dwarfed by the victory across the river. There, Jackson managed to negotiate a truce among bloodied survivors, even as hostilities continued in lower Algiers. Reinforcements raced across the river. "That night the Americans regained their lines on the [West] Bank, and by early morn Patterson had restored his battery." Vanquished, the British withdrew with only one trophy: a small flag snatched from one of the overrun West Bank batteries, inscribed: "Taken at the Battle of New Orleans, January 8, 1815."[16]

The events in lower Louisiana from late 1814 to early 1815 decisively ended the War of 1812, and January 8 became a holiday in New Orleans for decades. The disarray on the West Bank faded from public memory, and we can only ponder what might have happened if the British had sent more resources there and established themselves at Algiers Point.

As for the Baratarians, most accounts depict them as having fought heroically during the various engagements, although military historians debate whether their participation decided the outcome (probably not).[17] Afterwards, the pardoned outlaws mostly settled into legitimate trades, and the privateer era drew to a close. Jean Lafitte, meanwhile, returned to his old haunts on Galveston Island, still Spanish at that time, until the US Navy ousted him in 1820. His fate remains a mystery, but his destiny would become transformed: most people considered him a folk hero, even to this day, especially on the West Bank.

Patterson and Morgan are today aptly remembered in two street names along the Algiers levee. Jackson has a statue in his image and a prominent square named for him, and Jean Lafitte's name adorns a US National Historic Park and a town to its south.

4

The Formation of Villages

With its outlaw days behind it and a booming metropolis across from it, the West Bank in the early 1800s appeared to be a bucolic environment of plantations, farms, pastures, orchards, and light industry. But changes were afoot.

In terms of transportation, by 1803, "a system of relays set up every two leagues and maintained by dragoons" ran along the river road, while on the water operated an "active navigation system for several hundreds of leagues," allowing travelers to catch rides and circulated regionally. Americans at this time were establishing a similar courier service upriver, such that mail and communiques would take only four days to move between Natchez and New Orleans.[1] Locally, West Bankers used the ad hoc ride system, or their own slave-paddled pirogues, to cross the river for various needs and wants. Pierre Clément de Laussat recalled how faithful Catholics would arrive at St. Louis Church to attend "mass, some in boats which ferried them across the river [because the] parish includes both river banks for five leagues around."[2] So too East Bankers: "Folks from town go to Lake Barataria for [duck] hunting parties, which usually last a week or two."[3]

In terms of governance, the American administrators introduced new political jurisdictions that, for the first time, would be spatially fixed and administratively meaningful. In times past, rural spaces were demarcated loosely and tagged with vernacular monikers like "Ouacha" or "Allemands," or were borrowed from Catholic ecclesiastic *paroisses,* or *parroquias* (parishes). Settlers were too few, and the terrain too vast, to necessitate ratified jurisdictions with official borders, and the monarchists who ran the colony certainly had no need to draw up electoral districts.

Americans, on the other hand, had different notions and needs for governance, and they brought to Louisiana their way of organizing them. In April 1805, the Legislative Council subdivided the Territory of Orleans into twelve "counties," putting all of today's urbanized West Bank into Orleans County. Two years later, a parallel map of "parishes" was drawn, for judicial purposes as well as for civil government, while counties (sometimes called "districts") were retained for electoral and taxation purposes. It was also at this time (1807) that the Council created St. Bernard and Plaquemines parishes out of the once-vast Orleans County, using the rear backswamp edge of the West Bank's natural levee as the Orleans/Plaquemines line. Only one fragment of that shared line remains today, in the English Turn area by the Belle Chasse Air Base.

There were problems. Many county and parish limits did not coincide, and rarely did either align with ecclesiastic parishes, which is what most ordinary folks understood a parish to be. Confusion prevailed. Luckily for Orleans County and Orleans Parish, their lines were coterminous after 1807, covering today's Orleans and Jefferson Parish combined. But they too differed from the City of New Orleans, which in 1805 had been incorporated as a municipal entity entirely on the East Bank. Thus, from 1807 to 1825, today's urbanized West Bank was neither in New Orleans proper nor in not-yet-created Jefferson Parish, but rather in unincorporated Orleans Parish and Orleans County, plus a bit of Plaquemines Parish. Each was governed by police juries, elected by white males and answering to the territorial government until 1812, and to the state thereafter. (As for "counties," the state legislature mercifully did away with them in 1846, for their redundancy and unpopularity. Ever since, Louisiana has had parishes and parishes only.)[4]

With no city limits and two sprawling parishes, denizens of the West Bank perceived their space as they always had: by who owned what parcel. In 1815 there were around four dozen such long-lots along the forty river-fronting miles between Avondale and Fort St. Leon at English Turn. French Creole families with names like Duplantier, Degruise, Derbigny, Bienvenu, Lefevre, Dupuy, Andry, and Dela Croix lorded over the estates, living in stately but not necessarily lavish homes near the levee road.[5] Fronting the houses were ornamental gardens or oak allées; to their sides were garconnieres and pigeonniers; to their rears were kitchens, outbuildings, worksheds, barns, and cabins for the enslaved. Most parcels measured two to four times longer (forty arpents, the typical distance to the backswamp) than they were wide, and because they occupied the convex side of a yawning river meander, they widened and diverged with distance, unlike their counterparts on the concave East Bank, which narrowed and converged. Some West Bank plantations in the early 1800s were full-scale, self-sufficient operations focusing on cash staples like sugarcane, but more often, they were mixed-use "working farms" with food crops, citrus orchards, pastures, diaries, poultry, dovecotes, brick kilns, and mills, including sections leased to small farmers. Ditches separated the holdings, used for drainage or irrigation, and canals often extended into the backswamp to extract timber, shell, fur, or game. A visitor described the working-farm portion of one West Bank plantation as a "demesne," which, in feudalism, meant the land reserved on a manor for the owner's own use.[6] Of course, there was no true feudalism here, yet the antebellum West Bank landscape did not look altogether different from that of Old World feudal estates, with farms, fields, hamlets, and light industry interconnected by dirt roads and canals, radiating outward from the gardened manor houses along the river—and all resting on the brawn of enslaved "serfs."

Some estates were more prominent than others, chief among them that of Barthélémy Duverjé. A major landholder on the West Bank, Duverjé had acquired for $18,000 a portion of the former King's Plantation at today's Algiers Point from Martial LeBoeuf on August 9, 1805, leaving aside some space for a government-owned powder magazine and barracks.[7] Shortly after the sale, Duverjé sliced off the upper four arpents of his acquisition at today's Powder Street, immediately upriver from the magazine and barracks, and sold it to Toussaint Mossy of New Orleans, while later selling a small riverfront tract at the tip of the point to André Séguin of Le Havre. There, at the foot of what is now Seguin Street, the Frenchman would build the state's first marine way (slipway) for vessel construction and repair.[8]

In 1812 Duverjé had constructed upon his land an archetypal French Creole Louisiana country manse. It rose two stories high, with a steep, hipped, shingled roof, set upon sturdy pillars, with twelve rooms within its 72-by-52-foot walls, and a spacious gallery including an outdoor staircase. "Built with the strength of a fortress," the main house was adjoined by gardens, orchards, a dairy, and two rows of outbuildings.[9] Given its commanding position across from New Orleans, American troops occupied Duverjé's compound as the British approached in 1814–1815. Despite that no action occurred here, troops caused $2,100 worth of "injuries and losses" to Duverjé's property, for which the heirs of the late patriarch were indemnified by Congress in 1821.[10]

By that time, the main house was surrounded by four pavilions and a number of brick slave cabins directly behind it, plus a two-arpent brickyard and kiln with an inventory of lime made from shells and over 140,000 bricks. "On the batture in front of the habitation were two large sheds for wood, three slaughterhouses, and . . . two flatboats . . . used to deliver bricks to the city," wrote historians David Fritz and Sally Reeves. The outbuildings evidenced that, like many operations on the early nineteenth-century West Bank, the Duverjé family "habitation was not a sugar plantation, but rather a mixed-use agricultural and manufacturing site [devoted to] brickmaking, vegetable sales, cattle raising, and butchering."[11]

After the patriarch's death, Duverjé's widow, Alix Bienvenu Duverjé, herself from a family of West Bank planters, put the property up for sale. "The houses and buildings," read her 1821 advertisement in the *Louisiana Courier*, "are new and well made, and shall if required be bartered for brick houses well situated in the city of New Orleans, or for slaves." Savvy to the drivers of real estate value, the widow pointed out that "the establishment of a steam ferry which has just been put into operation . . . presents a fair opportunity to speculate."[12] She eventually decided to lease the house and farm instead of selling it, giving her a steady income for her retirement at 731 Royal Street.

Mme. Duverjé proved right about the ferry, which had begun service in 1818. Convenient city access made the rural tract ripe for residential development. In 1821 state surveyor General C. N. Bouchon sketched a plat for the Duverjé parcel, marking, after a hundred years, the first arrival of urbanization to Algiers proper, though not the West Bank (McDonoghville having been laid out in 1813; more on this later). Bouchon used the orientation of the Duverjé House to drive the entire street grid of future Algiers Point, starting with four surrounding streets parallel to the building's walls: Villere (now Morgan), Seguin, Barthelemy (now Bermuda), and Delaronde. This was unusual, because surveyors more typically designed a grand vision with its own spatial orientation, and would be averse to letting a couple of old buildings do the bidding for them. But perhaps due to the sheer prominence of the Duverjé House as well as its fortuitously centralized emplacement, it became optimal to spatially arrange the neighborhood around it, rather than despite it. The orientation of Duverjé House, and of the French long-lot which it occupied, thus explains the distinctive angle of Algiers Point's modern street grid. The new subdivision would be called Burg Duverjé or Duverjeville, and the mansion remained the neighborhood's central landmark for nearly the rest of the century.

It's worth noting that generic toponyms for West Bank subdivisions were usually of the "burg" or "ville" variety. The term "faubourg," which was de rigueur for the inner suburbs surrounding New Orleans, was rarely if ever used here, simply because there was no original urbanized core (-bourg) of which these subdivisions would be outside (fau-). Rather, early West Bank subdivisions were small riverside settlements with limited street grids, the likes of which most people would perceive as a bourgade (village), hamlet, or town. They certainly weren't cities; municipal incorporation would not arrive to the West Bank until 1870 and the early 1900s. Nor was the term banlieue (outskirts) used here, as it was on the East Bank. Instead, the whole land mass was simply the "right bank" to the people who lived there, and "across the river," "opposite the city," or "over the river" to the people who didn't.

After Alix Bienvenu Duverjé died in 1839, her daughter Evelina inherited the house, which continued as a residence until the police jury of Algiers acquired and renovated it in 1869 to serve as "the seat of justice of the right bank." A year later, Algiers was annexed into New Orleans city limits, and the former Duverjé House became "the third city court, fourth recorder's court and the eighth precinct police station."[13] It burned to ashes during the Great Fire of 1895, and was replaced the next year by the current Algiers Courthouse, built on the same footprint but with a Moorish-Romanesque style.

Barthélémy Duverjé's land sales proved consequential to West Bank development. André Séguin, who in 1819 bought the tip of Algiers Point, opened the first marine way and began building and repairing vessels. In due time, ship work would become a major industry in Algiers and the West Bank.[14] Just upriver was the land Duverjé had sold to Toussaint Mossy, who would become a financial tycoon and the city's premier public auctioneer. Mossy ran his plantation here until 1833, when he too yielded to the economic pressure to subdivide.

City surveyor Joseph Pilié undertook the plat sketch, and found himself confronted with a design decision. Should he lay out the street grid of "Mossyville" to match the angled arteries of Duverjeville? Or should he rotate the grid such that his blocks ran neatly parallel to the riverbank, along a north-south line, and in alignment with a neighboring subdivision to the south? That community, McDonoghville, pertained to John McDonogh, who in 1813 had purchased Francois Bernoudy's plantation just upriver from Mossy's land; shortly thereafter, McDonogh laid out lots on a portion of this holding, making it the first street grid on the West Bank.[15] Now, in 1833, with Mossy's land due to be surveyed,

Pilié decided to abandon the angled shape of Duverjeville's streets (1821) and straighten out everything to the south, conflating his new Mossyville with the extant McDonoghville. Maps of the era show a rather forced, awkward initial interfacing of the two systems, but this was later rectified with a straight artery, today's Opelousas Avenue.[16] To the south, the spatial fusion made Mossyville and McDonoghville visually indistinguishable, such that people referred to them by either or both names. "Mossyville" eventually fell out of the vernacular while "McDonoghville" persisted, for reasons we shall explore later.

As for Toussaint Mossy, his job as city auctioneer put him in a good position to market his lots. He pulled out all the stops in a February 26, 1833, *Louisiana Courier* ad, which reads like Chamber of Commerce copy. "The view" from Mossyville, wrote Mossy, is "magnificent and delightful[;] its harbor is excellent, and in point of security for vessels, greatly superior to that of New Orleans." Surely "this town . . . must rapidly increase, lying, as it does, between the two towns of Macdonogh [and] Durverges [*sic*]." Two steam ferries were about to be established, Mossy pointed out, which would make it easier to live in Mossyville and cross the river in "six or eight minutes" to reach the upper suburbs of New Orleans, than to endure "a walk through the mud or hot sun" three miles in each direction. "[T]he yellow fever never having been on that side of the river, and the elevation of the land . . . not exceeded by any other on the river, [Mossyville lots] will be sold without reserve. It is but seldom that such opportunities for good investments occur."[17] They sold well enough, along with his other enterprises, to make Mossy a wealthy man. His succession in 1849 included scores of shares in local banks and companies, including the Barataria and Lafourche Canal Company, along with ten slaves and nearly eighty land parcels, most of them in Mossyville and McDonoghville.[18]

Ask New Orleanians today the most notable figure of the historical West Bank and many would point to the man behind that latter village, John McDonogh. Born in Baltimore in 1779 and apprenticed by a merchant, the striking youth—"tall, spare, erect, with sprightly step and look"—made his way to New Orleans in 1800. The next three years saw ever-changing governments, laws, policies, and conditions, making for both economic uncertainty and opportunity. McDonogh played the scene masterfully, prospering as an international "mercantilist capitalist," importing and up-selling everything from wine and liquors to tableware and hardware.[19]

Over the next few years, his fortune now amassed, McDonogh shifted his portfolio from the high-stakes world of global trade to the safer realm of local real estate. The change seemed to parallel McDonogh's personal transformation from a local power broker and man-about-town, to what nosy neighbors viewed as an "eccentric," a "recluse," and a "miser," characterizations that would color his legacy to this day.

No better place existed for such a man than the West Bank of the early 1800s, which was just close enough to the metropolis to ensure rising land value, yet sufficiently removed to assure privacy and tranquility. McDonogh was not alone in viewing West Bank real estate as a form of currency—a safe place to park capital, almost like a brick-and-mortar bank, but with less risk, more prestige, and a restful residence to boot. He made the move in 1813, purchasing the Francois Bernoudy tract that originally pertained to Governor Étienne de Périer and, in 1737, to Chevalier Jean-Charles de Pradel, who had engineer Alexandre de Batz build a country house upon it. Known as Mon Plaisir (Monsplaisir), the 116-foot-wide chateau and gardens became a landmark on the West Bank horizon; a visitor from France in 1803 was astonished to see that "everything here was in the French style, even the old furniture, [with its] Parisian workmanship. No other residence in the colony was so elegant."[20]

Monsplaisir thus became, in 1817, the perfect place for the ever richer, ever more enigmatic John McDonogh to call home.[21] His plantation, including the early village layout sketched by J. V. Poiter in 1814, ran from what is now Homer Street at the riverfront (the channel has since eroded) down to present-day Hamilton Street, whose flailing angle reflected the French long-lot surveying system.[22]

Over the next two decades, McDonogh incrementally expanded Poiter's 1814 street grid, making the use of his property less agrarian and more urban, with two-acre tracts selling for $3,000. By 1834, everything from the riverfront to Hancock Street was laid out in squares, with streets parallel to the river named for American founding fathers (Washington, Adams, Jefferson, Madison, Monroe, the main artery of Franklin, and Hancock), as they are today, and those perpendicular named for famed thinkers, scientists, and explorers admired by McDonogh, himself something of a homespun philosopher and armchair intellectual. They included Newton, Socrates, Ptolemy, Magellan, Columbus, Copernicus, and Virgil, among others; many names have since been changed. McDonoghville in 1834 also included two interior parks, Mexico Square (since renamed) and Lima Square (gone), and riverfront open space, plus a canal running down the subdivision's main x-axis, present-day McDonogh Street, draining to the backswamp beyond Hancock.[23] In sum, this was no slapdash real estate deal; this was an articulate, enlightened urban vision, and it exuded all that John McDonogh was.

McDonogh's life and death played out at either end of McDonogh Street. He lived in Monsplaisir by the river, between today's Ocean Avenue and Hamilton Street, until his death in 1850. He arranged to be buried in McDonoghville Cemetery, laid out where his canal once emptied into the swamp. The crypt is empty today, his remains having been removed to his hometown of Baltimore, but its epigraph and surrounding tombs speak to McDonogh's humanitarian legacy. "Study in your course of life to do the greatest possible amount of good," reads one of the inscriptions. To that end, McDonogh bequeathed his fortune to the betterment of public education in Baltimore and New Orleans, giving rise to dozens of "McDonogh schools" and a fund which would last into the twenty-first century. "Do unto all men as you would be done by," reads another tomb inscription, and toward that end, McDonogh, though a slaveholder, grappled with the cruel institution, educated those in his custody, granted many of them freedom, and devised various liberation schemes to return Africans to their homeland. As far back as 1815, when McDonogh first laid out his village, he rented lots at low rates to working-class leaseholders and sold land reasonably to free people of color, making McDonoghville the West Bank's first free black settlement, "Freetown."[24] More African Americans would settle adjacently, especially after emancipation, and many are buried in McDonoghville Cemetery, near the tomb of the complex man with whom their histories are inextricably bound.

Today the neighborhood is home to the largest black community along the West Bank riverfront. It stands as a counterpoint to the East Bank trend in which historical black settlements usually coalesced in the "back" of town. As for Monsplaisir, grinding river currents finally swept away the old colonial home, along with most of Washington and Adams streets, probably in the 1870s. Metaphorically speaking, so too has gone John McDonogh's reputation: once celebrated by school children for bequeathing their schools, his name in recent decades has been removed from all but one schoolhouse, because he was a slaveholder.

~~~

On February 11, 1825, the West Bank was forever altered when the state legislature carved a new jurisdiction out of Orleans Parish's Third Senatorial District and named it for former President Thomas Jefferson. The impetus was a common one in this era, in which rural interests, namely sugar planters, felt they were being ill served by the city-dwellers dominating the halls of power. Ethnic tensions also played a role: while French-speaking Creoles predominated on both banks, English-speaking Anglos were on the rise and vying for power in New Orleans proper, whereas Jefferson Parish remained overwhelmingly Creole. Nearly all the men who sat on the new parish's initial organizing committee had French surnames.[25]

Jefferson Parish would span both banks and run from the Lake Pontchartrain shore down to Chênière Caminada and Grand Isle, while its older neighbor, including the City of New Orleans, would flare eastward to the Rigolets.[26] Where to divide the two parishes on the West Bank? By some accounts, the Canal Bernoudy, a drainage canal on the former plantation Francois Bernoudy (which he sold to John McDonogh in 1813), would form the dividing line. But there is a cross-bank curiosity here: if extended, the West Bank Orleans/Jefferson parish boundary aligns perfectly with the angled fortification that once constituted the upper limit of New Orleans, between Canal Street and Iberville Street at the edge of the French Quarter. If this is a coincidence, it's a remarkable one. Whatever its provenance, the Orleans/Jefferson parish line to this day slices across blocks and houses at a seemingly arbitrary angle, with zero regard to the boundaries of local properties. It even juts across the McDonoghville Cemetery (alas, McDonogh's tomb falls on the Orleans side of the line—barely). Only when the circa-1825 line reaches the former backswamp, which was developed much later, does the modern cityscape embody the jurisdictional border, in the form of a modern drainage canal—and that channel might well be traceable to the original Canal Bernoudy. Despite its peculiarity, this jurisdictional boundary has remained fixed for nearly two hundred years. Its East Bank counterpart, on the other hand, would move thrice in one-tenth the time. Later acts of the state legislature would refine a system of police juries to govern these unincorporated areas, in which voters (white males) would elect jurors or commissioners within eight to twelve electoral districts or wards, who in turn would elect a president among themselves.[27] Until the 1870 annexation of unincorporated Orleans Parish (Algiers) into the City of New Orleans and the twentieth-century incorporation of Gretna, Westwego, Lafitte, and Grand Isle, residents of all three West Bank parishes would govern themselves through the police jury system.

It was in this era when the name "Algiers" gained traction for the point bar formerly known as Pointe St. Antoine, Punta San Antonio, Pointe Marigny, Duverjeville, and Slaughterhouse Point. Various theories circulate as to its origins. Some claim the moniker alluded to the African slaves who landed here in colonial times, despite that they came from the faraway West African regions of Senegambia, Benin, and the Congo, not North Africa, and no one thought of them as Algerians. Others contend "Algiers" came from veterans of Spain's expedition against Algeria who, while serving in Spanish New Orleans, were reminded of the North African city on the shores of the Mediterranean across from France and Spain, when they saw this outpost, with its whitewashed buildings, on the Mississippi across from Franco-Spanish New Orleans. The third explanation harks back to the insinuations of "Barataria:" the Barbary Coast in this era was notorious for its pirate economy, in which cargoes were smuggled, ships seized, and crews kidnapped. Algiers was at the center of this action, and people on both sides of the Atlantic began to associate maritime mayhem with Algiers and the Barbary Coast, making them metaphors for piracy. The West Bank already had this repute inscribed into its map in the word "Barataria" (barratry), and as that reputation hardened in the early 1800s, the theory goes, the sobriquet "Algiers" began to stick to the area's main settlement.

A different angle on the Barbary Coast connection forms a more plausible explanation. During the Second Barbary War in 1815, American naval forces engaged pirate strongholds along the North African coast, and Commodore Stephen Decatur succeeded in bringing the cities of Algiers and Tunis under control. The action made Decatur a national hero, this being the first major foreign engagement of the young United States, and Americans thrilled to read of his exploits in Algiers and Tunis. Years later, New Orleans would rename Levee Street to honor Decatur.[28] In the late 1820s, France became increasingly active in both North African cities, economically and militarily, and colonized Algiers in 1830. To New Orleans's French-speaking population, who were pointedly proud of their mother country, the names of Algiers and Tunis took on patriotic meaning. Similarly, in this same era, uptown streets were named to commemorate Napoleon's conquests, with a principle avenue honoring the emperor himself.

It's unclear who applied the names "Algiers" and "Tunis" to these two particular West Bank subdivisions, but as to the question of why, it stands to reason that catchy names like these would help sell real estate, all the more so if they instilled a sense of pride. One early use of "Algiers" appeared in a July 1837 issue of the *Picayune* (without quotes or explanation, indicating readers would understand the reference).[29] By 1838, it appeared regularly in articles and ads, and in 1840 the term showed up in the city directory, a year after "Tunisburg" appeared on the 1839 Springbett and Pilié *Topographical Map of the City and Environs of New Orleans*. It too subsequently appeared in newspapers. Unlike "Algiers," which gained momentum in the vernacular and spread in its spatial domain, usage of "Tunisburg" and "Tunis" petered out in the early 1900s, and today only survives in parish assessor documents as a subdivision name.

This brings our attention to the area downriver from Algiers Point, toward today's Federal City and Old Aurora. Except for the one-block-wide parcels of J. B. Olivier (kin of the neighboring Duverjé) and the Widow Gosselin—that is, today's Verret Street to Vallette Street—this section of the West Bank traces its developmental history to Bienville's vast 1719 land claim, his subsequent leasing arrangements, and his final 1746 sale of his Bel Air plantation to Joseph Desdemème Hugon. In two sales in 1755 and 1760, Hugon sold this terrain to French official Jean Baptiste Destréhan, who used it to raise wax myrtle trees for making bayberry candles. Destréhan died in 1765, followed by his son in 1773, which left the son's widow, Felicité St. Maxent, to have to purchase the land back at a succession auction. Moving in powerful circles, Felicité married the Spanish governor, Bernardo de Galvez, and moved to Havana, whereupon she sold the West Bank land to her father, Gilbert Antoine de St. Maxent, who turned it into an indigo plantation and shipping depot. By 1794, some of the land came into the possession of the Macarty clan, Scottish Creoles who already owned the land immediately upriver and across. Overseeing twenty-six arpents from Vallette Street downriver, the Macartys ran a successful sugar plantation here until 1816, whereupon Jean Baptiste Macarty sold it to another prominent Creole landholder, the famed Bernard Marigny, who later shared ownership with his son Prosper. A messy divorce from his wife and cousin, Celeste Destréhan, forced Prosper Marigny to break up the property into narrow lots and sell. Some went to the LeBeuf family, which built a house in 1840 still standing in Federal City today, one of only a handful of surviving antebellum country villas or plantation houses on the West Bank.[30]

Members of the LeBeuf family intermarried with the Verret family, such that by 1834, the Verret and Marigny families together controlled seventy arpents downriver from Algiers Point. The two expansive holdings straddled the Verret Canal, a channel (today's Whitney Avenue) excavated under the direction of Furcy Varret (Verret) primarily for drainage but possibly also irrigation, mill power, and small-craft navigation, given that it had some sort of connection to the river.[31] That same year, 1834, the well-known surveyor-engineer Pierre Benjamin Buisson prepared a survey of the Marigny land, dividing it into twenty-five slender parallel lots for sale at public auction. Too narrow for plantation agriculture, the strips strongly suggest a first step toward subdividing the land for the surveying of streets.[32]

Relatedly, sometime between 1834 and 1839, the next plantation downriver from Marigny, pertaining to Pierre Cazalard, had been subdivided and labeled as Tunisburg.[33] Importantly, its streets, starting with present-day Murl Street, were laid out on north-south lines, parallel to existing property lines, as opposed to perpendicularly to the river, as had been done for Mossyville, Durvergéville, Olivierville, and Gosselinville. This established a spatial precedent emulated for most subsequent subdivision on this "lower coast." The subdivision's sobriquet alluded to Tunis in North Africa, which lies east of Algiers on the Mediterranean, just as Tunisburg lay east of Algiers on the Mississippi; the motivation for the rather exotic names probably stemmed from American and French military exploits along the Barbary Coast, both a source of local pride. While it is unclear exactly when streets were actually laid out in Tunisburg, the effort marked the farthest yet downriver urbanization on the West Bank. Its main landmark was the Cazalard Plantation House, which General Morgan had used in 1815 as a headquarters during the British assault. Later, Tunisburg was a home-away-from-home for Jefferson Davis, who bought a cottage there in 1853, only to have it confiscated by Congress in 1865. Around 1890, the McLellan Dry Dock Company moved into Tunisburg, which led to a semi-successful attempt to rename the community "McLellanville."[34] Neither name, however, endured into the modern era.

With Algiers at one end and Tunisburg at the other, economic pressure mounted to subdivide the 1.5-mile span of Verret and Marigny lands in between. Given its prime riverfront and convenient access via the Verret Canal right-of-way, this real estate was particularly suitable for industry and transportation. In the early 1840s, the Verrets sold the lowermost section to François Vallette, who built the Vallette Dry Dock there. The next section went to J. P. Whitney's Belleville Iron Works, and the subsequent layout of streets would become known as Belleville, the foundry being in the block closest to the riverfront. Next were lands sold to the Brooklyn Warehouse Company, which would become known as Brooklyn or Brooklinville, while the adjacent LeBeuf property became Lebeufville. On the other side of the old Verret Canal was Hendeeville, which extended down to Tunisburg. Some of these subdivision names were on paper only, while others circulated in the vernacular; many would conflate with their neighborhoods and fall out of use, surviving today only as the occasional street name.

By the late 1840s, the four miles along the lower coast exuded a village-like urbanization interspersed with industry and small farms. Some of the industry was impressive: the Belleville foundry, for example, "had immense front walls with turrets imitating a European castle," wrote historians Sally and William Reeves, where were "manufactured steam engines, sugar mills, vacuum pans, cotton presses, saw mills, [and] draining machines."[35] But hardly could the area be described as urbanized or industrialized. Streets were unpaved, and extended back only a few blocks. "From Algiers," wrote an advocate as late as 1885, "the entire distance down to Tunisburg is lined with beautiful residences, delightfully situated, amid orange and peach orchards, flowers and shrubbery."[36]

As New Orleans expanded on the East Bank, calls increased for improved cross-river access. The St. Mary's Market Steam Ferry Company began ferry service from the landing by the St. Mary's Market between present-day North and South Diamond streets, and by 1834, another ferry opened on the Jackson Avenue wharf. The two conveyances gave uptowners direct access to the West Bank, and replaced a three-hour slog through downtown and Algiers with a thirty-minute glide.

Ferries were economic and demographic lifelines. "Ferryboat connections with the east bank were the strongest determinants of how isolated from, or integrated with, the outside world, [the West Bank] was," wrote historians Fritz and Reeves. "Without them [it] would have been ten times more provincial."[37] This was even more the case when the operations upgraded from simple skiffs to steam-powered barges that connected with New Orleans's upper *banlieue*, where Anglo-American, German, and Irish migration had augmented populations, and where industries needed West Bank resources like lumber, firewood, and bricks. The New Orleans & Carrollton Railroad had just been established on Nayades Street (now St. Charles Avenue), with a spur down Jackson Avenue to the ferry terminal, giving East Bankers a way to roll and float to the West Bank with a minimum of walking. Where precisely would they disembark? At the landing of the lower plantation of the Destréhan family, where the Jackson Ferry pulled ashore.

If there is one historical clan most responsible for the present-day geography of the West Bank, it is probably the Destréhans, particularly when we consider the family's Marigny, D'Aunoy, Boré, Foucher, and Harvey branches. Their Louisiana grandsire was Jean Baptiste Honoré d'Estréhan, son of the king's councilor, who arrived at New Orleans in 1739 and later became colony treasurer. One of Jean Baptiste's sons rose to equal levels in the Spanish government, by which time the family had amassed land and wealth in St. Charles Parish where still stands the famed Destréhan Plantation House (1787). The main move to the West Bank came in 1821–1823, when Guy Noël Destréhan purchased the Derbigny and LeBreton (Robin) plantations, both of which had been carved from a 1790 Spanish land grant to the Ursuline Nuns. In 1833, the unified parcels came into the possession of Nicolas Noël Destréhan (more on those later), who by 1834 also controlled another parcel a mile upriver.[38]

With nearby McDonoghville, Mossyville, and Duverjéville already subdivided, new ferry lines up and running, and rising property values all around, Nicolas Noël Destréhan in 1836 decided to subdivide the lower of his two plantations. He hired Pierre Benjamin Buisson, a former soldier in Napoleon's army who had surveyed nearly half of today's Uptown and the Marigny land (1834) in lower Algiers.[39] The development would be called Mechanickham, or, in the variable orthography of the day, Mechanikham, Mechaniks Village, or Mechanicsville. Many of the initial settlers who moved here from Lafayette across the river were German skilled workers, called "mechanics" at the time, or *mechanik*. The town name may derive from the so-called "Mechanics' Home," an American communal-work phenomenon akin to a frontier barn raising. In this case, various mechanics—a "carpenter, bricklayer and plasterer [all] club together and assist in building a house for each other; they then labor for the lumber merchant and others, and by this means pay for the articles used."[40] No information survives as to early mechanics' homes here, but usage of the generic toponym "village" suggests there were more than a few, as opposed to a single lodge or boarding house. It's also possible that the development aspired to attract such home builders and such homes, rather than connote that some already existed.

Nicolas Noël Destréhan (1793–1848) was a singular figure in West Bank history: "a fine representative of French Louisiana creoles," by one historian's estimation, educated and cultured, yet at times impulsive, abusive, and altogether intense, having once commanded a slave to hatchet off his own arm (Destréhan's, that is) after he caught his *capeau* in a steam cane grinder.[41] He showed an aptitude for business, having developed the family-owned rear portion of the Faubourg Marigny in the late 1820s, just as its value rose on account of the Pontchartrain Railroad. In 1831 that enterprise became, with the help of a land donation by Destréhan himself, the region's first operational train. The railroad made the Faubourg New Marigny (today's Seventh Ward and St. Roch neighborhoods) "extremely profitable,"[42] and that success begged repetition.

Now, here on the West Bank in 1836, Destréhan worked with Benjamin Buisson to design a comparable development with an eye toward future railroad connectivity and, like McDonoghville, with a vision for a genuine civic community. Mechanickham got a scenic commons framed by twin boulevards (now Huey P. Long Avenue) addressing the river, space for a church and courthouse or college to the rear, and provisions for a railroad right-of-way, a foundry, and a ferry landing. Destréhan also set forth regulations for land-buyers, "allow[ing] the settlers to have their own government," but also imposing a proto-zoning ordinance prohibiting slaughterhouses of any type.[43] Why the concern? The West Bank formed the eastern terminus for Texas and western Louisiana cattle drives, thanks to its terrestrial contiguity with those regions. The commerce benefited the local economy, but the slaughtering produced repugnancy and reduced land values—not what Destréhan wanted. Better to ferry the beasts to Lafayette's flatboat wharves across the river, and let East Bank abattoirs do the bloody work.

As if to illustrate the symbiotic relationship between transportation and real estate, Solomon High, president of the St. Mary's Market Steam Ferry Company, expanded the Mechanickham street grid in 1838 with a seamless three-block annex immediately downriver.[44] From the company's perspective, the subdivision would give their ferry service more riders, while the ferry service would increase the value of the company's subdivision. Within a year, this development would gain the name Gretna, and in short time, the pithy appellation would eclipse the orthographically clumsy Mechanickham to mean both developments as well as later expansions. "Persons wishing delightful country residences, and to be near the centre of business," read one auction ad for Gretna lots, "[will enjoy] advantages too obvious to require description," to which was appended the note, "The directors of the St. Mary's Market Steam Ferry Co. will also grant to all persons purchasing property at the above sale a free ticket . . . to cross in the ferry boat for one year."

"Gretna" most likely comes from Gretna Green in Scotland, a border village famed for its runaway weddings due to Scotland's historically liberal matrimonial laws and geographical convenience to eloping English couples. What brought the toponym to the West Bank of the Mississippi, it is said, was a local Justice of the Peace known for granting marriages generously, coupled with a popular theatrical farce, *Gretna Green*, by Samuel Beazley, which played at four New Orleans theaters twelve times between 1829 and 1841.[45] "Gretna" started appearing on maps in 1838, in real estate ads in 1839, and in one whimsical article in 1840, where the *Daily Picayune* connected Gretna Green in Scotland, Gretna in Louisiana, a wedding of a couple who just happened to be named Green, and, lo and behold, a certain company with vested interests in all of the above:

> The happy parties were Mr. A. S. Green . . . and Miss Lucy Weyel, [and] a great deal of *éclat* was given to the affair through the liberality of the St. Mary's Ferry Company, by whom the happy pair were presented with a lot of ground in Gretna. The place is improving with a rapidity truly surprising. Seventy houses are already built, and a handsome hotel overlooks the landing place. Gretna is now in his green honeymoon, and may his joys be ever green.[46]

Moreover, Gretna was a popular weekend retreat for New Orleanians, known for its sports, regattas, hunts, and other amusements—the sort of scenic getaway that might also attract wedding parties. It was all good for business, aided by the famous name and its charming connotations. "The St. Mary's Ferry to Gretna is in full operation," newsreaders were reminded in 1842, "conveying passengers to pleasant entertainment across the river."[47] Benjamin Moore Norman, in his 1845 travelogue of the region, wrote of the pleasantries of Gretna and alluded to its appeal as a romantic getaway:

> The walk from Algiers to this village [of] Gretna . . . is spotted with comfortable residences, principally inhabited by the owners of the adjoining grounds. There is a steamboat [ferry] constantly plying from here to the city [and] Lafayette. . . . The village has a rural appearance, is regularly laid out, and exhibits some neat tenements. The forest approaches quite near; and, the idea that one may so easily lose himself in

the neighboring woods, gives to the place a touch of romance which only the denizens of a crowded city know how to appreciate.[48]

As part of a recreational economy that included romantic strolls, boxing, racing, and Choctaw *raquette*, Gretna as well as Algiers also occasionally hosted bullfighting and "bull-baiting," or animal fights. Algiers was the site of "possibly the earliest recorded Spanish-style bullfight in the United States[,] on Sunday, May 19, 1844." Behind it was an ambitious Minorcan named José "Pepe" Llulla, who moved to Algiers in 1840 and built a bullring by the ferry landing. Featuring visiting *toreros* and partaking of bulls coming in through the livestock trade in Algiers, the bloody spectacles were a hit. In 1852–1853, Algiers and Gretna held blood sports "contesting local Attakapas bulls against grizzlies imported from California or Mexico and drawing anywhere from 3,000 to 6,000 exceptionally unruly fans."[49] The human corollary of these sorts of ritualized bloodshed was dueling, and the rear of Algiers, like the back of New Orleans (today's City Park and Bayou Metairie), were favored spots for settling rows.

That sort of activity could only happen in a place that was both accessible to urban populations yet isolated from it, and as Norman implied in the above quote, that's what gave Gretna its appeal. One could "ferry from Gretna to Jackson street and [take] the two story car down Jackson and St. Charles to Tivoli Circle," noted an 1846 visitor, a two-leg commute that got you to downtown New Orleans in all of a long hour.[50] Yet the area was also isolated: unlike the Algiers-area subdivisions, which had developed adjacently, Mechanickham and Gretna spawned from farther-out ferry landings, and still had crops and pastures on their flanks and woodlands to the rear (thus the popularity of hunting). Among those agrarian parcels were those of W. Brown, R. Delogny, and J. S. David on the lower side toward McDonoghville, while on the upper side were the holding of Charles Derbigny and a vast tract pertaining to the Foucher family, which had at one time extended nearly to present-day Crown Point, largest on the antebellum West Bank.[51] In 1821 Antoine Foucher sold the upper part of his land to a man with the decidedly un-Francophone name of Stephen Henderson.

Much like his Scots-Irish neighbor John McDonogh, the Scottish-born Henderson made his money in East Bank investments, namely cotton presses, and sank it into West Bank real estate, purchasing in 1818 the former Duplantier sugarcane plantation from its new owner, Sosthene Allain. Previous owners going back a century included the colonist Richaume and surgeon Louis Vigé, followed by an array of titleholders, among them women and at least two free men of color, who used the land for timber, boat-building, and cash crops.[52] Upon his acquisition, Henderson, like McDonogh, was among the first to subdivide his West Bank land, having directed state surveyor General C. N. Bouchon to lay out lines in 1819. He also operated a sawmill, using an improved version of the circa-1740 Dubreuil Canal to haul in backswamp timber and, during high water, to power the saw mill.

Henderson would amass wealth and, again like McDonogh, would eventually bequeath it to charitable causes and call for the repatriation of the enslaved to Africa. In two regards, however, Henderson took a different path: his 1819 subdivision was not for urbanization, as was McDonoghville, but rather to create truck farms, such that Bouchon's "subdivisions" were really slender long-lots for food production.[53] And while the introverted McDonogh was famously a bachelor, Henderson, like other ambitious Anglophones moving to Francophone Louisiana, married into Creole high society. Henderson's bride, Zelia Eleonore Destréhan, traced aristocratic lineage to the early days of the French colony. Now, a hundred years later, the Destréhan family tree included a who's who of powerful planter families, and together they owned a substantial portion of the present-day metropolis on both banks.

Stephen Henderson died in 1837, at which time his will created a fund "to do the greatest quantity of good, and to the greatest number of persons and to the poorest people."[54] Some of his properties remained in the family, including one key parcel that in 1825 came into the hands of Henderson's brother-in-law, the same Nicolas Noël Destréhan who would create Mechanickham.[55]

Destréhan managed this second West Bank plantation for over a decade. In 1836, fresh off his successes with New Marigny and Mechanickham and creatively grandiose in his aspirations, Destréhan visualized a bold new project for this land. He named the subdivision Cosmopolite City, and designed for it a remarkable rendition of James Edward Oglethorpe's famous plan for Savannah, Georgia, in which broad orthogonal boulevards are separated into six smaller cellular "wards" (Oglethorpe's term), each structured around a central green nested therein. Side streets would have worldly names like English, Spanish, Italian, Russian, Persian, and Turk, which could only be outdone by his name for the grand boulevard: Paradise Avenue. The Oglethorpe Plan represented Enlightenment-era thinking on social equality, and Cosmopolite City represented an early attempt to introduce the progressive design to Louisiana. However, it was not the first: Milneburgh, Alexander Milne's envisioned community at the lakefront end of the Pontchartrain Railroad on Elysian Fields Avenue, exhibited a similar design two years before Cosmopolite City, complete with the nested greens and worldly names. Given Destréhan's involvement with land development along this railroad, he may have gleaned the Oglethorpe idea from Milneburgh, rather than Savannah.[56] In 1840 Destréhan hired Allou D'Hemecourt to actualize the vision, and sought permission to build a ferry line to Louisiana Avenue.

But however enlightened the inspiration, the plan was ultimately prone to the volatile late-1830s national economy and the vagaries of the local real estate market. Sitting across the river from a rather unpopulated part of New Orleans's upper *banlieue*, the parcels could not compete with those in closer, better-connected Gretna. Destréhan's ever-wandering mind shifted to yet another entrepreneurial idea, as we shall see in a moment, and he eventually abandoned his Cosmopolite City project, Oglethorpe Plan and all.[57] In broader developmental terms, however, a subdivision would eventually come to fruition here, though under a different name and form: today's Harvey. In terms of nomenclature, Destréhan's Cosmopolite City lived on in the Cosmopolite Brickyard (Cosmopolite Place), started in 1848 by a Destréhan in-law who would become a major West Bank figure. The brick operation was located "opposite upper line of Lafayette"[58]—that is, precisely on the site once slated for Cosmopolite City. Geologically, this locale proved good for brickmaking, because there Destréhan would soon dig a major waterway, and as the operator explained many years later, "the clay excavated [for it was] much stronger [than] brick made from batture [clay]."[59]

5

Canals, Railroads, Ships, and Industry

If the Destréhan clan had one winning strategy, it was their knack for economic diversification, in which land was used not only for monocrop staples but also for resource extraction, sugar processing, brickmaking, lumber milling, truck farming, citrus growing, pasture, and dairy.

Now Nicolas Noël Destréhan mulled regional transportation as a business endeavor, an idea he likely gleaned from his predecessors. A century prior, Claude Joseph Villars Dubreuil had a channel dug just to the east to connect with Bayou Barataria. More recently, the Barataria and Lafourche Canal Company bought a sliver four miles upriver and, using state-provided slave labor, dug the Company Canal to link with Bayou Lafourche to the west.

Destréhan's idea was to go straight south and connect with the bayou and bay of Barataria. In 1839 he supplemented his riverfront holdings with a purchase of backswamp and marshland southward toward Bayou Barataria, and on April 18, he wrote in his journal (according to a translation by historian William D. Reeves), "The next day I began opening a route across the cypress swamp and laying out the line of the grand canal."[1] So began the Destréhan Canal, today's Harvey Canal.

To augment the old sawmill canal, Destréhan contracted John McAuliffe, who appears to have hired "Irish ditchers" for the labor, the same source used to build the New Basin Canal on the East Bank during the previous seven years.[2] (Many Irish, as well as Germans, lived in Lafayette, today's Irish Channel, and could be conveniently ferried in as needed.) The task, as spelled out in a later lawsuit, entailed digging the riverfront segment "twelve acres in length, twenty feet wide at the top, eighteen feet at the bottom, and four and a half feet deep," with "all the dirt to be thrown on the west side, and the large roots and chips to be thrown on the east side." Canals in this flat region need guide levees, and Destréhan spelled out their specifications in his typically thorough manner: "The levée [is] to be made on the west side, to be exactly like the one already completed. . . . The east edge of the canal [is] to be cut plumb down, and the two feet difference in width at top and bottom, to be allowed for the slope on the west side." For this McAuliffe would be paid $1,200 and granted full title to "certain lots of ground in the village of Mechanicsham [sic]," worth an additional $800—a savvy negotiation on the part of Destréhan, in that in cost him no out-of-pocket cash and would bring external investment to a subdivision of his own making.

Work commenced in spring 1839 and proceeded in half-mile increments; by 1842, the waterway measured twelve feet wide, sufficient for small vessels. It was completed on July 15, 1844—at least by McAuliffe's understanding. According to the feisty Destréhan, the work fell short by a length of 12 feet, perhaps due to imprecisions of the measurement chain, or of an acre's length, technically 208.75 feet but often rounded down to 208 feet. Destréhan refused to pay McAuliffe, who sued, having completed 99.5 percent of the job by his opponent's own calculation. Destréhan met his match in court. "The defendant offered no evidence," the judge ruled, concluding tersely that Destréhan "must blame himself."[3]

A more serious shortfall of Destréhan's canal was its lack of a lock at the river, needed to reconcile differing water levels. Locks were always risky, and scouring currents made this spot especially dicey. So Destréhan doggedly designed his own solution, "a contraption of weights and balances to transfer boats [on tracks, over the levee] from his canal to the river and the river to the canal," a distance of 200 yards.[4] The mule-powered "submarine railway"—pure Nicholas Noël Destréhan—became a local curiosity, enduring in West Bank lore to this day. The contrivance got the job done, and by 1846, according to a visitor that year, the Destréhan Canal ran

> back six miles south to the bayou Oucha [Washa] which communicates with bayou and lake Barataria, connecting with the Gulf. [This] afforded not only ready intercourse with that region, but also facilities for bringing out hundreds of cords of ash and other kinds of wood fuel, supplied by that well-timbered land. . . . This wood

was [loaded] on the canal boat, a long, narrow double-ender, which when filled was cordeled to the river bank by a mule and driver, and [y]anked up on the levee, ready for the call of a steamboat captain. A brickyard near by was oft a scene of activity and a source of revenue. A princely income was thus brought in . . . from garden, orchard, dairy, wood-yard, and brick-kiln.[5]

Firewood was a key canal product because it fueled the hungry engines of countless steamboats. According to historian William D. Reeves, "slaves cut wood deep in the rear swamp [on a] quota [of] six cords per week . . . and if he could cut another cord he received a dollar."[6] Likewise, wild game, finfish, and shellfish; oranges and other citrus from the orchards; sundry esculents grown in the gardens; and milk and butter from the Destréhans' dairy cows, were moved by skiff through the canal for sale in city markets. Destréhan personally lorded over his assets and monetized every conceivable use. As per posted signs, he required that all "hunters, fisherman and promenaders" call on him at his house before using the waterway. He would charge hunters twenty cents for one gun and ten additional cents for additional firearms to hunt his lands, while each "fisher and promenader" would be charged ten cents, the former being limited to angling by line only.[7] In this manner, the Destréhan Canal would become a salient feature of West Bank country life as well as a vital artery connecting greater New Orleans with the estuarine abundance to its south. The flow of commerce transformed the Destréhan *habitation* into a key multiple-use production and distribution node and, in time, would breathe new life into Destréhan's abandoned Cosmopolite City idea—only this time, the canal-side community would have a more common street plan and a more down-to-earth name: Harvey.

"Harvey" came from Joseph Hale Harvey (1816–1882), husband of Nicholas Noël Destréhan's remarkable daughter Louise (1827–1903), who together rank as the most influential couple in West Bank history. Raised studiously amid splendor on her father's plantation, Louise had the opportunity, at age four, to take the inaugural ride of the Pontchartrain Railroad (1831)—the very conveyance, installed along the old Marigny Canal on Elysian Fields Avenue, that helped make her father a fortune developing the Faubourg New Marigny. She would remember that festive spring day for the rest of her life, and perhaps it internalized in her an appreciation for the connection between transportation and development.

Her father understood that relationship well, as he did relationships of the familial kind—even if they had to be arranged. In 1845, the elder arranged for 18-year-old Louise to marry 29-year-old Captain Joseph Hale Harvey, a Scottish-Irish Virginian and former Atlantic whaler, flatboatman, and all-around adventurer who, with his imposing presence and spirited personality, had won over his future father-in-law.[8] The union crossed a number of rivalrous rifts of the day—Anglo and Creole ethnicities, English and French tongues, Protestant and Catholic faiths, upper and lower southern cultural regions—all of which may have prepared the family well for the syncretic Louisiana society that would emerge.

But first came the nuptials, and they didn't happen in "romantic Gretna." Rather, after the complex marriage contract was signed in Lafayette across the river (the Jefferson Parish seat at the time), there was a Protestant wedding ceremony at the Congregational Church; a Catholic blessing at the St. Louis Cathedral; a voyage to Havana, Cuba; and then off to Europe for a nearly year-long honeymoon.

Their return in 1846 marked the young couple's ascent to the apex of West Bank society. As if to mark the occasion, they built themselves a castle—literally. A family descendant described the manse as a "medieval, two turreted baronial castle patterned from a faded old picture of [Joseph's] grandfather's and great uncle's home in Scotland." Inside were marble mantels, walnut finishing, and winding staircases up the crenelated octagonal towers—an architectural folly if ever there was one.[9] Its builders were said to be "non-slave Negro artisans of nearby 'Free Town,' who were among the best craftsmen in Louisiana."[10] According to historian Reeves, the castle was a Victorian Gothic answer to a comparably elaborate plantation house started ten years earlier by that endearingly overbearing father-in-law, Nicholas Noël Destréhan. It was called "the Big House," "Destrehan's Castle," and the "Louisiana Lyceum and Museum," for the elder's collection of art and curios—an eccentric touch that also earned it the nickname "Destrehan's Folly . . . by those who ridiculed his bringing of European art treasures to the country."[11] Folly or not, the five-story "vaguely Palladian" behemoth never quite reached completion and burned to ashes in 1852.[12]

Where did this palatial penchant come from? In the case of Harvey, it may reflect his years on the Mississippi, where elaborate adornment on steamboats had inspired comparable detailing on some plantation houses, the best surviving example of which is the "Steamboat Gothic" style of the San Francisco Plantation House in Garyville, Louisiana.[13] As for the Creole side of the family, it may have reflected a provincial yearning to showcase claims to an aristocratic lineage. Commented a tutor who lived with the Destréhans in 1846, the same year Harvey's Castle was constructed, "As had long been the custom here with Creole families of sufficient means, the sons . . . were sent back to the home of their ancestry to receive a more systematic and thorough training. Mr. Destrehan thus in early years imbibed tastes and ideas in La Belle France, [including] an architectural taste, and a wish to reproduce here some of the old baronial structures of that land."[14] Then again, the "castle look" was popular in the Romanticism-inspired architecture of this era, particularly for riverfront buildings visible from afar.[15] The Marine Hospital (1834), built in McDonoghville to care for infirm mariners, looked like a Gothic citadel, with crenelation on its towers and battlements, as did the twin Belleville Iron Works buildings in Algiers, with their "immense front walls with turrets imitating a European castle."[16] The West Bank skyline included a number of architectural curiosities, and it's worth noting that the present-day Algiers Courthouse (1896), an iconic sight from the French Quarter, too sports asymmetrical crenelated towers.

Harvey's Castle brought cross-river visibility to the Destréhan family operation and its eponymous canal. It also signaled the rise of Captain Joseph Hale Harvey as the heir apparent to the family patriarch, a transition the elder himself had choreographed. But Louise Destréhan Harvey would not be a passive voice in the marriage; it was not in her nature, nor was it in her unusual marriage contract, which was, frankly, more about personnel than the personal. After her father's death in 1848 at age 57, Louise, now all of 21 years of age, became the owner of the canal property plus 26,000 acres of Joseph's inherited Virginia land, as well as a co-owner, through a community estate, of many other assets, including $208,435 and 76 slaves inherited from her father. Joseph, meanwhile, went on to co-establish a commission merchant firm in New Orleans.[17]

The long 1850s were halcyon days for the Harvey-Destréhan clan. The couple would produce ten children; commerce bustled on the now-renamed "Harvey's Canal"; and the family enterprise generated far more income through its waterway and side businesses than through cash crops like sugarcane. In this regard, the Destréhan operation resembled that of the Durverje's a generation earlier, who at Algiers Point established the precedent of the West Bank mixed-use working farm with an enslaved workforce of specialists like "house servants, cow keepers, or gardeners [and a] shoemaker."[18] Likewise, "of [Destréhan's] 76 slaves, none were field hands," observed the historian Reeves. "The number of children and old people suggests a very stable society [of] family groups [in] headed households," and their work foretold "the tasks they would perform after emancipation, including brick making, merchandising, hostlering, and herdsmen."[19] Ever the diversifiers, the Harveys also looked toward subdividing some land for town development, the catalyst of which would be a transformational new industry on the West Bank: railroads.

〰〰〰

Riverine separation from the urban core was the West Bank's "original sin," a geographical happenstance intrinsic to its existence for which it has endured a despised subordination. Yet West Bankers have managed to turn that liability into an asset, and no one did it better than the railroad men.

Unlike the land mass across the river, the West Bank terrestrially adjoined the entire southwestern quadrant of the nation, a vast and growing region whose produce struggled to move eastward for lack of latitudinal waterways. Railroads could solve this problem, but without a bridge over the lower Mississippi, they could only reach the South's largest city via the West Bank. Thus railroads, which eventually subdued the commercial supremacy of the Mississippi and challenged New Orleans's monopoly on river traffic, would offer the West Bank some sweet revenge.

It would take awhile for the lightly populated Southwest to justify the expense of westward railroad construction, and for this reason, most of the early charter requests to the Louisiana State Legislature were for short rail lines on the East Bank. Among them were the aforementioned Pontchartrain Railroad and New Orleans & Carrollton Railroad, both built during the "railroad fever" days of the early 1830s.

The state needed internal improvements as much as private firms wanted profits, so officials bent over backwards in offering tax exemptions, granting railroad companies valuable rights-of-way on state land, legally empowering them with eminent domain, and often footing the bill for expenses.[20] Despite the subsidies, construction was difficult, logistics were complicated, and for those lines that did manage to open, service was limited at best and unreliable at worst. Louisiana railroads struggled through the 1830s and 1840s.[21]

By 1850, however, technology and construction methods had improved, while economic geographies shifted in a trans-Mississippi direction favorable to the

West Bank. The Red, Atchafalaya, and other western rivers had been improved for navigation, which brought commercial rigor to Louisiana's Acadian coast and prairie. Texas had joined the Union and, like southwestern Louisiana, produced an abundance of cattle. Cotton, sugarcane, and rice production all spread westward, as did slavery. The Mexican War and cession of lands up to the Pacific Coast broached the possibility of trade with the Far East, and the discovery of gold in California only added to the fervor.

New Orleans is not often remembered today as a jumping-off point for America's westward expansion—as are St. Louis, Kansas City, and Omaha—but perhaps it ought to be. One estimate made in 1853, when the migration was surging, put New Orleans's "floating population" (people in transit or staying briefly) at "125,000 strangers from the Western States; 25,000 Californians, going to and returning from California; [and] 125,000 immigrants, and strangers from Texas, Florida, Alabama, West Indies, etc."[22] Another estimate put the Californian traffic at 50,000. Whatever their true quantities (the above figures are possibly hyperbolic), migrants itched for westward access as much as New Orleans wanted western produce. Both called for better transportation toward the setting sun.

So began the second bout of "railroad fever." Financiers in 1851 convened in the Crescent City three times within a year, orating with such zeal that one historian compared the conventions "to old-fashioned revival meetings."[23] This time, the West Bank not only had a seat at the table, they had their own convention. Delegates at the New Orleans, Algiers, Attakapas and Opelousas Railroad Convention in June 1851 resolved to build a line connecting Algiers with the key Bayou Courtableau steamboat stop of Washington in St. Landry Parish—not quite the dreamed-of California connection, but a step in the right direction: westward.[24]

In the spring of 1853, investors led by Maunsel White, capitalized at $6 million, obtained a state charter for the New Orleans, Opelousas and Great Western Railroad Company to build tracks "to a point on the Sabine River most favorable for the purpose of constructing said Road through the State of Texas to El Paso [and] thence to the Pacific Ocean."[25] While the paperwork went through, company surveyors debated potential terminals and routes. The Opelousas contingent wanted the line to start at Donaldsonville or across from Baton Rouge, but the company's board of directors insisted on Algiers as the railroad's easternmost terminus. One reason was the importance of the New Orleans market; the other was that the police jury of Algiers had invested $75,000 in the company, paid in part by "a tax of one percent on the landed estate within their jurisdiction"[26]—a controversial case of government taxing the public to raise funds for private interests.

Next came route selection and right-of-way acquisition. For the eastern leg, Chief of Survey A. G. Blanchard made a strategic decision that would long affect the geography of the West Bank: the Algiers terminal station would be on the former Marigny holding downriver from the Point, where Furcy Varret had excavated a canal and left open an undeveloped corridor. The tracks would run along the grassy strip's upriver edge, near today's Atlantic Avenue. "By commencing at Verret's Canal," Blanchard explained, "it runs on the best route, without interfering seriously with any of the plantations," meaning the village-like settlements and small farms of Duverjeville (Algiers Point), Mossyville, and McDonoghville.[27] This move would influence the future location of the mile-long Algiers train yards and the lives of thousands for a century to come. From there the route pulled closer to the Mississippi, running 2,000 feet inland to avoid riverfront enterprises while still hugging close to the economic action and topographic high ground. The proposed 1852 route would become precisely the freight line still in use today, passing along 4th Street in Gretna, over the Harvey Canal on a drawbridge by Harvey's Castle, across the Millaudon and Zeringue plantations by the Seven Oaks Plantation House, and across Nine Mile Point to Thibodaux. Blanchard estimated the cost of the Algiers-to-Thibodaux leg to be $15,000 per mile for 51 miles, or $800,000.[28]

Not everyone was content. The succession of the late John McDonogh refused to pay the one-percent tax—and got sued by the Algiers police jury, while at the same time it resisted Great Western's demand for a 150-foot-wide right-of-way, triggering another lawsuit.[29] Railroad interests prevailed in both cases. Permissions elsewhere along the route fell into place, however reluctantly; most landowners saw the value the train could bring to their land, or understood that the company could seize it through eminent domain anyway. Construction was arduous, especially across swamplands, where track beds had to be shored up or placed on wooden trestles. But as historian Merl E. Reed pointed out, backswamp construction also "put the railroad close to usually inaccessible supplies of red cypress timber, the best wood . . . for ties. Consequently, the Great Western was perhaps the best timbered railroad in the South."[30] For the western leg, Civil Engineer Augustus Phelps started from a bridgeable point on Bayou Lafourche near Thibodaux, moved westward to Berwick Bay (today's Morgan

City) and onward to Opelousas following a series of topographic ridges (today's Highway 90 corridor), with eventual plans to reach Natchitoches and Texas.[31]

Work began in October 1852. By summer 1853, thirty miles had been graded, and by fall, seventeen miles of track had been laid—despite a yellow fever epidemic that killed 300 of the 350 railroad workers plus many Algerines, and would claim over ten thousand lives citywide.[32] Yet the project pressed toward completing its first phase, and held an inauguration ceremony on December 3, 1853, complete with music, toasts, speeches, and "an elegant repast in the open air." According to a *New Orleans Bee* reporter, "at 12 o'clock, [with] the aid of the locomotive "Natchitoches," we steamed . . . the distance of seventeen miles . . . in double quick time [on a track that] is admirably built, combining vast strength and solidity with entire ease and absence of jolting."[33] By fall 1854, the line spanned 52 miles, to Bayou Lafourche; a year later, it ran 66 miles; by spring 1857, it reached 80 miles, to Berwick Bay.

Expenses had run the Great Western into the red, until they were bailed out by the City of New Orleans's $1.5 million issuance of bonds to invest in the company.[34] The relief package demonstrated the wisdom of bringing the line into Algiers, rather than Donaldsonville or Baton Rouge. It also indicated that New Orleans did not see necessarily see West Bank improvements as a threat (at least not this one, this time). If the line brought in commerce without competing with the Mississippi, it could only be good for the city—as were the company's parallel investments on the East Bank. To facilitate cross-bank transshipments, the Great Western operated depots in both Algiers and on the Toulouse Street levee in the French Quarter, and kept an administrative office in the corner of the upper Pontalba Building on Jackson Square.[35]

From a broader economic standpoint, the Great Western was not an immediate success—"more of a convenience than an absolute necessity," in the judgment of the historian Reed, "important but not indispensable."[36] From a West Bank developmental perspective, however, this first railroad quite literally laid the groundwork for additional rail investments which *would* become indispensable, as catalysts for local industries. Together they would create a network of spur lines, depots, and stations, that, like the ferry landings of old, would seed and nourish human communities and further economic investments.

Less expected was the spatial effect of the tracks themselves, which would divorce the higher-elevation ten arpents or so fronting each holding, from the lower-elevation 30 to 70 arpents in the rear. The bifurcation led to a concentration of investment closer to the river and tracks, for reasons of greater access and more economic opportunities, versus a general divestment in the agrarian hindquarters. To be sure, this front-to-back pattern had long existed, but it had been a gradual differentiation; now it was a hardened demarcation, and the other side was, well, "the other side of the tracks." The railroad made the mid-nineteenth-century West Bank less of a plantation-based agricultural landscape (the trackbed made it awkward to get ploughs and wagons across, and runoff no longer flowed evenly), and more of a mixed-use landscape with industry between the river and tracks, hamlets and small farms just behind the railroad, and pasture and fallow fields farther back. Where West Bank subdivisions had preceded the railroad, residential streets and blocks occupied the riverfront in Duverjeville, Mossyville, McDonoghville, Gretna, and Mechanicksham. But where the railroad preceded the subdivisions, industry dominated the riverfront, and residential communities formed farther back, south of the tracks: witness Harvey and Marrero. As the tracks pulled away from the river, at Nine Mile Point, so did the industry, thus allowing residential blocks to form much closer to the river: for example, Westwego's Salaville and Bridge City. These patterns fell in place starting over 150 years ago, and hold true today.

☙☙☙

What were these industries? Operations that needed to be close to their customers, but not *too* close, gravitated to the nineteenth-century West Bank. That is, companies that needed to be convenient to port shippers and city dwellers (their main clientele) but also required ample space and resources unavailable on the high-priced urbanized East Bank, found a perfect home on the West Bank. Semirural West Bank communities had just low enough population density to minimize gripes and lawsuits over nuisances like malodor, smoke, noise, and detritus, yet also had just enough of a local work force to satisfy labor needs, thanks to cheap housing and ferryboat access. Its deep riverfront could dock any kind of river vessel; its truck farms could produce local food; its canals could handle the Barataria trade; and starting in 1853, its rails could roll in cars from points west. And it had space—lots and lots of available land. For these reasons, the West Bank became the industrial muscle of an otherwise mercantilist metropolis. Its specialties were shipyards, railyards, iron foundries, lumber milling, and sugar processing, along with a multitude of smaller value-added, and/or support industries, like brickmaking, cooperage, wheelwrighting, firewood collection, fish and game processing, warehousing and forwarding companies, and livestock corralling and slaughtering.

Slaughterhouses had operated at Pointe St. Antoine (Algiers Point) since colonial times, and continued after 1805, when Barthélémy Duverjé ran three small abattoirs at the foot of Lavergne Street. Dubbed Slaughterhouse Point, the spot was ideal for processing meat because it was just a short boat ride to the French Market's *Halle des Boucheries.*[37] Areas farther up the West Bank also had abattoirs, supplying meat to St. Mary's Market across the river, although Gretna developers banned slaughtering so as to make its real estate attractive for residential living. Relatedly, minutes from a Jefferson Parish police jury meeting in the mid-1800s recorded a proliferation of ordinances and regulations on nearly every aspect of livestock management, as would be expected in a jurisdiction of farms and pastures. Articles addressed sanitation, health inspections, waste disposal, the height of fences, the location of butchering (outdoors near roads was strictly prohibited), the handling of strays, even the conditions under which slaves could do the slaughtering. Attached to each article were fines for violators. Slaughtering was a main target of regulatory government, because it affected the health and quality of life of constituents.

Three factors drove the geography of stockyards and slaughtering: regional supply chains, local distribution networks, and metro-area spatial dynamics. During the antebellum era, most cattle consumed in New Orleans came from western Louisiana and Texas, including northern Texas herds driven to Shreveport and floated down the Red River. Others arrived along the Red or Mississippi and were barged down to New Orleans, to landings in Jefferson City or Lafayette City (present-day Uptown and the Irish Channel). Those that came from central Texas were driven to the tiny Matagorda Bay port of Indianola or Galveston, herded onto steam transports and shipped coastwise to New Orleans, coming up the river and unloading as needed.[38]

The circumstances that gave the West Bank a lock on incoming cattle occurred when the beeves were railroaded in on the New Orleans, Opelousas, and Great Western tracks, driven overland on a southern route, and/or floated in on the Barataria & Lafourche Company Canal from Louisiana's own Attakapas cattle country. The Southern Steamship Line, founded by Charles Morgan, dominated cattle-shipping between Texas and New Orleans; after the Civil War, Morgan acquired the railroad and made it into Morgan's Louisiana & Texas Railroad, while his ships docked at Algiers and discharged livestock by the thousands.

The West Bank's one disadvantage in this trade was the wide river separating beef on the hoof from beef on the plate. But this obstruction played advantageously, courtesy of that "close-but-not-too-close" spatial dynamic: the West Bank was close enough to reach thousands of East Bank consumers, but not so close as to pay high East Bank real estate prices.

That's where distribution came into play. Cattle could be barged from West Bank pastures and stockyards across to East Bank populations; at one point there was even a specialized cattle ferry. New Orleans butchers, most of them hailing from Gascony, had secured the right to slaughter at their neighborhood abattoirs, thus enabling them to meet demand just in time and deliver fresh meat to consumers swiftly. But what was good for business was bad for neighbors, as abattoirs, dispersed citywide, were notorious for discharging excrement, offal, and blood, causing disgusting stenches and health concerns.

After the Civil War, the discord heightened for a uniquely postbellum reason. Whereas most American cattle production during the conflict went straight to feeding combatants or civilians, Texas—with its huge herds, low population, and marginal seat at the theater of war—found itself with a surplus of over five million head. Cattle don't age well; the industry craves a timely market. New Orleans being the nearest major source of demand, the forces of the free market, pent up after four years of wartime disruption, let fly a great trafficking of Texas cattle into New Orleans kitchens.[39]

This put all the more meat on the hooks of the neighborhood abattoirs—and exasperation among gasping neighbors. Following the lead of other cities, citizens petitioned the state to relocate, concentrate, and regulate the abattoirs. Powerful interests, including the railroads, would also benefit from modernizing the city's antique abattoir system, and if centralization prevailed, as one legal scholar put it, "the expectation that New Orleans rather than Chicago could become the very heart of the world slaughtering industry seemed justified."[40]

In 1869, the biracial Reconstruction-era state legislature complied by passing "An Act to Protect the Health of the City of New Orleans, to Locate the Stock-Landings and Slaughter-Houses, and to Incorporate the Crescent City Live-stock Landing and Slaughter-house Company," which centralized slaughtering and granted a monopoly to one operator.[41] Citizens applauded the new law, and some invested in the publicly traded stock. As for its location, Slaughterhouse Point made the most sense, at least to East Bankers who were happy to push the nuisance across the river. Land was acquired and a makeshift livestock landing and processing facilities were hastily erected. "The slaughterhouses at Algiers," reported *The New Orleans Times* in July 1869, "are at the point which is henceforth to be the depot for the receipt of Texas and Opelousas cattle, and from which the slaughtered carcases [*sic*] of animals can be easily and speedily distributed to the various markets."[42]

Others, however, were outraged, principally the Gascon butchers. Supporting them were those who philosophically opposed monopolies, suspected corruption, or flat-out resisted the state legislature on racial grounds. The butchers filed nearly three hundred lawsuits, some of which went to the United States Supreme Court. Their argument rested on the recently ratified Fourteenth Amendment, which ensured broad federal protection against state infringements on basic rights such as practicing one's trade—not to mention freedom from slavery, the amendment's original intent.

In the meanwhile, the butchers formed their own association to rival the monopoly, and built an East Bank facility in what is now Arabi. The monopoly eventually acquired this new facility, and when workers "were given a choice between the company's fairly makeshift original abattoir [in Algiers] and a larger, better-equipped one located on the same side of the river as the city, the vast majority quickly abandoned the west-bank facility."[43]

In 1873, the US Supreme Court ruled in favor of the monopoly, limiting the Fourteenth Amendment to protecting the rights of newly freed slaves while avoiding the precarious postbellum federal/state balance of power. Essentially a victory for states' rights, the *Slaughter-house Cases* have been controversial ever since, lambasted by some legal scholars, heralded by others.[44] Regarding the case itself, however, the ruling was rather moot, because the original 1869 law had already centralized the meat industry, first in Algiers and then Arabi, where it would remain into the 1960s.

Yet small stockyards and slaughtering operations still persisted on the West Bank, and cattle, horses, mules, pigs, and sheep remained a part of everyday West Bank village life. In her elder years, Katherine Harvey Rogér, eldest daughter of Horace Harvey, remembered how cowboys would drive Attakapas ("Tucapaw") cattle by Harvey Castle in the late 1800s:

[I remember] the wild, long-horned Tucapaws cattle that periodically stampeded through Harvey. We knew they were coming by sounds . . . of fast-pounding hoofs, the pistol-like cracking of long whips and the whoops and howls of cowboys on wild Texas ponies, driving them from the Tucapaw country to the slaughter house pens in New Orleans. Everyone . . . ran madly for shelter. From our perch on Grandma's high raised gallery behind a stout wooden fence, we watched them sweep by for none of us would have missed that sight for the world. Always the stampeding cattle left a trail of wrecked fences and small houses . . . and sometimes death to those who were caught in their path. Once the Tucapaws ran through the corner barroom in Grandma's brick building across the canal. And all of Harvey could hear bottles and glass being smashed to bits.[45]

The West Bank's most critical industry was ship repair, without which even the most profitable vessel could become a costly liability. In colonial times, enough riverfront space remained open on the East Bank to accommodate this specialized activity. But with the advent of steamboats and the surge in Western commerce, wharfingers at New Orleans—that "grand mart of business, the Alexandria of America"—were forced to devote most space to round-the-clock loading and unloading. At any given moment, there was "the most extraordinary medley of . . . [c]raft of every possible variety,"[46] and with a nautical taxonomy to match: ships, barks, brigs, hermaphrodite brigs, schooners, sloops, barges, keelboats, flatboats, feluccas, galliots, ketchers, luggers, pettiauger, brigantines, batteau, steamboats, steamships, steam ferries, steam propellers, steam tugs, steam schooners, schooners, yachts—and more. During busy times, they all seemed to materialize simultaneously, jockeying for position and vying for space. Wrote one incredulous visitor in 1834, "the tiers of vessels, which extend for upwards of a mile along the levee, [await] three four and five abreast . . . at times six and seven deep," until a berth at the docks opened up.[47] The frenetic scene made New Orleans "the fourth port . . . in the world, exceeded only by London, Liverpool, and New York" and "the leading export city of the United States and one of the leading [in] the world."[48]

All this high-stakes bustle on the East Bank pushed the deliberative work of nautical engineering to the more spacious and placid West Bank. The New Orleans City Council in 1809 acted to clear its side of the river of ship repair activity, and in 1815 ordered French-born shipbuilder Pierre Séguin to remove his ship repair facilities from the Faubourg Marigny riverfront. Pierre died two years later, leaving his brother André to keep the business alive. André Séguin met Barthélémy Duverjé, master of the mixed-use West Bank plantation. Intrigued with this lucrative new waterfront use, Duverjé in 1819 sold to Séguin a sliver of riverfront land at what is now Patterson at Seguin Street in Algiers, where Séguin opened a marine ways, or slipway, allowing for vessel construction and repair.[49] From that moment, wrote historians David Fritz and Sally K. Reeves, "the process of converting Algiers from a semi-plantation into an industrial complex began."[50]

Captains of vessels docked at the Port of New Orleans, of course, would rather hire portside contractors to repair problems while their cargo was being transferred. But such work could take a long time, lengthening their stay and depriving the wharfinger of dockage fees. This issue became a flashpoint, to which the City of New Orleans responded by finally ordaining "it shall not be lawful to build, repair, heat or smoke any vessel, steam-boats, or other craft of any description whatsoever, in that part of the port, situated on the left [East] bank of the river Mississippi, and all builders, ship-carpenters and other persons, contravening the present article, shall pay for every contravention a fine of fifty dollars."[51] The fact that this 1829 ordinance penalized local contractors, and not visiting captains, further motivated anyone in the ship repair business to head to Algiers or McDonoghville to work—and probably to live as well.

The industry grew. Séguin's slipway was sold to ship carpenter François Vallette in 1837, who moored there "the condemned hull of a vessel, of about 200 tons, commonly called a hulk . . . to raise vessels [and] make repairs."[52] Functionally speaking, this may have been greater New Orleans's first dry dock, though by most accounts that credit goes to the New Orleans Floating Dry Dock Company, which had a specially designed unit built in Paducah, Kentucky, and floated down to the Algiers riverfront in 1837. A recent innovation at the time, a dry dock is simply a boat for broken boats: a floating barge-like chamber with gates, devised to fill with water and take in a damaged vessel, after which its gates are closed and the water pumped out, to gain access to the hull for repairs. Once completed, the gates reopen, the chamber refills, and the seaworthy vessel floats back into service.

The dry dock was a godsend for Algiers, because the alternative for getting under a hull—digging a pit and installing fixed piers on the riverbank—was costly, risky, and site-sensitive. Algiers' deep harbor, on the other hand, was ideal for moveable dry docks, even more so because the adjacent bank could be owned privately.[53] "Taking a stroll . . . through the bustling little village of Algiers," wrote a *Picayune* reporter in 1838, "we were enabled to examine every part of that admirable contrivance—the Floating Dry Dock." The contraption measured 225 feet long and 60 feet wide, with a double floor of thick timbers; at the stern was the gate to admit damaged vessels; at the bow were four steam pumps capable of draining the impounded water in six hours. "When we visited the dock, the steamboat *Levant* was resting in it, high and dry, in a perfectly horizontal position, at such a height from the floor that the workmen could get under any part of her." He concluded, "We regard this Floating Dry Dock as one of the most important collateral facilities for carrying on the operations of our commerce."[54]

Within a few years, similar operations opened nearby, such that in 1845, wrote a visitor, "Algiers [and] Macdonough [are] the great work-shop of New Orleans, for the building and repairing of vessels. It has its dry docks, and other facilities for the most extensive operations. In business times, it presents a scene of activity that . . . reminds one of the bustling and enterprise of the North."[55] The 1842 city directory listed twelve ship carpenters living in Algiers, plus eight regular carpenters, "three ship captains, two painters, two engineers, a joiner, a ship's blacksmith, a mechanic, a caulker, a blockmaker and two shipbuilders."[56] By 1849 the city director listed 34 Algerine ship carpenters, joiners, and painters, two "ship smiths" and three ship builders. By 1857 Algiers had twelve dry docks, one of them substantially longer than a city block.[57] Among them were Hasam & Anderson's Crescent Dry Dock, Hyde & McKee's Orleans Dry Dock, Hughes, Wallette & Co.'s Louisiana Dry Dock, Mooney & Girard's Gulf Dry Dock, and Piniger & Martin's Pelican Dry Dock. The last of these would be the largest dry dock erected in Algiers for the rest of the century, capable of receiving vessels up to 400 feet in length.[58] Seven of the firms organized the New Orleans Dry Dock Association and collectively set their rates (legal at the time) according to tonnage, length, and type. In 1860, for example, a sailing ship under 100 tons and 100 feet would pay $14 to $16 per day in dry dock, and a steamboat slightly more; those vessels 1500 tons and 600–750 feet long (the largest plying the river) would pay $126 to $138 per day.[59] Extra charges applied if cargo or ballast were aboard, and all payment had to be in cash. It was a busy scene, critical to river commerce, and by a later estimate in 1885, it provided the livelihood for three-quarters of Algiers households.[60] It was also perilous: workers toiled in dangerous conditions near gushing water and heavy moving parts, and the dry docks themselves could fall into disrepair. Some sank, and all battled incessant river currents, which ran fast and scoured deeply during high water.

Algiers and McDonoghville had a captive clientele for ship repair, as any damaged vessel at the Port of New Orleans had little choice but to limp over and pay a visit. Ship *building*, on the other hand, was more spatially elastic; so long as you had the materials, workforce, and a navigable waterway, you could build anywhere. Nevertheless, because Algiers fared well in all three regards—wood from the backswamp, skilled mechanics, and a deep harbor—it also boasted a rigorous shipbuilding sector. Of the ships registered at the Port of New Orleans between 1841 and 1860, Algiers had built at least 27 of them, including schooners, sloops, and yachts (all with one mast); brigs (two masts); barks (three masts); steam ferries, steam tugs, and paddlewheel steamboats, some of them massive.[61] The largest Algiers-built vessel in this era was the steamboat *Baltic*, at 192 feet in length, 29 feet in width, and 604 tons in weight. It was built in 1859 under the direction of James M. Penniger for John S. Walton's Ocean Tow Company, to be commanded by Captain William Chapman.[62]

Shipbuilding and dry-dock work required iron—iron boilers, engines, pistons, hardware—as did the metropolis across the river and the plantations all around. Iron foundries were big-footprint industries which required raw materials, lots of fresh water, labor, transportation, and proximity to their customers, but that also spewed nuisances, namely smoke and cacophony. This gave foundries that "close-but-not-too-close" siting requirement to which the West Bank catered.

No one understood this better than John P. Whitney. A Mainer born in 1806 to a family of Yankee shipbuilders, Whitney arrived at New Orleans in 1835 and saw opportunities galore, particularly on the West Bank. "Deeply interested in ocean navigation," he founded "an immense shipping business," and supplemented it by establishing the Louisiana Dock Company and opening Algiers' fourth dry dock. Both operations were in need of iron and brass fittings, as well as boilers and engines, so Whitney paid $25,000 for 400 feet of riverfront land from the Verret family just below Algiers Point, and in 1846 established the Belleville Iron Works.[63]

Covering 150,000 square feet and employing a skilled workforce of 300 men, Belleville would become the area's largest foundry.[64] It became many things to many people. To shippers and planters, Belleville was the premier regional "manufacturer of steam engines, sugar mills, vacuum pans, boilers, clarifiers[,] bagasse burners[,] cotton presses, saw mills, draining machines, and machinery of every description."

To shipbuilders, architects, and engineers of all stripes, including railroadmen, Belleville had "iron and brass castings of all kinds made to order," and the ability to forge rails.[65] To Algerines and New Orleanians across the river, Belleville would be known for its enormous twin pavilions with massive brick walls fronted by crenelated towers, said to emulate Penrhyn Castle in Wales—so prominent that people nicknamed the entire neighborhood "Belleville."[66]

To other industries dependent on iron, Belleville was a reason to locate in Algiers. When the Great Western railroad to Opelousas opened in 1852, it established its terminal just three blocks downriver from Belleville—a marriage made in industrial heaven, as each one benefitted from the other.

To John Whitney, Belleville represented what Algiers and New Orleans needed to nurture—that is, its notoriously weak industrial manufacturing sector. If nineteenth-century Algiers might be considered "the Pittsburg of New Orleans," then Whitney was a forerunner to Andrew Carnegie. As would become the famed Scottish steelmaker, Whitney was a creative entrepreneur and skilled businessman as well as a "cordial and kind" man with a generous public spirit. What set Whitney apart was his aim to integrate disparate economic sectors, in this case maritime shipping, the merchant sector, *and* value-added industry (unlike many local investors, who only knew the first two). Along with his dry dock and foundry, Whitney projected a steamer line between New York and New Orleans, and came to be considered "one of her most enterprising citizens and eminent merchants."

When his life was cut short in 1848 by scarlet fever, both the commercial community and civil society sensed it had lost a vital force. "Had that gentleman lived," lamented an editorialist who advocated for more local manufacturing, "he would have endowed the city with a branch of industry that would have done much to accelerate the march of New Orleans to the greatest . . . destiny. But his premature death seems to have nipped the enterprise in its bud, and all the enlarged plans which, in his public spirit, were associated with the [Belleville] foundry, seemed to have died with him."[67]

A well-run business ought to outlive its creator, and the Algiers operation did exactly that. "[The] Belleville Iron Works [is] a joint-stock company, capital $200,000, [with] exclusive building and ground," read an 1858 description. "This foundry fronts the river, and has a good wharf and landing [by] the depot of the

Opelousas Railroad, the track of which extends to the foundry."[68] Vital to river, rail, city and plantation, Belleville prospered during the late antebellum—but plunged with the outbreak of the Civil War, when not only its customer base dried up, but Confederates and later Union soldiers seized the operation for military purposes. It reopened afterwards with a different tenant, struggled economically, and burned down in 1883.[69]

Another source of income for Algiers and McDonoghville came in mooring fees, either for vessels idled for months or those in transit awaiting berths at the Port of New Orleans, which could take days. Mooring could produce income for owners of adjacent land, but it was also fraught with legal and nautical complications. In one 1842 case, the captain of the ship *Delaware*, struggling against a weak wind and unable to reach its berth, instead had his crew cable up to the idle dry dock ("hulk") owned by François Vallette and moored at the "Duvergsberg" (that is, Duverjeville, or Algiers Point) riverfront. Several days later, another ship owned by the same captain, the *Sheffield*, took shelter from rough waters by mooring itself to the *Delaware*. Soon Vallette learned of the two freeloaders and confronted the responsible parties, only to be ignored. "That night the wind blew across the river very strong," read a later lawsuit; "the ships pressed the hulk on the shore, [and] it sunk." Vallette sued for $500 to recoup his losses, but the case was not as cut-and-dried as it seemed. The defense argued that, according to Louisiana's Civil Code, "the banks of navigable rivers are free for public use, and that no one has a right to obstruct the use of them," and therefore the "the hulk was wrongfully at the bank of the river." They also argued that "the hulk was improperly and unsafely moored," and overvalued at $500. On appeal, the judge found in favor of the plaintiff Vallette, but awarded him only $250.[70]

❧❧❧

While dry docks, iron works, shipbuilding, and mooring dominated the Orleans Parish side of the West Bank riverfront, the Jefferson Parish side, with its smaller populations and greater distance from the city and port, devoted itself more to the handling and processing of Barataria Basin natural resources arriving on the Harvey (formerly Destréhan) Canal. That circa-1840s waterway so transformed the Destréhan-Harvey planter clan that, according to a family memoir, by the

1850s, "the plantation had long gone out of existence, [while the] canal remained the principal interest with its boat tollage[,] brickyard, tenant houses and boats as side interests."[71]

Under the skilled management of Louise Destréhan Harvey, the Harvey Canal monetized everything. There were fees for cargo stored in family-owned warehouses or laid out on quays. There were tolls based on tonnage for larger vessels, else thirty-five cents for pirogues, twenty-five cents for skiffs (each way), and, for conveyances using the tow path, ten cents for drayage carts, twenty cents for buggies, and thirty cents for pleasure coaches. Going hunting? Ten cents. Hunting on horseback? Fifteen cents. Fishing? Ten cents, unless you use a net (fifteen cents) or a seine (twenty cents). Just going for a stroll? Ten cents.[72]

Fishermen targeted species depending on how far south they went, and, correspondingly, how saline the waters became. "Waters that are slightly brackish . . . seem to be best suited to our 'green trout,'" reported one New Orleans guide, who was referring to largemouth bass. "In these waters where the lotus, or 'grandevole,' duckweed and water lily grow in profusion, these fish are found in the greatest abundance. Most of the . . . bayous west of the city, which are entered by Harvey's and 'the Company's' canal . . . are well stocked with them, [and are] easily accessible to the amateur fishermen."[73] A description of a trip down the Harvey Canal in 1885 painted a surprisingly pristine picture of the swamp environment even after decades of timbering and extraction of resources:

Opposite [uptown] New Orleans, on the right bank of the Mississippi, is a small canal, now used by fishermen and hunters . . . a few hundred yards of the river bank. The small craft that ply on this canal are taken up by cars [on] an inclined plane [Destré-han's "submarine railway"]. Five or six miles [down], you reach a deep, narrow and tortuous bayou [Barataria]. Descending this bayou, which for forty miles pursues its sluggish course through an impenetrable swamp, you pass into a large lake [Salvador] girt with sombre forests and gloomy swamps, and resonant with the hoarse croakings of alligators and the screams of swamp fowls. From this lake . . . you pass into another lake, and . . . another, until you reach an island [of] several elevated knolls [with] scant vegetation [and a] high mounds of shells [Temple midden], which are thought to mark the burial-place of an extinct tribe. The lake or bayou finally empties into the Gulf in two outlets [Barataria Bay and Caminada Bay], between which lies the beautiful island of Grand Terre.[74]

The whole course of the Harvey Canal and Bayou Barataria, from the submarine railway to the sea, formed a cultural as well as an economic realm. A Destréhan memoir recalled the "weatherbeaten characters who came up the canal by barge, pirogue, and sail boats bringing their 'catch of fish,' oysters, crabs and dried moss, calling their mixture of language, a Gumbo tongue, understandable to each other even though [we] did not understand them at all."[75] Recalled another elderly descendant, "It was by means of the canal that fish and other products of the region beyond, [including] cords of ash and other wood for fuel[,] were laboriously brought to market. It was a boon to the poor who would gather [Spanish] moss, free for the picking from live oak trees, and bring it to sell in New Orleans." The Harvey Canal brought the Destréhan-Harvey clan a "princely income," as did additional revenue streams from "garden, orchard, dairy, wood yard and kiln."[76] The waterway economically invigorated the entire central portion of the West Bank.

But it was not the only such waterway. Four miles to its west was the Harvey Canal's older rival, the "Company Canal," which passed through the marshes and bays to the southwest to reach the Attakapas country around Bayou Teche. Unlike the Harvey Canal, which was a family project, the aptly named Company Canal was a corporate endeavor—with ample state funding—stemming from legislation granting a franchise to the Barataria and Lafourche (B&L) Canal Company. A group of planters, merchants, and state representatives, capitalized at $150,000, formally organized the company in 1829 and in 1830 acquired a one-arpent-wide sliver of land from the plantation of Camille Zeringue.

This spot was optimal for a number of reasons. For one, it already hosted a man-made canal, dug sometime between 1759 and 1785, when Claude Dubreuil Jr. and later Jean Louis Trudeau owned the land. Trudeau sold a tract to Michael Harang in 1794, who in turn sold it to intermarried relatives in the Zeringue family. Decades later, Camille Zeringue, who had helped organize the B&L Company, would provide the key tract connecting with Bayou Segnette—key because this navigable bayou accessed the lakes Cataouatche and Salvador (known at the time also as Ouacha or Washa). From the lakes would extend the most critical and costliest stretch: a straight channel dug southwestwardly to Bayou Lafourche and then on to the Terrebonne, Teche, and Attakapas regions, to the Atchafalaya River port that would become Brashear City—today's Morgan City, originally named for Dr. Walter Brashear, cofounder of the B&L Company.

The company understood the same geographical advantage that railroadmen saw: if you wanted to connect New Orleans to points west beyond the reach of the Mississippi, you had to go through the West Bank. Ditto for points south, and in that regard, too, the Zeringue land was key, because it also connected through Lakes Cataouatche and Salvador down to the fishing village of Chênière Caminada (Caminadaville) by Grand Isle. All through here were vast stocks of cypress timber, hunting, and fur-trapping grounds, plenty of marketable Spanish moss, heaps of oyster and rangia clam shells at middens like Big and Little Temple, and productive estuarine fisheries.[77]

The Barataria and Lafourche Canal was actually a series of linkages dug to connect existing channels and natural water bodies. Unlike the Destréhan Canal, which was excavated by contracted ditchers paid by Destréhan himself, the B&L Company Canal was made by enslaved men, some owned by the company or its affiliates, others provided by the state's slave-owning Board of Public Works as part of its generous subsidy package. That board also provided a steam dredge to do the heavy cutting, while men did the rest, using wooden shovels and wheelbarrows. The main channel was paralleled by a shell road and two paths along the lower flank, while at the mouth by the river were planted China-ball trees among service buildings and dwellings for workers and toll collectors, many of them enslaved.

Work on the western reaches of the Company Canal would drag on for decades, but the main eastern trunk in present-day Westwego was completed within a few years, except for the lock. The 1834 Charles Zimpel map shows the canal in full operation, with twenty adjacent buildings. By 1841, workers completed the second stretch from Lake Salvador to Bayou Lafourche, where they installed a lock made of cypress timbers. That device was replaced in 1853 with a masonry lock, again with state subsidies. Transshipment activity there gave rise to today's Lockport, Louisiana.[78]

As for the challenge of building a lock on the Mississippi, a far more powerful current than that of Bayou Lafourche, the B&L struggled as much as did Nicholas Noël Destréhan. But whereas Destréhan and later the Harveys were on their own in resolving this problem, and ended up making do with their submarine railway for another half century, the B&L Company had access to state resources. Specifications called for a 130-foot-long, 25-foot-wide lock chamber with a draft of at least six feet, its cypress gate sills resting on cast-iron quoins (corners) sealed with hydraulic cement. "In determining the height of the locks," wrote historian Thomas Becnel, "engineers were careful to specify at least 2 feet above the high water mark of 1849," the year when the bloated Mississippi flooded both banks, including New Orleans via Sauvé's Crevasse.[79] Workers struggled to build the lock, finally getting it in partial operation by the mid-1850s. But it suffered constant problems, as did the larger B&L effort to reach the Attakapas, beset by poor management, tough conditions, and constant need to re-dredge natural waterbodies.

The Company Canal section that worked well from the outset was the route from river to Bayou Segnette to Barataria. In the early decades, logging, hunting, and shell- and moss- collecting kept the canal busy; after the Civil War, with the opening of a shrimp cannery on Grand Terre Island and breakthroughs in ice manufacturing, canal traffic shifted to seafood. In the holds of vessels "going to the front" were sacks of oysters; moss-covered barrels of shrimp, finfish, and crabs; ducks and other birds, turtles, alligators, and small game.

What the company really wanted, however, was steamboat traffic, and that required a lock that worked. State loans were secured for that purpose in 1851 and construction dragged for years.[80] The project entailed shoring up soil on either side of the lock and adjacent levee, forming, along with later alternations, what today is one of the highest points on the West Bank, at the foot of Louisiana Street and Sala Avenue ("The Hill"). The lock became a money pit, to the point that the Company lost ownership of the waterway through foreclosure when it failed to reimburse the state for the pricey improvements. In 1859 the canal came into the possession of Robert R. Barrow, a wealthy sugar baron with a need for west-to-east transportation for his output and "an interest in upwards of 700 slaves."[81] Barrow reorganized the B&L into a new company, Barataria and Lafourche Canal Company No. 2, and recommitted it to completing the canal's troubled western terminus.

The Barrow family, with controlling interests in Company No. 2, would operate what most West Bankers continued to call "the Company Canal" for decades to come. The flow of fresh seafood from the littoral margins of the West Bank up the waterway and into the pots and pans of New Orleans kitchens came courtesy of a veritable fleet of folk craft: barges, pirogues, bateaus, and skiffs, some powered by sail or steam, some towed by beasts, some poled or rowed. Perhaps the most picturesque vessels were luggers, small round-hulled wooden sloops with colorful sails mounted on sharply angled spars (lug rigs) tethered to a single mast. Because oysters comprised their principal cargo, the boats were commonly called oyster luggers, and their crews formed a sort of coastal/city subculture. Up to two hundred luggers plied regional waters in the early 1800s, each with crews of three to six men. They circulated daily from mid-September through late April, from across 80,000 acres of both natural and cultivated oyster reefs, and when the bivalves were not in season, they hauled fish, crabs, game, citrus, Creole tomatoes, and truck-farm produce—whatever sold. Those working the Barataria Basin usually came to market up the Company or Harvey canals, and upon entering the Mississippi, made a beeline for Lugger Landing by the French Market. There, at the floating wharf at the foot of Ursuline Street known as Picayune Tier, wrote Catherine Cole after herself sailing on a lugger from the Chênière Caminada, "you may see the red-sailed, felucca-like boats from the Barataria, and some day even buy redfish, or shrimp, or white pelican . . . from the olive-skinned captain."[82]

The jaunty craft were one of those romantic elements of the lower Louisiana landscape that gave the region an Old World charm. But to those inside the seafood industry, this was business, and players negotiated, competed, and litigated with each other relentlessly. The best oysters went to the storied restaurants and saloons of New Orleans, where they commanded upwards of $4 per barrel; topping the list were briny "counter oysters," shucked and eaten raw, which came from the saltier waters of Barataia Bay. At Lugger Landing, off-duty banana unloaders eager for work glowered at members of unions such as the Oyster Discharging Association, composed of "Turks, Russians, Austrians [Croatians from the Dalmation Coast in the Austro-Hungarian Empire], Italians, and other nationalities, some . . . engaged in the unloading of oysters since 1860."[83] Both suppliers and dischargers locked horns with authorities from the Louisiana Oyster Commission, who inspected the catch and collected taxes. After the bureaucracy was completed, the oysters were iced and sold to wholesalers at $1.25 to $3 per barrel. That cash flowed back to the West Bank, to the toll collectors on the canals, and to the remote camps and cabins of the luggermen's families.[84]

Because the dual waterways served overlapping hinterlands, they too competed. While the Harveys struggled with their clever but awkward submarine railway, the Company Canal toiled with its 1850s lock improvement. Not to be outdone, in 1854 Joseph H. Harvey sought and attained state permission to build an engineered lock at the mouth of the Harvey Canal, so long as the State Engineer approved the design, and Harvey paid all expenses and assumed responsibility for damages.[85] But the magnitude of the project and its risk led to years of delays, made worse by the Civil War and flooding concerns raised by the Jefferson Parish police jury.

Harvey finally won the right to build the lock in 1870, at which point he dusted off his late father-in-law's designs, amassed thousands of bricks, had heart cypress timbers cut to size, and imported pig iron from Pittsburg. Workers next bored into the same hard blue clay used to make the bricks, creating the chamber while leaving the levee in place. But when they laid the brick foundations, they unknowingly did so "on a deep down bed of quicksand," and proceeded to complete the walls and gates—"a fine expensive job," rued an aged descendant.

Soon the trouble started. "The river front end of the locks sank down all out of plumb[–] a failure, [and] for forty years they stood a failure." Fortunately, no flooding occurred, because the levee had been kept in place. The "old brick locks" instead became "New Orleans' first zoo," joked the descendant—"a deep red bricked pool of stagnant water [with] bull frogs and fat speckled trout and an alligator."[86] The Harveys persevered, using mules to drag vessels over the old submarine railway, just as Nicholas Noël Destréhan had designed all those years prior.

6

Crescendo and Calamity

By the middle of the nineteenth century, the economic geography of the West Bank formed something of a bifurcated spatial spectrum. At one end were Algiers, McDonoghville, and Gretna, which sat closer to the city and port and claimed the largest resident labor force, and for these reasons specialized in heavy industry, primarily dry docks and iron foundries. At the other end, farther from the urban core, were the communities on and between the Harvey and Company canals, which focused more on the extraction and processing of natural resources. While the downriver end of the West Bank cast its economic eyes across the river to New Orleans, the upriver end looked in the opposite direction, southward into the Barataria.

Between these two poles were the endeavors of the West Bank's hard-working smallholders and petty entrepreneurs: a necklace of truck farms, orchards, dairies, pastures, light industry, village mercantilism, and services, their spatial patterns punctuated by train stations and ferry landings. Ferries remained absolutely essential to cross-bank relations; by 1858, each of New Orleans's four municipal districts on the East Bank had its own ferry service to their West Bank counterparts, and hundreds commuted daily. One ferry ran from the foot of Elysian Fields Avenue in the Faubourg Marigny to the Belleville area of Algiers, a second connected St. Ann Street by Jackson Square to Powder Street in Algiers Point, a third linked the foot of Canal Street with McDonoghville, and the fourth connected the foot of Jackson Avenue with Gretna.[1]

Amid all this activity, the late-antebellum West Bank still had space for its colonial-era land use: enslaved cash-crop plantations. One of the largest pertained to Avignon-born Laurent Millaudon (1786–1868), a self-made tycoon with an incredibly diversified international investment portfolio that made him one of the richest men in Louisiana. In Jefferson Parish alone in 1850, Millaudon lorded over 3,700 acres on both banks, of which nearly two-thirds was improved—both top figures for the parish. On those 2,300 improved acres, Millaudon's slaves produced 272 hogsheads of sugar, 12,500 gallons of molasses, 10,500 bushels of corn, and grazed $3,800 worth of livestock. According to the 1850 Census of Agriculture, the cash value of just his land and equipment was estimated at $75,000, or $2.3 million today. The crown jewel of Millaudon's empire was his 1,800-acre West Bank sugar estate situated between the Harvey and Company canals, on the old colonial-era Bouligny holding, now Marrero.

Millaudon was also an inveterate amateur scientist, known far and wide for his sophisticated on-site labs and workshops where he "expended many thousands of dollars in experimenting with every new mechanical invention for the manufacture and refining of sugar and the distillation of rum." Neighbors gossiped whether Millaudon's tinkering would ever justify his "accumulated . . . mass of machinery, [for which] he was offered $40,000 by a thrifty ironmonger."[2] When Millaudon in 1859 sold "his large sugar plantation [of] thousands of acres [in] Jefferson . . . on the right bank of the river . . . worked by 443 hands, who are comprised in the sale," the price was "a sum of one million dollars"— and the buyer was his own son, H. C. Millaudon. This is the equivalent of well over $30 million today, and it represented only a portion of the elder Millaudon's total assets.[3] Most of the difference between the 1850 estimate and the 1859 sale price can be explained by the 443 men, women, and children included in the deal.

∽∽∽

The vast amount of southern capital taking the form of enslaved human beings, like the nearly 1,200 owned by Laurent Millaudon and his West Bank neighbor Robert Barrow, would grow in value if slavery spread to the Western territories. This became the single most volatile national issue in the late 1850s, and it rested on deeper intractable tensions between North and South—of industry versus agriculture, progress versus tradition, Anglo-Saxon versus Scottish-Irish and, as one New Orleans-based editorialist put it in 1861, of "the Puritan [versus] the Cavalier."[4]

The ultimate test of fraying national unity came with the contentious 1860 presidential campaign. After Abraham Lincoln won, seven southern states seceded, including Louisiana, on January 26, 1861. Each soon joined the Confederate States of America, which proceeded to outrage Washington, DC, by seizing federal assets and organizing armed forces. The United States military responded by readying its forces. Americans chose sides, and families were divided. "In *your* hands, my dissatisfied fellow countrymen, and not in *mine*," said President Lincoln in his March 4 inaugural address, "is the momentous issue of civil war."[5] A month later, violence erupted at Fort Sumter, and Lincoln promptly blockaded all southern ports. The critical lower Mississippi River region fell under the charge of Flag Officer David Glasgow Farragut's West Gulf Blockading Squadron, and the Queen City of the South was in the crosshairs.[6] "[G]et into New Orleans if you can," Lincoln instructed his military, "and the backbone of the rebellion will be broken."[7]

The West Bank had an odd seat at the theater of war. Economically, it was dependent on the vitality of New Orleans and its port, yet it was also able to feed itself with its truck farms and seafood canals. It also had a substantial stake in the plantation economy, which rested on slave labor, and by extension, the currency that was the slave trade and the credit represented by slave collateral. Sugar planters in 1860 had nearly $200 million invested, of which $105 million—over $3 billion today—took the form of owned lives. All of this happened under the dominion of the United States, and it would be cast into utter uncertainty by a sectional crisis.

New Orleans thus had mixed feelings about secession, and Robert Ruffin Barrow, owner of the Company Canal, personified the equivocation. Barrow was stridently pro-southern and pro-slavery, contemptuous of what he called the "Black Republican Party" now in control in Washington. Yet he viewed secession as impolitic, and he gently cajoled fellow partisans against the radical move. He and other Louisiana nabobs, after all, had done well under the status quo, which, among other things, had protected sugar planters from cheap West Indian imports. A new Confederacy, dependent mostly on cotton, might throw sugar to the vagaries of free trade—or otherwise might end in catastrophe. "When . . . the benefits [of] secession . . . are shown to me," Barrow wrote in December 1860, "by all means, let us secede; but until then, I shall advise moderation." Many of his powerful peers felt the same.[8]

The West Bank's small semirural population put the region at the mercy of decision-makers elsewhere, and as a result, it ended up exploited, run rough-shod, and stuck with the wreckage. Confederate authorities confiscated vessels and riverfront land, hastily erecting earthen fortifications in lower Algiers and along the Company Canal.[9] It also seized the old US Marine Hospital in Gretna and stocked the castle-like infirmary with, of all things, 10,000 pounds of gunpowder. The blockade, meanwhile, stilled Algiers's commercial dry dock and shipbuilding industry and clogged its bank, as idled vessels moored up in large numbers to wait out the crisis.

On the night of May 5, 1861, under unknown circumstances, the steamboat *Gen. Pike* caught fire, and "in less than one hour, eight steamboats were enveloped in the conflagration [which] spread with terrific rapidity . . . between Algiers and Gretna." Most were destroyed, along with infrastructure, costing at least $100,000.[10] Months later, at midnight on December 28–29, a "terrible explosion . . . at the old United States Marine Hospital at Gretna, blew up with a report that shook the whole city to its foundation stones." The detonation of the powder "shot . . . a pillar of flame . . . up to the sky, for an instant illuminating the whole heavens," wrote the *Daily True Delta*. "The explosion could not have been the result of accident. It must have been the diabolical work of some incarnate fiend, [of] traitors in our midst."[11] The blast utterly obliterated the hospital; even "the trees in the yard were broken, twisted and stripped as if by a hurricane."[12] Worse yet, it weakened the levee, causing a crevasse that flooded the McDonoghville riverfront, including the late John McDonogh's old plantation house.[13] Unbowed, Confederate authorities hastily erected two new "powder mills" to store 3,000 pounds of gunpowder behind the hospital ruins—and on March 10, 1862, they too erupted in "two terrible explosions," according to an East Bank diarist whose "house quivered as with an earthquake." Five operatives at the Gretna operation were "instantly blown to atoms."[14]

All this, and the war had barely begun.

The fiascos betrayed that Confederate New Orleans was woefully unprepared for conflict. A later inquiry found the region "almost entirely defenceless," unable to "make an hour's fight"; its soldiers "badly armed and had very little ammunition." Along many of those ad hoc earthen fortifications, "not a gun was mounted, a magazine built, nor a platform laid."[15] This was not to say that the spirit wasn't there, but rather that the Confederacy, as an administrative unit, was a fiction. When the war commenced, West Bank shipmen found themselves ready, willing and able to build or retrofit warships for the Confederate Navy.

They had everything they needed: nearby forests for timber, rail lines to import it, foundries for casting copper and iron, access to interior mines for metals, hemp for rope, cotton for sails, and most critically, "eight dry docks . . . in Algiers . . . with experienced builders and skilled mechanics." What they didn't have was competent oversight. Greenhorn agents squandered their budgets on ill-conceived naval contracts, and inducements from Richmond to spur private warship-building often ended up in the hands of swindlers and scammers. "New Orleans *was* equipped to turn out war vessels," wrote historian James M. Merrill, and it was in Algiers where the colors of the Confederate Navy first flew (April 22, 1861, under the command of Admiral Ralph Semmes). But the Confederacy's attempt to make warships instead became "a story of miscalculation, mismanagement, of corruption and confusion," which ended up producing "a patchwork flotilla of needlessly expensive intermediate type vessels."[16]

In late April of 1862, Farragut's Union fleet, following a ferocious naval engagement at the mouth of the Mississippi, dodged past twin Confederate forts and that "patchwork flotilla" and proceeded upriver unmolested. Word reached New Orleans, and rebels began the rash work of destroying their own assets. On the East Bank they put to the torch wharves, cargo, and watercraft, creating an apocalypse of flame and smoke. On the West Bank, "about the very first thing suggested by over-zealous patriots," according to an 1885 account, "was the destruction of the dry docks of Algiers, so that the Federal fleet should be deprived of . . . them"—an act deemed "suicidal in the extreme."[17] On the night of April 23, Confederate naval authorities set about scuttling or otherwise destroying all dry docks and shipyards on the West Bank, undoing a quarter-century of progress in a matter of hours.

On May 1, 1862, federal troops entered New Orleans on the East Bank, while across the river "the 21st Indiana was landed at Algiers [to seize] the New Orleans and Opelousas railway." One week later, Union Maj. Gen. Butler wrote President Lincoln, "New Orleans . . . is at your command."[18] So too was the West Bank, along with every river parish up to Baton Rouge. Union troops camped by the Company Canal, not to protect the waterway but the nearby New Orleans, Opelousas, and Great Western Railroad. As if to symbolize the historic changes afoot, that railroad, once a key West Bank artery serving so many slave plantations across lower Louisiana, would be held under Union control by free men of color enlisted in the 1st Louisiana Native Guard.[19]

The Civil War affected West Bank populations in various ways. To Southern partisans, the four-year confrontation began with a high-stakes casting of lots, followed by the exhilarating opening salvos of war, then desperate fighting and ultimately humiliating defeat. To planters like Barrow and Millaudon, it meant a scramble to replace enslaved labor, while to all slaveholders it meant the evaporation of millions of dollars' worth of "property." To thousands of young men, it meant conscription, grueling service, and for many, injury, disease, and death. To enslaved African Americans, secession seemed to seal their fate, while the outbreak of war raised hopes, to the point of euphoria as the Union suppressed the rebellion—only to transform to total uncertainly in the first hungry days of emancipation. To women on the home front, it meant assuming male roles and keeping families and local society and economies going under the most desperate of circumstances. To ship carpenters and dry dock operators, it meant total loss. To truck farmers, timbermen, fishermen, and canal operators, the situation was not so bad, as their nature-based economy was less intertwined with institutional structures, including slavery, and more resilient to trauma. Joseph H. Harvey, for example, continued to operate the Harvey Canal, and "came out of the war with capital to invest." Within a year of the surrender at Appomattox, he collaborated with a Swiss hotelier to start recreational boat excursions to Grand Isle "to enable New Orleanians to have 'a sniff of salt air.'"[20] But as if to demonstrate that Harvey's postbellum prosperity was the exception rather than the rule, the hotel wanted for guests, and it closed within a few years.

Changes were afoot on the West Bank—racially, socially, economically, politically, and geographically—and to these last two we will next draw our attention.

II

LANDSCAPE TRANSFORMATION, 1870S TO 1940S

7

The Political Chessboard

If one were to map the geography of power in the circa-1850 metropolis, the City of New Orleans would have had the lion's share, in all its forms: political clout, economic wherewithal, infrastructure, population and workforce, expertise, and social capital, in the form of civic associations and cultural prestige. What New Orleans did *not* have, but wanted, was developable land. What it *had*, but did not want, was competition—from the upstart cities of Lafayette, Jefferson, and Carrollton in Jefferson Parish on the East Bank, and potentially from Algiers in unincorporated Orleans Parish on the West Bank.

What transpired over the next generation was an epic reconfiguration of the political map whereby the "lion" gobbled up all four upstarts, and in doing so, birthed the modern political geography of the West Bank.

To understand how this happened, we have to go back to a different sort of geography, of settlement patterns in antebellum New Orleans. The older Creole population, locally born and mostly Francophone and Catholic, generally lived in the French Quarter and lower faubourgs, whereas the Anglo-American population, English in tongue, mostly Protestant, and recently arrived from points north, generally dwelled uptown, above Canal Street. The two groups and their allied immigrant groups competed relentlessly for political, economic, and cultural supremacy, each having different sensibilities on just about everything, from language and religion to governance, law, and social behavior.

The stakes were too high for compromise and reconciliation to win the day. The alternative was a municipal divorce, and that's exactly what New Orleans got. On March 8, 1836, the state legislature divided New Orleans "into three separate sections, each with distinct municipal powers."[1] Ethnic geography drove the new political map: the First and Third municipalities, below Canal and Esplanade respectively, would be mostly Creole, while the Second Municipality, above Canal, would be mostly Anglo-American. Each municipality would have its own Council of Aldermen, who together would form a General Council serving under a single mayor. Everything else was in triplicate, from police and fire service to public schools and port management.

The system was confusing, redundant, wasteful, inefficient, and egregiously divisive, pitting neighbor against neighbor and exacerbating intra-urban rivalry. Nevertheless, these were booming times, and New Orleans flourished despite its messy housekeeping. Commerce increased, capital flowed, and populations grew, all of which put a premium on living space, motivating owners of adjacent plantations to develop their land. New neighborhoods formed predominantly in an upriver direction, past Felicity Street, which since 1825 had become the jurisdictional line between Orleans Parish (New Orleans) and the newly created Jefferson Parish.

The separate jurisdictions broached questions of governance. To keep control in their own hands, residents of the new Jefferson Parish faubourgs above Felicity Street petitioned the state to grant them a charter to incorporate. On April 1, 1833, the City of Lafayette came into existence, comprising today's Irish Channel, Garden District and Central City. Lafayette would become a city of immigrants and transplants, with German and Irish making up nearly 60 percent of its 1850 population. This was the demographic pool that fed Gretna via ferry. As the seat of Jefferson Parish, Lafayette would also figure into West Bank lives by hosting the courthouse—an Egyptian Revival edifice still partially standing on Rousseau Street—where everything from marriage licenses to lawsuits were handled.

Similar transformations were going on farther uptown, abetted by the same new railroad (today's St. Charles Streetcar Line) that injected life into Lafayette. The line's terminus gave rise to a second Jefferson Parish community, named Carrollton, which was laid out in 1833 and incorporated as a town in 1845. With development underway at Lafayette and Carrollton, owners of the ten intervening plantations—the heart of today's Uptown—independently decided to develop *their* tracts and cash in on the boom. In 1846, they formed the Borough of Freeport, which in 1850 became a third new municipality, named Jefferson City, from Toledano Street up to Eleonore Street.

This was the Jefferson Parish of 1850: on the East Bank, three incorporated cities, with the parish seat in Lafayette, plus unincorporated plantation lands upriver, and vacant swamps and marshes toward Lake Pontchartrain; and on the West Bank, that necklace of riverfront hamlets running from upper Mc-Donoghville through Mechanicksham and Gretna to the Harvey compound and the Company Canal at future Westwego, and over to the plantation of George Waggaman known as Avondale. Swamps, marshes, and bays extended down to the three barrier islands, and a network of bayous and distributary ridges laced in between.

Back on the East Bank of New Orleans, the divorce was proving to be worse than the marriage. On February 23, 1852, power players beleaguered by the cockamamie municipality system got the state legislature to reconsolidate the three municipalities and, in a separate act on the same day, annex Lafayette into New Orleans.[2] Behind the move was the city's Anglo element, which recognized that bringing Lafayette's substantial Anglo-Saxon-Irish population into the municipal fold would help them win elections against Creole interests. And it did: the 1852 reconsolidation/annexation would nudge New Orleans's political and cultural destiny away from the Old World–oriented Francophone Creoles and toward American assimilation, while granting the city the opulence of today's Garden District and the busy Irish Channel riverfront.

The annexation cost Jefferson Parish its largest and most valuable city—over 10,000 people—and forced it to relocate the parish courthouse up to Carrollton, an inconvenience to West Bankers.[3] The Lafayette merger also set a precedent for land-hungry New Orleans to gobble up its neighbors at will.

Among them were all those tiny subdivisions in unincorporated Orleans Parish on the West Bank known collectively as Algiers. American authorities, upon taking control after the Louisiana Purchase, saw no reason to include this detached province in the new official charter (1805) of the City of New Orleans. Rather, Algiers would pertain to Orleans County, as one of twelve electoral and taxation districts coterminous with today's Orleans, Jefferson, St. Bernard and Plaquemines parishes. That county jurisdiction continued even after Orleans Parish was created in 1807, for civic governance and jurisprudence. Like Orleans County, Orleans Parish encompassed all of the present-day metro area, on both banks.[4]

For the next 18 years, 1807 to 1825, today's urbanized West Bank was neither in the City of New Orleans nor in not-yet-created Jefferson Parish, but rather in unincorporated Orleans Parish as well as Orleans County, plus a bit of

Plaquemines. It, as well as unincorporated Orleans Parish on the East Bank, was administered by a series of legislative acts set out in 1805 under the territorial government, and under the state after 1812. Governance would later come in the form of a police jury which oversaw unincorporated Orleans Parish on both sides of the river.[5]

In February 1825, the state legislature under Governor Henry S. Johnson created a new parish, named Jefferson, out of the Third Senatorial District of Orleans County. The East Bank Jefferson/Orleans parish line would be by Felicity Street, while on the West Bank, the boundary would be the Canal Bernoudy, and, as discussed earlier, possibly also a cross-river extension of the old fortification line in the French Quarter.

At first, Jefferson Parish was subdivided into twelve districts, each governed by a commissioner. This changed on January 30, 1834, when the state legislature created the "Police Jury of the Parish of Jefferson." On this body sat jurors, elected by white males within eight to twelve districts or wards delineated by parish judges as per the density and distribution of the population. According to 1834 police jury meeting minutes, the First Ward spanned from the Canal Bernoudy (the Orleans Parish line) to the upper edge of the Dugue-Harang plantation (roughly Klein Street in today's Westwego); the Second Ward went from there up to the Drouet property (in today's Waggaman), and the Third Ward spanned "to the upper boundary of Baptiste Paquet's plantation, f.m.c. (free man of color)" at the St. Charles parish line. All other wards were on the East Bank.[6]

Jurors, one per ward, would serve two-year terms, and were "empowered to make all such regulations as they may deem expedient" for the administration of their respective wards. First item on the list: "the police of slaves [and] pursuit and apprehension of fugitive negroes," followed by the building and maintenance of roads, bridges and levees, bank clearing, fencing, animal control, regulations on taverns and liquor, and other typical charges of local governance.[7]

For decades to come, various permutations of this ward-juror-parish police jury system would govern unincorporated Jefferson Parish, whereas the East Bank cities of Lafayette, Jefferson, and Carrollton had their own municipal governments. The West Bank at this time had no legally incorporated cities or municipalities, no mayors, and no official limits beyond those of wards (districts), ostensibly because populations were two small and rural to warrant them. When, for example, the police jury remapped all of Jefferson Parish into ten districts in 1836, each to elect a juror, it put all of "West Jeff"—McDonoghville and what would become Gretna, Mechanickham, Harvey and Marrero—in one single jurisdiction, the First District.[8] Lacking an agreed-upon vocabulary for such a liminal community geography, people used a wide range of terms, including *villages, towns, subdivisions, settlements, enclaves, -villes, -bergs,* even *cities.* The police jury, whose meeting minutes tended to limit use of *town* and *city* to incorporated entities like Carrollton and Lafayette, typically used the term *village* as a generic place name, as in "Village of McDonoughville," "Village of Mechanickham," "Village of Gretna," and so forth.[9] (Years later, the state clarified the terminology by defining a city as having a population over 5,000; a town between 1,000 and 5,000 residents; and a village having under a thousand. But this law, the Lawrason Act, was not passed until 1898, and it only applied to incorporated communities.[10])

A similar political geography emerged for unincorporated Orleans Parish on the West Bank—greater Algiers—as its population grew and residents clamored for more local control. In March 1840, the state designated the "Police Jury of the Parish of Orleans on the Right Bank of the River Mississippi," that last clause making, for the first time, a political distinction between the administration of the Left (East) and Right (West) bank of areas inside Orleans Parish but outside the City of New Orleans.

This Algiers body typically met in St. Charles Hall and included a president, attorney, treasurer, surveyor, syndic (public advocate), assessor, and tax collector. Elected jurors, serving as the legislative branch to the president's executive position, passed ordinances and oversaw everything from policing and leasing to education, improvements, and taxation. Similar police juries are in place today in about two-thirds of Louisiana's parishes, most of them rural.

The police jury system sufficed until Algiers started to develop formidable industries. Having more to lose economically, after all, means wanting more control politically. Capt. Augustin Seger, a primary force behind railroad and shipping improvements, had advocated for Algiers's municipal incorporation since the mid-1840s, as a way to ensure local taxes went to local improvements. The idea gathered momentum, and in 1866 local newspaper publisher A. B. Bacon went so far as to draft up incorporation papers, arguing that the geography of Algiers was, in the paraphrasing of the *Daily Picayune*, "superior to New Orleans, [what] with Texas now teeming with wealth, and West Louisiana [by] far the richest and greatest portion of the State." Algiers also had a longer riverfront with deeper draft and nearby railyards, which positioned it to attract midwestern-style grain towers (elevators), something new for the South. "Were New Orleans now to be founded," Bacon boldly ventured, "it would be placed on the right bank, instead of the left."[11] The state was not deaf to the demands for greater local control, having moved in 1855 to broaden the police jury's jurisdiction and authority, eventually giving it "independent governing power"—in many ways a de facto city, yet still without a charter of municipal incorporation.[12]

New Orleans recognized all too well Algiers's advantages and stirrings for independence. Its own shipping industry had limited wharf space, as everything above Toledano Street still pertained to the separate cities of Jefferson and Carrollton. (Lafayette by now had been annexed to the City of New Orleans.) It couldn't accommodate Algiers's dry docks, and needed cumbersome ferries to get rail cars across the river. Algiers also had over 6,800 residents who could boost the city's revenue coffers and clout in the state legislature. Plus, on account of a controversial new state law, Algiers had also landed (albeit briefly) a new, centralized slaughterhouse for Texas and Opelousas cattle, yet another money-maker that could be brought into New Orleans.[13]

So while Algiers mulled independence, New Orleans plotted annexation. The city had a track record of subsuming valuable neighbors: witness the 1852 takeover of Lafayette, and its ongoing ogling of Jefferson and Carrollton. One can almost see New Orleans's hands wringing in an 1869 editorial that read, "The port of New Orleans is not confined to its left bank. Algiers is as much within the port, though not within the city. . . . Let us see to what extent this additional district can be employed to supplement (our) maritime advantages. . . . It is about time that New Orleans should awaken to the very great advantages (of) Algiers."[14]

Many Algerines protested any talk of joining the City of New Orleans. They worried that taxes would increase, that revenue would stay across the river, and that East Bank politicians would not prioritize for West Bank problems.

Economic reasons, plus overwhelming political clout on the East Bank and deep ambivalence on the West Bank, ultimately explain the annexation of Algiers as New Orleans's Fifth Municipal District and 15th Ward. But Reconstruction-era racial politics formed the proximate cause for the March 16, 1870, state law that enacted the annexation. Since the end of the Civil War, tensions had mounted between white Democrats who had supported the Confederacy and the federally backed, racially integrated state government headed by Republican

Governor Henry Clay Warmoth. In an attempt to consolidate his power state-wide, Warmoth pushed to install political appointees in unfriendly municipalities, like Jefferson City, and if that didn't work, subsume these jurisdictions into adjacent friendly cities, like New Orleans. Toward this end, and after blood had been shed in an 1869 melee on Magazine Street, the 1870 law annexed Jefferson City to New Orleans, where it became today's Uptown. In an apparent attempt to counterbalance those likely new Democratic (white) voters, Algiers's annexation was included in the bill, under the presumption that its substantial African American population in Freetown would support the Republicans. Algiers thus became a throw weight in a postwar political and racial struggle, played out against a larger backdrop of economic geography.[15]

A few days after the Algiers annexation, delighted editors of the *New Orleans Times* published a spoils-of-war inventory. "The flourishing town of Algiers [comprises] six sugar plantations, and many vegetable and rice farms, having a total population of some ten thousand inhabitants," they wrote. "Several of our merchants have beautiful residences fronting on the river, from which they travel up daily to the city[,] returning in the evening. The Opelousas Railroad depot, situated at the lower part of the town, has been lately greatly improved, and is now one of the finest depots in the South." Getting down to business, the editors assessed the area's industry: "The chief business of Algiers is that of ship building and repairing; five large dry docks find constant employment for many artisans. . . . The Belleville Foundry, an immense brick building in the centre of the town, is now being . . . leased for a manufactory of oil and oil cake from cotton seed." All this heavy industry cluttered up the scenery, but fret not, they wrote: "If the visitor whose vision is offended by the ugly look of the riverfront of Algiers will go back of this, he will find as pretty a village as there is in the South. The streets are cleanly kept, paved banquettes, and some fifty or sixty street lamps. . . . Many handsome private residences . . . show as much good taste in their construction as could be found in the Second and Fourth Districts of our city [French Quarter and Garden District]."

Then the editors got down to brass tacks: "The right bank, financially, comes to us in good standing," they declared. Algiers's "real estate [has] a valuation of $1,943,650, her indebtedness being some seven thousand dollars, [while] the public buildings [of] Police Jury are valued at over thirty thousand dollars. We congratulate our neighbors on this good showing, and trust that they will prosper more than ever by their annexation to this great city."[16]

Algerines grated at such patronizing drivel. Wrote one editorialist in the *Algiers Independent*:

> The new arrangement will give speedy relief from the gang of thieves who are at present robbing the parish. But the relief is purchased at a dear rate of higher taxation and entire deprivation of all future self government. For years to come our interest may be distinct from those in New Orleans, yet in the control of these interests we are to have no par. . . . We have exchanged . . . an evil . . . for an evil.[17]

Of the three annexations, Jefferson City's was the most hostile, involving racial animus, power, corruption, greed and violence. Lafayette's 1852 annexation was less contentious, although it elicited a major shift in political power, from Creole to American. Algiers was somewhat in the middle—which is to say, quite controversial. That the neighborhood of Algiers Point still has a courthouse today speaks to its heritage of self-governance, and discontentedness with the loss of that power has resurfaced ever since—as early as 1877, when the *New Orleans Times* reported on "Aggravated Algiers—Why She is Unhappy in her Union with New Orleans," and in 1895, when the slow arrival of firefighters from downtown made a conflagration in Algiers Point that much worse.[18] Over a century later, in 2004 and again in 2015, State Representative Jeff Arnold sponsored legislation for Algiers to secede from New Orleans and become its own parish. Constituents, he said, were "tired of not being serviced" by city government and considered "the red-headed stepsister of New Orleans,"[19] echoes of the sentiments held by many Algerines in 1870.

Yet New Orleans, even after the 1870 double annexation of Jefferson and Algiers, had not sated its appetite. It next set its eyes on Carrollton City, seat of Jefferson Parish and home to high, dry, rail-accessed riverfront land. This was nothing new; an earlier version of the 1870 annexation bill had also thrown in Carrollton.[20] But it was removed at the last minute, probably because Carrollton's Democratic voters would have upset the balance of likely Democrats and Republicans that Jefferson and Algiers, respectively, would have brought to New Orleans's ballot boxes.

With a new lease on life, Carrollton in 1872 expanded up to Lebarre Road. But New Orleans by that time sat across Lowerline Street, as if knocking on Carrollton's door. When Republican Senator A. E. Barber introduced an annexation bill to the state legislature in February 1874, it aimed to absorb not just "all the city of Carrollton" but also "Jefferson Parish up as far as St. Charles Parish."[21] Had it passed, New Orleans today would span from Kenner to the Rigolets, and Jefferson Parish would be limited to the West Bank.

Instead, Barber's bill was trimmed back to Carrollton's original limits, and on March 23, 1874, it became law. Jefferson Parish thus once again lost its largest and most valuable city as well as its parish seat, while Carrollton became the Sixteenth and Seventeenth wards, and Seventh Municipal District, of the City of New Orleans.[22] The 1874 act settled seven decades' worth of spatial wrangling in cross-bank parish-level politics; a subsequent state law required that future annexations secure voter approval in both parishes, thus transferring this power from politicians to people.[23]

Much had changed in post-annexation Jefferson Parish: for the first time, the West Bank now had the preponderance of population and investment. Its own political geography had been transformed since 1836, when a single district lumped together McDonoghville to present-day Marrero and gave them one representative on the police jury. Subsequent growth led to a revamping of the system in 1856, in which each village got to elect three commissioners to oversee its own public works, and in 1858, when each bank got its own police jury, that on the West being "the Police Jury of Jefferson, Right Bank."[24] With each change, representation (and investment, taxation, and regulation) became more locally attuned, which brought more political meaning to the lines separating jurisdictions, which brought more identity and distinction *to* those jurisdictions.

The question now, with the loss of Carrollton, was, where to put the new courthouse?

None other than Louise Destréhan had an idea: in her own "castle," that crenelated curiosity overlooking the Harvey-Destréhan clan's canal-side operation. Moving the Jefferson Parish Court here would, finally, bring political power to the West Bank, plus rental income to family coffers and foot traffic to what would become Harvey.

In April 1874, the police jury of Jefferson, Right Bank, leased Harvey's Castle to use as a courthouse, and despite its lack of legal authorization to pay the rent, the body assumed occupancy. After three years of waiting patiently, Louise Destréhan filed suit for $3,400 owed, but judges ruled against her, even as she let the police jury stay while trying to persuade them to purchase the property. She finally evicted them in 1884.[25] Homeless again, the police jury of Jefferson, Right Bank, instead moved in June to William Tell Hall, a wood-frame structure still standing on the corner of Newton and Third streets. Gretna thus became Jefferson's fourth parish seat, and remains so today. That same year, the Right and Left bank police juries were reconsolidated back into a single parish-wide body. The new police jury continued to use William Tell Hall as its courthouse into the 1900s, by which time the building was becoming inadequate, not having been designed for this purpose.

In May 1905 the police jury formed a committee to contemplate a new courthouse, and dispatched members to other parish seats for design ideas. They found to their liking the Rapides Parish Courthouse in Alexandria, which had been completed two years earlier by builder William S. Hull of Jackson, Mississippi. Stylistically, the building was an eclectic mix of neoclassical, Romanesque, Renaissance, Baroque, and Beaux Arts, all recently fashionable. Hull submitted adapted sketches to the police jury that were inspected by the architectural firm of Soulé and McDonnell and found to be sound. Next, the committee "recommended that the new building be erected on the neutral strip in front of the Texas and Pacific Railroad station, on Copernicus Avenue, between Second and Third Streets."[26] The foundation was laid in 1906 and the courthouse completed in 1907, thus fulfilling the 1836 vision of Nicholas Noël Destréhan and surveyor Benjamin Buisson for Gretna (Mechanickham at that time) to feature a great public building behind the scenic commons.

The presence of a magnificent parish courthouse belied the fact that Gretna, like neighboring villages, still lacked corporate identity. This changed on August 20, 1913, when, through gubernatorial proclamation, Gretna was incorporated. Its limits would envelope both the original Gretna and Mechanickham as well as their 1870s annexes known as New Gretna and New Mechanickham, making them all officially the Town of Gretna. The peculiar old toponym "Mechanickham" soon faded from the vernacular; it appeared regularly in the police jury meeting minutes starting in 1834, but hardly ever after 1913. Today only history buffs know it.[27]

Now everyone living in what were previously four villages with diluted political control would be yoked into one town with a single name and government. In 1916 the state legislature incorporated Gretna as a city. Three years later, on January 18, 1919, the governor proclaimed the incorporation of Westwego (population 1,583) as a village, later that year a town, and in 1951, a city.[28] Both cities would get mayors, city councils, and official limits; the Jefferson Parish Courthouse would become Gretna City Hall, while parish government would establish itself in a series of adjacent complexes. In this manner, the atomized villages of the nineteenth-century West Bank began to cohere into the interurban subregion we know today.

Because of the late arrival of municipal incorporation and city government, which tend to solidify civic identity, denizens have long perceived and named their spaces with a multiplicity of overlapping designations, their interfaces being more like a painter's sfumato than a bureaucrat's line. The United States Census Bureau uses the clunky jargon "Census-Designated Places" (CDCs) to describe such unincorporated population clusters, but with no convenient handle in times past, observers loosely described them as *hamlets, enclaves, settlements, subdivisions, towns,* or *villages,* that last one being the term (*bourgades* in French) most frequently used by West Bankers themselves. Villages were not wholly informal spaces; in the mid-1800s, the Jefferson Parish population clusters (wards) that people often called "villages" did have the right to elect three public works commissioners to speak for ward needs. But ward lines would frequently change, and no state legislation formally decreed these villages to have standing in the eyes of the law.[29]

Toponyms were similarly soft, as was orthography. In antebellum times, for example, one person's Duvejéville (or is it Duvergsberg?) might be another's Algiers, which itself could, in certain historical uses, imply everything from Gretna to English Turn, or only from Algiers Point to the railroad depot—unless it was before 1830, in which case people might have called it Pointe St. Antoine, Punta San Antonio, or Pointe Marigny. McDonoghville (or Macdonogh, or Mac-Donough?), which by some standards bled into Algiers and Gretna, also went by Freetown and Gouldsboro. Tunis or Tunisburg got renamed Leesburg or McClellanville and later subsumed into Algiers, whose name now shares the map with Aurora and Cutoff—until you cross the Algiers Canal (aka the Intracoastal Waterway), which gets you to the Lower Coast of Algiers (except for the subdivision named English Turn—or is that a river bend?). Today's Gretna itself started as Mechanickham (Mechanikham? Mechaniks Village? Mechanicsville?), followed by another development explicitly named Gretna to which were added a New Mechanickham and New Gretna before becoming, en toto, the *Town* of Gretna and finally the *City* of Gretna. Harvey was originally Cosmopolite City; Westwego was also Salaville; Marrero, Amesville, and Bridge City, Belt City. Nowadays, there's little agreement on where and how McDonogh and McDonoghville (once rebranded Gouldsboro) straddle the Orleans/Jefferson Parish: at what point does the latter fall within Gretna—which begs the question, incorporated or unincorporated Gretna? So vexing was that confusion in Terrytown (created in 1960 in the back of John McDonogh's property, later Oakdale) that frustrated neighbors ran a "Terrytown, Not Gretna" campaign.[30] Marrero lies between Harvey and Westwego (which too has incorporated and unincorporated areas), and extends down through Estelle and the "back of Ames" nearly to Crown Point and Lafitte (legally incorporated as a village—as opposed to Grand Isle, which is a town). Spatial nomenclature of the West Bank grew even more complex with the advent of modern suburban subdivisions, whose corporate brands may or may not accord with neighborhood sobriquets, incorporated city limits, parish lines, or voting districts, much less with historical names.

It all makes for a popular topic of debate on the West Bank, and the more stridently someone defends the "true" name or borders of a particular space, the more likely you'll find someone who adamantly disagrees.

8

A Modern Economy Emerges

On the western bank of the river will be seen Algiers, Freetown, Gouldsboro, Gretna, and other suburban villages, with their dockyards, railroad repair shops, foundries, and mills, [above which] you pass an even more picturesque country[—] an almost continuous town . . . one succession of farms and plantations, sugar, rice, corn and tobacco.

—*Historical Sketch Book and Guide to New Orleans and Environs* (1885)

In early 1887, upon receiving various petitions for industrial leases in Gretna, the Jefferson Parish police jury held what today might be called "strategic planning." Meeting minutes did not document the discussion, but it likely spoke of attributes such as extensive open river frontage, cheap and abundant land, access to the Barataria, and railroad connections to points west. Jefferson Parish's West Bank had all these advantages; the East Bank of New Orleans had none of them—but did have what the West Bank lacked, namely capital and investor connections. The police jury concluded that the destiny of their domain lay in not just approving companies seeking licenses and leases, but in actively pursuing and enticing them. "Whereas we are informed that there are capitalists in New Orleans seeking to locate sites for various manufactories," read an April 7, 1887, motion offered by juror R. J. Perkins and seconded by W. M. Naudain. "Considering that the Parish of Jefferson offers desirable location therefore, and that it is in the interests of our parish to have such manufactories located in our midst, be it Resolved, That it is the sense of this Jury to offer every inducement and encouragement within its province to such enterprises and manufactories whenever located within our jurisdiction, and solicit visits to our parish to all such capitalists before locating elsewhere."[1]

The 1887 resolution did not precipitate the West Bank's industrialization; that process happened through free-market processes principally in the 1830s, when foundries and dry docks opened in Algiers. But it did mark the beginning of an intentional Chamber-of-Commerce-style policy. In the same month as the resolution, two cottonseed oil companies, Planters Crescent and Union, set up shop in Gretna; the next year, "the oldest and largest producer of cottonseed oil products in the United States, the Southern Cotton Oil Company . . . selected Gretna . . . as the company's new home because of its combination of railroad and riverfront facilities."[2] At these plants, the hard black seeds that had been separated from lint at upriver cotton gins, hitherto considered worthless, could be barged down to Gretna to be hulled and ground to extract a versatile oil for cooking, illumination, soap, and other uses.

By 1890, a statewide gazetteer described Gretna (population 4,000) as "chiefly a manufacturing town, [with] three large oil mills, one cooperage manufactory, the Union Stone company, the Louisiana Cypress Lumber company, two moss factories, a large brick manufactory, and other concerns," plus twenty retail stores of everything from food to shoes, various skilled tradesmen—and nine saloons.[3] By 1895, the successor of the New Orleans, Opelousas, and Great Western Railroad had established a spur and rail yard along Gretna's riverfront, where everything from ice manufacturers to coal distributors to molasses factories, and of course cotton seed oil companies, could be found.[4]

As economically vibrant as Gretna had become, it could not hold a candle to Algiers, which brought to bear all of Gretna's industrial siting advantages, plus a larger workforce, closer proximity to downtown, and, since 1870, a shared political destiny with the City of New Orleans. And while all West Bank villages had train depots of various sizes, Algiers had the main terminal by the river—and that made all the difference, because the broad corridor along Verret's Canal, acquired by the Great Western Railroad, would allow for the establishment of a bona fide industrial district.

That original Algiers-based railroad line, the New Orleans, Opelousas, and Great Western, had come a long way since its 1853 start and wartime damages. But since then, westward expansion had opened new markets and new lines connected with the growing track network. More and more cargo traveled by rails, to the detriment of river commerce. This trend did not bode well for the Port of

New Orleans, but did for the rail-friendly West Bank, and a new generation of railroad financiers cast their eyes in that direction.

After the Civil War, shipping magnate Charles Morgan acquired the financially troubled Great Western and renamed it Morgan's Louisiana & Texas Railroad. He aggressively expanded its Algiers rail yards to include nine tracks, a locomotive round house (turntable), depots and warehouses, and a new steam cotton press to reduce bale volume for export to the fabric mills. Now, increasingly, western cotton would arrive at New Orleans by rail rather than water, and the West Bank could do all the handling itself. "Morgan's Louisiana and Texas railroad," reported the *Galveston Weekly News* in November 1880, "has brought into New Orleans thus far this season 35,978 bales of cotton, against 8,400 last year."[5] The importance of the Morgan line stood out to a German traveler studying the region in 1880: "Now the line to Texas, universally deemed essential, has been completed after years of waiting. Today the iron horse roars straight from [Algiers] deep into the heart of Texas, [and] already the railroad's beneficial effects can be seen, [while] the Morgan Railroad Company has been building a branch line [into] the most beautiful and productive part of Louisiana [for] direct communication with New Orleans."[6]

Under Morgan's leadership and that of his successor, A. C. Hutchinson, after his death in 1878, the company went intermodal, building scores of vessels and becoming Morgan's Louisiana and Texas Railroad and Steamship Company, offering "Steamers and Rail Connections to Points in Texas, New Mexico and California, Havana, Vera Cruz, Cedar Keys and New York," all from a single spot in Algiers.[7] Now cotton could arrive from Texas, get pressed in Algiers and loaded onto Algiers-based steamers, and ship out to world ports without ever touching the East Bank. Likewise, Morgan Line ships, which were later taken over by Southern Pacific, would arrive from East Coast ports and connect with West Bank rails to anywhere from Texas to California. "Six or seven ships with names like *El Paso* and *El Monte* operated constantly," wrote historian Willian D. Reeves, "unloaded in Algiers, and their freight transferred to the cars of the Southern Pacific, which then dashed across the country. . . . Four hundred . . . longshoremen[,] both black and white[,] worked thirty-six hours to unload and reload each forty-seven-hundred-ton ship."[8]

The West Bank–West Coast connection affected passenger travel as well. To get to the Pacific Ocean, passengers in New Orleans first had to ferry to the Algiers depot on Atlantic Street. "One leaves Algiers, opposite New Orleans," explained a local advocate in 1882, "to Morgan City, and . . . after crossing some of the finest parishes of this State, reaches Houston and San Antonio [and] proceeds to Paso del Norte and thence along the Southern Pacific Railroad to Los Angeles, [where] it joins with the Central Pacific Railroad and reaches the distant city of San Francisco."[9] The Morgan yards now also had lumber milling facilities, machine shops, and its own foundry to construct railroad cars and steam locomotives—the heaviest of heavy manufacturing in a metropolis rarely thought of as an industrial town.[10]

The interconnected Southern Pacific Railroad, a larger company with which A. C. Hutchinson had affiliations, took over Morgan's rail interests, and while the shipping operation retained the Morgan name, the industrial district became known as the Southern Pacific Yards. "Few people have an idea of the magnitude of the plant of the Southern Pacific Company," wrote an Algiers advocate in 1896. "Standing on the river front, one notices extensive sheds and wharves with ships lined up in front, and looking back into the rear a series of buildings [and] industries which flourish [thereon] loom up into view. . . . The square mile of territory covered by them . . . is not unlike the famous town of Pullman, Ill. . . . It is the largest of its kind in the South, [employing] 3000 or 4000 men."

Many Southern Pacific worker families settled along Atlantic Avenue, which came to be known as "Silver City." The "SP Yards" stretched twenty-two blocks long by two blocks wide, from the river to the parish line, requiring that viaducts and a footbridge be built for traffic on Patterson, Newton, and Alix streets. From the 1880s into the 1960s, the track-laced strip was lined with long, solid industrial buildings up to four stories high, with intricate brickwork and imposing pediments. Inside were blacksmiths, machine shops, foundries, wood mills, paint sheds, and other spaces for the assembly of locomotives, rolling stock, and vessels.[11]

Southern Pacific was not the only rail yard in Algiers. Just upriver from the ferry terminals were five tracks of the New Orleans, Fort Jackson, and Grand Isle Railroad, established in 1888 to serve the lower fringes of the West Bank parishes. Its locomotives pulled into the company freight depot at the foot of Delaronde Street and onto the turntable and machine shops at Powder and Eliza.[12] Adjacent to the smoky cacophony of the rail yards were the more traditional riverfront industries, including an array of new dry docks (improved replacements for those torched during the Civil War), plus block-long industries on or near Patterson Street such as the Planters Oil Works and P. Fink's Algiers

Saw Mill. This was heavy industry, long a foible for New Orleans proper, but a forte for Algiers and the West Bank.

One indicator that the West Bank's population centers were growing to the point of subregional autarky was the rise in demand for interurban transportation, which indicated that West Bankers were increasingly circulating and working amongst themselves. Up to this point, they had little choice but to look to New Orleans across the river to satisfy their needs. "If the citizens of Algiers wanted to visit those of Gretna, or the ones of Gretna those of Algiers," wrote Hermann Zagel, who had worked as a teacher in Algiers in the early 1880s, "they had to go over to New Orleans on the ferry, ride three miles over there on the streetcar, and then cross the river again." Two entrepreneurs in the late 1860s attempted an Algiers City Railroad and a Right Bank Rail Road & Trading Company for local passenger service, but neither materialized.[13] Everything from labor to discretionary spending still tended to flow across the banks more so than circulate within the bank; it was easier to wake up in the French Quarter and work in Algiers than it was to wake up in Algiers and work in Gretna.

"Therefore, the need for a streetcar was great," wrote Zagel, "and the entrepreneur, Captain [Thomas] Pickles, saw it and decided to alleviate the condition." (In fact, Pickles had taken over the franchise from a man named William Bogel, who in 1881 had organized the Algiers, Gretna & Tunisburg Railroad for local passenger service.) Tracks were laid through Freetown, and a small steam engine and cars were acquired from across the river. Zagel's account, which is told in a picaresque style, recounts the 1882 inaugural run of the Gretna-Algiers Railroad:

> One morning there resounded below Gretna, in the vicinity of the river, a fearful, shrill, ear-piercing howl, which filled the otherwise quiet streets [and echoed to] the dark cypress woods behind the place. The cottonseed oil mills, a number of river steamers as well as several ocean-going ships . . . joined in a steam whistle concert from which the earth quaked. The whole city, black and white, rushed toward Front Street. Spraying sparks, with an Indian war whoop, a small locomotive with an attached streetcar came speeding around a sharp curve . . . and rushed into the city.[14]

Steam dummies provided the power, and electrical batteries powered the bells. To collect fares, the conductor remotely lowered a ceiling-mounted box among the passengers, and raised it afterwards for safekeeping.[15] "For some weeks everything went splendidly," Zagel wrote. "The passenger traffic between the cities was absolutely gigantic." Then everything seemed to go awry, and Captain Pickles' good idea fell on bad times, not the least of which included the Live Oak Grove Crevasse, which flooded the tracks.

But the forces of economic geography would soon redeem the concept, and the line returned to operation under mule power, in the form of the Algiers, Gouldsboro & Gretna Railroad. By 1890, Algiers had 3.3 miles of street or interurban rail lines; by 1900, the tracks ran 4.3 miles; and after 1915, about 9.3 miles. Electrification came in 1905, after which the Algiers Railway and Lighting Company ran constant service to Gretna, from its car barn at Pacific Avenue down to the Immigration Station at Horace and Flanders streets. At its 1920s peak, the entire West Bank streetcar system got passengers from that lowermost terminus, up Gen. Meyer Avenue to Algiers Point, along Monroe Street through Freetown and McDonoghville to Gretna, and along Fourth Street through Harvey, terminating at Barataria Boulevard in Amesville/Marrero.

In the years before automobile ubiquity, the interurban streetcars played a key role in unifying the West Bank and making it into a *bona fide* sub-region. But the era did not last long. Buses were on the rise nationwide, and cities gradually switched from rail to rubber for public transportation. During 1929–1931, the Naval Station Line, Marrero-Gretna Line, Algiers Line, Algiers-Gretna Line, and Gretna and Belt Line were, one by one, replaced by rubber-tire motor coaches—that is, buses.[16]

Typically, the West Bank, isolated from the urban core, retained old ways longer than the East Bank. This was an exception: while the extensive streetcar system in New Orleans proper would also diminish after 1929, when a labor strike interrupted service, many lines survived into the 1950s, and the Canal lines ran until 1964. The last day of streetcar service between Algiers and Gretna, by contrast, was January 22, 1931.[17] Some rails were removed from West Bank streets; in other cases they were simply asphalted over. Street repairs in 2019 uncovered rails buried for the better part of a century at 725 Patterson Road.

❧❧❧

Helping unify the West Bank economy was the fact that the upper end of the crescent had nearly as many geographical advantages as Algiers at the lower end. Railroadmen were among those to appreciate this. Shortly after the Civil War, as the South looked to railroads to rebuild its economy, the New Orleans, Mobile and Texas Railroad proposed to connect the Gulf Coast with northern Texas by building tracks from Mobile, Alabama, to the East Bank of New Orleans, and from the West Bank to Shreveport and on to Fort Worth. The eastern leg of the track-laying commenced in February 1869, followed by the western portion in May 1870.[18]

The big question was where exactly to site the West Bank terminal. Company officials might have preferred to pull into Algiers, given its busy riverfront and access to downtown. But right-of-way acquisition would have been costly, and competing rail lines would have fought the intrusion. Officials opted instead to pull up to the Mississippi along the upper guide levee of the Company Canal, at the opposite end of the West Bank, where open riverfront land made a perfect place for a terminal station, rail yard, and ferry dock. This was "the first place on the right bank," stated company engineer G. W. R. Bayley, "where the river bank is stationary, [without] accretion or caving." From here would be installed a ferry to carry entire trains across the river, on what would become the Walnut Street Train Ferry.[19]

With the site now identified, next came land acquisition. The parcel belonged to the renowned Camille Zeringue, whose manorial Seven Oaks home lorded over the entire lower half of Nine Mile Point. Zeringue resisted the railroad's offer, but backed by powers of expropriation, the company went to court to secure 183 acres of Zeringue's land, to his utter dismay.[20]

Zeringue's personal loss helped birth an important intermodal West Bank transportation node, with new tracks coming in from the west, a ferry to New Orleans, docks on the river, and the Company Canal to the south. In a display of pithy jocularity not normally associated with nineteenth-century railroad men, company officials, including engineer G. W. R. Bayley, named the site "West-We-Go," to advertise the western access at a time when all the nation was talking about the recent completion of the transcontinental railroad (1869).

The "Westwego" terminal facility was constructed throughout 1870, followed by forty miles of track by April 1871, after which the company would become widely known as the Texas & Pacific Railroad.[21] While the name Westwego initially applied only to the rail yards, it came to imply the community that formed adjacently—and form it did, given the workers needed at the facility. As for coinage itself, "Westwego" was a stroke of marketing genius: clever, whimsical, descriptive, promotional, euphonic, and unique. Locals like to point out it's the only town in the United States whose name forms a complete sentence. No wonder it stuck.

The Texas & Pacific Yards at Westwego became West Jefferson's answer to the Southern Pacific Yards at Algiers. Driven by profit and sitting all of two thousand feet from the South's largest city, both enterprises yearned to get their trains across the unbridged Mississippi River. The cumbersome solution: railroad barges, or "transfer ferries." The Morgan Company in 1878 put railroad cars on ferries in New Orleans, using mules to pull small wooden rolling stock onto rail-equipped barges of the Third District Ferry and crossing from Southern Pacific in Algiers to the foot of Esplanade Avenue. Texas & Pacific, which in 1880–1883 bought out New Orleans Pacific and parts of the Morgan line, installed a steam transfer ferry named *Gouldsboro* (named for railroad tycoon and Texas & Pacific president Jay Gould) connecting Thalia Street with McDonoghville. For this reason, McDonoghville and Freetown became known as "Gouldsboro," and the curving Mississippi channel as "Gouldsboro Bend," both names originating from the rail ferry.[22] The latter term is still used today by mariners.

Over the next fifty years, until the opening of the Huey P. Long Bridge in 1935, train ferries would grow in size and multiply in number, including one connecting the Algiers yards with a rail pier at the foot of Elysian Fields Avenue; a second for the Texas & Pacific Line to cross between McDonoghville and the Illinois Central rail yards at the Stuyvesant Docks (today's Lower Garden District riverfront); a third at Westwego connecting with Walnut Street by Audubon Park; and a fourth running between Harahan and Avondale for the Texas and New Orleans Railroad.

The largest ferry of all was a beastly hulk nicknamed "The Mastodon," measuring 366 feet long and 52 feet wide, its airtight sectional hull practically un-sinkable and capable of bearing over 1,700 tons. The barge fit two locomotives plus tenders and either 24 freight cars or 15 fully loaded Pullman passenger cars, broken into two segments on parallel tracks. Nearly half a football field in surface area, it was said to be "the largest barge in the world."

Wrote an intrepid *Times-Picayune* reporter riding the Mastodon in 1916, "the train moves slowly, rumbles over the trestled track and boards the transfer [barge] as cautiously as a thoroughbred mare walking a gang plank." Once the locomotive and cars were all secured, "two tugs, 'El Vito' and 'El Listo,' of 900 horse-power," one on each side, "guide the Mastodon back and forth against strong currents and difficulties of high water, day and night, through all weathers." For first-time passengers, crossing the Mississippi *on* a train *on* a boat was a triple novelty to be savored, and many disembarked to witness the spectacle. The Mastodon Transfer Barge, as it was officially known, crossed from a thousand-foot-long protruding rail dock at the foot of today's Hickory Avenue in Harahan to a point about a half-mile upriver at Avondale, which was the one spot outside the congested West Bank where the Southern Pacific tracks came the closest to the Illinois Central tracks on the East Bank. This proximity would later influence the siting of the Huey P. Long Bridge and the shipyards at Avondale, and help spur modern Harahan's extensive warehousing sector.[23]

What the Mastodon was to West Bank transportation, the Louisiana Cypress Lumber Company was to West Bank industry. Situated along the Harvey Canal, the sprawling mill, started by two Great Lakes timbermen who partnered with a local man named J. C. Turner, manifested a number of geographical advantages of the West Bank. Its 400 "workmen . . . about equally divided, white and black," felled around 300 cypress logs per day from the backswamp of Jefferson, Lafourche, and St. James parishes, floated them up the Harvey Canal via three tugs, and milled and planed them into "120,000 feet of lumber" per day—"dressed lumber, flooring, ceiling, molding, laths, shingles [in] a plant that is second to none in the State." Ferries, steamers, sailing ships, and schooners carried the output to market, as did trains, "about 100 car loads a month." Much of the material went into New Orleans housing stock, some stayed on the West Bank, and the rest shipped regionally. Workmen typically lived in Gretna or New Orleans and commuted daily, but since the plant's establishment in 1889, builders had erected "a number of cottage homes" where "some of the employees are putting up."[24]

Here we see all the elements of the quintessential West Bank at work: rich natural resources and a backswamp canal to access them; a mix of local and out-of-town money; tugs, railroads, and river vessels; hard work and integrated labor; that paradoxically advantageous mix of proximity and distance from New Orleans; plenty of waterfront space; the ability of working families to settle adjacently in decent affordable housing; and a landed aristocracy—in this case, the Destréhan-Harvey clan.

Consider their domain, circa 1894: in addition to the Harvey Canal, there was the Harvey Brickyard, both owned by Horace Harvey, who was also president of the Merchants' and Planters' Ferry Company, keeper of the local Harvey General Merchandise Store—and member of the local School Board. The steamer *Louise*

Harvey, named for Horace's mother, was captained by Capt. H. A. Harvey, while the *Frolic* fishing vessel was run by Capt. Frank Harvey, sailing up and down through "the big tract of Harvey land," on which worked dozens of truck farmers, all rented from Harvey kin. And the vast Louisiana Cypress Lumber Company? It leased Harvey land along the Harvey Canal.[25]

All this activity brought spatial coherence to what had previously been a smattering of houses in and around Harvey Castle, giving rise to the modern community of Harvey. It's hard to pin down a firm date for Harvey's founding; one can reasonably trace it to 1834, when Nicholas Noël Destréhan first envisioned its forerunner Cosmopolite City; or to 1839, when he began the canal that would become its raison d'être; or to after 1853, when it became a railroad stop. Certainly by the 1890s, folks were calling the area simply "Harvey," implying the community had town-like qualities. Unlike Gretna and Westwego, however, Harvey never incorporated, and to this day lacks a nucleus with something that feels like a Main Street. The Census Bureau labels Harvey a census-designated place (CDP), meaning an unincorporated population that is sufficiently concentrated to map out like a city, but has no city charter or borders.

So too is Harvey's upriver neighbor, Marrero. An early colonial record of this area appeared in 1732, stating that "SIMON, a mulatto" came into possession of the land by working it and by "purchase from a free negro named SCIPION," an unusual circumstance in the colonial era.[26] During Spanish colonial times, it became part of the Bouligny holding, and in the antebellum era, the Millaudon sugarcane plantation. After the war A. B. Merrill purchased the holding, of nine-thousand-plus acres, 20 percent of which was under sugarcane cultivation. Needing to replace his now-emancipated work force, Merrill experimented with Chinese laborers, as had other Louisiana planters and railroadmen, so much so that Donaldsonville started to form what one local newspaper called "the precincts of 'China Town.'"[27] In 1869–1870, over twelve hundred Chinese were brought into Louisiana, many landing in Gretna to take the train to railroad projects in Texas, while others went to Alabama or Louisiana plantations.

The largest single cohort of Chinese laborers on today's West Bank, numbering 141, came from San Francisco via St. Louis and arrived by steamboat at the Merrill plantation, future Marrero, on June 30, 1870. "These men were not brought from China *a la Coolie*," noted a visiting journalist, "but were already in the United States, each of his own enterprise, and each was contracted with the same as laborers of any other nationality." On the point of acculturation, "the climate of [their] part of China . . . is very similar to that of Louisiana, so that danger of acclimating sickness is to a great extent obviated."[28] Indications were that the Chinese labor experiment would work well on the West Bank, and that people of Asian descent would dominate the cane fields.

But when the journalist returned three weeks later, discontent prevailed. "The Chinese appear unwilling to engage as laborers," he reported,

> unless in large numbers[;] they pay little attention to any directions given, unless [they] come through the medium of the head man . . . of superior cast or rank.
>
> John Chinaman seems to entertain a very lively sense of his own interest in any bargain he makes; and the man of the Flowery Kingdom is not a whit behind the descendants of Canaan's conquerors in business shrewdness. . . . He has a keen relish, too, for getting hold of the right end of the asparagus—for having the best of the bargain.[29]

A few days later, in what the journalist described as "The Cabbage Revolt," the laborers rigorously disputed their contractual arrangements, which, among other things, included the right to grow and sell their own cabbages. Some Chinese were arrested, leading to more protests, and the experiment began to unravel.[30] By 1872, only twenty-five Chinese remained on the Merrill plantation, the rest having departed, or had their contracts terminated, for various dissatisfactions. Many resettled in New Orleans; some went into shrimping; and a small number remained on the West Bank. In the 1890s a tiny hamlet of Chinese gardeners formed a cultural landscape said to be unique in the region. "Just back of the Southern Pacific Railway track, a short distance above Gretna," wrote a reporter for the *Times-Democrat,*

> there is a small and rambling group of low one-story buildings [and] market garden, or small truck farm, [with] long rows of odd looking vines [growing on] low structures of light poles. . . . This is probably
>
> THE ONLY CHINESE MARKET GARDEN
>
> to be found in Louisiana, and one of the most important of its kind in America, east of the Rocky Mountains. It consists of sixteen acres of very rich, low-lying soil, leased . . . by the Ti Kee Company of Gretna, La. This little farm is all under cultivation, according to Chinese ideas of agriculture, and its products are in the main Chinese

vegetables, [sold] to the Chinese inhabitants of this city and vicinity, while large quantities are shipped to New York, Boston, Chicago, St. Louis and [beyond]. Four men, including a superintendent, his assistant, one Chinese and one colored laborer are employed on this little farm, while a Chinese cook . . . prepares their food in orthodox Chinese fashion. [Y]early net profits of the enterprise range from $1500 to $2000.[31]

As for those who resettled in New Orleans, they, with other Chinese immigrants, formed a Chinatown at 1100 Tulane Avenue and opened scores of laundries citywide. Many would learn English at the Presbyterian Church's Chinese Mission, among them ten-year-old Lee Bing, who had been brought to New Orleans by his father in 1913. The Lee family later opened laundries in Algiers and on Carondelet Street, where they "lived in the back room that barely held two double beds and a single canvas cot." One of the six children would become one of the most powerful and respected figures in recent Jefferson Parish history, Sheriff Harry Lee (1932–2007).[32]

The departure of the Chinese laborers informed A. B. Merrill's decision to sell his West Bank plantation to Oak A. Ames in 1873 for $180,000. Ames's motivation to purchase came in part from his illustrious family in Boston, whose company manufactured most of the world's shovels, and who made a fortune during the California Gold Rush and Civil War. Heavy investors in the Union Pacific Railroad, which had recently completed the transcontinental tracks, the Ames family had dispatched scion Oak to New Orleans to buy up key riverfront properties for an envisioned southern transcontinental railroad. The Ames group would soon meld into the Texas & Pacific Railroad, the outfit that created "West-We-Go."[33] Oak Ames stayed on to manage his acquisition of the old Millaudon and Merrill Plantation, withal his brothers Oliver and Frank, where their hired black workforce soon managed to produce about 5 million pounds of granulated sugar annually. The brothers also subdivided some lands to lease to small agriculturalists, known as the Southside, Front Place, and Estelle farms, a move that reflected an increasingly common land-use transformation in the post-Emancipation West Bank: the switch from a small number of large export commodity plantations, to a large number of small family truck farms to produce food for local consumption.[34] This meant more people living on Ames land, which meant a train station, which incentivized the opening of stores, which brought more services—the sort of "petty entrepreneurism" that invigorates an economy and lays the groundwork for industry. By the 1880s, people were calling the place "Amesville," and by 1894, "some three and a half miles of truck farms fill[ed] the space" near the river, along with "the big mill . . . eating up cane, disgorging juice, and [making] sugar. . . . Ames is a big place and a busy one."[35]

At around this time, Louis Herman Marrero, an Isleño-Anglo-American born in 1847 who fought for the Confederacy and had since become the most powerful figure in Jefferson Parish, purchased a flank of the Ames holding to subdivide for more farms. Marrero also constructed houses and stores and formed the Marrero Land and Improvement Corporation, which would later develop subdivisions for residential and industrial use. "Mr. Marrero has long been one of the conspicuous and dominant figures in the public life, not only of his parish, but of his state," wrote local historian Alcée Fortier in 1914.[36] Gradually, during the 1910s through 1930s, people began to refer to the corporation's subdivisions, and more and more of the Amesville area, as "Marrero," especially after Louis died in 1921, having served 24 years as parish sheriff and other positions.

Back in 1909, three thousand acres of these farmlands and soggy backfields had been organized into the Second Jefferson Drainage District, funded by the state's only ad valorem tax levied for this purpose. "Two large outfall canals were dug and a drainage station established [on] the Harvey Canal," reported the parish yearbook in 1935, "equipped with three Fairbanks engines using crude oil as fuel. As a result[,] farmers in the area do not suffer from excess rainwater." At around this time, laborers with the Works Progress Administration dug lateral canals and installed an additional 250-horse-power pump that would draw down the groundwater to the point that residential development could proceed.[37]

So grew Marrero. According to a 1939 US Geological Survey quadrangle map, Marrero was only around the Avenues A, B, C, and D subdivision just west of Harvey and east of Barataria Boulevard, whereas "Amesville" and "Walkertown" were ascribed to what is now the Ames Boulevard corridor. The 1966 update expanded the domain of Marrero, whereas Amesville fell off the map and Walkertown held its ground. The first black neighborhood in this part of Jefferson Parish, Walkerton began when, according to a local historian interviewed by the *Times-Picayune*, "Corrine Degree Walker, a widowed mother of 12 . . . purchased land in the area in 1921 to raise her family. . . . Walker's children eventually purchased property around her own, and they slowly built a community of African-American professionals, entrepreneurs and laborers."[38] Its main thoroughfare, Walkertown Road, is now Ames Boulevard. Today most West Bankers call everything between Harvey and Westwego "Marrero," as does the Census Bureau, while "Walkertown" survives as a local neighborhood name, and "Amesville" is all but forgotten.

The same decade that brought Walker to Walkertown also brought manufacturing to Marrero. In 1920 two northern industrialists—Bror Dahlberg and Carl Muench—investigated uses for bagasse, the cellulose cane fiber left over after the extraction of the sugar juice. They found that the pulp, used only as a low-grade fuel for sugar mills or dumped as waste, made excellent insulation boards for ceilings, walls, refrigerated cars, and other uses. Together with investors, Dahlberg and Muench established the Celotex Company in 1920 and secured a supply of Louisiana bagasse from the Southdown Plantation in Houma. They next conducted a region-wide site-selection exercise to determine the best location for their manufacturing facility, which would prove to be a lesson in the West Bank's geographical advantages, including its "close-but-not-too-close" attribute.

Muench explained that Celotex sought an "available a tract of land sufficiently large [,] at a reasonable price[,] located along the river [with plenty] of water [and] rail connections." The company found that "best available sources of supply for raw materials were west of the river, but our largest potential market for our finished product was on the east side." No bridge existed at the time, so the question became whether they wanted to pay high ferry costs for (all of) the wet bulky raw bagasse, or for (only that portion of) the light finished product to be sold locally in New Orleans, the rest being exported. Increasingly, their corporate eyes turned away from the East Bank. "We found a tract of land on the west bank of the river in Jefferson Parish [where] there was plenty of labor available [at a] rate . . . lower than in New Orleans proper. Fuel oil for our power plant could be delivered by barge at the river front, [and] it began to look pretty good."[39]

But industrial geography rests on the body politic, and the capitalists worried that some unwanted governance—in the form of an incorporated municipality— might one day intrude upon their best-laid plans. "We did not want to wake up some day and find ourselves incorporated willy-nilly into a new governmental unit with sovereign power to sock us for an additional tax," wrote Muench. "So we went down and conferred with the Parish officials [and came away feeling] they would do everything they could to make our stay with them pleasant. . . .

So finally we had found our location."[40] That locale, at 7500 Fourth Street in Marrero, would grow into a 150-acre facility employing 2,700 workers and producing hundreds of millions of square feet of rigid insulation board for countless drop ceilings and bedroom walls worldwide. Celotex got their geography right, because in subsequent years, Penick & Ford would locate adjacent to them and become the "largest cane syrup canning plant in the world," as did the Southern Shell Fish Company, the "largest seafood canning plant anywhere," and the Southern Cotton Oil Company, "another largest of its kind."[41] Celotex remained in operation into the twenty-first century—and Marrero remains unincorporated to this day.[42]

Westwego, which *would* incorporate, has always had a more coherent historical geography than Marrero and Harvey. Its provenance dates to the 1830 excavation of the Barataria and Lafourche Company Canal, and its name came from that 1870 rail yard branding. Westwego's population amassed to work the yards, wharves, and canal-side industries, and its incorporation came in 1919, giving it governance and borders. In the 1890s, the heart of Westwego gained another name, Salaville, and it would soon become home to one of the region's best-known industries.

Like Marrero, Salaville got its name from a man of Spanish descent. Whereas Louis Marrero hailed locally from colonial-era Canary Islander immigrant stock, Pablo Sala was born in Spain around 1827. Little is known about his early life, and in the annals of Westwego history, he seems to have come out of nowhere late in life to play a big role in the city's formation and then continue on. In March 1892 Sala acquired part of the plantation previously owned by Camille Zeringue and his son Jean Fortune Zeringue. The son lost it in a stock-mortgage foreclosure to Citizen's Bank, which sold the land to Sala, including the Seven Oaks Plantation House and "some old cabins near the [Company] canal built by Negro laborers and a house of Mr. Vallee."[43] Later that year, Sala hired civil engineer Sidney F. Lewis to lay out 162 lots immediately downriver from the Company Canal, named "Salaville." The first residents of the linear subdivision, all addressing Sala Avenue, were the aforementioned black families; the next were white families who previously had to ferry daily from New Orleans to their Westwego jobs, lured by Sala's offer of forty-dollar lots. By 1893, up to 200 people lived in Salaville and Westwego, five or six white families and about three times as many black families.[44]

Salaville was Pablo Sala's side project. The elderly entrepreneur's main venture was the conversion of Seven Oaks, less than a mile upriver from Salaville, into a weekend getaway for city dwellers. Named "Columbia Gardens" and opened to huge crowds in 1893, Sala's resort offered music, entertainment, food and drink, ornamental gardens, hunting and fishing, and the novelty of electrical illumination, plus riverside breezes from the mansion's scenic gallery, and even baseball games. "The resort was indeed ahead of its time," wrote historian Mark Matrana. "Such multifaceted attractions did not routinely develop until much later, and the use of the mansion as a tourist attraction was very unusual prior to the turn of the century."[45] Columbia Gardens did, however, continue the long-standing role of the West Bank as a recreational retreat for New Orleanians, something seen in the Algiers regattas and bullfights, the Gretna weddings and picnics, and the backswamp hunting and fishing.

Later in 1893 a terrible hurricane struck the Louisiana coast, and a year later, Pablo Sala died. His death led to the demise of Columbia Gardens, while Salaville ended up in the hands of his sister Maria Sala y Fabregas in Spain, who arranged for its expansion with a hundred new lots laid out toward Bayou Segnette. Her aim: to house coastal fishing families who, seeking refuge from the destruction of a powerful hurricane (more on this later), had sailed up the Company Canal to resettle in Westwego. Other coastal denizens had made the same move, but on a seasonal basis, floating up and down on houseboats and docking in Bayou Segnette like a floating neighborhood.

As technology advanced in ice-making, refrigeration, and canning, and as a wider rail network with ever-faster trains expanded distribution networks, demand soared for Louisiana seafood. Shrimp and oysters, once a rarity in the interior, became popular. Westwego found itself at the nexus of maritime bounty and insatiable demand, not the least in the gastronomic parlors of New Orleans. Westwego also had the rails, train ferry, river boats, and canal barges, and in Salaville, a seafood-savvy workforce in the form of coastal refugees. Luggers, bateaus, early inboard-motor "putt-putts," and other small fishing vessels moored side-by-side in the Company Canal, selling their catch to wholesalers, who around 1900 would establish a "cannery row" on and near Sala Avenue. In 1913 the *Daily Picayune* announced "WESTWEGO CANNERY—Big Oyster Industry to Be Established There," meaning the Dunbar-Lopez & Dukates factory and its "work[force] of a large number of men and women. . . . There will be no difficulty in getting all the oysters needed."[46] The nucleus of the scene was Sala Avenue at 2nd Street, where in addition to Durac Terrebonne's Fishermen's Exchange, there were two ice manufacturers, a crab meat processor, a shrimp factory, a cold storage unit, and a seafood retailer. They all operated only one block from the Company Canal fish wharf and shed (and only steps from residential houses, cafes, taverns, an undertaker, and two churches, including the True Vine Baptist Church, founded by former Zeringue slaves.[47]) The routine at a Westwego shrimp factory went like this:

> The shrimp on being unloaded at the cannery are washed and sorted under the direction of the inspector, who discards [those] unfit for canning. The shrimp are then headed and peeled[,] thoroughly washed, [and] boiled in brine[,] a process known as blanching. The meats are cooled and sorted according to size, either by mechanical sorters or by hand. They are next packed into cans, which are sealed before being placed into the retort for the final processing under steam pressure. The shrimp are then ready for the labeling and the consumer.[48]

The labels themselves were works of art, featuring placid bayou scenes, vibrant color schemes, majestic typeset, and proud proclamations of product quality.

By 1942 five major processors—Ed Martin Seafood, Robinson's Shrimp, Louisiana Blue Crab, Hudson Seafood, and Cutcher Seafood—employed 567 people in Westwego (population 5,000), of whom 83 percent were women and nearly 60 percent were black.[49] In a typical shrimp or crab processing operation, the women, white and black, would stand elbow to elbow around two 40-foot-long wet tables, and, wearing hair bonnets and aprons, place the extracted meat in bowls and the shells in buckets, while hoses flushed organs and fat into a central drain. Men typically shucked the oysters and handled the canning.[50] The workers' dominant language was Acadian and Creole French; their ethnicity reflected lower Louisiana's rich cultural heritage; their handiwork embodied the delta's ecological abundance; and their workplace exemplified all the West Bank's geographical advantages.

Those same advantages made the seafood scene but one of the area's economic sectors. "In Westwego are many nationally known concerns," boasted the 1936 *Jefferson Parish Yearbook*. There was also "the American Aluminum

Company handling as much as three shiploads a month of bauxite ore from South America. The Texas & Pacific yards are here, [as are] the Southern Pacific yards. Here also is the bulk plant of the Sinclair Refining Company, the North American Trading & Import Company, dealers in bulk molasses, the United States Industrial Alcohol Company[, the] General American Tank Storage & Terminal Company, and many other industrial activities."[51]

9

The Battle for the Intracoastal Waterway

The great nineteenth-century shift from riverine to rail transportation forced the Port of New Orleans to retool for the new century. Restructured as a state agency in 1896, the Port, now under the direction of a Board of Commissioners (the Dock Board), moved aggressively to improve its East Bank facilities. What this meant, in essence, was to make the East Bank more like the West Bank: to build its own railroad yards to match those in Algiers and Westwego, to erect its own grain elevators to match those in Harvey and Amesville (Marrero), and to create new, leasable, deep-draft wharf space, of which the West Bank had an abundance. What resulted, during the 1890s through 1920s, was the creation of major new East Bank port features, such as the 4750-foot-long Stuyvesant Docks between Louisiana and Napoleon avenues, with their integrated railroad networks, pavilions, platforms, power generators, and grain elevators; the New Orleans Public Belt Railroad, which gave private rail operators consolidated access to port wharves; and the Inner Harbor Navigation (Industrial) Canal, dug through the Ninth Ward for barge traffic, shipbuilding, and value-added industries—all niceties the West Bank had developed on its own.

One valuable advantage the East Bank could never duplicate, of course, was the West Bank's access to the Barataria Bay via the Harvey and Company canals. But even in this seemingly secure ambit, times were changing and so was the infrastructure.

The Harvey family—frustrated by the 1870 failure of the Harvey Canal lock and unable to get the Jefferson Parish police jury to fork over the rent for Harvey's Castle—seemed on the verge of giving up. Joseph and Louise moved the family to Prytania Street in uptown New Orleans in 1873, and in 1880, they sold a portion of the Harvey Canal for $100,000 to the Barataria Ship Canal Company. That firm had been authorized by Congress in 1878 "to construct and operate a ship canal from New Orleans to the Gulf of Mexico . . . and to grant to said company the right of way for that purpose."[1] Envisioned as a wide, deep-draft seaway to open Gulf waters, the proposed waterway aimed to "be the only gate through which the largest ships will reach the Port of New Orleans, [i]f the Eads jetties should prove a failure."[2]

That last condition referenced the treacherous shoaling that persisted at the mouth of the Mississippi, a costly frustration to ships calling at the Port of New Orleans. Some men proposed solutions to the problem; others devised alternatives. Skeptics scoffed when the brilliant nautical engineer Capt. James Eads proposed a simple solution: to construct parallel jetties at South Pass to constrain the flow, increase velocity, mobilize sediment, and scour out the channel. Among those proposing alternatives were the men behind the Barataria Ship Canal Company, who saw Mississippi shoaling as an opportunity to build their own lucrative "river" through Jefferson Parish.

There was just one problem: Eads's jetties, installed during 1874 to 1879, worked brilliantly. With the mouth of the Mississippi now reopened to deep-draft vessels, the Barataria Ship Canal lost its rationale and the project eventually faded away, although the concept of a West Bank seaway would return seventy years later.

The river revival encouraged the Harvey clan, namely matriarch Louise, to reinvest in their old asset. The family moved back to the West Bank and regained full control of their ancestral waterway. Louise, now a widow and personally in debt on account of a second failed attempt at constructing a lock, sought to professionalize operations and rectify financial affairs. In 1898 Louise, age 71, decided to incorporate The Harvey Canal Land and Improvement Company. To keep control within the family, she issued shares to relatives and required that any stock sales be offered first to board members or the company. She then promptly sold her own personal ownership of the canal and adjacent lands to the company, and installed her son Horace as manager.[3]

The new management endeavored to bring the operation into the twentieth century. A valuable new commodity was being extracted from the Barataria

Basin—petroleum—and in no way could the Harvey Canal's antiquated submarine railway stand between the oil wells of south Louisiana and the gas tanks of American engines. Likewise, the sprawling Louisiana Cypress Lumber Company, the largest leaseholder along the canal, depended on the waterway and needed it to meet modern standards.

Meanwhile the Harvey Canal's longtime competitor to the west, the Company Canal at Westwego, had come under the control of the son of owner John Ruffin Barrow, who died in 1875. Young and pugnacious, John Barrow Jr. pieced back together the troubled Bayou and Lafourche Canal Company No. 2, rebuilt the lock at the Mississippi, saw traffic increase when Bayou Lafourche was dammed in 1903 (thus allowing for the lock to be removed at Lockport), and soon finally achieved the dream of opening the Company Canal in its entirety, from New Orleans to the Attakapas country.[4] Barrow was now poised to eat Harvey's lunch.

Harvey needed a lock. His consulting engineer Rathbone DeBuys investigated canals nationwide and settled on a design of twin concrete walks, 30 feet wide and 180 feet long. Because the removal of the levee on which the submarine railway operated would disrupt the public road atop the levee, the company received permission from the police jury to install a drawbridge instead. The company also built its own dredge, to deepen the channel to six feet, while cutting off points (bends) and digging out bars (shoals). In an April 1902 article headlined "Harvey Canal to Be Made a Waterway for Fuel Oil," the Daily Picayune predicted the improved channel "will be the shortest and safest route for the transportation of fuel oil, [and will help] develop the adjacent country, affording . . . quick transportation of produce. The government has already awarded the company a contract for carrying the mail to Grand Isle."[5]

The lock project seemed cursed—again. While the request for construction proposals ran in local papers, one of Horace Harvey's children fell out of a carriage, the sight of which "shocked" his wife Sallie, who subsequently died, probably of a heart attack. A year later, Horace's mother, materfamilias and company founder Louise Destréhan Harvey, died at age 77, marking the passing of a key generation in one of the West Bank's founding families.

Between the loss of Harvey's wife and mother, and while the lock research was underway, the Harvey Canal became the scene of a curious ecological disaster. In early July 1902, millions of buffalo fish, carp-like suckers considered an important food source, died and clogged six miles of canal. All maritime operations shut down, as did adjacent industries, at great loss of profit. A noxious stench "beyond the limit of human endurance" forced a residential evac- uation, and livestock had to be restrained from imbibing the tainted waters. Some theorized that a recent storm had pushed saltwater inland, trapping the fish in a salinity regime they could not tolerate and leaving them "smothered by the lack of oxygen [and] gasping for air." Whatever the cause, everyone agreed the solution was to cut the levee and let the river water flush out the festering carrion—which was exactly what Horace Harvey needed to do anyway. "One of the first and immediate results of the fish plague," reported the *Daily Picayune* on July 9, 1902, "will be the building of modern locks connecting Harvey's canal with the Mississippi river." Declared Horace during the crisis, "We will build the locks at once. This will hurry the matter."[6]

The levee was blasted and ploughed open on the morning of July 12, at which point the high river water gushed through "to thoroughly cleanse the basin of the rotten fish." By July 20, the Harvey Canal was clean.[7]

No one quite knew it at the time, but the resolving of the great fish-kill of 1902 would lead to the creation of a major piece of American shipping infra- structure. As Harvey foresaw, the cut levee forced lock construction to be fast- tracked. A contractor was hired; designs were finalized, materials secured, and with a budget of $75,000, work commenced in 1903. The lock would take the form of a 184-foot-long basin flanked by massive earthen levees and 30-foot-high concrete walls, set upon 284 pilings. A pair of equally high steel gates were installed at either end, one facing the river and the other the canal. The gates swung upon a miter sill (bottom closure unit) seven feet underwater. One gate would open to receive a vessel from the adjoining water body; once inside the basin, the entrance gate would close and the exit gate slowly opened. Water lev- els would equalize, raising or lowering the vessel along with it. The vessel would then sail out, and the process repeated for the next customer. "The opening of the Harvey Canal locks," foretold the *Daily Picayune,* "will give the shortest and most direct route from New Orleans to the Barataria country . . . and the noted fishing grounds and oyster banks of South Louisiana, and will undoubtedly boom the industries of those sections."[8]

Testing of the lock in August 1905, however, revealed a nasty old problem: that same bed of quicksand that caused the 1870 failure, which allowed im- pounded water to seep under a gate. To seal it, engineers drove a hundred feet of ball-and-socket sheet piling into the earth across the soft spot, doing with steel what they had hoped natural clays would accomplish. The effort took an additional two years and upped total expenditures to $155,000, plus $300,000 for adjacent land and building purchases, putting the company in debt and its future in question.

Things got better. The completed locks passed testing by the state board of engineers and the local parish in early 1907, and officially opened with a ceremony on March 30. The inaugural vessel was Captain McSweeny's steamer *Grand Isle,* personally selected by Horace Harvey because "the Captain is the pioneer of the trade down in the Grand Isle district, and Mr. Harvey wanted to pay him the compliment of being the first to pass through."[9] What Harvey had his eye on was the lucrative seafood trade, currently at Salaville in Westwego, now sure to come his way. As if to evidence the promise, on the occasion of lock completion the *Daily Picayune* reported that "an ice factory will be erected near the mouth of the canal to accommodate the fish, game and oyster boats coming up from the gulf."[10] After years of impediments, ranging from quicksand to fish-kills, and after losing his wife, mother, and nearly his business, Horace Harvey had finally, truly completed the canal first built by his grandfather, Nicholas Noël Destréhan, 68 years earlier.

The new lock shined a favorable light on the Harvey Canal in the eyes of the federal government, which for a century had been officially committed to building "internal improvements"—what we now call national infrastructure. The concept was first articulated in an influential 1808 report by Secretary of the Treasury Albert Gallatin, "Public Roads and Canals," which called for federal leadership and public funding for transportation networks to spur private investment and economic development. Federal and state subsidies would underwrite a number of the private companies that were driving the transportation revolution of the nineteenth century—and this was as true in Louisiana as anywhere, as the Company Canal had demonstrated. A subsequent 1819 report by John C. Calhoun identified military as well as economic justifications for such transportation projects, which led to the General Survey Act of 1824, the law that permitted the deployment of Army Engineers on civil works projects. "Thus began the continuous association between the Corps of Engineers and [the building of] waterways," wrote historian Lynn M. Alperin, and the Corps's "historic responsibility to maintain the navigable waters of the United States."[11] By the late 1820s, legislation authorized initial surveys for canals connecting the Atlantic to Gulf coastal plains.

New Orleans, of course, benefited from any navigation improvements on the Mississippi River and its tributaries, and regional investors had no problem accepting government support for local canal construction. But the city and its port would decidedly suffer from federal or state promotion of valley-wide canals, roads, and, in time, railroads. Such vectors would allow western trade to flow eastward, circumventing the Port of New Orleans—and that is exactly what happened. In the two decades after the Louisiana Purchase, New Orleans controlled over 99 percent of trans-Appalachian shipping, halcyon days for the new American city. Then the New York State–supported Erie Canal opened in 1825, followed by railroads and other canals. Produce could now flow faster, better, and cheaper straight eastward to the major coastal metropolises, rather than going down through New Orleans and coastwise around Florida. The cost of shipping a ton of wheat from Buffalo to New York City plummeted from $100 to $10. New Orleans's control of western trade dropped to 80–90 percent in the 1830s, to 60–70 percent in the 1840s, and to around 50 percent in the 1850s.[12] "The flow of western trade reversed itself," wrote two historians; "the economic unit known as the Mississippi Valley had been turned on its head, so that the Mississippi River was flowing north."[13]

This was alarming news for the East Bank of New Orleans, but a potential opportunity for the West Bank. In the same way that western railroads could only approach New Orleans via the West Bank, so too could a western waterway—that is, an interconnecting "intracoastal" canal.

Such a facility had been envisioned as early as the 1820s, only to be put on hiatus as railroad mania and western expansion distracted the nation, followed by Civil War and Reconstruction. The intracoastal idea resurfaced in 1873, when the Rivers and Harbors Act authorized a survey for a route from the Rio Grande to the Mississippi River, to be dredged or otherwise pieced together through natural bodies of water or offshore trenches. Early discussions identified Bayou Lafourche as the connector to the Mississippi at Donaldsonville, which would cut both the West Bank and New Orleans proper out of the picture. Work overseen by the Corps of Engineers ensued in small segments, if and when Congress appropriated funds. Hidden from public view and only indirectly beneficial to voters, the "inglorious ditch" ranked as low in priority as it did in glamour.[14]

But after oil wells were discovered and lucrative new bulk-transport needs sprouted on the Texas and Louisiana coasts, attention refocused on the waterway, and both private and public interests found their goals in alignment. On the private side, in 1905 businessmen from Victoria, Texas, formed the Interstate Inland Waterway League, aimed at creating an 18,000-mile network of interconnected waterways from the Great Lakes through the Mississippi Valley to the Gulf Coast. This group would become today's Gulf Intracoastal Canal Association, the nonprofit trade organization that coordinates with federal authorities on that asset's management. On the public side, President Theodore Roosevelt, who saw railroads as an overly powerful trust, welcomed alternatives, and in 1907 formed the Inland Waterways Commission. "The fall of 1907," wrote historian Lynn Alperin, "witnessed an unprecedented crop of conventions and support for waterway improvements.[15]

This being the same time that the Harvey Canal completed its locks, one might presume the year 1907 was a serendipitous moment leading to the addition of the Harvey Canal to the Gulf Intracoastal Waterway. But in fact, the Harvey family at first saw the Corps of Engineers project as a threat—yet another source of unwelcome competition for Gulf shipping traffic, along with the Barrow family's Company Canal in Westwego and the new Plaquemine Lock and Canal (1909) south of Baton Rouge, which let Atchafalaya Basin traffic reach the Mississippi.

What changed the presumed foe into a potential friend was a 1914 letter from the Secretary of War recommending that the route "be as near the business portion of the city of New Orleans as practicable," for both "economy of construction and saving of time in movement of freight."[16] Toward that end, it called for "the construction of an inland waterway . . . 7 feet deep and 75 feet bottom width . . . *to follow either the Harvey or Company Canal.*"

That was good news for greater New Orleans. For the West Bank, the big question was, which canal would the feds select? The report spelled out the attributes of the two longtime competitors:

The Harvey Canal is connected with the Mississippi River by a lock [with] a width of 29 feet 11 inches, an available length of 150 feet, and depth of 7 feet over the miter sills. From the lock the canal has a depth of about 6 feet and width of about 70 feet for 5.4 miles to Bayou Barataria, through which . . . ample depth exists for a distance of 12.4 miles to Lake Salvador. The route across that lake is almost 12 miles to the entrance to the Harang Canal, as this [section] is named, it having but recently come into their possession. This Harang Canal, 7.3 miles long, connects Lake Salvador with Bayou Lafourche. It was the intention of the company to extend their route by cutting a canal from Bayou Lafourche to Bayou Terrebonne; a survey party was in the field making the location, but was withdrawn when the act of Congress directing this report was passed. . . . The ownership of the canal is in the Harvey Canal & Land Improvement Co., legally a corporation of a small number of stockholders, but practically a partnership. Its right of way is about 300 feet wide.[17]

The other canal . . . ordinarily known as the "Company Canal," [was] constructed about 1830 by the Barataria & Lafourche Canal Co. It is owned at present by Mr. R. R. Barrow. It is connected with the Mississippi . . . by a lock having a width of 25 feet, a length of 160 feet, and a depth of 6 feet. The canal is about 2 miles long to Bayou Segnette. This bayou is very crooked and several cut-offs have been made to relieve navigation, and through them the distance traversed from the canal to Lake Salvador is 8.8 miles. The route usually followed across the lake to the mouth of Bayou Des Allemandes is about 13 miles in length. [Then] the canal runs through swamps for about 13 miles to Bayou Lafourche at Lockport. From this point it has been extended 8 miles through the swamp and across Lakes Field and Long to Bayou Terrebonne about 8 miles below Houma. Boats run regularly from Houma to New Orleans. The canal is supposed to have a depth of 6 feet, but . . . parts have shoaled to 4 feet. . . . The right of way of the canal varies, being 1 arpent (about 192 feet) wide at some points, 208 feet at others, and 300 feet in one or two places.[18]

Government authorities contacted both families to gauge their interest in selling. Both played coy, as they tried to feel out how much the feds needed *their* channel, and divined how much they stood to lose if the government built its free-toll waterway elsewhere.

Then war broke out in Europe, and priorities got rearranged again. This time, however, the distraction abetted the waterways argument. As if to prove the concerns of the War Department and former President Roosevelt, the vast quantities of American matériel heading for the western front overwhelmed the nation's rail system. Just within greater New Orleans, whose population soared during the war years, traffic increased 300 percent on backswamp waterways. "For nearly a century," wrote the *New Orleans Item*, waterways like the Company and Harvey canals "waited for transportation demands [such as those] of the World War to force recognition of the value to the state and nation of inland waterways—5000 miles of navigable streams and bayous, through the medium of gasoline-propelled freighters."[19] The current government moved quickly to reinvigorate inland canal usage by building a fleet of modern tow barges, and the Corps of Engineers came away with a newfound commitment to the intracoastal waterways system.

In January 1917 the Corps sent a second round of letters to the Harveys and the Barrows, asking their price. The Harveys responded with a request for $531,300 for the canal bed, lock and appurtenances, buildings, and bridges, plus $5000 per acre for adjacent land. The Barrows stalled, fearing that selling a portion of their waterway would "make the rest of the canal useless by cutting off its head."[20] Officials found they were having better rapport with the Harveys. Making matters worse was rising water in the Mississippi, which in April damaged the Barrows' locks but not the Harveys.' They were forced to close the Company Canal, sending their customers to the competition at the worst possible moment.

In 1919 the Corps made its decision: the Intracoastal Waterway would use the Harvey Canal to adjoin the Mississippi. The Barrows' damaged lock and too-narrow right-of-way spelled doom for the Company Canal, whereas the Harvey Canal was in full operation, had or could acquire the 300-foot right-of-way, lay nearly four miles closer heart of the city and port, and had responsive negotiators. An agreement was reached in 1921, followed by three years of land acquisitions, and "on March 10, 1924," wrote historian William Reeves, "The Harvey Canal Land and Improvement Company finally sold its canal to the United States Government. The check [for] $515,000 was received and deposited at the Canal Commercial Bank,"[21] itself an institution that began as a private canal-builder in the 1830s, when Nicholas Noel Destréhan had his canal idea. After eighty-six years of floods, war, occupation, failed locks, attempted takeovers, castles, quicksand, fires, fish-kills, and a parade of colorful characters, Destréhan's ditch was now a national asset. The government promptly got to work updating the facilities, demolishing Harvey's Castle in 1924 (last used as tenement apartments), widening and dredging the channel, and in 1934 spending $2 million on a new 425-foot-long, 75-foot-wide, 12-foot-deep lock.[22] The Harvey Canal became the most vital link in a toll-free 3000-mile navigable channel running from Boston to Brownsville.

Stung by the success of his rival, John Barrow Jr. got something of a consolation prize when, on June 18, 1925, he sold the western Lafourche-to-Terrebonne portion of his Company Canal to the United States government for incorporation into the Intracoastal Waterway. But he came home with a check for only $84,000, far less than his original $300,000 asking price, and a fraction of what the Harveys got. Barrow's tepid negotiating might have been attributable to various ailments he had been enduring. Worse still were his marital problems and disputes with his daughters who, behind his back in late 1925, sold the original Westwego portion of the Company Canal for $75,000.[23] A year later, the patriarch died, bringing to an end the century-long story of the Company Canal and the Barrow family's seven-decade ownership of it.

Might the Company Canal have won out if Barrow had negotiated more effectively? Some mariners continued to see a role for the old channel. "Only five years after the present-day Harvey Lock was completed," wrote mariner-historian Daniel Hubbell, "the marine industry was already complaining that it was too small. In 1939, there were suggestions that another, larger lock should be built at the site of the old Westwego lock."[24] Instead, in the early 1950s, the Corps of Engineers dug an alternative "cut off" route for the Gulf Intracoastal Waterway through West Plaquemines and Orleans Parish. This is today's Algiers Canal, and its wide lock (opened 1956) shares the daily traffic with the Harvey Canal route.

The impact on the West Bank of the 1919–1925 decisions in piecing together the Gulf Intracoastal Waterway can been gleaned from any satellite image. The Harvey Canal today forms a thousand-foot-wide corridor of scores of marine services and other industries and warehousing, with three bridges over it, a tunnel beneath it, and a steady stream of barge traffic on it. As of 2008, there were 7,226 jobs along its banks, nearly all of them directly related to the waterway.[25]

The Company Canal, on the other hand, is now nominally reduced to its Bayou Segnette trunk, with two relic concrete lock walls remaining at the river levee. The Salaville end of the channel, which after the Barrow era had come under the ownership of the Westwego Canal and Terminal Company, was filled in during 1959–1962; its span along Louisiana Street is now a nondescript landscape of open yards, metal sheds, a furniture outlet, and Las Maracas Mexican Restaurant.[26] Today everyone in greater New Orleans recognizes the name "Harvey," as a community and a body of water. Very few know "Barrow," and those few who know the Company Canal are either in the business of fishing or flood control.

Yet the Company Canal lives on, in the form of the seafood economy of the West Bank. To this day, coastal fishermen sail up Bayou Segnette, as they did 75 and 150 years ago, and up the extant section of the Company Canal, where a number of seafood processing plants remain in operation. Some of their catch of shrimp, crabs, oysters, gators, and whole fish is sold to the public through a dozen or so open-air vendors at the Westwego Shrimp Lot. Located at 105

West Bank Expressway in precise alignment with Salaville and the now-filled channel, the picturesque market is a living vestige of the West Bank's legacy as a nexus between Barataria Basin waters and Crescent City kitchens. And while the Harvey Canal bustles with activity as part of the Gulf Intracoastal Waterway, in the judgment of one historian, it was not the Harveys or the Destréhans or even the Corps of Engineers, but rather the Barrows who "were truly the founders of the inland waterway system," having been the first to actualize a navigable connection to points west.[27] That system has been described as 'the longest canal in the world,' from Boston to the Rio Grande."[28]

10

Landscape Change in Three Acts

One day in the early 1940s, Katherine Harvey Rogér, eldest of Horace Hale Harvey's eight children and now a grandmother, stood on a West Bank levee and cast her eyes over her ancestral lands. Fighting melancholy, she marveled at the grand sweep of history, in which her forebears were premier agents. "Leaving the ferry at Harvey," she wrote, "a feeling of nostalgia for the past came over me." She continued, "I stood looking out over the country-side for something, besides the canal, to pin my memories to. Nothing at all of my remembered childhood was there."

Then I listened, but no sound from the past came to me. . . .

Then I sniffed, for surely one of those many crowding sweet smells of the long ago would be lingering somewhere, [a] whiff of that air of my childhood[,] the smell of orange blossoms, or the pungent odor of those old magnolia flowers, or from jasmine or the overly perfumed butterfly lillies that grew in the border of Grandma's beautiful garden.

I stood there hoping for even a faint breath of the salty wet smell of the sea [from] dripping fish and seafood [or a] wagonload of fish or oysters. . . . I sniffed hard, but none of it was left[,] none came.

The great heavy hand of time had passed over all this land that had belonged to us, leaving nothing. . . . All that was gone now. All but the canal was gone in the cause of progress.

From the changes I saw[,] I knew that the Harvey and the Canal of today had progressed even beyond the wildest dreams of all those old ancestors of mine. . . . and all traces of nostalgia for the past quickly slipped away from me.[1]

If we were to attain the sweeping perspective that Mrs. Roger had over her sixty years and extend them over the entire West Bank for three hundred years, three prevailing eras would come into focus. The first would last for much of the eighteenth century, during which forest would predominate, decreasingly so toward century's end. The second era, mostly agrarian, would endure over the long nineteenth century. The denouement, during the twentieth century, was the transformation of a subrural condition ("subtopia") to a sort of "suburban interurbia," with green fields and woods giving way to gray concrete and edifice.

That's the historical geography of the West Bank in three acts: Forest-Field-City. Trees-Crops-Buildings. Arboreal-Agrarian-Urban. Rural-Subrural-Suburban.

This liminal pageant of place through time brings our attention to the exceptions—the outliers, the holdouts, the first evidence of the future or the last gasp of the past. And there are plenty, of course, as our three-act play is intentionally oversimplified. Algiers Point, for example, has been urbanized across two of the three acts. Bayou Segenette has been a swamp for all three. Patches of woodlands persist amid modern subdivisions, slipping through the cracks of progress, while a few antebellum plantation homes still stand, evading the ravages of time.

If there is one part of the West Bank in which the Forest-Field-City sequence is so replete with exceptions that the rules simply don't apply, it's Nine Mile Point. This promontory, so named for its riverine distance from the French Quarter, is unique in that it retains acreage of nearly every landscape ever known to the West Bank. Though its swampy hydrology has been drained, the point bar still has large tracts of pasture, forest, and, until recently, agriculture, set within the last undeveloped French long lots within the conurbation. It has industry, electrical energy production, grain storage, warehousing, and maritime services—yet also suburban subdivisions, an urban grid in nearby Bridge City, even one of the West Bank's last surviving plantation houses, the circa-1830 Magnolia Lane. And it has transportation: freight railroads and highways swirling on and off the gradual incline of the Huey P. Long Bridge; barges and vessels moored along the bank or tending to grain elevators.

These land uses have always evolved, and sometimes, they have clashed. For that we have the story of Seven Oaks, the grand plantation mansion that lorded over Nine Mile Point.

Originally named *Petit Desert* (Little Wilderness), this estate came into the colonial fold as part of a sprawling three-section 1719 concession from the Company of the West to three French officials who initially used it as a transshipment depot to develop the other two sections. In 1720, settlers from L'Orient arrived under Captain Ignace Francois Broutin to turn the wilderness into croplands. Over the next two generations, various portions of Petit Desert would pass in and out of the hands of illustrious colonial families: Villars Dubreuil, Bouligny, Trudeau, and after 1785, the intermarried Harangs and Zeringues, one of whose offspring, Camille Zeringue, was born around 1790.[2]

By 1812 Petit Desert spanned thirty-four arpents along the Nine Mile Point riverfront. Under Camille's direction, the holding expanded, the sugar harvests increased, the Zeringues entered the patrician class, and their plantation became the largest holding in the region. With an eye toward diversifying his income streams, Zeringue in 1830 sold an arpent to the Barataria & Lafourche Canal Company (in which he was invested) to connect the river with points south and westward, a project that would take years but prove profitable in the interim.

All that was missing from the operation was a manor house to match, and in the late 1830s, Camille Zeringue had just such an edifice erected. In the words of architectural historian Samuel Wilson Jr., the mansion was "an excellent example of the style of Greek Revival as adapted to the Louisiana plantation house[:] large and almost square in plan, [with] twenty-six massive brick columns of the Doric order [and] a huge pyramidal slate roof" topped with four symmetrical chimneys and a "belvedere [with] a magnificent view of the city and the river."[3] It would be called Seven Oaks, either for the surrounding trees or the seven-columned galleries. Its grandeur reflected the affluence of Louisiana's antebellum sugar barons, just as the hundred-strong slave force, lodged "back o' the big house," explained its provenance. It was a golden age for the former, time on the cross for the latter, and in retrospect, it wouldn't last long.

For Zeringue change would come first in 1852, when the New Orleans, Opelousas, and Great Western Railroad pressed for a right-of-way through his plantation, to which a court ruling forced Zeringue to acquiesce. The tracks were built through in 1853, and by year's end, trains were puffing across Zeringue's land, making money for other people at his expense.

Nine years later, when the Civil War broke out, the tracks became a potential ingress for Union troops—and the Zeringues were enthusiastic secessionists. Soldiers built an earthen fortification along the Company Canal, and the plantation became an encampment, costing Zeringue more crop space, while the Union blockade quashed his exports. Federal occupation in May 1862 and incremental emancipation over the next three years would upheave the plantation economy. Yet Zeringue, unlike many of his colleagues, managed to hang on in the war's aftermath.

His new enemy was the railroads, which, granted the power of expropriation, coveted Zeringue's land—"183 acres . . . between the master house and the Company Canal"—for a major rail terminal.[4] The aging patriarch indignantly rejected a purchase offer of the Texas & Pacific Railroad, so in 1870 the company sued to seize the land. T&P's court victory, wrote historian Marc R. Matrana, himself a family descendant, "demonstrates the greatly declining social, political, and economic status of . . . plantation owners" vis-à-vis the "political dominance of the railroads in the postwar South."[5] Attesting to this power shift is the fact that we call this area today not by the name "Petit Desert" or "Seven Oaks" but by railroad company neologism, "Westwego."

After Camille Zeringue died in 1872, his heirs found their fields crisscrossed by track beds, an annual struggle to secure a labor force, and a huge house in need of constant maintenance. A bank foreclosure in 1891 put the plantation in the hands of Pablo Sala who, realizing changing times would call for new uses, converted the place into Columbia Gardens, a day-trip resort for New Orleanians. Immensely popular at first, the venture did not survive Sala's death in 1894, after which the house changed hands repeatedly, and railroad interests gained control over more land.

In 1912 the Missouri Pacific Railroad Company bought the old house, and over the next twenty years, the former Zeringue Plantation became a veritable train yard strewn with storage tanks and fronted by the smoky Walnut Street Train Ferry terminal.[6] Amidst it all stood Seven Oaks, increasingly forlorn yet still imposing, its eighteen rooms rented out to tenants. One woman who lived there as a child remembered being able to hear the roar of lions at Audubon Zoo, less than a mile across the river.[7] After the last occupants departed in 1954, the mansion fell into a state of disrepair, hastened by vagrants, looters, and Hurricane Betsy's winds in 1965. Suburban Westwego had grown to its south, and Bridge City to its west, while oil tanks arose practically in its shadows, like mushrooms on damp fallow.

By the 1970s the belvedere atop Seven Oaks had collapsed into the attic. Wisteria-entwined columns stood free of the roof, looking like a Mayan ruin. Preservationists pleaded with the Texas Pacific–Missouri Pacific Railroad Company to at least stabilize what remained and make it into a heritage park. But state and local authorities offered only half-hearted support, while company officials remained intransigent. On August 27, 1977, they had the ruins bulldozed—and Westwego has regretted it ever since.[8]

Few spots tell the story of the West Bank's three hundred years of "scene changes," from arboreal to agrarian to industrial, as poignantly as Seven Oaks, even as Nine Mile Point does the opposite, retaining elements of all three scenes. Camille Zeringue would recognize only a few aged live oaks still standing on his land; even the Company Canal has been filled. Yet he and his predecessors laid the groundwork for nearly everything we see there today, going back to 1719, and this end of the West Bank would look very different had other decisions been made.

Fifteen miles downriver, at the opposite end of the West Bank, stood a counterpart of Seven Oaks, and it too would transcend the standard sequence of landscape transformation. This was the Stanton Plantation, on the lower coast of Algiers, its dense forests among the first on the West Bank to become fields and crops. Trees first fell here shortly after New Orleans was founded, and by 1723 land grants to French colonials Sieur Bourbeau, Sieur Massy, and Sieur Jean Hebert were already in operation as plantations. In the Spanish and early American eras, members of the Scottish Creole Macarty family would own parcels here, being neighbors at one point with a wealthy free woman of color named Constance Larche (L'Arche), who grew rice with thirty slaves in Plaquemines Parish, down from old Fort St. Leon.[9]

In 1811 the Macartys decamped for the East Bank, selling their West Bank land to the Andry family.[10] In 1822 the Andrys erected a stately mansion comparable in some regards to that of the later-built Seven Oaks. The largest plantation houses in their locales, both had spacious two-story wrap-around galleries and hipped roofs with dormers and belvederes. Unlike Seven Oaks, however, the Andry Plantation House was rectangular in shape and more Creole in its aesthetics, redolent of French and West Indian traits, with graceful spindle colonnades instead of austere classical columns. The design accommodated local climate conditions; wrote an impressed visitor to a similar edifice in 1803: "Galleries along the four sides of the house provided coolness when it was hot and warded off the chill when it was cold."[11]

In 1836 and 1841, Jean Baptiste LePretre purchased the Andry plantation in two sales, the latter for $85,000, which included 35.5 frontage arpents, the main house, outbuildings, a sugar mill and steam engine, tools, carts, wagons, 100 head of livestock, sugarcane in the field, and 82 slaves along with their cabins. To give an idea of its productivity, the LePretre Plantation produced 440 hogheads of sugar during 1861–1862, despite the wartime blockade.

Profits subsequently plunged, as they did throughout the Louisiana sugar sector. Production had dropped by 98 percent (230,000 tons to 5,000 tons) between 1861 and 1864, and total value, estimated at $200 million before the war, was at most one-eighth that figure by war's end.[12] LePretre sold the plantation to Thomas P. Stanton in 1869; a dozen years later, Stanton was only able to produce 305 hogsheads of sugar.[13] His heir Charles Thompson Stanton was unable to keep up with expenses, and in an 1885 sheriff's sale, title to the plantation switched to the ownership of his mortgagor, Richard A. Milliken, though the plantation would retain the name "Stanton."

Milliken, born in Ireland in 1817 and later a Confederate soldier and president of the Louisiana Sugar Exchange, would bring Stanton out of its postbellum malaise. He partnered in 1888 with William A. Rutledge, and together they purchased the Devron, Delacroix, Orleans and other adjacent parcels, including Madame Larche's former land, and installed all the latest agricultural and transportation equipment. After Milliken died in 1896, his widow Deborah Allen Farwell Milliken took over the partnership with Rutledge, and together they made Stanton even more successful.

By the early twentieth century, as every other sugar plantation folded in Orleans Parish in favor of urbanization or industry, the Stanton Plantation went in the opposite direction, growing to an unprecedented seven miles of riverfront, covering 1,600 acres, with 150 buildings, a workforce of up to 400, its own harbor and rail lines with a hundred cars, a drainage system and electrical plant, and the area's largest sugar mill, capable of processing 500 tons per day. It was practically a company town, with workers living near or on site, some in what appear in old photographs to be either former slave cabins or none too different. Saturday nights at the Stanton Plantation were notorious in this era; reports of fights and murders among workers were common back-of-the-paper new items.

As the biggest and last commodity plantation within New Orleans city limits, Stanton Plantation was an extraordinary paradox, both a paradigm of the latest technology and a relic of times past. Among the smoke stacks and locomotives still stood the elegantly aging 1822 mansion. In 1908 Stanton became a woman-run plantation, as Mrs. Milliken bought out Rutledge's interests; four years later, she sold it to a corporate entity named the Stanton Plantation and Manufacturing Company.[14]

It proved to be a timely move, because Louisiana sugar was about to sour. Reasons were many. The American Sugar Refining Company had built a state-of-the-industry refinery (1912) in Chalmette, directly across the river, giving Stanton competition for contract milling. Around the same time, mosaic disease and root rot struck the regional sugar crop, while years of erratic rainfall and late frosts diminished harvests. On the political front, Congress in 1913 passed a bill to reduce duties on sugar imports, which, though later rescinded, scared investors away from American sugar and into foreign markets. Even the Stanton Company looked to foreign shores, as it sold some of its sugar mills in 1915 to the new El Porvenir Plantación in La Ceiba, Honduras, started by a group of local investors that included the Vaccaro Brothers and Canal Bank.[15] The Great War in Europe provided temporary relief, as increased demand coincided with bumper crops, but by then the damage was done. Sugar-related professional offices in New Orleans declined in number and size, the two sugar refining plants on the French Quarter riverfront were sold off in 1917 and 1920, prices collapsed in 1920–1921, and consistently bad yields during 1923–1928 led to numerous plantation closures.[16]

The economic forces that had done in so many other sugar outfits were now bearing down on Stanton. And so was the Mississippi River: the channel curve at this spot steered currents obliquely into Stanton's riverfront, grinding away company land. In 1916 the Corps of Engineers and Orleans Levee Board decided to realign the levee, which required the expropriation of 80 valuable riverfront acres. Then, during the extremely high water of 1922, a major levee cave-in occurred by the mansion, with all the marks of developing into a catastrophic crevasse. After a contentious refusal of support from federal authorities, the Orleans Levee Board hastily excavated a "crib" as a "supplementary bulwark [to] confine the water in the river if a break should occur in the original embankment."[17] The frantic intervention prevented a full crevasse flood, but it turned the main plantation compound into a muddy mess, with water ponded all around the 1822 mansion.

Sometime after the 1922 cave-in, either by hasty deterioration or prompt demolition, the woebegone manse was gone. "Part of Famous Plantation Will be Subdivided by Firm," read a headline four years later, when 225 acres of Stanton Plantation cane fields were sold.[18] As for the remaining land, in 1930 the Stanton Plantation Company sold 2,400 acres to Russell Clark for a mere $100,000; Clark's plans for what the *Times-Picayune* called "the last remaining plantation in the city limits"[19] were to build "a country home [with] driveways [and] trees and shrubbery."[20] After Clark sold most of it, dozens of smaller lots hit the market in the 1940s for isolated country homes, by which time the industrial-agrarian landscape of circa-1900 had largely reverted to small farms and hamlets amid a patchwork of fields and forest.[21] By this time, few still called the area "the Stanton Plantation," and Stanton Road is the sole remaining use of that toponym today.

Like Nine Mile Point and Seven Oaks at the upper end of the West Bank, the lower coast of Algiers and Stanton Plantation represent a scrambling of the West Bank's Forest-Field-City landscape sequence. Both were exceptions to the rule, or perhaps evidence that there never was a rule in the first place. Wherever humans make decisions about land—or just about anything else, for that matter—contingency prevails at every stage.

11

Flood, Wind, and Fire

One of the great natural advantages of the West Bank has long been its uncluttered riverfront, boasting plenty of space for specialized industries like shipbuilding and dry docks. These deliberative, deep-draft activities were ill suited for the highly congested East Bank, where "broad wooden piers for oceangoing ships extend into the river[,] about 100 above [Canal Street and] 60 below it," forming a maze of maritime activity upon shallow waters in constant need of dredging.[1]

The same forces that made the West Bank riverfront deep, however, also made it vulnerable.

Disasters often trigger adaptations and inscribe lasting changes in the landscape, making them inflection points in the history and geography of a place. On the West Bank of the long nineteenth century, such traumas usually took the form of bank cave-ins, crevasses, and floods.

Waters in a river like the Mississippi, flowing in a soft-bottomed channel across a deltaic plain, move like a bobsled. Where the track runs straight, the bobsled glides down the middle. Where it turns left or right, the bobsled banks oppositely, with a velocity and force commensurate with the acuity of the bend.

Likewise, where the channel runs straight, the force of the water is evenly distributed across the channel, making the bottom generally flat, without a deep trench (thalweg). But where the river meanders, the thalweg, like the bobsled, swings out upon the concave (outer) side, running fast and strong, while on the convex (inner) side, the water slows, loses its kinetic energy, and deposits its suspended sediment to create a beach, or batture. "The inhabitants consider themselves fortunate when a batture begins to form [by] their land," wrote Pierre

Clément de Laussat, recalling his time as Louisiana's last French colonial ad-
ministrator in 1803. "But one bank builds up firmly only at the expense of the
opposite bank; one is always in proportion to the other."[2] Usually, that "opposite
bank" was the West Bank.

As the Mississippi comes around Nine Mile Point and enters the Greenville
Bend, its thalweg, running about 150 feet deep, rebounds from the East Bank
by Carrollton to the West Bank by Westwego, where it gets as deep as 180 feet.
There it remains, running past Marrero, Harvey, Gretna, around the Gouldsboro Bend by McDonoghville, to Algiers Point. Depths vary depending on the
season, year, and dredging, but along this particular stretch, the West Bank side
of the river is two to three times deeper than the East Bank side. It so happens
that just off Algiers Point lies the deepest point in the entire Mississippi River
system, at times over 200 feet. The flow next bends sharply past the French
Quarter, sending the "bobsled" into East Bank's Third District Bend (Marigny
and Bywater), after which the channel straightens out, and the bottom flattens,
for the next five miles.

Because New Orleans expanded upon the convex flank of a broad crescent,
where water slows and sediment drops, its riverfront runs shallow and forms
sandy point bar deposits. The main portion of the West Bank riverfront, on the
other hand, flows deeper and faster, with greater friction and abrasion against
the levee.[3] The erosion on this cut-bank meander was worst during high water, perceptible to observers, like a garden hose shot obliquely into a mud pile.
Sometimes ancient cypress logs or stumps would get dislodged. Other times the
erosion happened invisibly, during normal river stage, as currents scoured below
the water level and burrowed subterranean passages—called an *anse* (cove) by
French-speakers and a cave by English-speakers—weakening the bank until it
unexpectedly caved in.[4]

If sufficiently deep, or the river sufficiently high, a cave-in could develop
into a crevasse—"a fissure or breaking of the Levée," explained a local writer
in 1823. These breaches "are occasioned [firstly by] the yielding of the Levée;
and secondly, the sinking of the bank of the river."[5] That latter phenomenon
was also called *éboulis* or *éboulemens*, meaning landslides of the river bank.[6] If
severe, wrote one observer in the early 1800s, "the waters rush [through] with
indescribable impetuosity, with a noise like the roaring of a cataract, boiling and
foaming, and bearing every thing before them. Like the breaking out of a fire in
a town, it excites universal consternation."[7]

The historiography of New Orleans is punctuated by famous East Bank crevasse floods. The 1816 Carrollton (Macarty) Crevasse, the 1849 Sauvé Crevasse, and the 1871 Bonnet Carre Crevasse are remembered because they affected people and property en masse, and we tend to declare them "disasters" only to the extent they impact us. But in truth, the West Bank, from Westwego to Algiers Point, was far more prone to massive river flooding than the East Bank, and suffered some of the largest deluges, in terms of surface extent, in the recorded history of all southeastern Louisiana. There were just fewer people living there for the historiography to remember them as disastrous.

Of course, deltaic rivers naturally writhe and scour, and crevasses are what enabled the Mississippi to jump and dump and make the delta in the first place. Humans responded in two ways. Natives moved out of the water's way, viewing floods as a condition rather than a problem. Imperialists viewed floods as intolerable problems and, bent on permanent colonization, endeavored to solve them by "raising up" (*lever*) embankments as man-made levees. The effort started as early as 1719, when the Mississippi's waters first washed over early New Orleans.

Later in the colonial era, the channel began shifting at New Orleans. Its thalweg leaned into the West Bank, while its opposite currents ran increasingly slack off the Faubourg Ste. Marie (St. Mary) riverfront on the East Bank. Sand began falling out of the shallow waters off Tchoupitoulas Street, forming a batture. According to the Roman civil law in effect in Spanish New Orleans, such *terre d'alluvion* was understood to be public space. Anyone could promenade the batture; you could even cart off some fill if you wanted. But you could not own it.

Jean Gravier, who lived at what is now 800 Tchoupitoulas, thought differently. The year was 1803; dominion of the colony was about to transfer to the United States, which practiced English common law. Unlike civil law, common law viewed such riparian depositions as pertaining to whomever owned the adjacent land. This was music to the ears of Jean Gravier and his lawyer, Edward Livingston, who recognized the value of this new terrain, forming precisely at the right place and time to capitalize on the impending shipping boom in this new American city. Gravier hired workers to build a levee around "his" batture, essentially privatizing a public space. Locals protested, and the Creole-dominant Conseil de Ville reproved Gravier's actions—only to be contradicted by the American-controlled Territorial Court.[8]

What ensued was an epic, years-long court battle. "The Batture Case" pitted two divergent legal philosophies, involved powerful figures including President

Thomas Jefferson, and put at stake fundamental national questions about public access to western rivers. As for the "St. Mary Batture," as locals called it, Livingston and the city negotiated a compromise in 1820. "All the soil between the present Levée and the river shall in future be held by the city for the purposes of navigation," explained John Adems Paxton in 1822, "but that no buildings whatsoever shall be erected thereon." In other words, land outside the levee would have a public maritime servitude, as it does today. As for the new land inside the levee, Paxton wrote, "This piece of property, which has made so great a figure in the history of litigation, is now divided among a great number of proprietors, [to] be improved and made useful to the public, as well as a source of profit to the owners." He concluded, "All [our] commerce centers on the Batture, and it would be difficult to select in any city in the world a spot in which more extensive business is done in the same space. The property then must soon become invaluable."[9]

Paxton would prove right. The St. Mary Batture would eventually swell to 200 acres, forming today's Warehouse District, a fortuitous natural gift now worth billions of dollars.

All well and good for the East Bank—but a calamity for the West Bank. For every acre of land gained across the river, roughly the same space would disappear from the upper Algiers and McDonoghville riverfront. A circa-1798 map updated in 1875 shows that from Jackson Square to the Irish Channel, and from Algiers Point to Gretna, the curving Mississippi channel shifted its position 500 to 1,000 feet straight eastward, *into* the (counterintuitively named) West Bank.[10]

The resulting land loss took two forms: chronic and acute. Chronic riverfront land loss occurred nearly constantly, rarely made news, and earned the consternation of only riverfront landowners, who saw their holdings erode at the same rate their lucky cross-river counterparts saw their holdings aggrade. All of Montgomery Street and most of Washington and Adams streets would disappear. The intersection of Jefferson and Americus in 1845 lay 870 feet in from the levee; today that same space *is* the levee.[11] An 1853 account put the erosion of "the Mcdonough and Algiers," and the accretion across the river, "at the rate of one square in ten or fifteen years."[12] Total land lost amounted to about 200 acres, among them the spaces of most the plantation houses from the 1700s and early 1800s from Algiers to Gretna, including the famed French colonial Monsplaisir chateau later occupied by John McDonogh. As early as 1803, French prefect Pierre Laussat reported that "landslides caused by the river had already gouged out an arpent of land and threatened [Monsplaisir] only a few years away." It is said to have finally washed into the river in the 1870s.[13]

Chronic bank erosion was punctuated by acute events, the likes of which affect humans dramatically and make history. They happened when high water, strong currents, or that drifting thalweg encountered a weak spot in the levee, leading to cave-ins and crevasses. Such incidents occurred in or affected the West Bank at least in 1802, 1840, 1842, 1844, 1847, 1849 (English Turn), 1850, 1851, 1852, 1855, 1858, 1865, 1867, 1881, 1882, 1884, 1891, 1892, 1893, 1894, 1920, and 1922 (Myrtle Grove).[14]

In stipulating how to respond to levee failures, the police jury of Jefferson Parish focused on labor, not engineering. "If any rupture (crevasse) should happen," read Article 17 of the 1834 parish regulations, "the syndic of the district . . . shall immediately repair to the spot and require the inhabitants . . . to send a sufficient number of negroes to remedy the accident, [with] no compensation." Each planter had to have on hand sufficient "pickets and clubs" and "a deposit of straw and moss," as well as "a white overseer" to guide the effort, without specifying his qualifications. If more laborers were needed, the crevasse owner was compelled to hire others' slaves, else face stiff fines. Moneys earned by hired-out slaves would go to their master, and if the slaves "should happen to drown [or] be wounded[,] the owner . . . shall be entitled to an indemnity."[15] That no specifications were issued as to *how* to plug a crevasse indicates that an ad hoc strategy usually prevailed until the river dropped. More advanced tactics included building a ring levee around the rupture, or obtaining a steam-driven pile driver to fence it in with planks, after which the hole might be plugged by sandbagging or stuffing in bagasse, moss, or hay. Sometimes an old steamboat or barge would be towed in and scuttled in the opening. Preemptive measures included building double levees, or realigning and strengthening them against the worst currents. The best prevention was to inspect and maintain levees vigilantly, catching problems at their embryonic stage.

Cave-ins and crevasses varied in nature, size, and effects. One Algiers incident occurred in sudden sequences one night in late February 1842, as "slide after slide occurred, until the whole neighborhood quietly walked off and disappeared gracefully into the Mississippi," taking with it a large popular hotel, a bowling alley, and a recreational boathouse, part of Algiers's weekend tourism scene.[16] Five years later, in May 1847, a crevasse two hundred feet wide and five feet deep put up to four feet of water in the area by Powder Street, destroyed various houses, and probably caused some people to drown, along with horses and livestock.[17]

The spring of 1849 high waters that triggered the famous Sauvé Crevasse flood of New Orleans had, a month earlier, ruptured the Fortier Plantation levee in present-day Waggaman, unleashing a "rush of water [of the] most awful destructive appearance" with a "noise . . . heard from a long distance."[18] It later tore a 100-foot hole in the Tunisburg levee, "doing an immense amount of damage in the vicinity" of today's Odeon Avenue.[19]

This was not always the case. A February 1850 failure on the Lacoste Plantation six miles below Algiers typified the type of crevasse that caused a headache and some crop damage, but was hardly disastrous, as "the water fortunately has not spread to any great extent over the neighboring fields, flowing mostly in a direct course towards the swamp."[20] Indeed, incidents like this could, under certain conditions, yield more benefit than cost. As the *Daily Picayune* explained later in the 1850s: "As soon as the water passes the breach and begins to spread over the lower plains, its velocity is diminished, and its earth matter . . . is deposited, the heaviest particles [first] and the finer atoms of soil at. . . . greater distances. Thus the cultivatable lands along the margin of the river become greatly widened by every Crevasse, and the subsequent increase in the fertility of plantations is a measureable compensation for the disadvantage of an overflow."[21]

Not so the Bell Crevasse, which everyone agreed was perfectly catastrophic. It occurred on John M. Bell's plantation about four thousand feet upriver from the Harvey Canal, where once coursed the Bayou des Familles distributary, making this a natural fork. In the Spanish era, this parcel had been a rice plantation, for which the fields were flooded (to kill weeds) through the reuse of the old natural distributary as a flume network with a sluice gate. After rice gave way to sugarcane, which suffers from excess moisture, the old "sluice was removed [and] filled with earth. But the earth does not appear to have been packed with sufficient solidity, and when the river rose[,] it found the weak spot."[22]

The crevasse opened on the morning of April 11, 1858, and soon all of Bell's land was under water, followed by neighbors' lands, including Harvey's to the east and Millaudon's to the west. The gap expanded to 250 feet across and a frightful 22 feet in depth, meaning the disappearance of the entire artificial levee and the natural deposits beneath it. Floodwaters reached "the inundated tomb of John McDonogh" about 3.5 miles away, putting the entire West Bank under water, except for the immediate riverfront. Even the Marine Hospital, a stone's throw from the river, took on water. The Harvey family's waterway operation was swamped, and its channel made things worse, communicating the deluge far down into Plaquemines Parish.[23] Floodwaters were reported in late April, fully twenty-seven miles downriver from the metropolis; by mid-June, they extended a staggering "sixty-five miles [south and] still spreading out further, until there is a strong probability that the Mississippi will soon be connected by an unbroken sea of water with the Gulf of Mexico."[24]

For weeks in mid-spring 1858, the West Bank and nearly its entire watershed ceased to exist as a landform, disrupting everyday life and an entire season of economic activity. Ecologically, "the whole country was a lake" meant that creatures of the swamp and bayou—"spiders, lizards . . . snakes, leeches . . . buffalo fish"—were on the move into new areas.[25] "In every direction dead horses and other cattle are seen lodged in trees or floating . . . All the game has either been destroyed or has fled. . . . There are no deer, no rabbits, no coons, nothing. . . . The snakes have been washed out to sea, and the oysters have been killed." The deluge swelled slowly and predictably enough for people to take evasive action, making fatalities rare but refugees common. Importantly, there was no back levee to impound the water; instead, it flowed steadily in one vast sheet, from river to sea. "Hundreds of poor people who lived about Barataria have fled from the scene[–] and yet, in the midst of all this destruction, we have heard no word of complaint from the losers."[26]

As often happened during big crevasses, the rushing water attracted popular interest, and ferry operators cashed in on the curiosity seekers. One contented client of this early disaster tourism was the English-born architect Thomas K. Wharton, who after dinner on May 18 joined companions on "the omnibus to the Gretna Ferry, crossed the river, and after a pleasant walk of ½ a mile on the Levee," arrived at the "'great 'Bell Crevasse,' which has been pouring its relentless flood . . . into the opposite country [and] buried [it] under a brown, soaking deluge as far as the eye can [see]." The tourists seemed unfazed by the news of two men who, just an hour earlier, had been swept into "the furious torrent and have not been seen since," much less by the ongoing suffering throughout the West Bank. On the contrary: "Quite a number of familiar faces from the city had been, like us, attracted to the spot," Wharton wrote in his diary. "We reached home about dark, tired indeed, but amply repaid by our visit to the 'Bell Crevasse.'"[27]

In the first two months, at least forty plantations went under. Damages to the sugar crop were estimated at $5 million, over $150 million today, and ended up much higher. Thousands of houses were inundated, farms were wiped out, and long stretches of the New Orleans, Opelousas and Western railroad tracks were submerged under four feet of water.[28]

By autumn, river stage had dropped, but still the crevasse let water pass, on account of its capacious size (three hundred feet wide in early October). Not until December did workers stop the flow, by surrounding the fissure with ring levees designed by engineer J. A. d'Hémécourt and built at a cost of $115,771.[29]

After the floodwaters drained out of the bayous and into the Gulf, the entire eastern portion of the Barataria watershed was one vast mucky debris field. The Bell Plantation itself had been scoured into a half-mile-long trench between what is now Avenue A to Avenue E in Marrero, five to forty feet deep, clogged with mud-caked driftwood, with sediment ridges splayed in a pattern that reminded one observer of snowdrifts. For years, a two-thousand-acre, slip-like indentation remained along the riverfront where the crevasse had scoured.[30]

Total losses were exorbitant, and lawsuits were filed—only to be interrupted by the man-made disaster of the Civil War. In a stinging irony, the only economic assets spared by the Bell deluge—the riverfront shipbuilding and dry dock industries—were precisely the ones burned and scuttled in the ensuing conflict. Meanwhile, the Marine Hospital in Gretna, repurposed as a Confederate powder depot, mysteriously exploded in late 1861, causing another crevasse that flooded McDonoghville—which all along had been steadily losing land to bankside erosion.[31] Two weeks after the Confederate surrender in April 1865 came yet another serious West Bank crevasse, on the Magee Plantation in lower Algiers, where workers dug into an earthen Confederate fortification to help seal the hole.[32] The late 1850s through 1860s were probably the single most tumultuous era in West Bank history, hydrologically, politically, and militarily.

Up to this time, levee construction and maintenance had been a local matter, the responsibility of landowners and parish governments with varying levels of state funding and oversight. That approach, to say the least, was not equal to the task. After the Civil War, as Washington's power and influence grew, a consensus formed that western river control ought to be a national priority. Federal expenditures for waterway improvements rose from under $5 million in the 1850s to $65 million in the 1870s.[33] In 1879, Congress created the Mississippi River Commission and charged it to work with the Army Corps of Engineers in advising and funding state and county or parish governments in controlling the river for both navigation and flood control. In subsequent decades, with the Mississippi

River Commission "offering advice, serving as a clearing house for technical data, and providing two thirds of the funding," wrote environmental historian Ari Kelman, "levees in Louisiana reached a new level of sophistication."[34]

If the end of cave-ins and crevasses seemed on the horizon, it was a mirage. "I beg leave to call your attention to the condition of the bend from Westwego to Algiers," pleaded New Orleans & Pacific Railway Company president E. B. Wheelock to Maj. Amos Stickney of the Corps of Engineers in 1883. "The caving in this bend has already destroyed [our] depot. . . . It threatens the entire commerce [of the West Bank] and may occur again at any point."[35] Stickney concurred, and had his staff work out plans for bank stabilization. But while federal support was ample, it was also slow, and would take years to complete, during which the problem only worsened.

In early March 1891, a man named Bidstrup needed to cut the levee on the plantation owned by the Ames brothers (formerly Millaudon) in present-day Westwego/Marrero, for the purposes of inserting a pipe. Installations like this, though risky, had been permitted by a state legislative act in 1890, and Bidstrup made sure police jury president Louis H. Marrero was present to assure the pipe cut had been adequately sealed.

Marrero thought so. Bidstrup surely did. The Mississippi proved otherwise.

High springtime waters and hungry currents exploited the cut, which had been filled too loosely. As it widened into a crevasse, word got out, and communities rushed to sandbag their houses, while villages like Gretna and enterprises like the Brooklyn Stockyard, Southern Pacific, and Texas Pacific shored up their own private ring levees. By March 20, the Ames Crevasse was 250 feet wide; next day, 375 feet, as river water came within a foot of the top of the Company Canal locks, threatening to turn that waterway into a veritable distributary. By March 24 the crevasse measured 400 feet wide and 23 feet deep; by March 28, it was 678 feet wide; by mid-June over 1,000 feet. Its waters flooded from Algiers through Gretna and spread all the way to Vacherie and Bayou Lafourche, leading some to compare the disaster to the 1884 Davis Crevasse, which wiped out $4 million in sugar and rice harvests alone, and even the Bell Crevasse of 1858. In early May, Frank A. Ames himself, distraught over the calamity on his property, acknowledged the Ames Crevasse might "prove to be the most destructive ever known."[36]

Unlike during the Bell Crevasse, when the local police jury could only look to itself for a solution, now federal resources could be called upon. The Mississippi River Commission in Memphis appropriated $250,000 for emergency repairs and monitored other needs up and down the lower Mississippi, as crevasses broke out in multiplicity. There was another difference: whereas the Bell Crevasse flooded southward into Plaquemines, the Ames Crevasse, though only a mile from the Bell, moved westward into Lafourche. "Some curiosity was felt over this phenomenon," reported one journalist. The reason, he speculated: "the floating or trembling prairies of southern Louisiana." Also known as flotant, these *prairies tremblantes* are thick mucky entanglements of organic matter that are unanchored to the underlying earth, and can shift about with wind or current. "There are quite a number of these in [Lake] Salvador," the journalist explained, and "the current from the Ames crevasse has carried these floating islands down stream," forming a dam of sorts and routing the floodwaters upstream instead.[37]

Once again, entrepreneurs saw an opportunity to make money off morbid curiosity. "Ho, for the Ames Crevasse," called J. B. Arleans of the Steamer *Neptune*, who offered Sunday excursions to the breach from the foot of Henry Clay Avenue for 20 cents.[38] By late April, Arleans had lots of competition. The crevasse was directly across the river from Audubon Park, site of a world's fair six years prior, and recreationists could see the turmoil from afar.

There was no one heroic moment when the Ames Crevasse was sealed; rather, it gradually let through less water as other crevasses opened upriver and relieved the pressure. This made it easier for the two hundred workers—in toiling once done by slaves, now by convicts—to build a bulwark behind the 1200-foot gap of waist-deep mud.[39] The trapezoid-shaped crib levee remained in place for decades, and its imprint can still be seen today in the conspicuously angled levee between Avenue C and D along the Westwego riverfront.

Both the Bell Crevasse of 1858 and the Ames Crevasse of 1891 illustrate the shaky nature of a fluvial delta. In both cases, had the river swelled at the wrong time and the fissures widened just so, it's possible the Mississippi could have torn a new path through Harvey and created a new deltaic lobe in the Barataria Basin. Both crevasses, after all, formed near an earlier distributary fork, whose route traced a shorter path and steeper gradient southward to the sea, compared to ninety-five miles of wending river to the southeast. Both disasters, taking place between the Harvey and Company canals, also suggest their owners were wise in being extra-cautious about building their locks. If an improperly filled sluice gate and pipe hole nearly redrew the map of North America's greater river, imagine what a failed lock on a major navigation canal could have done.

Cave-ins and crevasses had been perennial West Bank worries, if not annual nemeses. A year after the Ames Crevasse, multiple levee failures, including one in St. James Parish traceable to "a big crayfish hole," caused additional flooding, while in mid-August 1892, the 200-foot-wide "Algiers Cave" swallowed the beautiful new train depot of the New Orleans, Fort Jackson and Grand Isle Railroad.[40] More followed in 1893 and 1894. But with more federal capacity directed at the problem, their frequency would finally slow in the new century, the last significant one occurring in 1922. In addition to bigger and better levees, two devices helped bring the problem under control. One was the spur dike, an L-shaped rock or timber jetty laid out perpendicularly to the cutbank, confected to tame currents and stabilize thalweg shifts. Four spur dikes had been installed on the Gouldsboro Bend (Gretna/Algiers) in 1884–1888, and two at the Greenville Bend (Westwego/Marrero) in 1889–1890, and yet the Ames Crevasse occurred precisely between them the very next year. Another thirteen were placed along the East Bank Carrollton and Third District bends between 1889 and 1891.[41]

A more effective tool for bank stabilization was the revetment—that is, retaining sheaths made of various materials (matted-willow "mattresses," rock gabions, creosote planking, sand asphalt, or concrete slabs) laid out to shield cutbanks. Revetments were nothing new; what was new was their professionally engineered design backed by adequate funding. In 1883, the Corps devised a plan for three sections along the West Bank, spanning eight miles from Seven Oaks in Westwego to De Armas Street in Algiers, particularly "the entire third section [along McDonoghville, which] is a caving bank, and if not protected it will in time cut away Algiers, and change the whole front on the opposite side of the river."[42] Estimated costs for the mattress and dike protection system were $1,150,000, or $30 million today, for which congressional authorization and appropriation had to be secured. During 1887–1906, the Corps installed a series of revetments from Anson Street to the parish line, and from there down to Seguin Street during 1898–1899.[43] Around the same time, the New Orleans Harbor Improvements project conducted bank stabilization work on both sides of the Mississippi, including the Greenville Bend Revetments (where both the Ames and Bell crevasses had occurred), the Gretna Bend Revetments, and the Gouldsboro Bend Revetments (where those 200 acres had eroded away in Algiers and McDonoghvillle) during the 1890s to 1930s.[44] They successfully deflected the high water of spring 1922, though they tended to shift the problem to unarmored levees, such as those at the Stanton Plantation in lower Algiers, where, after a refusal of federal support, the Orleans Levee Board hastily excavated a "crib" as a "supplementary bulwark [to] confine the water in the river if a break should occur in the original embankment."[45]

Later in the 1900s, the Army Corps devised stronger concrete mat revetments made of thousands of concrete slabs, twenty-five feet long, four feet wide, and three inches thick. Slabs are wired together into 140-foot-wide sections of lattice and laid out upon submerged banks smoothed over by draglines, then covered in riprap.[46] Cast in a yard in St. Francisville, the heavy mat, as well as sheet-piling-based floodwalls, not only controlled cave-ins and crevasses but also reworked the hydrological dynamics of the river, by absorbing energy as the current leans into cutbanks. This explains in part why there are now placid battures along the West Bank where once deep swift water flowed. But the thalweg is still very much there, just a few hundred feet offshore, and the ever-shifting "Algiers Hole" still lurks off the Point, at times over 200 feet below the anything-but-lazy Mississippi River. Where goes the scouring, up comes history: in 2004, Army Corps repairs on a collapsed section of the Westwego riverfront unearthed the remains of a number of old vessels, among them the 1864 USS *Chickasaw,* an ironclad that saw action in Mobile Bay and later became the *Gouldsboro* train ferry. Ending its career as a coal barge, the heavily remodeled warship was scuttled in 1944, and remains embedded in the Greenville Bend.[47]

Despite the repeated disasters buffeting the Barataria Basin, Grand Isle at its southern rim had managed to become a special place. Once the haunt of smugglers and pirates, later home (along with neighboring Chênière Caminada and Grand Terre) to the coastal fishing fleet, the sandy barrier island had since the Civil War become the resort of choice for affluent New Orleanians to escape the torrid metropolis.[48] Mandeville, Biloxi, and Galveston were also summertime getaways, and each billed itself as a healthy antidote to miasmas and disease. But Grand Isle was different. Here the Creole gentry let down its hair, "shed[ding] city clothing and some degree of inhibitions," according to three historians, in "an exotic, almost erotic atmosphere, markedly different from the rigid mores" of the era.[49] Splendid hotels and picturesque cottages accommodated the guests, and yachts took them sightseeing at old Fort Livingston or to the curious Asian shrimp-drying community at Manila Village. No wonder some of Louisiana's best-known writers of the "local color" literary genre, Lafacadio Hearn, George Washington Cable, and Kate Chopin, all wrote extensively of Grand Isle. It was Louisiana's Riviera.

Most New Orleanians got to Grand Isle via the West Bank, by steamboat on the two canals or by train from Algiers. Investors affiliated with these conveyances were also hoteliers and restaurateurs on the island—vertically integrated tourism operators in today's parlance. The arteries also carried the islands' seafood harvests into New Orleans, with the West Bank transshipping and adding value to the catch. Economically speaking, Grand Isle was "in" the West Bank; the two spaces occupied the same watershed, and Grand Isle answered to the same Jefferson Parish police jury as Gretna and Westwego. What happened on Grand Isle affected the West Bank.

In late September 1893, a tropical storm developed off the Caribbean coast of Honduras and rapidly strengthened to 85-knot winds before weakening over the Yucatan Peninsula. Once in the central Gulf, the track swung to the northeast, where warm surface waters fueled winds to 115 knots—what today would qualify as a Category 4 hurricane. In its path: the yawning mouth of the Barataria Bay, with the Chênière Caminada peninsula and Grand Isle to its west, the mouth of the Mississippi to its east, and the West Bank dead ahead.[50]

Tropical storms over the Barataria Basin were hardly rare. Over seventy systems of various sizes passed there since record-keeping began in 1851, and five had struck near Grand Isle since the deadly Isle Dernière (Last Island) Hurricane of 1856. What distinguished this latest system was its power—the strongest recorded to date for that spot—and the populations in its path.

With minimal warning and full force, the tempest made landfall in the twilight of an otherwise beautiful Sunday, October 1. Highest levels of human exposure lay to the northwest of the storm track, and there the mayhem would be the most terrible. Because of the Coriolis Effect, however, the strongest winds and surge spun off the vortex's counter-clockwise churn in a northeasterly direction, into the Barataria Basin and around the mouth of the Mississippi. Rivers can't flow uphill, even a hill of water, so the Mississippi reversed and spilled over the levees in Plaquemines Parish, adding more water to the bloated Barataria. Grand Isle's hurricane thus became the West Bank's flood. "The first point below New Orleans where the storm commenced to do its work of destruction was the old "Poydras' plantation," wrote Rose C. Falls in a detailed account published later in

1893. "From there down, Stella, Monsecour, Old Harlem, Myrtle Grove, Savoy, Belleview, Hebert's, Livaudais, [an]d Sardelot's" all flooded:

> Houses were unroofed or blown down, fences were leveled, the crops of cane and rice were badly injured, animals were killed or drowned, and sugar houses were badly damaged. . . . At Point Celeste a large negro church was torn [and] carried over a quarter of a mile . . . across the track of the New Orleans, Fort Jackson and Grand Isle Railroad.
>
> All along the Mississippi, on both banks [for] nearly a hundred miles, were strewn the wrecks of boats and luggers, the debris of houses, the bodies of animals, and the ghastly corpses of men and women and little children, [amid] a thick mantle of sea weed swept in from the Gulf of Mexico.[51]

Floodwaters crept up the rear streets of the West Bank, while gales whipped above. An Algiers benevolent hall lost its roof; the Methodist Church lost its steeple; a house of worship in Freetown completely collapsed. On the riverfront, dry docks jostled dangerously and craft strained at their moorings. Inexplicably, at 9 p.m., the crew of the Algiers transfer ferry "*Gouldsboro,* of the Texas and Pacific [Rail]road, started to cross the river in the teeth of the gale[,] loaded with passengers and freight cars." The hulking craft spun across the turbid waves, dodging the unmoored ferry *Jerome Handley,* the steam launch *Harry Shannon,* and the steamer *Grace Pitt,* which had broken free of wharves in McDonoghville, Gretna, and Algiers. All three unmanned vessels were smashed and sunk, while another half-dozen ferries and barges ended up grounded or damaged. The *Gouldsboro* crew redeemed itself by managing to moor to an East Bank wharf, saving the locomotives, cars, and terrified passengers from a fateful plunge.[52]

Monday dawned clear and sunny, bringing to light the magnitude of the catastrophe. At least 822 of Chênière Caminada's 1,471 residents were dead or missing, 396 of its 400 structures were destroyed, and another 1,300 people had perished throughout Louisiana and Mississippi. Grand Isle, perched upon a slightly higher ridge, lost about 30 of its 300 permanent residents, and would have lost hundreds of visitors had the storm struck in summer, as all beachfront hotels and cottages were wrecked. "More than 400 corpses were unburied," reported one traumatized survivor; "many could not be found for they had been carried out to the gulf," among them 63 "Chinamen" from Bayou Andre. "The odor emanating from the dead bodies, both of man and beast, made the situation all the more unbearable. . . . We began to feel the want of fresh water [and] provisions."[53]

Lifelines came from the West Bank, even as it recovered from its own mess. The first was the Gretna-based steam yacht *Grace,* led by Horace H. Harvey himself, with the parish coroner aboard. He took the Harvey Canal and arrived to the disaster zone to find "hordes of haggard and starving people [with] ungovernable damnable thirst."[54] Westwego ice makers sent provisions down on the Company Canal. "The arrival of two boats laden with ice was hailed with joy," wrote Rose Falls. "Other boats came from the city with provisions donated by the charitable people of New Orleans."[55] More followed—luggers, schooners, and steamers, sponsored by churches, social clubs, newspapers, business associations, the Red Cross, ordinary folks who organized a Citizen's Relief Committee, even theaters and music academies. In Algiers, the Fort Jackson and Grand Isle Railroad commenced cleaning debris and repairing its tracks, and set out picking up survivors.[56]

The West Bank had become the staging ground and jumping-off point for rescue efforts. But the boats and trains bringing relief *to* the coast soon found themselves transporting refugees *from* the coast. Lack of basic provisions motivated the inland move, but there was a longer-term issue: the entire fishing fleet and infrastructure had been destroyed. Worse yet, the Barataria oyster reefs, best in the region and a chief source of local income, had been buried in sand and would take years to recover.[57] The storm victims, particularly Chênière Caminada survivors, had absolutely nothing but bankruptcy and grieving. Of all the greater New Orleans region, the coastal fishing families knew best the Harvey-to-Westwego corner of the West Bank, because for decades they had sailed there via the Harvey and Company canals. Those economic interactions had produced familiarity and social networks, which made those communities attractive as a resettlement option.

The generosity of the Harvey family played a key role. Horace afforded space along his canal for a temporary refugee encampment, where the Sisters of Charity coordinated the distribution of donated supplies. By October 9, up to seventy-four Chênière families found refuge along the Harvey Canal, with space for fifty more.[58] The diaspora would later grow to 126 families, and by April 1894, according to the *Daily Picayune,* "some had moved further up towards [the] Company canal; others are now living in Gretna [or New Orleans], while the majority went down to Barataria and along Bayou Lafourche."[59] The late Pablo Sala had recently subdivided Salaville in Westwego, parallel to the Company Canal, and parcels could be bought cheaply along Sala Avenue. By the end of 1894, twenty refugee families built homes there, and in time their breadwinners returned to guiding luggers to and from Grand Isle—only now from the inland end.[60] Kin and kith would later settle nearby, through a domestic version of chain immigration.

The coastal migrants imparted to the West Bank a lasting cultural change, as they were mostly Acadian (Cajun) in ethnicity and culture, with varying amounts of Houma Indian, French Creole, and other bloodlines. Their names were a who's who of Louisiana Cajun clans: Terrebonne, Pitre, Chabert, Guedry (Guidry), Bourdro (Boudreaux), Gaspard, Ducos, Broussard, plus a few of Italian (Sicilian), Spanish, Croatian, and Anglo origin.[61]

The 1893 storm had made Westwego and adjacent communities the closest greater New Orleans would have to a "Cajun neighborhood." A 1942 study estimated that Westwego's population had nearly tripled between 1893 and 1899, to about 500, with most of that increase directly or indirectly attributable to the hurricane. "Most of the people speak a French dialect," wrote the researcher. "Even the people who speak Spanish speak French also, [namely] Creole and Arcadian ('Cajun). . . . The High School offers a course in Classical French, but it is not generally popular."[62]

Into the late twentieth century, the main Westwego census tract comprising old Salaville and the former Company Canal had fully 2,952 residents who claimed French as their "mother tongue" (1970), by far the most throughout greater New Orleans in both absolute numbers and relative (42 percent) to the census tract population. Other tracts from Westwego to Harvey had similarly high numbers. Thirty years later, in the 2000 Census, more people claimed "French" ancestry in the main Westwego census tract and from Marrero/Harvey down to Lafitte than anywhere else in the metro area.[63] More recently, the 2013–2017 survey-based estimates of the American Community Survey show that the heart of Westwego (Census Tract 272) was the only one in the metro area in which a measurable percentage of respondents (7.05 percent) identified "Cajun" as their ancestry. Combined with those who claimed "French" ancestry, as many Cajuns do in open-response surveys, fully one out of every three residents in this tract claimed this heritage, one of the highest rates in the region.[64]

French is no longer heard in the streets of Westwego, but Cajun ethnicity is very much alive. Names like Pitre and Terrebonne are still prominent, and a walk around the Westwego Shrimp Lot, with its fresh seafood, boudin, alliga-tor meat, and nearby fishing fleet on Bayou Segnette, is like a trip to Acadiana practically within sight of downtown skyscrapers. It is a happy ending to a story that began with tragedy.

As for Grand Isle, it would take years for (some) hotels to rebuild, only to be set back again by storms in 1909 and 1915. (Horace Harvey would again perform heroic rescue work after the Great Storm of 1915, earning him the sobriquet "The Little Father of the Baratarias."[65]) Chênière Caminada would never truly recover. By the time an auto road (Highway 1) linked the islands to the mainland in 1932, New Orleanians no longer felt a need to flee each summer for health reasons, and could sooner drive Highway 90 to the beach in Biloxi. Grand Isle would remain popular for fishing and light bathing, but the opulent resorts would never return, nor would that steady exchange of people and commerce with the West Bank.[66]

⁂

Two years after the Chênière Caminada hurricane, and after four crevasse floods since 1891, another calamity struck the West Bank. Shortly after midnight on Sunday, October 21, 1895, a fire of unknown origins ignited in a crowded tene-ment near the Algiers Point riverfront. Northeasterly winds fanned the flames throughout the two-story tenement known as "The Rookery," sending a dozen poor, mostly Italian families fleeing onto Morgan Street. Among them were the wife and children of Paul Bouffia, who operated a fruit stand at 307 Morgan.[67]

Three horse-drawn fire trucks arrived from Engine 17 House on Pelican Ave-nue, and firemen arranged for their largest steam pump to draw from the river. Two other crews with shorter hoses tapped ground wells a block from the fire. Streams of water arched into the blaze, and neighbors breathed a sigh of relief.

But because it had been a dry autumn, the wells "were emptied of water (within) half an hour," wrote local historian William H. Seymour.[68] This left only the river pump to do the dousing, and it wasn't enough. By 2:00 a.m., the 300 block of Morgan and both sides of 200 Bermuda were ablaze.

Chief Daly of the Algiers Fire Station had larger pumps ferried from down-town. By the time they arrived, the fire had consumed most of 200 Morgan, plus the Eighth Precinct Police Station and the Duverjé Plantation House serving as the Algiers Courthouse. Reams of archival records combusted in the aged wooden manse, and "when the old roof fell in, it sent up a shower of sparks . . . windward" into more doomed houses.[69]

Neighbors carted valuables to the river, dodging skittish horses pulling tanks back to the pumps. Mayor John Fitzpatrick and his fire chiefs witnessed the litany of inadequacies: wells too dry, pumps too weak, hoses too short, firemen too few, and fuel too plentiful, in the face of that fateful wind. They watched helplessly as the blaze consumed both sides of 300 Delaronde, 300 Bermuda, 200 and 400 Delaronde, most of 100–400 Pelican Avenue including the fire station, and 100–300 Alix—plus Bermuda, Seguin, and Bouny down to Powder.

The fire might have destroyed the entire neighborhood but for three interventions. Workers at the nearby Hotard & Lawton Saw Mill started their steam pumps and, with a 1,300-foot hose tapping into river water, soaked rooftops and saved everything downriver of Lavergne Street. Tug boat crews, meanwhile, drenched moored coal barges so they wouldn't ignite. Most importantly, the wind shifted direction and blew the flames into ruins. The fire burned itself out.

By dawn, all that remained of Old Algiers was "a vast forest of gaunt and grim chimneys."[70] At least 193 houses on ten blocks were destroyed and dozens more damaged, along with commercial structures and infrastructure. Though no one perished, roughly 1,200 residents were left homeless. Losses were estimated at $400,000, or $12 million today.

Some blamed the debacle on Algiers' low prioritization from City Hall. Others faulted the firefighters. "The principal causes of the rapid spread of the flames were not only the scarcity of water and a furious wind," judged the *Picayune*, "but the poor work of the fire department. When they lost control of the fire they became demoralized." Or was it an institutional problem? A monograph published earlier in 1895 pointed out that "Algiers and Gretna, are without protection [of] a fire-boat[,] sadly needed on several occasions," including on New Year's Day 1894, when "a good blaze in Algiers . . . demonstrated the need of a water works system for that suburb." Longtime Fire Chief Thomas O'Connor had himself reported on "the prospect of adequate water supply [and] dangerous conditions of fire service in the Fifth District (Algiers)."[71]

Rumors circulated about the fire's origin. Some said Paul Bouffia, the occupant of 307 Morgan, had recently acquired fire insurance, raising suspicions in some minds. The *Picayune* described Bouffia as "heartily disliked," with "a very bad reputation." Others claimed "he had [started] two fires in the place before, which narrowly escaped being disastrous."[72] Police located Bouffia and carted him to a provisional police station, where enraged survivors gathered, "some . . . bold enough to openly cry out to lynch him." Others, according to Seymour, spoke of "a contemplated expulsion of the Italian element of the population." Bouffia could have met the same fate as the eleven Italians who had been lynched across the river in 1891, after having been acquitted of murdering the city's police chief. Only in a later court appearance did evidence show Bouffia had been on the East Bank when the fire started. He was set free.

Meanwhile, a mob of a different sort gathered on the ferry, this one of gawkers from across the river. So many crowded the Algiers Ferry House that the iron gangway collapsed, and a hundred spectators became victims. Twenty were injured, two girls disappeared, and a woman was later found drowned. The aftermath was more deadly than the disaster itself, and both the lynch mob and ferry collapse gave Algiers some highly unflattering national press.[73]

What got less attention was the charitable response of many more Algerines and New Orleanians. Citizens formed a Relief Committee that Sunday and secured food and shelter for victims. Nearly $16,000 in donations came in, or $457,000 today—enough, along with insurance claims ($300,000, or $8.5 million today) and social support, to get victims back on their feet.[74]

The neighborhood recovered speedily, as the fire had occurred during a prosperous era inspirited with public investment. Streets were paved; electrification arrived; a new waterworks plant was built to resolve pressure problems; and a viaduct was installed to decongest riverfront activity. The city erected a new Moorish-style Algiers Courthouse with asymmetrical crenelated towers on the spot of the old Duverjé House, and all around arose handsome new frame houses with exuberant millwork. As early as 1896, wrote Seymour, "a walk along those attractive streets make it difficult to realize that this was the same so lately in ashes and ruins."[75]

The Great Algiers Fire of 1895 ranked as the worst urban conflagration in the West Bank's history. It was a disaster by any measure, but it was also an impetus for improvement. A 1902 article in the *Sunday Daily States,* which never mentioned the 1895 inferno, flattered the new Algiers for its "more metropolitan air."

The town is electrically lighted, the same as the big city just across the old Mississippi's murky waters; its waterworks can compare with that of towns of much greater size, [as can] its ice plant. . . . There are several paved streets in Algiers, asphalt and vitrified brick, [and] an excellent drainage system. The Algiers pumping station is one of the finest. . . . A telephone exchange . . . is another much-to-be-welcomed institution. . . . The New Orleans Lighting Company will extend its mains [here] for the purpose of supplying fuel and illuminating gas to the public [and] is now laying mains through the town as quickly as possible.[76]

One might go so far to say that, if Algiers had to burn, it picked a good time, during a golden age of American urbanism. A walk today around this 300-year-old community evidences the point.

12

Bridging the Banks, Draining the Swamps

St. Louis got one in 1854. Rock Island and Davenport had theirs by 1856. St. Louis got a better one in 1874, and it's still in use today. Why couldn't the Queen of the South bridge its stretch of the Father of Waters?

The will was certainly there. As early as 1826, an engineer named Jean Jerome petitioned the state legislature to build a European-style stone segmental arch bridge, complete with rows of dwellings on each side. The very concept strongly suggested that Monsieur Jerome had never actually seen the Mississippi at New Orleans.[1] Idle talk and editorials calling for a span would circulate for decades, but not until the 1880s did a serious engineering proposal come forth.

It came from Elmer Lawrence Corthell, one of the nation's most respected civil engineers. Corthell gained experience with the Mississippi through his work on the Eads Jetties. Before being called off to St. Louis to oversee the construction of the Merchants Bridge, Corthell proposed for New Orleans "a belt road, a bridge across the Mississippi, and a union depot." Although not a full metropolitan circumvallation, Corthell's span proposal was nonetheless revolutionary in that it linked the banks with a crescent-shaped belt of tracks, from downtown New Orleans to Westwego, Gretna and Algiers, without cumbersome transfer ferries.

Where to cross the river? Reported the *Daily Picayune* in January 1889, Corthell "adheres to the opinion that the best site for a bridge is at one of the straight reaches about Nine-Mile point, [which] will allow the Southern Pacific and the

Texas Pacific to . . . connect with the belt road and run into the union depot."[2] This was the one spot were East and West bank railroads came the closest across a mostly undeveloped space, thus minimizing right-of-way acquisition costs. Corthell estimated a bridge "125 feet above the water, with fixed spans and cantilevers which would admit any vessel passing under it," would cost $3 million, or $83 million today.[3]

In early February a bill was introduced in Congress authorizing "the Southern Bridge and Railway Company of Louisiana." The corporate entity had been formed by railroad interests, including magnate Jay Gould, for the express purpose of "construct[ing] and maintain[ing] a bridge over the Mississippi river, above New Orleans, for the passing of railway trains, wagons, cattle and foot passengers."[4]

Other engineers argued for a drawbridge, which would allow tracks to run lower on a more favorable grade with shorter inclines. Soon Corthell had competition, as the New Orleans Terminal Railway & Bridge Company organized to propose just such a drawbridge between Algiers and present-day Bywater. "Mississippi River mariners can be forgiven for laughing at the notion of a drawbridge right below Algiers Point," wrote mariner-historian Daniel Hubbell. "The main dispute here was between river steamboat interests and oceangoing shipping interests. The former wanted the bridge to be below the city; the latter wanted it built above the city."[5] Newspapers took sides, arguing about designs, locations, and vested interests.

The debate caused delays, as did geological concerns, which opened up time for other political priorities to intervene. Shipping interests, for their part, grew increasingly nervous about aiding railroads at their expense. Nevertheless, Corthell moved forward with his design, and in 1897, sketches of a span bearing a striking resemblance to the future Huey P. Long Bridge appeared in newspapers as far away as Idaho.[6] By this time, the Union Depot had been constructed in New Orleans, as Corthell envisioned, but sans the beltway and bridge.

Years passed. Funding fell short, political deals went awry, disputes arose over whether a private or public entity should build and run the bridge, and key advocates died, including Corthell in 1916. "There would have been a bridge bearing his name, across the Mississippi at this point," wrote the *Times-Picayune* in his obituary, "but fate intervened and proved too strong for the man who had several times mastered destiny and shaped it."[7]

But the year 1916 also saw a breakthrough, when the state legislature defeated a bill calling for private construction and, in its stead, passed a constitutional amendment for the City of New Orleans to build the bridge through its Public Belt Railroad Commission. This meant that New Orleans would own a major piece of infrastructure entirely within Jefferson Parish, between Nine Mile and Twelve Mile Point. In July 1918 the City Council passed an ordinance for the creation of a Board of Advisory Engineers within the Public Belt Railroad Commission, to research all angles of the project, from the type and location of the crossing to geology, engineering, usage, and financing.[8]

Over the next year, the Board of Advisory Engineers fulfilled its duties, despite wartime limitations and members' bouts with the global influenza pandemic. In 1919 it released a thorough report in which members affirmed "the general feasibility of the plan of river crossing and terminal" from both an economic and construction viewpoint. "This is the most important message it is able to transmit," the committee stated, and construction "should be immediately undertaken."[9]

The next major question involved the aptly named Bridge and Tunnel Committee. The Corps of Engineers, sensing that the soft bedload of the river would not support piers, favored a prefabricated sectional tunnel laid along a trench. Members even considered a *transbordeur*, an aerial transfer bridge in which cars would be loaded into a cage (gondola) raised by cables and rolled across a span built high enough for ships to pass.[10]

What the members recommended would please the railroad men—perhaps unsurprisingly, this being a railroad commission committee—and raise the ire of everyone else. They called for "a low-level two-track [bridge] with a total of nine (9) spans between levees, including a vertical-lift central span [and a] track grade [of] one per cent," a design good for trains and bad for ships. "If a low-level bridge is not acceptable," the members allowed, "a single track tunnel is the recommended alternative, [but] a high-level bridge is not recommended."

This latter point put the committee at odds with powerful military officials, especially during wartime. Ships on the nation's greatest river patiently awaiting trains to pass for the bridge to lift? Others saw the tunnel as equally unfeasible. The only consensus regarded the location, "between Nine-Mile and Twelve-Mile Bends . . . between Avondale and Westwego," although the board did consider crossing sites at Chalmette, in present-day Bywater, and in Carrollton.[11] The final site would be at River Mile 106.1 above Head of Passes.

Over the next few years, military officials and shipping leaders mulled options, while the commission hired the famed Dr. Ralph Modjeski, the Polish-born, French-trained American bridge builder. Modjeski steered his clients away from the tunnel or low-lift bridge options, as well as the zany *transbordeur*. In 1925, he won a War Department permit for "a high level cantilever bridge, having a vertical clearance of 135 feet above high water, and a central span of 750 feet clear."

Motorists had by now become a lobby of bridge users, and with the support of the Louisiana Public Service Commission and later Gov. Huey P. Long, they called for the addition of two pairs of nine-foot-wide auto lanes, which necessitated the addition of truss supports to the cantilever design. The "permit expired before financing could be arranged," wrote the Modjeski firm in a later report, at which point the Great Depression made money matters only worse.[12]

Finally, in 1932 parties agreed on a financial solution: the commission would issue bonds, the federal government would underwrite them, the city and state would build the bridge, and Southern Pacific would pay annual rent to offset expenses. Total cost would be $13 million, over four times Corthell's 1888 estimate, but a bargain given the engineering miracle underway by lead engineering firm Modjeski, Masters and Chase, and primary contractor American Bridge Company.

To solve the problem of the soft river bottom, Modjeski and Frank M. Masters designed caisson wells of steel walls within which alluvium could be dredged down to "a stratum of hard sand . . . as firm and as unyielding as hard rock," probably a relict barrier island.[13] With the caissons in place, the wells were packed with fine sand to create artificial "islands" that were ringed with timber cofferdams, filled with concrete, and built up with granite blocks to form five towering piers.

To meet the War Department's height requirement, Modjeski and Masters greatly lengthened the track span to create the 1.25 percent grade surmountable by freight trains. To accommodate motorists, at the urging of Gov. Huey P. Long, they incorporated two narrow—*very* narrow—auto lanes on either side of the tracks, and even added pedestrian walkways. To bear the immense load, they created both a cantilever and truss design with a striking vaulted profile, spreading the weight over a great length. What resulted was a veritable work of engineering art, sturdy and colossal yet graceful and sinuous.[14]

Three months before opening day, Sen. Huey P. Long, former Louisiana railroad commissioner and governor, was assassinated in Baton Rouge. For his advocacy of the project and other public works, the span was officially named the Huey P. Long–Public Belt Bridge. It is said that Long, whose appeal to rural Louisiana folk was matched by his animus toward New Orleans power brokers, would only support a metro-area bridge if were outside city limits. Surely the rural Jefferson Parish site pleased the reputedly anti-urban Long, but as we have seen, the bridge's outlying location had been identified, if not fixed, since the 1880s.

Placing the marvel "amongst the Pyramids, the Obelisk and Pantheon," the local press on dedication day published "outstanding facts about the Public Belt Railroad Bridge:"

> The new Mississippi river bridge . . . is of the cantilever type, with eight spans. The center span is 790 feet long. The length, with approaches, is 4.4 miles—longest railroad bridge in the world. Height of the main span is 135 feet above high water level. From the lowest point of the foundation of the central pier to the top of the superstructure is 409 feet, equal to the height of a 36-story building.
>
> Total width of 78 feet accommodates double railroad tracks in the center and two 18-foot vehicular roadways with two pedestrian walks 2.5 feet wide cantilevered on the sides. Materials used include 413,370 tons of concrete; 4400 tons of granite; 60,100 tons of steel; 131,500 cubic yards of sand; 1,189,034 lineal feet of piling; 3,500,000 board feet of timber decking; [and] 537,500 square feet of mattress protection around the piers.
>
> Average number of workmen employed for three years was 200; maximum employed at one time was 1000.[15]

During dedication ceremonies on December 16, 1935, a speaker declared the crossing of the Mississippi meant, after nearly a half-century of planning, that "East is West and West is East."[16]

Indeed it did. The "Huey P." compressed space and time by turning a cumbrous trek into a swift glide, seemingly uniting the cross-bank divide. Fiscal resources on the East Bank would now have efficient access to the attributes of the West Bank, and western West Jefferson would surely flourish. It was no coincidence that the police jury launched its pro-development *Jefferson Parish Yearly Review* in 1935, just as the bridge was opening, and that the main features of the first edition would be all about the new asset.[17]

To an extent, the bridge did catalyze West Bank development. "The Southern Pacific is completing a 400-car yard at Avondale near the west approach to the bridge," proclaimed the police jury in the 1935 *Review*. "A large roundhouse and turntable is being built and light car and locomotive repairs will [employ] one hundred men, [while] at East Bridge Junction an auxiliary yard for 200 cars will be built [by] an additional fifty men."[18]

The bridge created new opportunities as it rendered others obsolete, among them the no-longer needed transfer ferry railyard of the Texas and New Orleans Railroad. Its space caught the attention of river pilot Captain Harry Koch, marine operator Perry Ellis, and ship repair executive James Viviant because it had the right equipment and location for a major new shipyard. In 1938 the threesome formed Avondale Marine Ways, Inc., and together with engineers James H. Bull and Fred Wilson, the company secured the lease from the railroad company to establish a shipyard for vessel construction and repair. By the early 1940s, Avondale had hundreds of employees building Merchant Marine convoy ships and repairing tugboats, tank barges, and other war-support vessels; it later would become the largest private employer in Louisiana, with upwards of 12,000 on the payroll, and the apotheosis of the West Bank's 200-year-old ship-building legacy.[19] Subdivisions for workers sprouted up in Avondale and Waggaman, the western-most anchors of the urbanized West Bank. The bridge also made good the 1926 promise of Belt City, laid out "at the spot where the automobile approach of the new bridge will reach ground level," to finally start house construction, prompting its mid-1940s renaming to Bridge City.[20] None of this would have happened had not the Huey P. killed the old transfer ferry and made its site available for shipbuilding.

But the Huey P. Long Bridge also diminished a key advantage of the West Bank, namely its monopoly on access to points south and west. No longer was the West Bank the place New Orleans *had* to go through to get to the Barataria, Attakapas, Texas, and beyond. Now a good portion of that commerce could flow straight to the East Bank before even reaching Westwego, much less Gretna and Algiers. Seafood could now get from bays to markets via refrigerated trucks taking the bridge, rather than on luggers floating up the Company Canal to the canneries in Salaville. Western passenger trains could now pull into the elegant Louis Sullivan-designed Union Depot in downtown New Orleans rather than the wooden Algiers Station and transfer ferry, while freight trains would only need to traverse the West Bank if they had business there. Southern Pacific's Algiers Yards would still keep busy, but the fulcrum of action would shift away from their plant; the yards declined after World War II and eventually closed in the 1960s. The bridge also killed the specialized jobs associated with the transfer ferries, diminished regional boat traffic, and reduced passenger ferry usage and toll collections. Westwego had received a percentage of the ferry company tolls as a source of city revenue, and "the loss of this traffic . . . seriously affected [its] income [and] the town is finding it difficult to meet its obligations." In 1937, Westwego, already mired in the Depression, "defaulted on interest on its outstanding bonds"—this in shadows of one of the region's greatest engineering achievements.[21]

As for the West Bank's human geography, the Huey P. Long Bridge did not fundamentally alter the main Algiers-to-Westwego urban corridor. For one, "its failure to accommodate adequately the cross-river highway traffic for the City proper became obvious," admitted the Modjeski firm, in part because of the narrow lanes but mostly for its outlying location.[22] Most New Orleanians in these times still lived neighborhood-scale lives, walking to school and taking the streetcar to work. Most households did not have cars. Riding the ferry made more sense than driving 15 to 20 miles circuitous miles, and nearly 9,000 vehicles and 27,000 pedestrians still ferried across the river *per day*.[23] In 1938 you could ride from Canal to Bouny Street in Algiers; Jackson Avenue to Copernicus Street in Gretna; Louisiana to Destrehan Avenue in Harvey; Napoleon Avenue to Barataria Road in Marrero; and Walnut Street to Sala Avenue in Westwego— for pennies, on regular schedules, all but one for 24 hours a day. For thousands of folks, the slow but convenient ferries, most of them run by the Bisso family, worked better than a speedy long drive to an outlying bridge.[24]

≈≈≈

What had a greater effect on West Bank urbanization than the bridge was the less-glamorous engineering feat of drainage.

Swamp reclamation was a long time coming to New Orleans. The city had little more than a gravity-driven runoff removal system for its first century, followed by three mediocre attempts at steam-pump-assisted drainage during 1830s through 1870s. Not until 1893 did the city commit to expert engineers to design a comprehensive municipal drainage system. They set out mapping and measuring the city like never before, creating an elevation map of one-foot contours, including a 948-acre section of Algiers Point, and used those data to devise a citywide system of gutters, drains, pipes and canals. The runoff flowed off the high ground through underground infrastructure and into enormous pump stations, which propelled the water through outfall canals and ejected it into adjacent water bodies. Under the aegis of the New Orleans Sewerage and Water Board, established in 1899, workers installed the intricate apparatus into the cityscape, along with a separate water treatment and distribution system as well as the city's first sewerage system.

The transformation over the next decade was radical. Wrote George Washington Cable in 1909, "there is a salubrity that could not be when the mosquito swarmed everywhere, when the level of supersaturation in the soil was but two and half feet from the surface, where now it is ten feet or more. . . . The curtains of swamp forest are totally gone. Their sites are drained dry and covered with miles of gardened homes."[25]

Algiers and other West Bank communities endured similarly muddy, puddling conditions. The solution devised for the East Bank was the same essential concept to be deployed across the river, with Bayou Barataria serving as the runoff receptacle. "The drainage of Algiers on the right bank of the Mississippi," declared the Engineering Committee of the Drainage Advisory Board in 1895, will entail a "system of gutters, branch and main drains, and branch canals leading into a main or intercepting canal located on Canal [now Whitney] Avenue. From a main pumping station, located near the intersection of Lawrence Street and [Whitney] Avenue, the total run-off of the section, amounting to 671 cubic feet per second, may be reduced to 400 cubic feet per second, and will be lifted . . . and delivered into the outfall . . . canal, leading into Bayou Barataria."[26] Additional feeder ditches would run on Vallette, Eliza, and Lapeyrouse streets, which delivered runoff by gravity for the pump station to lift and eject over a rear protection levee.

Work got underway in the early 1900s. Algiers streets were torn up, drains and pipes laid, the pump station installed, and in 1907, workers commenced digging the three-mile-long Algiers Outfall Canal to connect with Bayou Barataria.[27] Concurrently, networks of main lines and connectors for water distribution and sewerage removal were laid—right down to residential meter boxes—with the Algiers Water Company's new treatment plant built at the riverfront, and a sewerage treatment plant at the backswamp. The systems went online in 1909, sending Algiers from the eighteenth to the twentieth century.[28]

Not to be left behind, the Jefferson Parish police jury set about in 1910 creating a drainage district for McDonoghville, Gretna, and Harvey, matching those in place for Amesville (Marrero) and Westwego. They were about to create piece-meal systems, as had Algiers.[29]

But one man had a better idea.

George Alfred Hero, born in 1854 to a Swedish immigrant, gleaned a fascination with drainage as a youth while visiting his brother's plantation in Assumption Parish. There he saw land going unused on account of standing water, and, after some toil with muck and pluck, succeeded rather handily in figuring out how to drain it. Hero moved on to a highly successful career in finance and cotton trading, becoming director of the New Orleans Cotton Exchange, but never lost his interest in the art and science of removing the "wet" from wetlands. Motivations to do so multiplied in this era of progressive improvements and civil engineering: New Orleans in 1893 had appointed a Drainage Advisory Board to figure out how to dry out its backswamp, and soon got to work installing a system under the auspices of the Sewerage and Water Board. Then in 1905 came yet another yellow fever epidemic, further intensifying the call for drainage. Having gained a taste of the West Bank through his various investments, Hero in 1912 restlessly schemed how to drain its morass—and despaired at landowners' lack of interest in doing the same.

That same year, the Louisiana State Legislature, having been lobbied by Hero, passed an act empowering police juries to form "drainage districts," within which taxes could be raised and bonds issued to pay for mechanized drainage. Private land owners could count their bottomlands as part of these parish districts, and share the risk, as well as potential rewards, of converting them into developable real estate. And if private parties owned enough acreage, they could pool their holdings and become their own drainage district.

Having been "instrumental in the establishment of the system which the State used to drain many of the lowlands," Hero endeavored to partake of the opportunity.[30] He went about purchasing ten thousand supposedly useless acres in the backswamp in Jefferson and Plaquemine parishes. Hero's genius was in getting the parishes to work together, no easy task in Louisiana. The holdings qualified to become the Jefferson-Plaquemines Drainage District, and Hero became its president.

Orleans Parish, meanwhile, wanted in on Hero's project. None other than the mayor of New Orleans, Algiers-born Martin Behrman, became "the director of the West New Orleans Realty Company, which had bought 200 squares [at] $500 per square . . . out of the George A. Hero drainage district and is prepared to market them." Said Mayor Behrman to the *Picayune* in October 1913, "I did this because I know the work being done by Mr. Hero . . . is the most monumental task that has ever been attempted by any man in this city in the last generation. . . . I know the land and the values—and the success of the undertaking is absolutely assured."[31] The city contributed $9,000 a year to the effort, making it the Orleans-Jefferson-Plaquemines Drainage District, covering over thirty-nine thousand acres across parts of "Algiers and Gouldsboro . . . McDonoughville, Mechanicham and Gretna [and] the Harvey Canal [down to] the lower line of the Cedar Grove Plantation" in Plaquemines Parish, plus the "Aurora, the Orleans, the Stanton, the Delacroix, and the Beka" plantations of the lower coast of Algiers.[32] Five thousand owners had chips on the table, Hero having the most. Marrero, meanwhile, being hydrologically separated by the Harvey Canal, organized itself as the Second Jefferson Drainage District in 1909 and funded its drainage through an ad valorem tax. Westwego, on the other hand, did not drain its backswamp, much of it owned by the Marrero family, in part because it contained the economically valuable Bayou Segnette. It remains the only community within the conurbation that still retains an honest-to-goodness backswamp.[33]

Through the tenacity of George Hero, the three parishes for the first time collaborated on a single major project, and the West Bank took a front-and-center seat at the table of metropolitan attention. How to pay for it? That's where the 1912 Louisiana law came in. The owners voted to tax themselves seventy-five cents per acre per year for forty years, for which state-backed drainage bonds were issued to front the money. Snapped up quickly, the bonds raised over $200,000 to spend on construction.[34]

Working with astonishing speed, engineers John F. Coleman and Allen S. Hackett designed for Hero a system of interconnecting drainage ditches and canals, and contractors dug them into the landscape. They worked within the existing framework of 1700s French long-lots and 1800s roads and ditches, and in so doing laid out the geometry of future West Bank urbanization. Aiding the engineers' efforts was the amphitheater-like topography of the West Bank, with higher natural levees running along the broadly looping riverfront, and a low "stage" at Bayou Barataria's juncture with the Harvey Canal and the natural Bayou Fatma-Ouatchas River drainage, making it clear where the main pumping station should be located.

In 1913 came another serendipity. A young Sewerage and Water Board engineer named Albert Baldwin Wood perfected his design for an enormous impeller capable of drawing water out of a suction basin and into a discharge basin at a remarkable velocity. Wood's screw pumps worked wonders for the East Bank system, and were just what were needed at the main West Bank station where the Harvey Canal joined Bayou Barataria. Built and installed in 1914, the pump would draw water through five gigantic tubes at a speed said to be the fastest in the world, capable of removing over one million gallons per minute. So phenomenal was its capacity that some reporters got carried away and put the discharge at 45 million gallons per minute, even a billion![35]

By early 1915, all components were in place to pull the plug on the West Bank backswamp. Everyone seemed confident, *supremely* confident, that everything would work, and that a civic bonanza awaited. Whereas it took Holland 75 years and $3.2 million to drain a similarly sized lowland, one journalist pointed out, "construction of the drainage plant opposite New Orleans, under way for less than a year . . . will [cost only] $234,000, and it will require only three days to draw off the water and increase the value of land . . . to a minimum of $300 per acre—[plus], mosquitoes will perish and human health and comfort will increase."[36]

This being New Orleans, merriment would mark the starting of the pump— on Carnival weekend, no less. "'Hero Day'[,] regarded by land men as one of the great events in the history of the state," would be Saturday, February 13, 1915, three days before Mardi Gras.[37] Arrangements had been made for President Woodrow Wilson to activate the motors with a button in the White House, connected via telephony to the rural fringes of the West Bank.

That morning, after a sumptuous banquet at the Grunewald Hotel, dignitaries including Governor Luther Hall, Mayor Martin Behrman, Chief Engineer John Coleman, and Hero himself gathered on St. Charles Avenue by the Garden District. There an automobile parade, fronted by two marching bands, police on foot and horseback, and "mounted heralds wearing shields with letters spelling 'Hero,'" rolled down to Canal Street and on to the river.[38] There they joined 300 guests aboard the steamboat *Hanover,* which took the party into the Harvey Canal, where they transferred to the yacht *Daisy* and proceeded on to the pump station. The predominant occupation among the celebrants was that of real estate agent, followed by politician.

At the pump site, twelve hundred citizens cheered the arrival of the entourage. Local and national press took their places, and honored guests gave soaring speeches. Hero, ever the doer, announced his plan to drain a million more acres, from the Mississippi to Bayou Lafourche, and predicted that only four million dollars of drainage investment would make Louisiana a billion dollars richer. More formalities followed. "Then came the President's message, handed up by a hastened messenger. And then the pumps began to whirr."[39]

Whirr they did. Torrents rose from the ponded swamp water, up the five tubes, through Wood's screw pumps, and out into Bayou Barataria south to the sea. The calculations were spot-on: most of the standing water in the district disappeared within three hours, after which the pumps were slowed to permanent duty to remove rainfall and river infiltration.

In only two years—and two hundred minutes—the West Bank had achieved, through a private-public partnership across three jurisdictions, what New Orleans on the East Bank took the better part of a century to achieve. Land valued at \$3 per acre increased to between \$200 and \$500 an acre almost overnight.[40]

The only thing that didn't work that memorable day was the President of the United States. A miscommunication at the White House led to a delay, giving President Wilson an excuse to step out "for his usual Saturday morning of golf link."

Instead, some unremembered aid pressed the button to drain the West Bank of New Orleans.[41]

There is a postscript to this story. The drainage happened so fast that no one really knew what to make of all this "reclaimed" land, and different parties projected their interests upon it. New Orleanians viewed it as their new suburban annex. Sugar planters envisaged new cane fields. Truck farmers saw new truck farms. Industry foresaw new plant sites, for which Peters Road was paved down to the pump stations, and on which the Southern Pacific extended its track bed. Developers saw new subdivisions; bankers, new mortgages; homeowners, new houses.

George Hero had another idea, and it would nurture all of the above. Together with his engineer Allen Hackett, he proposed an auto bridge across the Mississippi from Race Street to Gretna. His lands had not been selling well since their reclamation, being too far from potential buyers across the river, and a bridge would fix that. His span plan came to be known as the Hero-Hackett Bridge, and in 1925 it won the enthusiastic support of the Jefferson Parish police jury.

Two years later, Hero and Hackett applied to the War Department for a permit, and that's when the delays began. The military made an issue of the height of the bridge; redesigns were repeatedly rejected, and cost estimates ballooned. The War Department finally issued a permit in 1929 for a 1,760-foot-long cantilever bridge with unusual helical approaches, intended to save right-of-way acquisition costs (at the risk of dizzying motorists—and surely precluding modern tractor-trailers).

But by then the stock market had crashed. This being a costly private initiative during the Depression, investment monies dried up and the "structure could not be financed."[42] As the competing Nine Mile Point bridge plan finally gathered momentum, the Hero-Hackett Bridge went dormant—although Allen Hackett would keep the concept alive until it saw a second life twenty years later.

Hero died of a stroke after having been struck by a car outside his Garden District home in December 1932, just as work began on what would become the Huey P. Long Bridge. He might have been chagrined to know that the headline of his obituary identified him as "Span Advocate," his one disappointment, rather than "Drainage King," his greatest success. The tribute's closing paragraph did mention Hero's other gifts to the West Bank: his land donation to Orleans Parish to become Martin Behrman Playground in Algiers, and to Plaquemines Parish to be the West Bank's first airport in Belle Chasse. Hero had purchased that terrain as part of his drainage district project, and when it didn't sell, he tried harvesting maidencane (Pifine) grass from the prairie marsh and processing it to feed to mules. After a drought nixed that effort in the mid-1920s, he parlayed his son's wartime aviation service into the making of an airfield. "All you had to do was grade off a cow pasture and have a couple of fifty-five-gallon drums of gasoline," laughed grandson George Harry Hero III in a recent interview, "and you could be an airport."[43] It would be called Alvin Callender Field, named for a local flying ace killed in the late war, and it would become today's Belle Chasse Naval Air Station, one of the most important assets of the region. The facility moved to Hero's donated tract only after an alternative version of the original Hero-Hackett Bridge finally got built in 1958, as the Greater New Orleans Bridge.[44] And the Belle Chasse Highway, connecting the bridge to the air station on Hero's donated land? George Hero built that too.

13

Booming Times, Bombastic Visions

Whatever West Bank growth may be attributed to Hero's entrepreneurship or Modjeski's engineering would be more than matched by the regional boom triggered by World War II.

The South in general, and New Orleans in particular, played outsized roles in the conflict. Government war programs invested $4.4 billion in southern plants, including $1.77 billion into strategically positioned oil-rich Louisiana, more than any southern state save Texas. New Orleans got its share thanks largely to Andrew Jackson Higgins, the brilliant Nebraska-born boat builder who for years specialized in shallow-draft vessels for Louisiana's bayous and swamps—exactly what would be needed to land millions of troops on the beaches of two overrun continents. Winning lucrative Navy contracts, Higgins Industries made New Orleans, long a mercantilist city, into a heavy manufacturing center, producing 20,094 boats and employing up to 30,000 people across seven gargantuan city plants.[1] None were located on the West Bank, but many workers were residents of the West Bank or adjacent rural areas, among them Cajuns, the same stock that built ships in Avondale or repaired them at Algiers and Gretna.

The war permanently shifted rural south Louisiana away from its nineteenth-century economies of fur, fisheries, and crops, and toward one of petroleum extraction and refining. New Orleans proper swelled from 494,537 in 1940 to an estimated 545,000 by mid-1943, "caused by worker migration to the city," and 559,000 by 1945.[2] The West Bank, from Algiers to Avondale, would grow from 55,000 in 1935 to over 85,000 in 1948, and as one Jefferson Parish advocate emphasized, the jump was not a "synthetic war boom [because] none—absolutely none—of our industries are purely war plants, subject to abandonment afterward."[3]

The East Bank in 1945, having hosted all those once-busy Higgins plants, did feel sudden abandonment, exacerbated by a postwar recession which also affected tourism and shipping. The West Bank, with its stable legacy industries, found itself on better footing, having boomed enough to benefit but not enough to bust. To wit, in 1939, before the war began, a solid 55 percent of locally made products shipped out of the Port of New Orleans were manufactured on the West Bank. A decade later, after so many East Bank industries evaporated, that same figure rose to 60 percent—despite that the West Bank was home to only about 15 percent of the metropolitan population.[4]

With all those good jobs and living space, the West Bank attracted the attention of famed New York transportation planner Robert Moses, who consulted for the Louisiana Department of Highways on how to bring the region's tangled gallimaufry of old roads into the modern era. Moses sensed that the next frontier of New Orleans was the West Bank, and it featured centrally in his influential *Arterial Plan for New Orleans* (1946), in which he proposed a "Waterfront Expressway" to connect points east with a new downtown bridge, to open the West Bank to full-scale suburban development (more on this later). Civic advocate Thomas Ewing Dabney, writing in 1948, viewed Moses's plan as an outside expert's validation of the promise of (what Dabney called) the "west side," and admonished East Bankers for their blinding conceit:

> The Huey P. Long bridge in 1935 merely recognized a movement which had already begun; and the Moses report of 1946 emphasized the new direction [of] the city's growth when it said, "*The natural area of residential expansion at New Orleans is in the direction of Algiers and Gretna.*"
>
> Many in New Orleans are unaware of the amazing progress the west side has made.... They speak, on occasion, of Greater New Orleans, but the term has no real meaning for them, and for the most part they think of the westside as the vague and remote wilderness of Lafitte's day, known only to the jolly pirates.... They have no conception of how close this *proposed development* is to their own front yards. They know that New Orleans has become unwieldly and crowded, but they do not see the great opportunities of this frontier.[5]

The "proposed development" to which Dabney alluded was not a bridge or a high-way; it was a seaway, one with the capacity of permanently rerouting American shipping while replumbing the entire Barataria Basin. The vision was a revival of that 1878 plan to dig a major oceangoing shipping canal to the Gulf of Mexico. It would become known as the Mississippi Valley Seaway or West Bank Seaway.

The ambitious monikers were a sign of the times. Historian Gary Bolding called this era the "seaway movement[,] the realization of a century-old dream for a shorter and safer water passage from New Orleans to the open sea."[6] Other ports were doing the same thing, cutting deep-draft channels to make a call to their facilities more enticing for world shipping. New Orleans did as much with its Inner Harbor Navigation (Industrial) Canal, opened in 1923, though that wa-terway was designed for barges and maritime industries, not oceangoing ships.

A dozen years later, the call was for exactly that—like the old Barataria Canal plan, but scaled up for modern cargo vessels. The Jefferson Parish police jury first floated the idea in 1935, and after eight years of garnering support, local officials and shipping magnates met in 1943 with the Army Corps of Engineers. Parties agreed that a tidewater seaway would put New Orleans and the Missis-sippi Valley inland waterway system back in competition with traffic flowing in and out the Panama Canal.[7]

Where exactly to place this theoretical seaway pitted East Bank and West Bank interests. The East Bank argument was to cut a channel eastward from the Industrial Canal and continue along the north shore of Lake Borgne and out the Mississippi Sound to open seas. Its main proponent was former Dock Board president Col. Lester F. Alexander, who had advocated for it since the early 1900s.[8] The "Alexander Seaway" route had momentum on its side: the Gulf Intracoastal Waterway (GIWW) had just been dug along this very path and inaugurated on July 15, 1943, having been fast-tracked to protect vessels from German submarines.[9] Converting it to a seaway would require widening, deepening, and extending it out to the Chandeleur Sound.

The West Bank argument involved a resurrection of the venerable Company Canal, that 120-year-old slave-dug channel sidelined ever since it lost out to the Harvey Canal in the 1924 federal purchase. What advocates now planned was truly radical: all of Salaville and much of Westwego would be dug out into a capacious harbor lined with slips and covered with wharves. At the head of the harbor would be a gigantic lock connecting it with the Mississippi; beneath it would be tunnels for cars and trains to cross; and to its south, after a slight elbow at Bayou Segnette, would be a deep-draft seaway cut straight through the Barataria to the west end of Grand Isle, where a gulf-side harbor would be built with easy access to open seas.

Fifty-five miles long, this Mississippi Valley–West Bank Seaway would cost $75,000,000, including "an $18,000,000 twin ship lock of 40 ft. depth over sills from sea to river level, a saving of $37,000,000 of the taxpayers' money over the East Bank route."[10] Cost savings was but one of about a dozen arguments for the West Bank option. Another point invoked a curious geographical axiom: "UP-RIVER is the normal direction of expansion for river cities; west bank seaway plan goes *with* the grain of this trend, east bank project goes *against* it."[11] Other arguments spoke to nautical pragmatism: the seaway's "entrance at the Gulf will be free from the difficulties and hazards [and] current and silt [deposits] always present at the river passes, [and] it is straight except for slight curves."[12] In other words, the Mississippi Valley–West Bank Seaway would become, for all navigational purposes, the new mouth of the Mississippi River.

Raising the stakes even higher was a parallel debate: congestion at the Harvey Locks had created a bottleneck along the GIWW, and domestic barge companies called for an alternative route to reach the Mississippi. Various proposals in the 1940s would either conflate or separate the initiatives into one or two proposals. Some wanted both seaway and GIWW to go through Westwego; others wanted the seaway in Westwego and the GIWW in Algiers; those on the East Bank wanted the seaway in their preferred eastward Alexander route, and were agnostic about the GIWW alternative route on the West Bank.[13]

What resulted were two major decisions that would permanently reconfigure the metropolis. The East Bank would get the seaway; its backers had the political clout, and were not about to send all that maritime action to a rival bank *and* a rival parish. Adding to their argument was Robert Moses' *Arterial Plan for New Orleans*, that 1946 diagnosis of metro-area transportation needs conducted for the Louisiana Department of Highways, which called for a titanic East Bank Tide Water Ship Canal and harbor—and nothing for the West Bank.[14]

After years of political maneuvering for funding, a bill to fund the seaway was signed into law by President Eisenhower on March 29, 1956. It would be dug in four phases during 1958–1968. No longer would it have Col. Alexander's proposed route; instead, it would cut southeastwardly through forty miles of St. Bernard Parish marshland into the Breton Sound. And no longer would the seaway bear Col. Alexander's name, nor even be called a seaway. Instead the

Oblique satellite perspective of the West Bank (*center*) and its relation to Barataria Basin (*bottom and lower right*), the Pontchartrain Basin and East Bank of greater New Orleans (*upper left*), and Lake Borgne, the Mississippi Sound, and the Gulf of Mexico (*upper right*). Graphic by Richard Campanella; imagery from ESRI.

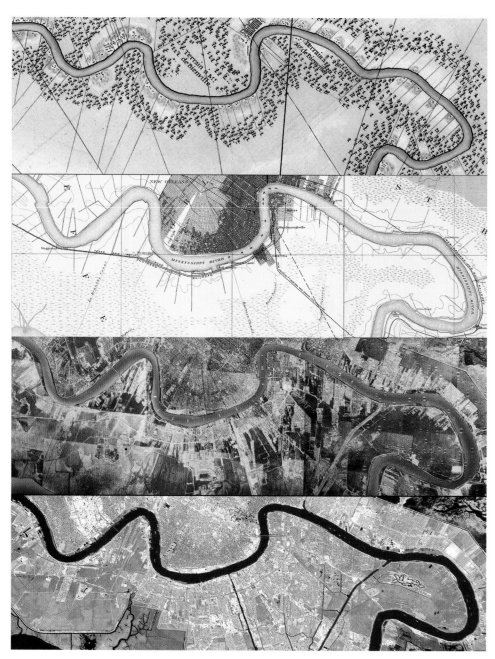

The West Bank as seen in a 1732 colonial map, an 1891 topographical map, an aerial photo mosaic taken 1961–1964, and a satellite image from 2005. Graphic by Richard Campanella; images from Library of Congress, US Geological Survey, New Orleans Public Service, Inc., and Landsat.

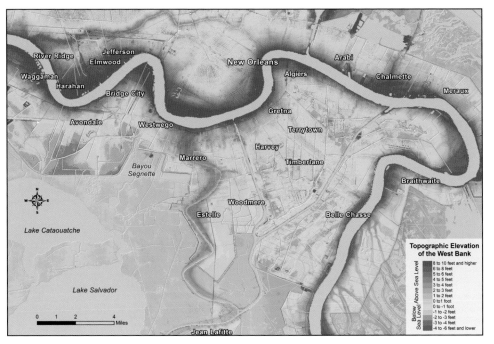

West Bank topographic elevations. Map by
Richard Campanella using LIDAR elevation
data from FEMA/State of Louisiana.

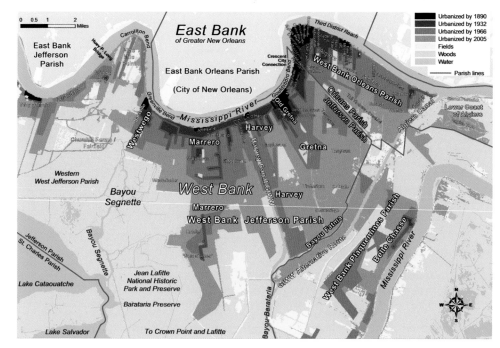

West Bank urban growth, overlaid with historical and present-day place names. Interpretation and map by Richard Campanella.

Detail of *Carte de la côte de la Louisiane,* by Jean-Baptiste Bourguignon d'Anville (1732), showing bayous and bays of Barataria Basin (*lower center*) and the future West Bank across the Mississippi (Fleuve St. Louis) from Nouvelle Orléans. Courtesy Library of Congress.

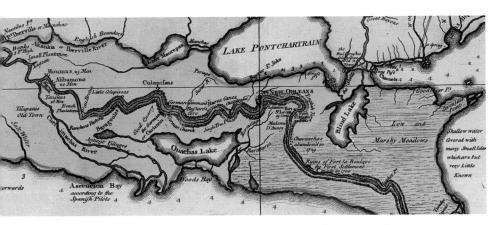

Detail of *Course of the River Mississippi,* by Robert Ross Sayer (London, 1772), showing King's Plantation (Algiers) across from New Orleans. Courtesy Library of Congress.

Detail of *Birds' Eye View of New-Orleans*, by John Bachmann (1851), showing the West Bank from the US Marine Hospital in McDonoghville (*lower right*) to Belleville Iron Works in Algiers (*upper right*). French Quarter appears at top. Courtesy Library of Congress.

Detail of *New Orleans from the Lower Cotton Press,* by David William Moody, published by J. W. Hill and Smith (1852), showing the Belleville Iron Works at far left and the West Bank, from Algiers to Gretna, in left distance. Contrast the bucolic West Bank landscape with the busy port activity and high urban density of New Orleans across the river. Courtesy Library of Congress.

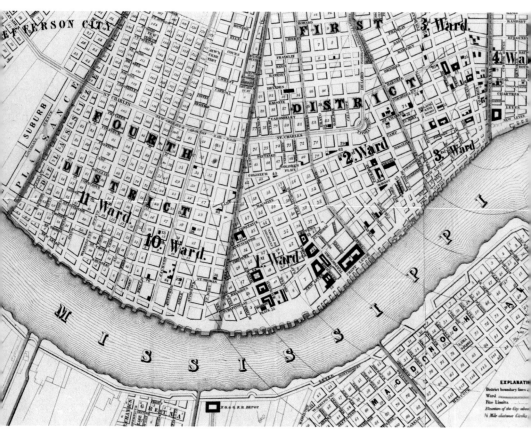

West Bank subdivisions (*bottom*) and their cross-river relations to New Orleans neighborhoods, as depicted by Benjamin Moore Norman in *Norman's Plan of New Orleans and Environs* (*detail*), 1854. Courtesy Library of Congress.

Detail of *New Orleans, La. and Its Vicinity*, by J. Wells and W. Ridgway-Virtue Company (1863), showing the West Bank from the US Marine Hospital (destroyed 1862) down to Algiers. Courtesy of Library of Congress.

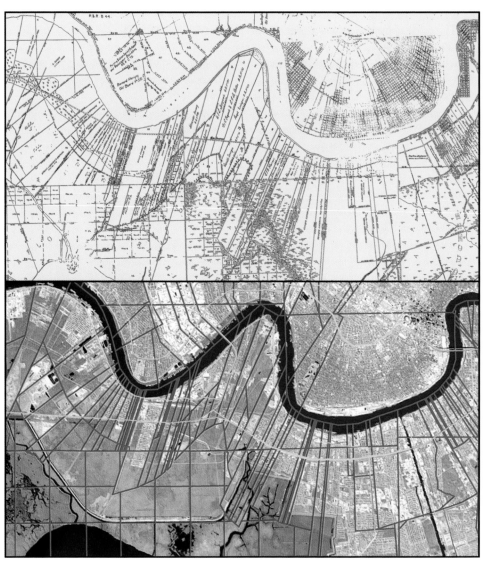

Comparison of 1830s French long-lot plantations (*top*) to present-day irregular sections of the Public Land Survey System (*red lines overlaid on 2005 satellite image*), showing their provenance. Grid pattern in swamps at lower left of each map reflects standard American rectangular township-range-section survey. Historic maps and red section lines courtesy Louisiana Office of State Lands; interpretation and graphic by Richard Campanella.

CAPTURE OF NEW ORLEANS.

The fall of Confederate New Orleans to the Union in May 1862 meant the destruction of the West Bank's shipbuilding and dry dock repair industry. From *Youth's History of the United States,* by Edward Sylvester Ellis (1887), British Library/British Museum.

Depiction of a Louisiana bayou, like those in Barataria Basin south of the West Bank. From *Picturesque America* (1872-74), by William Cullen Bryant, British Library/British Museum.

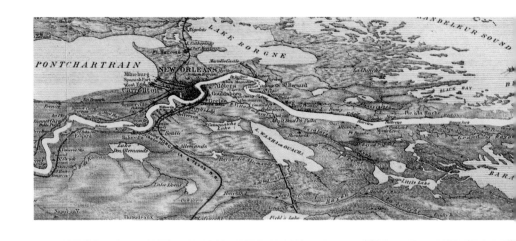

Left: Detail of *Bird's-Eye View of the Missis-sippi River* (1884), by Edward Molitor, show-ing the West Bank's railroad connections to Texas (*tracks at left-center*) and access to Barataria Basin and Bay (*lower right*). Cour-tesy Library of Congress.

Below: Dry dock in Algiers around 1903. Courtesy Detroit Publishing Company, Library of Congress.

Nine Mile Point retains examples of nearly all historic and present-day land covers of the West Bank, from forest and pasture in the shape of French long lots to industry, shipping, subdivisions, and railroads. The Huey P. Long Bridge is in the foreground. Drone photograph by Marco Rasi, 2019, used with permission.

Seven Oaks Plantation House (1840), on former Zeringue Plantation of Nine Mile Point, photographed by Frances Benjamin Johnston in 1938. Courtesy Historic American Buildings Survey, Library of Congress.

Above: Looking into the West Bank and Barataria Basin toward the Gulf from over Lake Pontchartrain, circa 1950. Courtesy US Army Corps of Engineers.

Right: Articles by West Bank advocate Thomas Ewing Dabney in the *Jefferson Parish Yearly Review* (1948), foreseeing the "West-Side" as a "new frontier" of New Orleans, with a seaway connecting it to the Gulf of Mexico. Courtesy Jefferson Parish Police Jury.

NEW ORLEANS from the air, looking
downriver. Proposed west bank seaway
would enter river at Nine Mile Point,
center foreground, just beyond bridge.

Go West-Side,
New Orleans, to your
NEW FRONTIER

By Thomas Ewing Dabney

New Orleans is today frontier, as it
was at its founding two and a half centuries ago. Not frontier in the literal
sense of Bienville when he stood in the
wilderness that is now Jackson Square
and hoped the insignificant port he laid
out would serve the Mississippi Valley
when and if; but frontier in the philosophical, the true meaning of the term
to which the advance into the unknown

is merely incidental to the use of the
opportunities thereof.

Human activity, since the beginning
of life, has always possessed the land
and has cluttered the earth with the
shards and broken columns of civiliza-
tions which tried to meet the future
with the past and went down under
those better able to pick up the new and
larger challenges of every advance.

By this definition New Orleans has
always been frontier and always will

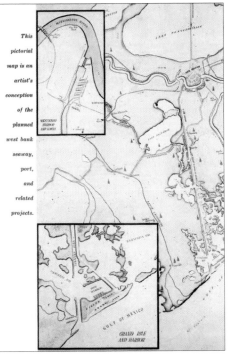

This

pictorial

map is an

artist's

conception

of the

planned

west bank

seaway,

port,

and

related

projects.

36

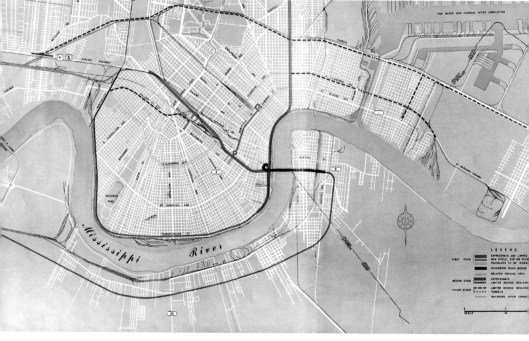

Map from Robert Moses's *Arterial Plan for New Orleans* (1946), envisioning the future Mississippi River Bridge and West Bank Expressway, as well as "Waterfront" (Riverfront) and Pontchartrain Expressways on East Bank. All but one came to fruition.

Aerial view of Southern Pacific Yards in Algiers, 1922. Courtesy National Archives.

Semirural Gretna, Harvey, and Marrero (*at top*) stand in contrast to high-density uptown New Orleans, 1923. Courtesy National Archives.

Aerial view of downtown New Orleans in foreground, and Algiers-McDonoghville area of West Bank in background, 1923. Courtesy National Archives.

Algiers and McDonoghville (*lower left*) at midcentury. Within a few years, the Mississippi River Bridge would be built across the foreground, the Southern Pacific Yards (*trackbeds at right*) would close, and the West Bank would rapidly suburbanize. Note the McDonoghville Cemetery at lower center. NOPSI photo courtesy Entergy/Private collection of Richard Campanella.

Before (1952), during (1957), and after (2006) construction of the Mississippi River bridges, named the Crescent City Connection in 1989. Graphic by Richard Campanella based on imagery by US Geological Survey, Del Hall/US Air Force, and Digital Globe.

The greater New Orleans Mississippi River Bridge just after its 1958 opening, which triggered permanent change of the West Bank from a landscape of towns, industry, and truck farms to one of "interurban suburbia." NOPSI photo courtesy Entergy/Private collection of Richard Campanella.

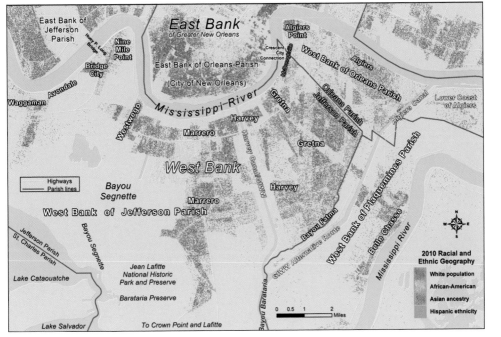

Racial and ethnic geographies of the West Bank, 2010. Map by Richard Campanella based on block-level data of the US Census.

The Crescent City Connection with Algiers Point in background. Drone photo by Marco Rasi, used with permission.

Top left: Algiers Point during low water in spring 2017. Drone photo by Lorenzo Serafini Boni and Marco Rasi, used with permission.

Bottom left: Algiers Point during high water in May 2019, looking toward Gretna. Drone photo by Marco Rasi, used with permission.

Holy Name of Mary cemeteries in Algiers, looking toward Federal City and lower Algiers. Drone photo by Marco Rasi, used with permission.

Crescent City Connection superstructure overlooking McDonoghville Cemetery and former Fischer Projects along Orleans/Jefferson parish line. Drone photo by Marco Rasi, used with permission.

View of Woodland area of lower Algiers, into petrochemical facilities in Chalmette across the river. Vietnamese gardens and fruit trees are discernible at left-center, between houses and forest; Algiers Canal at lower right. Drone photo by Marco Rasi, used with permission.

Old Gretna during high water, May 2019. Drone photo by Marco Rasi, used with permission.

This photo of St. Alphonsus Church and St. Mary Church in old Lafayette (*foreground,* now Irish Channel of New Orleans), and St. Joseph Church in Gretna (*distant center right*), illustrates the proximity of these two cross-river areas. German and Irish immigrants in Lafayette rode the ferry to settle in Gretna, and Redemptorists were involved in the construction of all three original churches. Photograph by Marco Rasi, used with permission.

Historic cityscapes of Algiers, McDonoghville, Gretna, and Marrero. Photographs by Marco Rasi with Richard Campanella, used with permission.

Ethnicities and foodways in the West Bank cityscape. Photographs by Marco Rasi with Richard Campanella, used with permission.

Lock of Harvey Canal, whose channel was originally excavated in 1839, looking south toward Bayou Barataria. Drone photograph by Marco Rasi, used with permission.

Industry along Harvey Canal (Intracoastal Waterway); downtown New Orleans in distance.
Drone photograph by Marco Rasi, used with permission.

The West Bank's economic interaction with the Mississippi River includes riverfront dry docks for ship repair, mooring of barges and other vessels, shipbuilding, local transportation, and support of shipping activity at the Port of New Orleans. Photos by Marco Rasi and Richard Campanella.

The West Bank Expressway in Marrero looking toward Harvey; Hope Haven is in the foreground along Barataria Boulevard. Drone photograph by Marco Rasi, used with permission.

The cemetery along Ames Boulevard, relic of an era when Marrero was an array of hamlets and truck farms known as Amesville. Photograph by Marco Rasi, used with permission.

Channel of Company Canal emerging from Bayou Segnette (*foreground*), looking into Westwego and Salaville, where the original Barataria and Lafourche Company Canal (1830) was dug from the Mississippi River. The channel was later used by Acadian (Cajun) families to bring seafood into Westwego canneries; to this day, Westwego and Marrero have substantial Cajun populations. Note fishing fleet in foreground. Drone photograph by Marco Rasi, used with permission.

Looking down Bayou Segnette, last undrained swamp on the West Bank, toward Lake Cataouatche and Barataria Basin. Drone photograph by Marco Rasi, used with permission.

A sinking delta surrounded by eroding coasts and rising seas means a West Bank cityscape rimmed with levees, floodwalls, barriers, gates, and pumping stations, many of them upgraded as part of the $14.5 billion post-Katrina Hurricane Storm Damage Risk Reduction System. Photographs by Richard Campanella.

Scenes of the West Bank/Barataria Basin environment and its denizens. Photographs by Marco Rasi and Richard Campanella.

Algiers Canal lock at Mississippi River, 2019. Drone photograph by Marco Rasi, used by permission.

Cross-bank relations at their best. Photograph by Marco Rasi, used with permission.

canal would be called the Mississippi River–Gulf Outlet—"MR-GO," a chipper sobriquet that, in time, would become perfectly infamous.[15]

Algiers, meanwhile, would get the GIWW alternative route. Monies eventually totaling $14 million were authorized in 1948 to dig a trench from the main channel of the Intracoastal Canal (which here shared the natural channel of Bayou Barataria), following along the Plaquemines Parish boundary, and to build a lock at Cut Off along the lower coast of Algiers.[16] In the early 1950s, backhoes and bulldozers gnawed away at 9.4 miles of West Bank earth, aiming for a channel 12 feet deep and 125 feet wide. Following in the long tradition of West Bank lock problems, engineers encountered unstable soils and had to dredge down to 25 feet, pump out the water, and drive 6,000 pilings into a layer of sand to provide a sufficiently strong foundation for the 760-by-75-foot concrete lock chamber. The channel itself effectively severed the Algiers and English Turn promontories, and finally opened in April 1956.[17]

The new waterway forced some infrastructural reshuffling. For ground traffic, new connectors had to be built concurrently with the ditch digging. They included a $1.8 million bridge with 100-foot clearance for Highway 1509 (today's Green Bridge on Gen. DeGaulle Drive–Woodland Highway 407), and for the price of $3.6 million, a railroad bridge, auto bridge, and auto tunnel to access Belle Chasse in Plaquemines Parish. All were opened around the same time as the canal.[18]

As for drainage, the GIWW Alternative Route made for a convenient new outlet to eject runoff from subdivisions in all three abutting parishes. New pump stations would be built on both sides, and the channel would become the premier outfall drainage canal of the eastern half of the West Bank.

Viewed from afar, the GIWW Alternative Route, or "Algiers Canal," represented perhaps the most radical single-project alteration to West Bank geography to date. While the new channel would create a great economic opportunity for Plaquemines Parish—in the form of job-rich Engineers Road, which, like the Harvey Canal industrial corridor, became a haven for the oil-and-gas services sector—it would also create new risk, as a potential entry for hurricane storm surges. The danger would become increasingly perilous as ground levels subsided below sea level on account of mechanized drainage, as populations increased in sinking neighborhoods, as wetlands eroded in the Barataria Bay, and as sea levels rose.

As for Westwego, it lost out on both accounts, and the Company Canal, denied its resurrection, would instead get rejected twice again. Dead for all economic purposes, the 130-year-old canal was buried, literally, during 1959–1962.

Surely West Bankers were dismayed by the defeat, for the second time in seventy years, of their seaway. In hindsight, they should count their blessings.

No one knew it at the time, but Westwego and the West Bank landed on the winning side of the seaway decision. The tragic losers were eastern New Orleans, the Lower Ninth Ward, and St. Bernard Parish. Their nemesis was the Mississippi River–Gulf Outlet.

At best, the MR-GO fell short of economic expectations. Incessant bankside erosion necessitated costly dredging, else the draft got so shallow that ships had to lighten their loads, losing millions. Shippers hesitated relocating their container cranes and facilities to the envisioned "Centroport" wharves by France Road, which additionally dissuaded potential clients. The MR-GO was supposed to replace the Mississippi River; instead, it carried only 11 percent of port tonnage by 1990, and barely 5 percent by 1998.[19] Risk-adverse maritime firms instead reinvested in riverside containerization facilities in uptown New Orleans. Old Man River beat out MR-GO, and the upstart seaway became an expensive liability.

Environmentally, the MR-GO was a disaster. Its excavation destroyed eight thousand acres of wetlands; its channel allowed salt water to intrude and kill cypress swamps; its water surface formed a minimum-friction pathway for storm surges; and its guide levees, together with those of the GIWW, effectively funneled surges into the metropolis, increasing water volume, speed, and power. It happened in 1965, during Hurricane Betsy, when the MR-GO was under construction. It happened again forty years later, when Hurricane Katrina's surge entered the GIWW/MR-GO funnel, breaching floodwalls catastrophically, flooding tens of thousands of homes, and killing hundreds of people.

Had the West Bank Seaway been built instead, a comparable scenario could have played out in the Barataria Basin. Had the perfect storm come in a particular direction, a similar surge might have penetrated populated regions. Indeed, the extant network of man-made waterways, including both routes of the GIWW/Harvey Canal and Bayou Segnette/Company Canal, already were cause for concern; a full-blown seaway would have made matters that much worse. And this is to say nothing of the giant harbor envisioned for Westwego, which, if it all worked, would have been rimmed with towering cranes and intermodal arteries. Mammoth maritime traffic jams likely would have formed at the lock, as containerized vessels awaited passage through the bottleneck. From a residential perspective, the area would have been all but unlivable.

The West Bank Seaway was a disaster narrowly averted in every conceivable way, and West Bankers should savor the suffering they were spared. Perhaps some individuals foresaw that things might go awry, even during the halcyon days of the "seaway movement." Thomas Ewing Dabney, that well-intentioned public intellectual who had advocated for the West Bank Seaway, said as much in a moment of unrecognized prescience in 1948, though he failed to bring his observations to their logical conclusion. "The hurricane of September 19, 1947, and the rush of water under which it submerged the east-side route made [leaders] think more deeply and constructively on the problem; and many influential men who formerly favored the east-side now see that the west-side route is better."[20]

≈≈≈

The West Bank at midcentury brimmed with optimism—and bumper-to-bumper traffic. Atomic-age development had overwhelmed Victorian-age infrastructure, and postwar leaders knew the status quo was untenable. Gretna Mayor William J. White spoke of "dangerous high blood pressure throughout the parish, as the traffic congestion on the West Bank's one main highway from Avondale to Algiers got heavier and heavier and the ferries huffed and puffed and strained to handle a situation that is a generation too fast for them."[21] All indicators pointed to an unprecedented boom, but only if it were accompanied by requisite improvements.

With the end of World War II on the horizon, federal legislation in December 1944 created the Interregional Highway System. The Louisiana Department of Highways followed suit by taking stock of its state highways, and among other things, sketched in a possible Julia Street-to-Algiers bridge. As the war ended, the department hired as a consultant Robert Moses, the lordly planner who almost single-handedly reconfigured greater New York, to diagnose the region's transportation ills—road, rail, water, and air—and devise a visionary "arterial plan" for New Orleans.[22]

Working with his consulting engineers Andrews & Clark, Moses released his report in November 1946. In time, the document would prove to be as influential as it was controversial. Moses's central finding was that "the natural area of residential expansion of New Orleans is in the direction of Algiers and Gretna, [where] the land is fairly high, reasonably cheap, and ripe for further development."[23] That realization drove his recommendation for an eastbound "Pontchartrain Expressway" and a westbound "Waterfront Expressway" fronting the French Quarter to converge upon a new Mississippi River bridge between Calliope Street (present-day John Churchill Chase) and the blocks bounded by Lamarque and Socrates streets. That the main aim for all three pieces of infrastructure was not downtown New Orleans nor Metairie nor eastern New Orleans, but rather Algiers and McDonoghville, evidenced the promise Moses saw in the West Bank. Moreover, the planner circumvented that narrow old bottlenecked 4th Street corridor along the West Bank riverfront, and instead sketched out a capacious grade-level boulevard over a half-mile away—the birth of today's West Bank Expressway.

Urbanists today, who scorn Moses for favoring expediency over people in New York, would despair at his painstaking avoidance of the industrial West Bank riverfront—yet his wanton disregard for New Orleans's most historic neighborhood, having proposed for *its* riverfront an unsightly elevated expressway. But at the time, most power brokers on both banks backed Moses's arterial plan. East Bank leaders supported what would become known as the Riverfront Expressway, as well as the later-added Claiborne Expressway, and West Bankers loved the as-yet unnamed expressway on the West Bank, which would course through largely vacant land and surely create valuable real estate.

What the parties disputed was where exactly the bridge should go, and who should pay for it. A survey conducted during World War II indicated most people preferred a Julia Street-to-Algiers route. Those results were skewed, however, by the many ferry-riders destined for the Todd-Johnson Dry Docks and Algiers Naval Base, who used that trajectory to get to work. Jefferson Parish officials especially disliked that option, calling Julia Street overly congested, but their real gripe was its Orleans Parish location.

What they and state leaders wanted was a reincarnation of the circa-1920s Hero-Hackett proposal, crossing from Race Street to Perry Street in Gretna. (Allen S. Hackett's New Orleans-Gretna Bridge Co., Inc., continued to run ads for the Hero-Hackett Bridge into the mid-1930s.) This position, advocates magnanimously argued, could equally serve Orleans, Jefferson, and Plaquemines parishes while minimizing right-of-way expropriations, given its two helical ramp approaches.[24] The Race-to-Gretna "section was chosen," explained a Jefferson supporter in 1943, "first because it is central to the business development of both sides of the river, and second because the Mississippi is relatively narrow there, [only] about 1700 feet wide. And hydraulic conditions are favorable."[25] The main reason was its location well within Jefferson Parish.

The 1946 arterial plan essentially split the difference, putting the bridge half-way between Julia and Race. But the apparently judicious compromise was not the work of Solomon; it was the work of Moses. The prescient planner nurtured a parallel idea of unifying various downtown passenger train stations into a "Union Passenger Terminal" on Julia Street, and so as not to interfere with that chess-move, he shifted the bridge crossing up to Calliope Street.[26] This positioned the span to soar over the West Bank riverfront precisely at the Orleans/Jefferson parish line, and while its main traffic exchange fell within Orleans, the trajectory of the vehicles flowed directly into Jefferson; motorists would have to exit and loop back around to get into Algiers or Belle Chasse. (Moses also put to rest the preposterous notion of continuing the Mississippi River bridge as a fifty-mile causeway across the entire Barataria Basin to reach Grand Isle, where a state park would await city vacationers—the original "bridge to nowhere." Writing with polite restraint, Moses said, "It is difficult for outsiders, however imaginative and park-minded, to see any economic justification for this proposal." He listed the main reasons why, starting with "too costly" and ending with "[un]needed."[27])

The financial dispute rested on the question of bridge tolls. New York and other northeastern states had experimented successfully with the issuance of bonds backed by motorist tolls to underwrite bridges, tunnels and turnpikes. The local champion of the idea was naval engineer and civic advocate Capt. Neville Levy, who found a willing partner in New Orleans Mayor deLesseps "Chep" Morrison, a self-styled reformer and transportation advocate. Others wavered. State Senator Alvin T. Stumpf of Gretna, for example, introduced a bill in 1948 calling for a toll bridge, but two years later supported a constitutional amendment for a toll-free bridge. Regardless of the funding mechanism, West Bankers strongly supported the bridge, and Gretna property owners voted overwhelmingly in November 1951 for a $45 million bond issue to finance construction.[28]

So mandated, the state legislature passed the Bridges and Ferries Authority Act in 1952, which empowered public-private "authorities" (commissions) to build, operate, and repair bridges, highways, and ferries. The law's first spawn, in June 1952, was the Mississippi River Bridge Authority, on which were seated board members from the City of New Orleans, Jefferson Parish, the Louisiana Department of Highways, plus Modjeski and Masters as consulting engineers.[29] On the same day the authority incorporated itself, pilots on two key downtown ferries went on strike, stranding thousands of angry commuters growing ever more impatient with their "inadequate and unsatisfactory . . . horse-and-buggy mode of life [in this] auto age."[30]

The authority tackled myriad project questions. First on the list: bridge or tunnel? Moses opined bluntly on this matter: "Never build a tunnel if you can build anything else."[31] The Authority concurred, finding a tunnel to be costly and incompatible. As for the exact path, another consulting group, Masters and Henderlite, knowing of Moses' rejection of Julia Street in favor of a Calliope-Lamarque crossing, suggested an adjustment. They pointed out that Thalia Street, "at the site of abandoned T.P.M.P train ferry, where no dock of wharf existed [and] property damages were clearly less, [would make] the best connections . . . to the Pontchartrain Expressway." The authority debated Calliope versus Thalia, and concluded that a bridge at Calliope, being longer, would increase costs by $20 million. So the route was finalized at the Thalia-Bringier Street crossing, at River Mile 95.7 above Head of Passes.[32] (It's worth noting that while the Lamarque-to-Bringier route ran through the historic black settlement of old Freetown, it also intersected the only spot on the West Bank that earned a positive rating on those notorious 1939 government "redlining" maps: an all-white area along Bodenger Boulevard where lived a "[g]ood class of executives-business and professional men."[33] The bridge was an equal-opportunity displacer.)

Next question: suspension or cantilever bridge? Soft clay deposits below the river caused engineers concern about tipping anchorages and sagging suspension cables; besides, Modjeski and Masters wrote, "110 miles per hour [hurricane winds] would be very damaging to a suspension bridge."[34] Instead, they opted for a cantilever and truss design, like the Huey P. It would have four auto lanes, a decision that made financial sense at the time but would prove to be an overly conservative estimate of future usage.

The bridge would rest on a series of land and water piers, the latter two reaching as high above mean low-water level as they were below, over 160 feet in each direction, and would run 13,428 feet maximally, including approaches and ramps. The main channel span measured 1,575 feet long, peaking at 362 feet high, and providing 153 feet clearance to vessels during highest river stage. That extraordinary height made the Mississippi River Bridge "unique among the three greatest cantilevers in the world" in its shape; other spans had a more arching profile, which meant their trusses could be arranged differently. This was an exciting project even for the seasoned Modjeski firm, because at the time it represented "the largest cantilever span in the United States . . . and the longest highway cantilever span in the world."[35]

Who would pay? That Neville Levy became Authority chairman meant the pro-toll side had prevailed. The reasoning came from financial advisors who suspected rural Louisianians would rebuke their tax dollars going to the sole benefit of urban New Orleans, and recommended instead that users bear the cost. The law thus provided "that the bonds be backed by toll earnings of the bridge," until the $45 million price tag was paid off.[36] Here too, Moses's influence was at work: "it is obvious that it would have to be a toll structure," he wrote back in 1946, and backed up his position with ample usage data projections.[37]

On August 9, 1954, leaders signed a "Tripartite Agreement," in which the Mississippi River Bridge Authority would finance and construct the bridge, most approaches, some ramps, and the toll plaza; the Louisiana Department of Highways would focus on the Pontchartrain and West Bank expressways, among other things; and the City of New Orleans would commit to building key interchanges and improving connecting streets.

Building a bridge means timely construction of scores of interconnected parts, each predicated on permitting, right-of-way acquisitions, expropriations, demolitions, soil testing, and site preparation. For the Pontchartrain Expressway on the East Bank, this meant clearing the former New Basin Canal bed, the Calliope/Gaienne street corridors, and associated ramps, for which scores of old buildings were purchased for $3.5 million and razed. Among them were the magnificent Delord-Sarpy House (1815) on Howard Avenue and St. Paul's Episcopal Church (1893) on Camp Street.

For the expressway on the West Bank, the right-of-way work was easier, due to its relatively sparse urbanization. Once again, it was Moses who first conceived this artery in 1946:

A new location for a highway is recommended, from the Westwego approach to the Huey P. Long Bridge at Route 90 to Algiers south of the present winding highway. This will bypass the main streets of the communities. At Algiers it would connect with the approaches to the new Mississippi River crossing. This artery should be developed in its initial stage as a conventional boulevard with a wide neutral ground so that grade separation structures could be added at important cross streets as the need for them develops.[38]

Nineteen fifty-four was a big year for the West Bank. Work began in winter on the "West Bank Four-Lane Expressway" (the "Super Expressway") running at grade level from Algiers to the Huey P. Long Bridge across mostly small farms and fields. On March 16, the Corps of Engineers issued a bridge construction permit to Modjeski and Masters. To replace the infamously bottlenecked drawbridge at the Harvey Canal, work began on June 28 on "the world's first fully automatic vehicular tunnel," 1,080 feet long and four lanes wide plus a walkway, costing $4.4 million.[39] On August 18, officials convened for a ceremony on the Gretna riverbank. With Authority chairman Neville Levy presiding and cameras at the ready, a pile driver began hammering the first test piling into the river bottom. "This symbolized the 'Go Sign' on construction," beamed the Sheriff Frank J. Clancy, one of the most powerful men in Jefferson Parish.[40] The West Bank would buzz with activity from that moment on. "To tell the truth," wrote Gretna Mayor William J. White, "Gretna has been preparing for this bridge for nearly thirty years, for it was Jefferson Parish public officials, back in 1926, who first broached the idea [of the Hero-Hackett plan] and practically picked the spot."[41]

Using floating derricks with concrete mixers and gantry cranes, workers in 1955 bore into the river bottom and began pouring caisson concrete. Pier shaft construction came next, and the four main towers, two on land and two in water, rose in steady increments over the next two years, while the approaching expressways and ramps were built on either bank. The first steel anchor arms and grillwork went up in the fall of 1956; by spring, the dramatic profile of the bridge came into shape as the main cantilever spans and their interconnecting trusses progressed toward each other, like outstretched arms reaching for a handshake. Work paused during hurricane season, and by Christmas, only a one-hundred-foot gap remained. On January 3, 1958, the last members were fitted into place, and the "hands" shook across the East and West banks.

Their task completed, the derricks and barges were sent away. Now came the roadwork, electrical illumination, painting, completion of approaches and plazas, and finishing touches. At 12:01 AM April 15, 1958, the Greater New Orleans Mississippi River Bridge partially opened to the public, six months ahead of schedule, and 17,584 vehicles crossed on the first day. Formal dedication ceremonies were held on October 18, 1958. After 240 years of watery separation, the East and West banks of New Orleans proper were linked, and neither would ever be the same.[42]

≈≈≈

Nineteen fifty-eight was a culminating year of postwar modernization. In the five prior years, the metropolis got a new causeway across Lake Pontchartrain, two expressways, two tunnels, bridges small and large, widened arteries, new civic centers, track consolidation into the new Union Passenger Terminal, expansion at Moisant Airport, the Algiers Canal, and plans for a new seaway, not to mention scores of road-rail grade separations and intersection redesigns. Now, in 1958, five weeks before the bridge opened, Jefferson Parish replaced its century-old police jury with a parish president and council form of government—and a new courthouse to boot, a gleaming, nine-story Modernist edifice in Gretna, "tallest all-glass building on the west bank of the Mississippi south of the City of St. Louis."[43] Even Plaquemines Parish, farthest from the action, reaped the benefits of the forthcoming bridge as it dedicated Allen Callender Field as the nation's first "joint operating field [for] the Air National Guard, Air Force Reserve, Naval Aircraft, Marine Air Reserve and the Coast Guard" (today's Belle Chasse Naval Air Station), a move ten years in the making and actualized when the bridge opened in April 1958.[44] Populations were larger than ever in all four metro-area parishes; New Orleans proper surpassed 600,000 for the first time, while Jefferson Parish more than doubled (103,873 in 1950 to 208,769 in 1960) and the West Bank passed the 100,000 mark. It was an exhilarating time, and nearly everyone hailed the progress.

III

LANDSCAPE SUBURBANIZATION, 1950S TO PRESENT

14

From Subrural to Suburban

Amid all the change was a very different kind of progress—only in this case, half the populace fought it bitterly. "SEGREGATION VOID IN PUBLIC SCHOOLS," read *Times-Picayune* headlines on May 18, 1954, one day after the United States Supreme Court ruled unanimously in *Brown v. Board of Education of Topeka* that state laws racially segregating public schools were unconstitutional. Calls for civil rights gained momentum throughout the South, as whites resisted and authorities dragged their feet on integration. They used, to their advantage, the "with all deliberate speed" clause in the ruling, which neglected to put a target date on the integration mandate. Their legal nemesis was Judge J. Skelly Wright of the District Court for the Eastern District of Louisiana, who worked assiduously in enforcing *Brown*, striking down state segregation laws and, in 1960, fixing a date by which the racial integration of the public schools had to begin.

On November 14, 1960, four little black girls marched past furious crowds and into two previously white-only public elementary schools in the working-class Ninth Ward. So began the grade-by-grade end of *de jure* segregation in public schools—only to be matched by *de facto* segregation in residential living patterns, courtesy of "white flight" to suburbs like the West Bank, making geography do what the law no longer could. And how does one flee to the suburbs? By driving all those new highways and bridges, and buying those ranch houses and split-levels in all those new subdivisions on all those recently drained lands.

Starting in the late 1950s but especially after 1960, a wholesale demographic resettlement transpired. White families abandoned the urban core for the metropolitan periphery, taking their buying power and tax dollars with them. Those in the downtown wards tended to move eastward into St. Bernard Parish; those uptown or lakeside typically moved westward into Metairie; and those along riverfront neighborhoods such as the Irish Channel showed a preference for the West Bank, where many had ferried for years to jobs or had cross-river kin. Moving there would simply complete the socioeconomic relationship, and now they had both means (the bridge) and reason (school integration) to do so.

As if in fulfillment of Robert Moses's 1946 prediction of the West Bank as the next frontier of New Orleans, builders raced to erect homes for eager buyers. Two neighborhoods epitomized the thrust: Aurora Gardens in Algiers, and Terrytown near Gretna.

Taking its name from the old Aurora (Jourdan) Plantation, whose antebellum mansion still stood along the river and where sugarcane grew only fifty years prior, Aurora Gardens comprised a square mile of curvaceous streets and terraced lots on which 4,000 contemporary, air-conditioned, single-family homes would be built—"the most perfectly planned community," according to developers Ernest B. Norman Jr. and J. Robert Norman. The initial phase began two decades earlier, when patriarch Ernest B. Norman Sr. began selling lots in 1940 along Newton Highway (later Gen. Meyer Avenue), aiming to house some of the four-thousand-plus employees soon to work at the Todd Shipyards and Naval Station. The Normans had close ties to this land; some family members lived in the Aurora Plantation House, and in 1947, they gifted forty acres to the Marianites for the operation of their normal school, later Holy Cross College.[1]

The new phases of Aurora Gardens lay south of Gen. Meyer Avenue, and their houses were larger, costlier, and more fashionable than the earlier bungalows. Properties sold steadily throughout the late 1940s and especially after 1951, when the Sewerage and Water Board agreed to install municipal sewerage facilities (septic tanks having been used previously), and after 1954, when bridge construction began.[2] Some Aurora houses were planned by Barbara C. Gibson, who became so adept at design that she would sketch blueprints in real time for visitors at the New Orleans Home Show. "Spectators seemed amused that a woman should design floor plans and elevations," Gibson told a reporter, adding, "Frankly, I think the woman's angle is most important in house design, [e]specially the kitchen floor plan."[3]

Priced at $18,000 to $32,000, or about five times the area's median household income, the contemporary ranch-style residences were aimed at the upwardly mobile white middle class. "Aurora Gardens is full of wonderful, friendly people you'll be proud to have as neighbors and as personal friends," assured a mid-1950s marketing brochure that, together with the models in the photographs, signaled what those neighbors would look like. "Aurora is THE community for the successful young families of New Orleans."[4]

Public schools, of course, had been strictly segregated since Reconstruction, and racially restrictive covenants in house-sale contracts had been standard in new subdivisions for decades. But the legal overturning of these practices in the 1960s hardly equated with integrated living. Schools did not have to be *de jure* segregated to make this and other new suburban communities white, nor were deed covenants needed to preclude blacks neighbors. Rather, steep prices, social pressure, coded marketing, and, according to one source, the real estate strategy of "block-busting," accomplished segregation *de facto*. An octogenarian interviewed in 2001 recalled that her childhood neighborhood around 500 Homer Street in Algiers Point was "mixed[;] we had white neighbors and white across the street," and black households in other houses. "That's how it was[;] that was all over." Indeed, demographic data from 1939 show that 500 Homer was 41 percent white on the downriver (north) side and 21 percent across the street.[5] She explained why the area later became all black, as she understood it: "But when integration came[,] the real estate agents . . . . told [white residents that a] black was moving in, [so] they sold their property and was told there's *a good place down [in] Aurora and they all moved down that way*. . . . So the real estate agents knew how to make money."[6]

White Algerines from the Point joined other New Orleanians from across the river and became neighbors in lower Algiers. The 1960 Aurora Gardens census tract recorded a population that was 99.8 percent white (3495 out of 3501 residents); ten years later, after Jim Crow laws fell and white flight accelerated, the three 1970 census tracts covering the neighborhood were 97 percent white (17,037 out of 17,532). Aurora remains majority-white today, though less so than 50 years ago.[7]

One might get the impression that modern American suburbia and modern American sociology were finally catching up with the West Bank, making the past history, and the future now. Yet in the region's remarkable capacity for retaining historic land uses, one only had to take a twenty-minute walk down from Aurora Garden's sunken living rooms and backyard barbeques to find farmers growing crops and mules pulling ploughs as if it were 1890. Into the 1950s, fully 110 farms operated just within New Orleans city limits. They averaged 74.3 acres in size and yielded more sales per acre ($76.27) than any other Louisiana parish. At least ten were in lower Algiers, just below Aurora Gardens along the Cutoff Road, their "narrow but deep" shapes reflecting the old French long lots. Among the owners of the 20- to 30-acre slivers were members of the extended Pittari family, who "lived well—what with chickens, eggs . . . turnips, shallots, cabbage, carrots, beets and cauliflower [plus] tomatoes, peppers, egg plants, corn[,] beef cattle, milk, [and] hogs, [all] right on their farm [and sold at] a comfortable profit [at] the French Market." Family members did all the labor, with the latest machinery or sometimes with mules or horses. "It is hard to beat this land," marveled the family patriarch. "We live good [and] have as much money as [with] a very good job. *It is a good life.*"[8] Similar operations could be found on Nine Mile Point and along the fringes of Marrero and Gretna, representing the remarkable persistence of a nineteenth-century landscape in the Space Age, within what, into the late 1940s, still ranked as the South's largest city. Piece by piece, that agrarian landscape would lose ground to tract housing and strip malls, though it would never quite fully disappear.

One of the many truck-farming areas that did succumb to suburbanization occupied an unincorporated tract known as Oakdale, bounded by the parish line, Gretna city limits, McDonoghville by the river, and the former backswamp. If ever there was a space between and betwixt, interstitial and liminal, this was it.

All that changed with the 1952 decision to build the Mississippi River Bridge at the Thalia Street–Bringier Street crossing, which positioned ramps at Victory Drive (renamed Gen. DeGaulle in 1961). While the entire Victory Drive Interchange sat within Orleans Parish—it had to, because the City of New Orleans paid for it—the lanes directed West Bank–bound motorists on a trajectory that, within seconds, would land them upon Oakdale's fields and forests. That made those acres perfect for Jefferson Parish's first fully planned "town," complete with a major shopping center.

The man with the plan was developer Paul Kapelow, the "town" would be named for his daughter Terry, and the name of the shopping center would recall what previously stood there: Oakwood.

Whereas Aurora Gardens predated the bridge and expanded after it opened, Terrytown spawned entirely from the bridge. In 1959 Kapelow's company, Terrytown, Inc., purchased the 1,200-acre Oakdale tract—"which not too many years ago was way out in the country and considered an excellent spot for deer hunting"[9]—and began construction that summer. The first 500 homes went up nary a thousand feet from the toll plaza. Plans were ambitious: 4,000 three- and four-bedroom houses of various sizes and styles set back on 60-by-110-foot lots, along curvilinear streets within six adjoining neighborhoods accessed by grassy boulevards. Terrytown, explained Kapelow, would be "a unified, harmonious community, beautifully landscaped, with all big city utilities including a central sanitary sewerage system, subsurface drainage and reserved areas for schools, churches, parks and neighborhood shopping."[10] Best of all, proclaimed one Terrytown advertisement, "It is only seven minutes from Canal St. You'll be home in less time than it takes to smoke two cigarettes."[11]

Terrytown's first phase opened on March 6, 1960, little more than a year after the land purchase and within two years of the bridge opening. The speed of construction resulted from revolutionary new building methods, for this was the area's first completely planned community of prefabricated houses, all with central air conditioning and heat and other modern appliances. Foundations were poured concrete slabs; prebuilt walls were raised into a frame in a matter of hours; and all plumbing was set into a single wall. Buyers could choose among 23 predesigned styles and sizes and select their lot for prices in the $12,750 to $15,500 range, substantially less than Aurora Gardens.

After Terrytown, Inc. developed the first phase, other companies took over subsequent construction. One of them, Kesk, Inc., became "the first developer in Louisiana to utilize the 'Town House' concept of apartment planning," which would later become a signature feature of Terrytown's streetscape. "A complex of twelve buildings of varying sites," explained a parish advocate, "the Town House will contain seventy-two 2- and 3-bedroom luxury apartment units in a beautifully landscaped park-like setting, each [with] a different elevation and exterior finish and . . . a private, Vieux Carre-type rear patio opening onto a center garden mall with swimming pool."[12] All Terrytown developers retained the same basic design of traffic-calming curved streets named alphabetically, starting with A (Arrow, Apollo, etc.) at the northern tip of the parallelogram-shaped expanse, and proceeding down to M (Mystic, Morningside, etc.) two and a half miles to the south. "Thus," wrote local historian Judy Dobbins Mills, "the Terrytown of today, although the result of a master plan, is not a single development, but rather a series of interconnected, coordinated communities built by a variety of companies."[13] On its tenth anniversary in 1970, Terrytown was home to 13,643 people, of whom 13,397 were white—98 percent, nearly the same as Aurora Gardens.[14]

In a very short time, an open space became a place with the identity and character of working- to middle-class former New Orleanians with deep local roots. Yet Terrytown's appearance made it seem rather placeless; by design, it could have been anywhere in the United States of 1960. In a way that would recur as the West Bank transformed from subrural to suburban, the Oakdale tract's prior liminality got passed on to Terrytown's spatial identity, such that people never quite knew how to think of it or where to place it.

Which parish was Terrytown in? Entirely Jefferson, but abutting the Orleans line, and approached by bridge ramps entirely within New Orleans.

Is it really a "town"? No, nor is it a city. Terrytown, though officially recognized, is unincorporated and answers to the parish government—Jefferson, that is.

What is its relationship to McDonoghville? Terrytown is separate and behind what most people call McDonogh or McDonoghville, which straddles the parish line along the river—although John McDonogh's land did originally include parts of what is now Terrytown.

Is Terrytown part of Gretna? The US Postal Service initially viewed Terrytown as a private company name and not a recognized place name, so it assigned it a Gretna mailing address and zip code (70053). Seeing "Gretna" on their mail, some new residents reasonably surmised they indeed lived in Gretna, and called Gretna city offices for service requests—only to be told they did *not* live in Gretna. "Census figures were confused," wrote Judy Dobbins Mills of the mounting headaches, "affecting representation and funding; voters were confused about candidates for office and where they could vote."

In 1989 community advocates launched a "Terrytown, Not Gretna" campaign and got the Jefferson Parish Council to pass a resolution officially recognizing Terrytown as "bounded by the City of Gretna, the Orleans Parish line, the Plaquemines Parish line and the center line of the Belle Chasse Highway."[15] The next year, representatives in Washington, DC, got Terrytown added to the official US Post Office directory of deliverable destinations, and the Census Bureau recognized the community as a Census Designated Place, where demographic data would be aggregated as if it were a city. Ergo, Terrytown: the official, unofficial, recognized, unincorporated corporation-created non-town comprising six subdivisions within a single master plan in or near three parishes in the former backswamp of a former village, to which you may mail a letter, but within which you will never find a city hall.

A suburban subdivision is incomplete without a shopping center, and in 1963, the influential local developer Edgar B. Stern Jr. met with co-investors at the Timberlane Country Club to unveil plans for "the first regional shopping center in the area with a covered, completely air-conditioned mall, which will be cooled in the summer and heated in the winter." At 400,000 square feet and with 3,000 parking spaces across fifty acres, the enormous outlet reflected budding investor confidence in this side of the river. "We know that folks . . . . will appreciate the nice living on the West Bank," said a Sears executive planning an anchor store. "Sears is constantly pursuing the location and relocation of stores near where people live."[16] Oakwood Mall opened in 1965.

Fittingly, the investors met at the exclusive Timberlane, "the first new country club in the New Orleans in recent years," announced within months of the bridge opening and adjoined in 1963 by Timberlane Estates, "one of New Orleans' most exclusive residential areas."[17] With golf rising in popularity among the upwardly mobile middle class, and the concept of a "golf-course community" spreading nationwide from its origins in Florida in the 1920s, the West Bank, with its ample space and incoming bourgeoisie, offered ideal locations. In accordance with the time-honored real estate formula of transportation access plus amenity equals pricey subdivision, various developers over the next fifteen years built an intricate maze of golf-course subdivisions south of the Belle Chasse Highway, in and among the old natural waterways of Bayou Fatma and the Ouachas River. As a whole, they may be viewed as iterations of the Terrytown design formula of curvilinear streets, wending boulevards, variable parcel sizes and structures, and shopping centers—except that these new developments affixed themselves, spatially and psychologically, to the tranquility of the exclusive greens. (No one seemed to worry that if golf declined in popularity, so went property values.) Most were aimed at middle-class price levels; some, namely Timberlane Estates (1970 population: 3,588, of whom 98 percent were white), boasted bigger lots, huge houses, and higher prices—the sort of prestigious subdivisions that, by century's end, would gate themselves off from their neighbors. To wit: whereas Terrytown in the 1980s fought to separate its identity from that of Gretna, residents of Timberlane Estates voted overwhelmingly in 2009 to join Gretna. The reason: "because Jefferson Parish had rejected their efforts to turn their subdivision into a gated community, [to prevent] motorists [from] using Timberlane Drive as a shortcut between Belle Chasse Highway and

Lapalco Boulevard."[18] Annexation into Gretna got Timberlane residents a new gate-friendly governance, while Gretna got a nice addition to its tax base. The city even partially paid for the gates.

The 1960s-1970s developments around Timberlane exemplified the West Bank's counterintuitive class geography, in which affluent home-buyers did not monopolize the high ground closer to the river, as one might expect in a flood-prone region. Rather, they settled in drained areas specially designed for affluence, despite their low elevations and adjacency to surge-prone water bodies. Levees and pumping systems had convinced moneyed home-buyers, and the developers who catered to them, that they no longer had to worry about topography and hydrology. So why bother living on the limited space of the natural ridges, which so often abutted noisy industry and railroads? Wealthier people thus settled on lower ground, while higher ground remained significantly working-class, quite the opposite of typical class settlement patterns elsewhere.

The 1980 Census confirmed this trend, which did not exist prior to the 1958 bridge opening (and of course would have been impossible prior to the 1915 drainage of the backswamp). Those data showed that 100 percent of the census tracts lying south of Lapalco Boulevard (farthest from the river, lowest in elevation) had fewer lower-income households, whereas those on the river side of the West Bank Expressway (highest in elevation) had the largest percentage of lower-income households. Those tracts on intermediary ground between Lapalco and the expressway had a 50/50 mix of wealthier and poorer tracts.[19] This reversed relationship of wealth and elevation, while exceptional in human geography generally, was not unique to West Jefferson. The West Orleans equivalent of Timberlane Estates was English Turn, an exclusive golf-course community created by the Jack Nicklaus Development Corporation and built in the late 1980s in the backswamp of the Lower Coast of Algiers. Of the 1,030 acres needed for the gated subdivision, around 70 percent had been officially identified as wetlands, for which over a million cubic yards of sediment were brought in to fill.[20]

Nor was the flipped pattern limited to the West Bank. After drainage apparatus was installed in the early 1900s to dry out the East Bank of New Orleans, the white middle class living near the river, four to eight feet above sea level, "leapfrogged" over the mostly poor, mostly black, topographically lower "back-of-town" to settle in the *lowest*-lying places such as Gentilly and Lakeview, which would subside four to eight feet below sea level. In East Jefferson Parish, both black and white residents historically found space on the high ground along the river; only after drainage did most of Metairie and Kenner transform into subdivisions, and that's where white flight went—even as they too subsided below sea level.

༄༅༄

As West Bank development sprawled southward and westward, new residents found themselves increasingly distanced from the very transportation arteries that got them there. The first houses of Terrytown, for example, sat only a thousand feet from the Mississippi River Bridge toll plaza, whereas the latest subdivisions in Algiers, Gretna, Harvey, and Marrero lay three to five miles away. Avondale Shipyards, largest employer in the region, was even farther west. As it became clear that commuting *on* the West Bank was becoming more onerous than commuting *from* the West Bank, stakeholders contemplated solutions. No one called for less development, nor greater housing density, but rather for additional bridges and expressways.

In 1964 the Jefferson Council presented plans from an engineering firm owned by David de Laureal and Warren G. Moses to build an Interstate 29 splitting off from the earlier 1946 plan of Robert Moses (no relation) for an expressway to points east, which by the 1960s was coming into fruition as Interstate-10. The I-29 spur of I-10 would form part of the New Orleans Outer Belt (or "Outer Loop") that would run southward along Paris Road, cross a new river bridge from Chalmette to lower Algiers, run parallel to the recently completed Algiers (Intracoastal) Canal, continue westward along the Louisiana Power and Light Company (LaPaLCo) transmission right-of-way south of Lapalco Boulevard, and recross the river at another new bridge from Luling to Destrehan. The West Bank portion of the beltway was dubbed the "Dixie Freeway," and the reason why it swung fully three miles south of the just-completed West Bank Expressway was to "open up more undeveloped land . . . south of the Timberlane Country Club and Terrytown."[21] In an article subtitled "Parish Prepares for Interurbia," the *Jefferson Parish Yearly Review* announced in December 1968 that Congressman Hale Boggs had won federal approval for the Outer Belt. The term "interurbia," not often used, perfectly describes the modern West Bank that was coming into form: the region had spots that were genuinely urban, surrounded by suburbia, yet it still had spots that were subrural, and all three land covers meshed together as interurbia.[22]

As contractors built I-10 and authorities pursued the $200 million needed for the Outer Belt, traffic increasingly overwhelmed the 1958 Mississippi River Bridge. Booming suburbanization had driven daily crossings to thirty-five thousand vehicles, which rocketed to fifty-two thousand per day when tolls were lifted in May 1964, in fulfillment of a campaign promise by Gov. John McKeithen. Funds would instead come from "a pledge of annual State stipends as security and support for the revenue bonds."[23] By the late 1960s, daily usage began exceeding the design capacity of sixty to sixty-five thousand per day, making commuters "fight a daily 'battle of the bridge.'"[24] It would only increase as the West Bank's total population swelled from under one hundred thousand in 1960 to over one hundred seventy thousand in 1970, and as oil and gas investment grew throughout the coastal region.[25]

The Mississippi River Bridge Authority responded by broaching a third bridge proposal, meaning that greater New Orleans might go from zero to five bridges within a single generation. The Authority wanted this latest span in uptown New Orleans, running from South Claiborne Avenue down Napoleon and crossing onto Barataria Boulevard—a modification of the old Hero-Hackett route, realigned to link with the Dixie Freeway and give the Outer Belt something of a figure-8 configuration.[26]

The extravagant plan reflected the zeitgeist of the mid-1960s. A robust national economy brought incomes up and unemployment down, Americans were pulling ahead in the space race, and gasoline demand was insatiable. While turmoil was brewing over the growing military engagement of the United States in Viet Nam, optimism generally prevailed. The West Bank had a stake in each of these ambits—NASA Michoud engineers buying homes, oil and gas suppliers establishing service bases, military contractors at Todd and Avondale shipyards, airmen at Belle Chasse—and talk of new beltways and bridges all made perfect sense. And for the first time in a century, African Americans, in the dispersed concentrations where they lived, could guardedly share in a sense of optimism.

15

Geographies of Ethnicity, Race, and Class

West Bank census maps exhibit an apparent crazy-quilt of racial and ethnic settlements. Groups with very different lived experiences may be found residing on high or low ground, near or far from industry, more heterogeneously or homogenously, with seemingly little regularity.

Closer inspection, however, reveals prevailing tendencies and replicating explanations with deep historical roots. People, after all, do not randomly or evenly spread themselves across the landscape, particularly on this delta and in this society, where habitability and power are unevenly distributed. Humans gravitate to spaces that enable them to survive and thrive, and avoid those of higher risk or scant resources; empowered groups tend to monopolize the former, and relegate others to the latter. In Louisiana, power meant race, and racial and ethnic geographies have inscribed themselves across the West Bank since its earliest occupancy.

Prehistorically, numerous *petites nations* (small tribes) of two language groups (Muskogean and Chitimachan) thrived in two cultural economies (ridge-top maize farming and coastal shellfishing) in the vicinity of the West Bank, their identities, alliances, and settlements in constant flux. With European colonization, Francophones from French Canada, the French Caribbean, and France proper came to live and work at a depot and plantation at today's Algiers Point, along with enslaved peoples from fifteen different ethnic groups from the Senegambia region, Ouidah on the Bight of Benin, and Cabinda in the Congo. By the

1720s, German-speakers settled at the nearby Côte des Allemands; by the 1760s, Acadian refugees arrived at the Côte des Acadiens; and by the 1780s, Spanish immigrants from Granada, Malaga, and the Canary Islands settled regionally. Native peoples, their numbers diminished by conflict and disease, found themselves displaced to the fringes or subjugated into assimilation, but nonetheless able to trade with the colonials and persevere.

These varied groups interacted and often intermarried with members of French and Spanish charter groups, and their offspring "creolized" as they came of age locally, becoming less like their forebears born elsewhere and more like their locally born peers. West Bank populations morphed into a Creole society, mostly French in tongue and Catholic in faith, and during the 1700s, its ethnic geography was spatially intermixed—a French Creole family on one plantation, a Spanish don or Parisian colonial on the next—while its racial geography was spatially stratified within each plantation. The white planter family and staff lived in larger abodes by the river; the black enslaved families in rows of humble cabins to the side or rear. Some free people of color lived thereamong, a few major landowners and slaveholders themselves.

During the early 1800s, as the West Bank landscape transformed from commodity plantations and timber-cutting to a mixed village-industry-farm-plantation scene, its settlement geographies became attenuated derivatives of those across the river. "Derivative" because West Bank transplants came from East Bank source regions, and "attenuated" because the newcomers found on the West Bank different geographical circumstances: lots more space, far fewer people, cheaper real estate, market-gardening opportunities, skilled-labor jobs, and transportation access shaped by the point-to-point nature of ferry routes.

Of these cross-bank contrasts, the most important was space, of which the East Bank had little and the West Bank had lots. Low population density was not simply a facet of West Bank life; it was a driver. It kept housing affordable, land use mixed, lifestyles bucolic, air and water cleaner, and lives more salubrious. "The air over at Algiers today was sweet and fresh," wrote diarist Thomas K. Wharton (1855) in what would have been a common assessment, "[s]o different from the gaseous oppression of the city."[1] Yellow fever and other viral diseases did occur on the West Bank, but were less frequent and less deadly than those across the river. This was because the main vector, the *Aedes aegypti* mosquito, bred better in the hard urban environments of the East Bank, where there were lots of tiny water pockets, and because fewer people and more green space on the West Bank helped curtail contagion. Low density also made residents more dependent on their local (West Bank) community for basic needs, and more reliant on transportation (to the East Bank) for special needs. You could buy bread, milk, rope, and nails down the block in Algiers or Gretna, but if you needed a bank loan or a Mallard bed, you probably needed to ferry to New Orleans.

Most significantly, low population density affected ethnic, racial, and class settlement patterns, in ways that differed from New Orleans across the river. To answer the question of who settled where, it helps to address who did *not* settle on the West Bank.

The aristocracy did not. Bourbons and nabobs had little interest in the rustic and provincial West Bank unless they owned land or investments there. They preferred the sophisticated world port that was New Orleans; in its halls of power they wielded their clout, and in its tony precincts they displayed their wealth. (To be sure, the occasional patrician did move to the West Bank, such as John McDonogh. But he did so specifically to get *away* from the aristocracy.) There has never been a West Bank equivalent of the Garden District.

Likewise, white-collar professionals—financiers, bankers, factors, agents, merchants, lawyers, underwriters—needed access to the commercial core. Because Anglo-Americans tended to dominate these professions, their families predominated on the East Bank and had little reason to live in the West Bank's Francophone villages. Thus as New Orleans increasingly anglicized and Americanized in the mid-1800s, the West Bank retained its French-speaking Creole society—an early form of the region's capacity to preserve culture. Whereas the French language declined in the French Quarter in the early 1900s, it remained common in Westwego into the 1950s.

Wealthy urban families were more likely to use their slaves as domestics, so their paucity across the river meant that urban slavery (as opposed to field slavery) was uncommon on the West Bank. Urban slave quarters—those distinctive slant-roofed dependencies appended to townhouses and cottages throughout the older neighborhoods of New Orleans—were all but unknown on the West Bank. Slaveholding families who did live in West Bank villages usually had enough space on their farm-sized lots to house their slaves in outlying cabins, rather than in attached quarters.

So who *did* move to the West Bank? Mostly it was the white working- and middle-class cohort composed of jack-of-all-trades laborers, merchants, and skilled craftsmen: French Creoles; German, Irish, Italian, Spanish, and Slavic immigrants; American rivermen; peoples of the Mediterranean and Caribbean basins; an assortment of mariners and seamen with nautical skills; plus neighbors from the German and Acadian Coasts or south into the Barataria. A significant number of *gens de couleur libres* (free people of color), particularly those with ship-related trades, also settled on the West Bank, or had gained their freedom there, though the bulk of this nine-thousand-strong caste remained in the lower faubourgs of New Orleans. Jewish families and institutions were rare on the West Bank, and remain so today.

West Bankers in this era lived in door-to-door ethnic heterogeneity. City directories and census schedules for Algiers and Gretna show French-surname heads of household next to Germans or Anglos, next to three more French, a Spaniard, and an Irishman. To be sure, kin and kith would often live adjacently, forming micro-enclaves of one ethnicity or another; for example, Morgan Street in Algiers Point in the 1890s had a two-story tenement building where Italian immigrants lived in crowded conditions. A larger ethnic enclave was Mechanickham-Gretna, where ferries brought plenty of German "mechanicks" (craftsmen) families from the Lafayette riverfront. Decades later, the 1893 Chênière Caminada hurricane sent a wave of Acadian refugees up the Company Canal to the West Bank. But even here, heterogeneity prevailed, and one could typically find a Podesta and an O'Brien living next to an Abadie, Kramer, Williams, Baranich, Hernandez, or Landry.

The great unifier was class, regardless of ethnicity. The great divider was race, regardless of class.

People of African ancestry first formed a West Bank enclave, if it may be called that, at the Company Plantation behind the present-day Algiers Courthouse. Wrote the compound's architect Le Page du Pratz:

> The camp for the negroes [comprised] a square in the center, and of three wide streets where I laid out their cabins, between which I left an adequate space [for] strong palisades. I left only one gate [outside of which] I had two cabins built, one of which was for the white commander, and the other for . . . medical supplies and [the] young negro who . . . I learned several years afterwards [became] one of the good surgeons.

The compound had 32 cabins with vertical timber walls and tree-bark roofs, where lived a revolving cohort of up to 154 enslaved people, the largest concentration of African people in early Louisiana.[2] For the next century, the geography of the West Bank's black population mostly took the form of the back-of-the-big-house morphology of plantation life. Subjugation, control, and surveillance were designed into the layout, with cabins arranged for the gaze of the master and the drive of the overseer.

When the daily agony of bondage proved too much, some slaves created their own geography, by escaping to the wetlands behind the plantations. They were known as maroons, from the Spanish *cimarrón,* meaning the ruddy brown color associated with feral cattle; the term implied that which had been domesticated but had gone wild. The West Bank's Barataria region was ideal for maroonage, with its bayous, bays, ridges, middens, wild foods, and potential Indian allies, and while little is known of the maroons who traversed there, much is recorded of the white fight against them. The Spanish administration responded with everything from amnesty to armed patrols to harsh punishment. At one point the colonial government funded the anti-maroonage efforts with a half-*real*-per-slave tax, and appointed West Bank planter Don Francisco Bouligny to lead a guerrilla war against the runaways, chiefly the charismatic Jean (Juan) St. Malo and his band. Racial violence and the threat of insurrection made maroonage a top Spanish priority in the 1780s, and it continued under the American regime, when slave smugglers prowled the same marshes as the beleaguered fugitives.[3]

It is somewhat ironic that the Spanish would crack down mercilessly on slaves escaping to freedom, because it was also the Spanish who, through their *coartación* and manumission policies, enabled some slaves to buy or be granted freedom. These policies gave rise to Louisiana's free people of color population, which increased sixteenfold during the Spanish colonial era. A small number would settle on the West Bank, and against all odds, a few became planters and slaveholders themselves.

The first free black settlement on the West Bank formed probably in the 1820s in John McDonogh's subdivision. According to an analysis of conveyance books by Algiers historian Kevin Herridge, McDonogh sold property to at least eight free women of color and ten free men of color between 1827 and 1836, earlier records having been lost.[4] The famed philanthropist would later liberate many of his own slaves, who joined their free brethren and grew the community. Nicknamed "Free Town" or "Freetown" by 1841 (when the term appeared in a *Picayune* advertisement), this part of upper Algiers, though majority white, would become home to the largest concentration of free blacks on the West Bank.[5] According to a census analysis by Algiers Historical Society member

Tom Yalets, 120 free people of color lived in Freetown in 1850, making up nearly one-third its population; the remainder were born in Germany, France, Louisiana, Ireland, and America, in descending order. Of the free blacks, most were Louisiana-born; three were born in Ste. Domingue and two in Africa, the latter among the last living connections of African American Algerines to the African continent.[6] It was probably in Freetown where writer Dominique Rouquette described in 1850 how "the negroes and mulattoes of New Orleans" gathered in Algiers "almost every Sunday [to] have a game of raquettes [a lacrosse-like sport of Choctaw origin] of which they are passionately fond."[7]

Freetown's elevated, riverfronting topography speaks to the influence of low population density on the West Bank's human geography. On the East Bank, populations were large and land scarce, and disenfranchised people got pushed to the "back of town." On the West Bank, people were few and land abundant, so there was enough high ground for everyone, even the disenfranchised. The portion of the original subdivision of McDonoghville within Orleans Parish, now known by the official neighborhood name "McDonogh," remains an African American neighborhood today, and it is as topographically elevated as anywhere on the West Bank.

After the Union seizure of New Orleans in 1862, enslaved people, though still technically in bondage, read the tea leaves of history and gradually began self-emancipating. In May 1864, the biracial state legislature officially abolished slavery in Louisiana, and freedmen held an Emancipation Jubilee in June. "Slavery's chain is bound to break, and Massa and I must part," they sang at Congo Square, "I'll never feel your lash again, for freedom's got the start!"[8]

But what also started was utter uncertainty, and right behind it, the pressing exigencies of basic human needs. How to survive? Former slaves and former masters recognized their economic interdependency: planters had all the land but lacked labor, whereas the freedmen could do the labor but lacked the land. Black families worked out uneasy truces with planters and became paid field hands, dwelling as tenants in hovels nearly identical to slave cabins. In this manner, the antecedent geography of West Bank plantation slavery implanted the future geography of at least four African American neighborhoods.

One such neighborhood arose from the old slave quarters along the lower boundary of Camille Zeringue's Seven Oaks Plantation at the base of Nine Mile Point. In 1865 freedmen here established a church in the dwelling of Martin Tilton. As the railroad arrived in 1871 and the cannery industry formed along the

Company Canal, giving rise to today's Westwego, the congregation grew and in 1893 purchased a parcel on Sala Avenue from Spanish developer Pablo Sala. The new church, erected in 1898, gained the name True Vine Baptist Church, and members would work in the Westwego railyards, riverfront industries, or Salaville's seafood processing plants.[9] Other African Americans moved nearby for the social and economic opportunities, and the community thrived into the 1900s.

Both the enclave and the church made an appearance in novelist R. Emmet Kennedy's 1929 book *Red Bean Row*. Following in Lafcadio Hearn's literary tradition of "local color" and inspired by his friend and fellow writer Edward Laroque Tinker, the Gretna-born Irish-American Kennedy wrote of the West Bank's poor black communities, having previously written *Gritney People* in 1927. Though works of fiction and told from a white outsider perspective, Kennedy's books did draw on actual places and people, including True Vine Baptist Church and Red Bean Row, the nickname for the black fishing families along Westwego's Company Canal.[10]

The True Vine Baptist Church, where generations of Zeringue slave descendants worshipped, endures today in historic Salaville, proud of its status as the oldest church in Westwego.[11] Congregant Mrs. Doris Hooper Pitts, interviewed on the church's 150th anniversary in 2015, is living testament to the African American experience in this part of the West Bank. "She was born on Norton Street in Westwego in 1920," reported the *Times-Picayune*, "and christened at True Vine Baptist Church." Mrs. Pitts remembered how a "pot belly stove [kept] the area warm [and] children . . . sat on the floor around the altar, [later] played games, sack races and [had] plenty of food." This being Cannery Row, Mrs. Pitts worked at three Westwego seafood processors; hers being the World War II generation, she served in the Office of Strategic Services in Washington, DC; being intellectually ambitious, Mrs. Pitts earned a master's degree in library science and became "the first certified African-American public librarian in Jefferson Parish."[12] Although her roots and her Sundays are in Westwego, Mrs. Pitts actually came of age in Marrero, home to the largest predominantly black neighborhood in West Jefferson.

Marrero's black population, like those of McDonoghville and Westwego, also traces its origins to antebellum times. Its progenitors were the twelve hundred people formerly enslaved by Laurent Millaudon and Robert R. Barrow on their adjoining plantations. After the war, brothers Oliver and Frank Ames bought the land and hired the freedmen for sugarcane cultivation, or leased small truck farms to them. The hamlet of black agriculturists became part of Amesville, or Ames Farms, which was later renamed for its sheriff Louis Herman Marrero.

In 1921 a black woman named Corrine Degree Walker, a widow and mother of twelve, purchased land along Marrero's principle artery; her children did the same, and kin and friends moved adjacently. A community formed, named Walkertown, and its main thoroughfare, Walkertown Road, became Ames Boulevard.[13] Segregated schools and a library were later established nearby, which attracted more African Americans. Marrero and parts of adjacent Harvey would become the most expansive predominately black neighborhood in the West Bank.

Gretna's black population partially derives from the McDonogh slaves and the free people of color of the Freetown section of McDonoghville. An 1841 advertisement posted by the owner of the US Coffee-House Ball Room illustrates how the three communities tended to fuse their identities, regardless of racial divisions (emphasis added): "Mrs. P. J. Auth respectfully informs her friends *of Algiers and Free Town of Gretna*, that she will give a public ball . . . at her house *in Algiers*.[14] Thirty years later, an 1871 article in the *New Orleans Republican* provided insight into the postbellum status of the Freetown/Gretna area:

> Freetown is a growing village on the right bank of the river, about a quarter of a mile above the [parish] line. . . . [It was] settled more than two generations ago, principally by free people of color, hence its name. Some of these people possessed considerable means, as may be judged from the style of many of the older houses, which exhibit considerable architectural taste and, surrounded by fruit trees and shrubbery, are desirable residences. . . .
>
> Of late years, however, the character of the population has changed and Freetown is now, to a great extent, peopled by Germans, who live by fishing, gathering moss in the woods and catching drift wood. . . .
>
> For many years the people of Freetown had no other means of education for their children than to send them to the school in Gretna, about two and a half miles distant. . . . But last year [1870], a public school was organized in [Free]town. . . .[15]

Other small black enclaves formed adjacently, behind the railroad tracks among farms and fields. In his 1927 novel *Gritny People*, R. Emmet Kennedy wrote in dialect about black life in East Green, "far across the pasture . . . away on the other side of the town."[16] East Green was an actual place in Gretna (or "Gritny," as black folks were said to say). There was also West Green and Johns Town.[17] East Green happened to be the home of the Big Easy Negro dance hall, a hopping venue that burned down in August 1911 but would live on in the memories of pioneering jazzmen.[18] Pops Foster, born on a plantation in 1892 and interviewed in 1967, recalled performing around 1908 "over in Gretna [at] the Big Easy Hall and the Drag Nasty Hall (it's still in Gretna)."[19] The term "Big Easy" returned into the parlance thanks to writers in the 1970s and the 1987 movie, and has since become the favored nickname for New Orleans, surpassing "Crescent City" and "The City That Care Forgot." But the original coinage came from black Gretna on the West Bank.

Another historical black settlement coalesced in the Cutoff area in lower Algiers, so named for its shortcut across the English Turn promontory to get to the Belle Chasse area. Here, sugarcane plantations thrived well into the 1900s, among them the Devron, Delacroix, Orleans, and particularly the Stanton operation, all using black labor. By 1918, about 500 African Americans lived in and around Cutoff, and while they had two churches, the nearest public education for the 103 local children, the Lawton School, sat three miles away. A philanthropically funded "Rosenwald school" opened to educate the black children of Cutoff. As in Marrero and elsewhere, this helped strengthen the spatial coherence of the settlement. The institution lives on today as the Rosenwald Middle School and Collegiate Academies.

While slavery and emancipation laid the groundwork for the black residential geography of the early-1900s West Bank, it was *de jure* and *de facto* racism as well as the geography of poverty that drove the patterns to today. After Reconstruction, West Bank communities, like the rest of the region, had been strictly segregated in their public facilities. Everything from schools to waiting rooms were created in racial redundancy, always separate, never equal. So were public spaces in the private domain, including lunch rooms and theaters, and private companies in the public service—such as the Algiers Public Service Company, which assumed ferry operations in 1925 and promptly installed signs reading "'For Ladies' and 'For Gentlemen' for whites, and 'For Negro Women' and 'For Negro Men' for Colored patrons."[20] Even McDonogh Cemetery, where the famed philanthropist had been entombed alongside his slaves, and where caretaker and former McDonogh slave Edward Thornton had continued the tradition of integrated burials, came under a segregation order by New Orleans Mayor

Shakespeare in 1891. By the 1930s, "the negroes all [lay] at the southern end the cemetery," and by the 1950s, as if to ensure no interracial mingling among the living or the dead, "a fence separating the two sections" had been added.[21]

Segregation in residency figured somewhat differently. The aforementioned historical enclaves were not the products of law; rather, they emerged organically from a racially divided and unequal society, and they were not spatially absolute. "Segregation always existed," said Martha B. Mallory, an African American woman born in 1930 and interviewed in 2000, "but most of the whites and blacks got along. We lived side by side, we were in and out of each other's houses, and the children played together."[22] Some blocks in Algiers were downright integrated, with white and black living door-to-door like in the faubourgs across the river. In 1939, for example, the thirty-four riverfront blocks between Slidell and De Armas streets had a mean block-level racial composition of 57 percent white and 43 percent black.[23] Even in the more prosperous, mostly white, blocks across Opelousas Avenue, there were no legally codified white-only areas, though it certainly felt that way to blacks. Resident Lillian Alveris Williams, born in 1912 and interviewed in 2000, recalled "that African Americans could not cross Opelousas Street unless they were working as domestics in the area"—"unwritten rules," the interviewer added, that made certain spaces "off-limits to African Americans, not by law, but by intimidation."[24]

One reason for the absence of *de jure* neighborhood segregation was that white supremacy was so powerfully emblazoned into the social order that most white families would not have felt their status threatened by having black neighbors, and none of their white peers would have confused that spatial proximity with social equality. This began to change as racist sentiment got codified in Jim Crow laws, as real estate became a profession, as decisions to create new subdivisions moved from aging planters to corporate developers, and as swamp drainage opened up new spaces for codified racial animus to take root in housing patterns. Here would be created new high-value, auto-friendly subdivisions that, in the mind of the white power structure, could well be "threatened" by black residency. Keeping them white, and white only, would keep them valuable.

But how? In 1924 the City of New Orleans passed a racial zoning ordinance, whereby, in accordance with a recent state law, neighborhoods would be legally designated for white or black. Jefferson Parish contemplated the same in 1926, when whites of the Seventh Ward filed a request to District Attorney J. E. Fleury "for zoning of white and colored residents."[25] But government-led racial zoning was of dubious constitutionality, even by 1920s standards, and the United States Supreme Court in 1927 ruled against New Orleans's racial zoning ordinance in *Harmon v. Tyler.*

Not to be outdone, white real estate operators circumvented the legal ruling by used housing deeds and covenants to commit white buyers not to sell or rent to nonwhite families.[26] The tactic had been around for a while. When, for example, the Gentilly Terrace Company in 1909 subdivided East Bank land to become "Little California," complete with terraced gardens and California bungalows, it assured builders and buyers, in a section subtitled "THE COLOR LINE," that "each purchaser binds himself and his heirs and assigns to never lease or sell to a negro and negroes . . . nor can a Chinaman build a laundry shack on the corner next door to your home."[27] State courts viewed such building restrictions as private contractual matters not in the purview of courts. The real estate sector eagerly stewarded the ministerial end of this sort of paperwork racism, because they knew what kept real estate valuable was white money. Two agents, J. A. and W. G. Moran, explained to the *Times-Picayune* in 1927, shortly after *Harmon v. Tyler,* how things would work:

> Individuals and associations who perform any of the functions incidental to ownership [would] pledge not to participate in any transaction in which either white or colored would attempt to obtain residence in any section reserved for the opposite race. The real estate man would decline to sell or lease, the lawyer to examine title, the notary to pass the act, the insurance man to protect, the architect to design or remodel, and the homesteads to grant loans, where any such invasion would be intended. Co-operation along those lines would be more effective than formal law. . . . The outcome would guarantee that both races in New Orleans would continue to reside here in peace and tranquility.[28]

The "sections" mentioned above were not official zones that might appear in a government ordinance, but rather internal decisions of private developers to draw lines on their plats reserving for whites or blacks. For example, the 1936 plat of the Belt City subdivision, which would become Bridge City, depicted a "restricted section for colored."[29] Afterwards, homebuyer contracts would do the trick of controlling who lived where.

That courts had deemed discriminatory deeds as private matters, and therefore constitutionally acceptable, did not stop local government from protesting publically when one was violated. In 1937, it came to the attention of the Jefferson Parish police jury that developer Stafford, Derbes, and Roy, Inc., which had sold lots in Suburban Villa "to numerous persons with the understanding that said subdivision would be a strictly white residential section [but] are presently selling lots . . . to the negro or African race in violation of its agreement with the original purchasers. . . . The continuation of such acts will promote ill-feeling, hatred and contempt."[30] The police jury officially condemned the sales as being "in bad faith," mandated their cancellation, and forewarned any continuation of the practice. Passed 14 to 0, the resolution signaled clearly to both developers and buyers that "white only" meant *white only.*

Real estate players also adopted a tactic that would later be described as "redlining," in which areas thought to be fiscal risks were marked on maps. Residents therein would be handled differently in the home loan or services marketplace, sometimes to the point of denial of credit or insurance, higher interest rates or premiums, or other impediments to successful homeownership. Among the market players who used this tactic was the United States government, which, during the Depression, got into the business of being a mortgage lender and a landlord to struggling Americans. In 1939, the Home Owners Loan Corporation (HOLC), a New Deal agency established in 1933 to refinance troubled home mortgages to avoid foreclosure, teamed with local real estate experts to assess the "residential security" of greater New Orleans, including the West Bank. Using a number of criteria, ranging from "Building Type and Size" and "Predicted Price Trend" to "Foreign Families %" and "Negro %," the mapmakers drew green lines around those areas deemed the "Best" risks, blue for "Still Desirable," yellow for "Definitely Declining," and red for "Hazardous." Not all redlined neighborhoods were black, but most black neighborhoods were redlined. So too were many mixed or mostly white downmarket districts, especially if they abutted industry, wharves, canals, or railroads.

That did not bode well for the West Bank, which was ridden with industry, wharves, canals, and railroads. The HOLC mappers deemed fully 95 percent of its nineteen separate population centers, from Westwego down nearly to Cutoff, as being Definitely Declining or Hazardous. Most in the former category were predominantly white; most in the latter were predominantly black. Only one tiny area in Algiers—along Ptolemy Street and Bodenger Boulevard, described as "Good class of executives-business and professional men" and with zero foreign or black families—warranted a Still Desirable rating, and not a single spot anywhere on the West Bank earned a green Best.[31]

As for the Hazardous areas, the HOLC described the "100% Negro" area near the US Immigration Station in Algiers as comprising "low class Negro laborers [in] very cheap properties . . . mostly shacks [in] a very dilapidated appearance." The "50% Negro" blocks along the Algiers Yards got a Hazardous rating for a litany of nuisances: "open drainage ditch on Whitney Ave . . . railroad tracks . . . streets unpaved . . . pumping station . . . Southern Pacific shops. . . . ." An area by the Harvey Canal ("single and double cottages . . . fronting on the main highway being occupied by white people and fairly well maintained, while those not on the highway are occupied by negroes and . . . very dilapidated") got a blanket "Hazardous" rating. So too did the Cajun folks on Cannery Row along Westwego's Company Canal—"predominately lower class fishermen, factory workers, wage hands"—recorded as 95 percent white and entirely Hazardous.[32]

While it is unclear how these maps affected West Bank housing, it cannot be assumed that redlined areas received no loans. Research by historian Amy Hillier has shown that HOLC-redlined areas in Philadelphia were not categorically excluded from lending; some Hazardous areas actually received more loans than better-ranked areas, though they were typically charged higher interest rates.[33] More recent research by Todd Michney and LaDale Winling has shown that these maps were made *after* HOLC's loaning phase, when the agency focused on selling off its housing inventory, and that during the loaning phase, the HOLC "lent on black-owned properties to a much greater extent than previously understood," and that African Americans "received HOLC assistance in rough proportion to their ownership rates in most locales."[34] Hillier's research also showed that lenders inside and outside of government had already been steering clear of maligned areas prior to the making of the maps, and that the maps had not been widely distributed. So while the HOLC maps should not be viewed as the "smoking gun" of government redlining, nor as the premier agent of urban decay, the practice of preemptively stigmatizing needy areas, as illustrated in those maps, could and did set targeted neighborhoods on a path of divestment and decline, by hardening preexisting patterns of racial isolation and impoverishment. Most of the West Bank areas deemed Hazardous on the 1939 maps remain socially and economically troubled today.

Regardless of redlining, the low land values for which indigents had to settle, and to which industry also tended to gravitate, often put the poor, mostly black, next door to environmentally beleaguered areas. This partially explains why the historic Algiers/Freetown black population spread up along the vast Southern Pacific railyards, and why the old Marrero and Harvey black communities abutted the flanks of the Harvey Canal. There was another reason: industry didn't just pollute; it also created jobs. The longshoremen employed at the juncture of the Morgan (Southern Pacific) ship docks and the SP Yards "were both black and white. Four hundred men worked thirty-six hours to unload and reload each forty-seven-hundred-ton ship."[35] This meant round-the-clock work, which encouraged workers to live near their workplace, where they also found cheap housing. What resulted were racially mixed blocks of working-class neighbors living adjacent to industry. In 1939, for example, the twenty-seven blocks on either side of the SP Yards averaged 40 percent black, with those closer to the river more white and those farther back more black.[36]

Then came the modern post-drainage subdivisions with their racialized contracting language, and fields and farms became all-white neighborhoods positioned in a seemingly erratic pattern that was anything but. When the white Aurora subdivision of Algiers was first laid out in 1940 and expanded in the 1950s, its street grid neared but did not traverse the predominantly black blocks of Cutoff, thus forming one of the West Bank's many racial dividing lines. This was the same era in which the Algiers Canal was dug (opened in 1956), which had the effect of severing Cutoff from the lower coast and directing future African American residential expansion southwardly along the canal.[37]

Likewise, in West Jefferson, two varieties of segregated neighborhoods—market-rate subdivisions racialized through private deed covenants, and subsidized public developments racialized by local housing authorities—were fitted among the preexisting patchwork of older settlements. Parish advocates spoke matter-of-factly of the new 97-unit "Garden Plaza All Colored Subdivision on Silver Lily Lane in Marrero," and of "District No. 3's new white subdivisions—the Shady Moss Homes on Richland Drive in Marrero" and "the housing projects of Manor Heights on Belle Terre Road with 80 new homes under construction . . . all white." In Westwego: "There is also the $1,570,000 hundred unit Low Rent Housing Project—divided into two sites, one with 78 dwellings for white occupancy and the other with 22 for colored [to be] completed late in 1962."

Pressure had been mounting on Jim Crow since World War II, and after the Supreme Court ruled against separate-but-equal in 1954, black citizens increasingly pressed for civil rights. The movement gained momentum. Television coverage of subsequent protests brought worldwide attention to brutal white resistance, putting segregationist officials on the defensive. One of their responses was to try to save "separate" by making concessions on "equal." Into the late 1960s, the West Bank saw a cynical new emphasis on public investment in black facilities, even as the real goal was to keep blacks separate. The *Jefferson Parish Year Review,* mouthpiece of parish government and commerce, mentioned "Negroes" or "colored" only in passing in its 1930s and 1940s editions, mostly in patronizing historical allusions. But from 1952 to 1967, articles cheerfully heralded new investments in black spaces, while not-so-subtly doubling down on segregation. To wit:

- " . . . new buildings of McDonoghville High School, for colored . . . ."

- "QUITE modern is the addition to the high school for colored, at Gretna . . . ."

- " . . . the newly constructed Elm Grove School for Colored Children in Harvey. . . . ."

- " . . . the recently completed Lincoln Memorial School at Marrero, another of our gilt edged investments in the future of our colored youth. . . . ."

- " . . . the new Lincoln Consolidated High and Elementary School at Marrero for colored children—a well designed, well lighted, efficient temple of education."

- "Construction of the new Negro Park at the end of Huey P. Long A, [with] a ball park, wading pool and other facilities like the white park area. . . . Swimming pools for both the white and colored parks will be provided [soon]."

- "A new colored Elementary School is being erected off Ames Boulevard."

- " . . . construction was authorized . . . for stadiums at the Lincoln and Bunche Negro Schools."

- "Opening day at the new [white] swimming pool in Mel Ott Park in Gretna . . . A pool for Negroes also was opened on June 1 [1962] at Gretna Park."

- "Gretna's four outdoor Recreation Centers—Mel Ott Park, McDonoghville Park and Belle View Park for whites and Gretna Park for its colored youth—continue to grow in popularity."

- "Of the Negro schools . . . on the West Bank, Elm Grove Elementary will receive 6 new classrooms, Fourth Ward Elementary 12, Frederick Douglass 4 and McDonogh #27 Elementary 4 new classrooms."

- ". . . new football field and stadium [for] the Negro Lincoln High School in Marrero."

- ". . . two new swimming pools—the one at Mel Ott Park accommodating 900 white swimmers and the one at Gretna Park accommodating 300 Negro swimmers. . . . Special days will be reserved at each pool for the use of handicapped and retarded children."[38]

The last explicitly segregationist pronouncement in the *Jefferson Parish Yearly Review* came in its 1967 edition, in which the editors, seemingly oblivious to the social changes ongoing around them, lauded the "two additional playgrounds . . . added to the city's recreation facilities, one in McDonoughville section of Gretna for colored children and one on Lafayette for white children."

By this time, however, the Civil Rights Act of 1964 and the Voting Rights Act of 1965 forced change upon Southern society. Integration ensued in many spaces, such as lunch counters and public facilities. But most neighborhoods, and by extension schools, merely shifted from *de jure* to *de facto* segregation, in a manner that intertwined with spatial separations by class. Most whites were wealthier than most blacks, some far wealthier, and many were able to move into subdivisions in which few blacks could afford to live. In the decades following the civil rights movement, the West Bank's former white working-class neighborhoods would become remarkably diverse racially and ethnically; its new gated and other expensive subdivisions would become mostly white and middle- to upper-class; and its former black neighborhoods would remain mostly black and mostly poor, a chief example of which was the Fischer Projects.

The Fischer Housing Development, started in 1964 and opened in 1966, occupied an almost encyclopedic example of an "urban interstice," a space betwixt and amongst, isolated and marginalized, neither here nor there. Cusped within the curving Mississippi River Bridge ramps and toll plaza, it bordered the old Southern Pacific tracks, lay behind the Donner Drainage Canal, sat between Algiers and Gretna along the parish line, near the former backswamp of Mc-Donoghville, and behind its cemetery. Yet just a few decades earlier, it was sunny and green, part of the Oakdale Tract subdivided in 1932 into a grid of "small farm homes." Oakdale had been designed for "the city worker to cut living expenses by raising . . . vegetables, fruit, berries or chickens, pigs and a cow"[39]—a viable idea during the Depression, and perfect for the subrural West Bank, long home to truck farms. Dozens of farming homesteads of two to three acres operated in Oakdale into the 1950s, on the fringes of a major American metropolis.

The bridge that unified that metropolis killed the Oakdale farming community. Some homesteads were expropriated for the toll plaza; others would make way for Terrytown. Those that found themselves enveloped by ramps and traffic congestion ended up cheap, inconvenient, unpleasant, and unwanted—the perfect place for public housing.

After the Housing Authority of New Orleans (HANO) acquired the land, the architectural firms Mathes-Bergman and August Perez and Associates adapted their Internationalist designs used for the Calliope and Guste projects on the East Bank, to the 48-acre Algiers site.[40] Towering over the complex was a thirteen-story Modernist apartment with 168 units for elderly tenants, the tallest building in the vicinity. Surrounding it were fourteen long three-story structures with galleries set upon a grassy quad, their sections slightly zigzagged and connected by breezeways. Named for a former HANO director, the William J. Fischer Public Housing Development had 1,002 subsidized rental units, two schools, a library, a health center, and other facilities. Though it was conceived in the last days of Jim Crow and slated for black residency, Fischer opened after the Civil Rights Act, and had no explicit racial restrictions. Nevertheless, nearly all residents would be African American.

Only a year after it opened, HANO began shifting its policy toward "scattered site public housing," as opposed to the original super-block design strategy for American public housing. Concentrating poverty in big isolated "projects" was proving problematic; better to weave subsidized housing into the urban fabric such that the poor might live amongst other classes, as they often did historically. Scattered-site housing could be achieved through arrangements made with private landlords and nonprofit organizations paid through floating vouchers allowed under the eighth section of the Housing Act of 1937, which would become known as "Section 8 housing." There were also so-called "turnkey" housing programs, in which rental payments could be applied toward home ownership at off-project sites, which not only dispersed poverty but gave poor families financial equity and a stake in the neighborhood. In the late 1960s, HANO began dispersing some residents of the projects into adjacent neighborhoods, including

"56 housing units . . . to be located 1 ½ miles west of the Fischer Housing Project in Algiers."[41]

Fischer would be the last of the old-style projects to be built, and to many West Bankers, it was none too soon. While it provided affordable living to hundreds of families, Fischer also became a locus of crime and racially tinged police tensions. The public began to associate "public housing" with violence and mayhem. As early as 1969, headlines would strike a soon-to-be-familiar refrain: "Algiers Residents Oppose Public Housing Proposals."[42] The nadir came a decade later, when New Orleans Police Department Officer Greg Neupert was killed at Fischer, and subsequent police action led to the shooting deaths of three black suspects. Fischer residents saw the response as brutality, to which police answered that the suspects had fired first.[43] To many West Bankers, "Fischer" had become a stigmatized word, and its shabby, Stalinesque architecture a cause for shuddering as they drove off the bridge.

Only three decades after the farms and gardens of Oakdale, Fischer had become West Bank's version of a new socio-spatial euphemism in American English: the "inner city." It wasn't really the inner city, of course. Fischer was a cross-river outlier to the divestment and decline going on in the true inner city, on the East Bank, and as such, most West Bankers could literally and figuratively *drive around it*—avoid it, ignore it, view it as a sacrifice zone, and hope it didn't spread.

16

Connecting the Crescent City

Commuters sped past Fischer and its problems in ever-growing numbers, forcing planners to readdress traffic congestion barely fifteen years after they thought they had resolved it. The problem was not simply more motorists clogging the bridge; in 1974, only 7.7 percent of West Bankers commuted daily to downtown New Orleans. The new congestion came from local traffic: fully 59 percent of those who now lived on the West Bank also worked there. This drove vehicular movement in all directions—upriver, downriver, toward the river, away from the river—which caused lengthy waits at intersections along the grade-level West Bank Expressway. "Cross expressway traffic patterns are [seeing] heavy congestion at all major intersections," state planners found, and "pedestrian movement is hazardous."

The proposed solution: raise the expressway so that "both foot and vehicular traffic will be able to cross the corridor," thus "encourage[ing] and strengthen[ing] neighborhood linkages among areas now separated by the expressway."[1] As the *Times-Picayune* put it, "Since a single road cannot be both a restricted-access expressway and an unlimited-access city street, the solution has been to leave the local traffic on the ground and elevate the through traffic."[2]

A consensus formed in separate studies in 1970 and 1972, the latter "recommend[ing] upgrading of the expressway to freeway standards from the Harvey Canal Tunnel to the Greater New Orleans Bridge as soon as possible." That same year, the West Bank Council of the New Orleans Chamber of Commerce and the Jefferson Parish Council formally endorsed the concept. In 1973 the Louisiana Department of Highways found strong support at various public hearings, and "received . . . no negative responses" from 88 stakeholder agencies and organizations.[3] The department released a preliminary engineering design study in 1974, recommending

> the expansion of the existing expressway . . . from four lanes to six (three in each direction), and elevation of that portion from Barataria Boulevard across the Harvey Canal to Terry Parkway/General DeGaulle with erection of twin high level bridges over the canal. Interchanges, with grade separations, will be proposed at all major cross streets. Parallel service roads will be widened from two lanes to three lanes each and converted [to] one-way [directions]. The Harvey Canal Tunnel will be retained for local traffic use with the service roads.[4]

That recommendation would produce a dominant element of today's West Bank. But it would take years to actualize, during which time anxious merchants frequently expressed concerns about customer access and inconvenience. Planners responded with a construction timeline of four years and no more than eighteen months at any one site. They also decided to divide the highway to allow sunlight to reach landscaped greenspace below, and "to reduce the appearance of a vast concrete ribbon."[5] Each three-lane-wide artery would expand to a fourth lane when an on-ramp adjoined from the service road below, and then contract to three as the extra lane descended down the next off-ramp.

Around the time construction began, word came from Louisiana's congressional delegation regarding the Dixie Freeway, that 1964 vision for a West Bank–traversing Outer Belt superhighway. An environmental impact statement had determined the project would be overly damaging to wetlands; besides, the case for its necessity had never been strong, particularly in the face of growing anti-freeway sentiment, born of the stunning 1969 defeat of the French Quarter Riverfront Expressway. The Dixie Freeway's federal moneys were instead reallotted to interstate mileage in northern Louisiana.

Cancellation of the Dixie Freeway brought urgency to the expansion of the West Bank Expressway, and weakened the case for an uptown bridge, which was supposed to connect with the freeway. Now that the expressway would be the West Bank's only major artery, the argument strengthened to build the second bridge downtown near the extant span, so that both would feed into the improved expressway. And everyone agreed a second bridge was needed, as 1978 "average traffic volumes . . . exceeded design capacity [by] 35 percent," with over 100,000 vehicles per day "not uncommon."[6] The cancellation of the Dixie Freeway also helped quash the Chalmette-to-Algiers bridge, although segments of the Outer Belt would eventually be built, namely I-610 from Gentilly to Lakeview, I-310 from Destrehan to Luling, and I-510 from eastern New Orleans to Chalmette.

Work began on the new $200 million West Bank Expressway in late 1977, starting with the frontage roads, "to carry traffic while an elevated modern structure is built."[7] Every step involved the removal and relocation of utilities, drainage apparatus, lighting and signage. In early 1979, concrete piers were erected for the new high-rise bridge over the Harvey Canal, and steel superstructure work began in autumn.[8]

While builders built the new expressway, planners planned the new bridge. Legislation in 1976 had arranged for financing for the "Greater New Orleans Mississippi River Bridge No. 2" in the form of $200 million in general obligation bonds, and afterwards, an equal amount in revenue bonds to be backed by the reintroduction of tolls (suspended since 1964). Federal grant dollars were also in the mix.[9]

As for designs, planners duly considered a wide range of options, even if many were probably dead on arrival. Among them were a no-build option (not "prudent"), an expansion of either of the two existing bridges (not "viable"), a new crossing from the Press Street railroad yards in Bywater to the former Southern Pacific Yards in Algiers (also not "prudent"), and a "twin tube tunnel," which was rejected with a stridency reminiscent of Robert Moses's old dictum, "Never build a tunnel if you can build anything else."[10] Previous committees had also considered crossings at Causeway Boulevard to Nine Mile Point and, mostly controversially, from Napoleon Avenue to Barataria Boulevard.[11] In fact, preliminary planning had been going on well before the 1976 legislation; as early as January 1973, Robert Tannen, head of the planning division of Curtis and Davis Architects, "said the consultants' recommendation on a new bridge will be within the corridor [or] general vicinity of the existing Mississippi River bridge."[12]

To the relief of preservationists and activists aghast at the specter of a massive bridge cleaving historic uptown New Orleans, the planners recommended the "Parallel to Existing" option, meaning "a new, high-level, multimodal bridge . . . located about 400 feet downstream and parallel to the existing Greater New Orleans (GNO) Bridge." Why 400 feet? Were they any closer, soil-pressure bulbs associated with the pier caissons might overlap with those of their counterparts, potentially causing tilting. Were they any farther apart, the right-of-way requirements for the approaches would increase, driving up expropriation costs and complicating "the exit geometry for the transit ramps." Originally planners had proposed a separation distance of 350 feet, but they widened it to 400 feet to allow barge-mounted derricks to move safely among the piers, and to minimize the chances that a catastrophic accident on one span (like a ship collision) would damage the other.[13]

The new span's four lanes would flow unidirectionally onto the East Bank, except for two additional high-occupancy vehicles lanes. "Upon completion of the Downstream Parallel Bridge," planners wrote in 1978, "the existing Greater New Orleans Bridge would be designated one-way and serve traffic destined to the West Bank."[14] The crossing would be from Calliope to Lawrence streets, not too far from the circa-1950 proposed path for the first bridge. Selecting the extant corridor was "viable" in that it minimized impacts by utilizing the existing Pontchartrain and West Bank expressways, and "prudent" in that it kept land acquisitions costs low and linked the two most congested spots on both banks.

Later that year, the Mississippi River Bridge Authority (MRBA), which owned the first bridge, got absorbed into the Louisiana Department of Transportation and Development (LaDOTD), itself a fusion of four other state agencies, including the Department of Highways. LaDOTD and MRBA selected the E. Lionel Pavlo Engineering Company to build the new bridge's substructure, and Modjeski and Masters to build the superstructure. It would be the latter firm's third major bridge project here within fifty years.[15]

The decision on the new bridge forced modifications on the West Bank Expressway. Gen. DeGaulle Boulevard had to be widened; the Gretna cloverleaf had to be reconstructed; and service roads had to be expanded around the dizzying can-of-worms to be built at the foot of the bridges.[16] Costs mounted, and construction time lagged. The complications led Marrero and Westwego representatives in 1981 to question "whether the West Bank Expressway should be elevated west of the Harvey Canal, [where] present service roads are carrying traffic 'three times as efficiently' as the old expressway."[17] The state decided the elevated portion would go no farther west than Cohen Street in Marrero.

Work progressed: in September 1982, Boh Brothers constructed the elevated expressway from Manhattan Boulevard to Lafayette Street, and a year later began work on the most congested portion, from Manhattan to Stumpf. Traffic began to flow over the new Harvey Canal Bridge in the summer of 1984. The last section, from Stumpf to the bridge, was put out for bid later that year, after which "a motorist would be able to drive uninterrupted from Marrero to the Central Business District on . . . 'the Cadillac of the transportation industry.'"[18]

But first, of course, the second span would have to be completed—along with connecting ramps and roadways ten times longer that the Mississippi River was wide. After two years of design work and soil testing, LaDOTD took bids for pier construction in June 1980 and contractors began work in March 1981. Like the first span, the new bridge would be a cantilever-and-truss design, its longest segment measuring 1575 feet, with 150 feet of navigation clearance above high river stage and a total length of 3,018 feet. It behooved the engineers to emulate the profile of its "fraternal twin," since both would function as a single piece of infrastructure and an icon of the city's skyline. Beauty mattered. The new span differed from the old span in three regards: it would be wider (94 feet to 52 feet), heavier (28,000 tons to 17,200 tons of structural steel), and costlier, $550 million to $42.4 million.[19]

The piers, which alone cost more than the entire 1958 project, numbered four, with Piers I and IV anchored on the New Orleans and Algiers land sides, respectively; Pier II in seventy-foot-deep river water; and Pier III by the Algiers riverbank. Each would be aligned precisely using geodetic monuments on the Pilie Street floodwall and at a brass survey disc on the Algiers levee, and for aesthetic reasons, paired side-by-side with their 1958 counterparts. The piers would go as deep as their twins, 100 to 180 feet into the hard Pleistocene clays of the suballuvial surface. The two inner piers were designed to withstand a blow from a 40,000 ton vessel moving at eight miles per hour. Pier II, being in the river, was the only one to be supported by a caisson. Its construction began with nineteenth-century technology: the laying of a 300-by-400-foot mattress of brush willows to protect the bottom sediments from scouring.[20] In the fall of 1981 a two-section open-dredge caisson with fourteen wells, one of the largest ever made, was floated in, dredged inside its wells, filled with 13,813 cubic yards of concrete, and built up into Pier II. All four piers were completed between June 1982 and June 1983.[21] By this time it became clear that the bridge would not be ready in time for the 1984 Louisiana World Exposition.

"Construction of the Greater New Orleans Bridge No. 2 was a complex project," Modjeski and Masters later wrote in classic engineer's understatement. "It required constructing one of the world's largest cantilever bridges adjacent to an existing bridge in a wide, deep and often swift river in the presence of ocean going ships transiting the site."[22] Timing was everything, and everything was interdependent. For example, superstructure work began in November 1982, after a long process of selecting optimal steel grades and refining bolting and sealing techniques, and in less than a year, the build-out of the steel cantilevers came within a stone's throw of the just-in-time completed piers.[23] Using the Algiers bank as a basecamp, the contractors operated three large floating derricks to raise and piece the beams into place. The Algiers cantilever arm reached completion in March 1984, just as work began on the New Orleans side. In August, after seventeen months of assembly, the two halves finally joined, in full view of fairgoers at the Louisiana World Exposition (and those riding the hair-raising gondola car over the river). To citizens' eyes, it looked like a completed bridge by late 1984, and Modjeski and Masters officially completed its contractual obligations on August 1, 1985.[24] But to the frustration of West Bankers, it would take another three years to complete deck work, electrical wiring, illumination, and painting, plus the various approaches and ramps running from the Superdome and tying into the elevated West Bank Expressway.

On Friday morning September 30, 1988, officials gathered to dedicate the Greater New Orleans Mississippi River Bridge No. 2. At 1:00 p.m., with helicopters overhead and reporters gathered, "a vanguard of white Mississippi River Bridge Authority police cars" led an advance of civilian cars, "four abreast . . . like a noisy, slow-moving wave," with horns blaring and onlookers cheering. The happy convoy rolled across the span at 15 mph, among them an Algerine named Kelly Ragland, eager to put an end to "25 years of waiting." "[For] the rest of my life," Ragland told the *Times-Picayune*, "I'll tell people[,] I was the first . . . unimportant person to cross it."[25]

The "important" people also had something to say. The $500 million bridge had been the costliest project in Louisiana history, said Transportation and Development Secretary Neil Wagoner, but "also the most needed." Gov. Roemer acknowledged that a $1 toll would be collected to defray the remaining $120 million of expenditures, for which Sen. Fritz H. Windhorst of Harvey jokingly offered the governor a one-dollar bill in the hope it would be "the first and last toll on the new bridge" (it was neither.) On a cheerier note, Representative Francis Heitmeier of Algiers declared that "today, the West Bank will begin a new era in transportation and economic development, and we'll take our place as the best bank in the entire state of Louisiana."[26]

17

Troubles Wash Ashore

That beautiful fall Friday was a red-letter day in the history of the West Bank, and it earned two articles and a beautiful photograph on the front page of the *Times-Picayune.*

But it didn't get the headline. That went to a story with a very different tone, and it would not bode well for the region: "OIL PRICES PLUNGE, THREATEN LOUISIANA'S RECOVERY."[1]

In truth, the 1988 bridge inauguration was a rare bright spot in an otherwise bleak era. Petroleum prices had plummeted starting in 1983, stilling oil and gas extraction worldwide; the market slightly rebounded in 1986 only to slip again in 1988. While the fuel savings delighted consumers, production zones suffered terribly, principally on the Gulf Coast, which had grown heavily dependent on the oil sector. Roughly half of Louisiana's one hundred thousand oil and gas (O&G) jobs disappeared. White-collar petrol workers in downtown New Orleans either got pink slips or tickets back to Houston, which itself was undergoing upheaval. Gleaming skyscrapers on Poydras Street lost their tenants. Well-paying blue-collar O&G service jobs on the West Bank vanished, and pipe fitters, welders, oil-rig contractors, caterers, and helicopter pilots found themselves unemployed. Ship workers met a similar fate: less demand for vessels and fewer to repair quieted shipbuilding and dry docks. Meanwhile, containerization technology had zapped unionized longshoremen and dockworker jobs, and whatever few crane operator jobs there were went to East Bank containerization facilities.

Fewer basic-economy jobs (those that bring in outside money) meant less revenue circulating in the West Bank's nonbasic (local) economy, including retailers and home builders. These sectors hemorrhaged jobs and brought down real estate values, leaving families with outsized mortgages they could no longer finance. The state, which had been dangerously over-dependent on O&G for revenue, laid off employees and cut social services. To add insult to injury, highly unpopular toll booths opened in 1989 to pay for the new bridge, beleaguering West Bank commuters with rush-hour traffic slowdowns and yet another daily expenditure.

Folks appreciated the amazing engineering marvels, and took pride in their beauty and great new name, "Crescent City Connection," coined by a Metairie schoolgirl. But the oil crash quashed the cheerful optimism of the West Bank, and nearly all indicators of vibrancy—from population to median household income to investment—would at best increase at diminishing rates, and at worst flat-line or decline. Once home to most of Jefferson Parish's population and economy, the West Bank by the last decade of the twentieth century accounted for only 42 percent of the parish population, collected a mere 20 percent of the parish's occupational license taxes, and had double the unemployment rate of East Jeff, peaking at 17 percent around 1990.[2]

To be sure, some projects conceived during the boom, like the 1985 renovation of Oakwood Mall, opened during the bust. But whenever people sense that their tomorrows will not be as good as their yesterdays, they react accordingly, and that is especially true of investors. New subdivisions on the West Bank, which once opened unremittingly, became rarities. Older subdivisions did not age well. Strip malls became shabby. Industry closed and left weedy fields. The *Jefferson Parish Yearly Review,* that sunny cheerleader since 1935, whose roseate prose read like a Fox Movietone newsreel voice-over, ceased publication. Crime rates increased, especially in the so-called inner city, and the crack cocaine epidemic hit public housing hard, namely Fischer by the Orleans/Jefferson parish line. In response, the Gretna-based Jefferson Parish Sheriff's Office, under the leadership of the charismatic Sheriff Harry Lee, adopted tough policing policies that found enthusiastic support among some populations—and accusations of racial profiling among others. Social discord mounted as the regional economy struggled, exemplified in ongoing race-related parish council redistricting controversies and culminating in the 1991 gubernatorial runoff pitting the charmingly corrupt three-time former Gov. Edwin Edwards against Jefferson Parish state senator and former Grand Wizard of the Ku Klux Klan David Duke. The bitter campaign attracted international attention and ended in a decisive victory for Edwards ("Vote for the Crook—It's Important" was the winning argument), though Duke won the majority of white Louisianians' votes, including many in West Bank precincts.

Rising crime and declining investment also had the effect of diversifying the "white flight" of the 1960s into a broader exodus of various races and ethnicities seeking suburban lifestyles and better schools. Whereas the West Bank in 1960 and 1970 was 75 percent white, by the 2000s it was 50 percent nonwhite (as the United States Census Bureau defines "race," and higher if "ethnicities" such as Hispanic, Middle Eastern, and South Asian are included). White families on the move mostly went northward to the exurbs of St. Tammany Parish.

Meanwhile, southward across the marshes, brewed a crisis largely unrecognized during the halcyon days of the West Bank, and one that darkened the view of its future.

Fluvial deltas are among the most dynamic places on Earth. They are just as much waterscapes as landscapes, a viscous mix of fresh water, alluvium, and nutrients spilled out along a tide-washed littoral.

All of this fluidity is anathema to urbanization. Settlements need hard earth beneath to grow into permanent cities; only so much sogginess can be tolerated. If a hydric environment nevertheless presents itself as highly strategic to human movement—in the case of New Orleans, of connecting a global oceanic foreland with a vast hinterland—then human agents will endeavor to impose rigidity on that fluid firmament, in the form of engineering structures that control water and drain land, to dry it out and make it habitable.

Rigidity here meant levees, earthworks, floodwalls, barricades, embankments, berms, revetments, canals, sluice gates, channels, locks, and pumps. It took nearly two hundred years, but engineers ultimately prevailed in hardening the soft environment. By the 1920s, the West Bank no longer endured crevasse floods from the Mississippi or cave-ins along the banks; its swamps had been drained, and its waterlogged soils dried into developable space. And develop they did.

Those same structures, however, interrupted the processes of delta-building. By straitjacketing the Mississippi and restraining the channel from storing excess water laterally, man-made levees uselessly jettisoned freshwater and sediment into the Gulf of Mexico, instead of diffusing them broadly across the coastal plain. Seawater (30–35 parts per thousand salinity) thus worked its way inland, into freshwater regimes and toward populated areas. Whereas in the year 1900 freshwater (nearly 0 ppt) prevailed as far south as Little Lake, halfway between the West Bank and Grand Isle, by the 1960s that area had a salinity level of 7 ppt and would continue to rise by about one ppt per decade. Lafitte, a freshwater community in 1900, had become brackish by 1960.[3]

Five factors drove salinity intrusion: the level of the sea was rising on account of a warming climate; the elevation of the land was sinking on account of sediment deprivation; freshwater (including runoff) no longer moved outwardly from the river on account of levees and drainage systems; a maze of recently excavated canals provided rising seawater with various ingresses; and their paralleling guide levees (spoil banks), acting as barricades across once-open marshes, steered and concentrated seawater in certain areas and thus augmented their salinity.

Canal excavation near the West Bank had a history as old as colonization. Trappers dug *trainasses* for pirogues or skiffs; planters excavated irrigation and timber-extraction canals; companies dug navigation channels; and drainage districts made outfall canals.[4] But these new channels, which dramatically augmented saltwater intrusion, were different. They had been dug speedily, in intricate and lengthy fractal networks, to reach wellheads with pipe-laying barges for the purposes of extracting oil and gas. Large corporations such as Louisiana Land & Exploration "owned most of the coastal marsh," wrote historian Jason Theriot, while "regulatory agencies supported the canalization [and had] few, if any, restrictions, [as] most people viewed wetlands as wastelands."[5] Hundreds of linear miles were dredged just in the Barataria Basin, mostly during the 1930s to 1950s, and on each one were floated barge-mounted drills to hunt for hydrocarbons. The inimitable A. J. Liebling, trying to understand Louisiana oil and politics in 1959, described one such drilling barge on the West Bank of Plaquemines Parish as "a creature at once reminiscent of a giant sucking insect," with "shafts, called jacks, [as] the barge's feet." After being floated out the canal to the lease site,

she thrusts down the lower extremities of the great rods until they dig into the sea bottom and hold her fast. She then rises on them, like an automobile on jacks, until there is a good clearance between her bottom and sea level. . . . Next she extrudes from her belly the business end of the drill that she will thrust ten or fifteen thousand feet beneath the bed of gulf or ocean until she reaches oil or gas—or the charterer gives up[,] to be towed to her next job. . . . She is a specialized succubus, a great pipette, moved about to wherever her manipulators think there may be blood worth sucking.[6]

The sucking and piping made southern Louisiana a premier corridor in the movement of petroleum from production to processing to distribution, through which today passes a quarter of the nation's fuel consumption. West Jefferson in particular enjoyed a share of the riches. In 1955, the parish ranked as the fifth largest oil producer among the state's sixty-four parishes, while Louisiana ranked third in the nation. The petroleum sector became Jefferson Parish's largest industry, bringing in over $2 million per month just in crude, not including value-added products. Its premier production spot was the Lafitte Oil Field in lower Barataria Bay, which had yielded 200 million barrels since 1935. Along with other spots, it sent its black gold through pipelines laid in dredged canals or on barges sailing up the Intracoastal Waterway and arriving in Harvey—"the Little Houston of Louisiana," according to one industry advocate—"with nearly two hundred concerns serving the oil industry lining both banks of the [Harvey] Canal." He waxed poetic on the process: "To the oil fields via its waterway goes the tools, the mud, and the equipment. And from the oil fields [come] the crude petroleum . . . by barge [from] the water wilderness."[7]

The alacrity went out of the industry's voice in the late 1960s, by which time scientists, regulatory agencies, and the public came to understand the value of wetlands and the damages incurred in their scouring. Crude production by now had shifted to offshore wells, and with an environmental movement now afoot and the 1969 National Environmental Policy Act giving it legal leverage, petroleum companies adopted a new strategy. They formed a consortium to build floating mooring stations twenty miles offshore, for supertankers to discharge crude oil into a network of pipelines leading to "a hollowed-out underground salt dome for storage prior to distribution to regional and national refineries."[8] Legislation enabled the Louisiana Offshore Oil Port (LOOP) in 1972, and construction, including the building of Port Fourchon at the mouth of Bayou Lafourche, finished in 1981. LOOP had environmental impacts all its own, but it also, for the first time, engaged environmental scientists in the design and operation of a major oil facility. No longer would large quantities of crude flow directly into the urbanized West Bank, but the damage to its coastal apron had already been done, because those myriad channels would never be filled. Instead, they widened, creating more erosion-prone banks, particularly because they forked off from older, wider man-made navigation canals, such as the Barataria Basin Waterway, which opened in 1925.

While many factors drive coastal land loss in Louisiana, and some are hotly debated, most coastal scientists view canal excavation and river levees, in that order, as the weightiest. According to one analysis of aerial and satellite imagery, the Barataria Basin lost 433 square miles of land in one human lifetime, having covered 1,480 square miles in 1932 and 1,047 square miles by 2016. The loss began at a rate of two to five square miles per year in the 1930s to 1950s, peaked at eight to nine in the 1970s and 1980s, and has since declined to less than one square mile per year today—not because the problem has been solved, but because the most vulnerable land has already disappeared. The shape of that rate curve seems to implicate the oil and gas extraction canals; had the erosion been largely attributable to levees, we would see a more steady linear relationship, since levees date to the 1700s but oil and gas extraction canals date to the mid-1900s.

Recent research utilizing droves of seismic data provided by the oil and gas industry points to another factor: the role of sedimentary faults in the deeper Holocene and Pleistocene layers. Scientists who attribute land loss and relative sea level rise to these shifting subterranean interfaces, including many oil and gas industry geologists, see the problem as largely beyond human causation and control. Coastal advocates and environmentalists, on the other hand, view the fault hypothesis suspiciously, seeing it as convenient for the oil and gas industry to absolve itself of liability. They also point out that the withdrawal of petroleum fluid may open cavities in these layers and induce fault slumping, making it an industry responsibility. Academic scientists tend to parse their words carefully in pinpointing causation, and readily admit we do not know enough about these deeper geological dynamics. As to the role of oil and gas extraction, scientific studies involving industry geologists tend to attribute around one-third of the land loss to the petroleum industry, whereas their academic peers put it as high as four-fifths. Everyone agrees that many factors are at play variously in different areas; the culprits in the Breton Sound, for example, may be different from those in the Barataria Basin.[9]

Whatever the causes, the crisis comes ever closer. Some of the red pixels (indicating lost land) on the researchers' digital maps lay within a few miles of the urbanized West Bank, by Lake Cataouatche, Bayou Barataria, and Bayou Segnette near Westwego. Even the loss in the lowermost reaches of the Barataria Basin, where the vast majority of erosion has occurred, affects the West Bank in that it diminishes terrestrial impedance against hurricane-induced surges and replaces it with minimum-friction watery surfaces.[10] West Bankers, for their part, have moved closer to the problem, by settling into former backswamps. Worse, as those lowlands were "reclaimed" through artificial drainage, they began lowering even more—by fractions of an inch, then inches, then feet, even yards. The Aurora area of Algiers, for example, once sat entirely above sea level (ASL); now it straddles the level of the sea. The Gen. DeGaulle Drive corridor, once 1–2 feet ASL, is now 3 feet below sea level (BSL). The Park Timbers and Tall Timbers subdivisions are 3 to 6 feet BSL, and areas between the Belle Chasse Highway and Harvey Canal, once around 2 feet ASL, now lie as low as 6 feet BSL. The West Bank's single largest deep "bowl" is in the rear of Avondale, around 6 feet BSL, and while it is currently mostly forested, it is slated for a massive residential and commercial development project.[11]

What happened was anthropogenic soil subsidence. The soils of the delta contain five components: sand, silt, clay, water, and organic matter. If the water component is removed, air takes its place, which oxidizes the organic matter, which shrinks and creates more air pockets—into which the clay, silt, and sand particles consolidate, like a dried-out sponge with a weight upon it, and drop below sea level. Managers made matters worse by drawing down normal water levels of drainage canals so as to store more rainwater in the event of a sudden downpour, but this also had the effect of lowering the adjacent groundwater and exacerbating soil compaction.

Being below sea level is not a natural condition here; the Mississippi River created its deltaic plain entirely above gulf waters. Today, throughout metro New Orleans south of Lake Pontchartrain, only the natural levees and distributary ridges remain above sea level, while the drained swamps and marshes have dropped below. (As if to prove that artificial drainage causes urban subsidence, the only West Bank lowland that remains above sea level is Bayou Segnette—which is, not coincidentally, the only West Bank backswamp that was never drained.) Sunken areas now had to be rimmed by levees and floodwalls to prevent outside water from pouring in—more so as the coast eroded and the sea rose. People settled in the "bowls," secure that engineering technology had resolved any threats, and that those levees and floodwalls would never fail them. The drainage of the West Bank occasioned more than "just" a topographic change; it also altered its ecology, hydrology, soils, and possibly even the climate. In 1918, Weather Bureau forecaster Isaac Cline noted an eight-degree increase in summertime temperatures and a four-degree increase in wintertime since 1900, precisely the era of drainage-system installation on both banks. "Water absorbs heat more slowly than the earth during the day and loses it less rapidly at night," Cline explained. "New Orleans, entirely surrounded by water and with its soil saturated, formerly boasted of a more uniform climate. In late years, however, levees have prevented overflows, reclamation projects have [drained] swamps and, finally, sub-surface drainage . . . has eliminated surface water [and] ground moisture [by] eight or ten feet."[12]

As a result of these and other environmental manipulations, the West Bank witnessed a remarkable reversal of its sources of risk. From the 1700s to the 1920s, West Bankers feared flooding from the Mississippi River, courtesy of levee scouring, cave-ins, *éboulemens*, fissures, and crevasses. They also dreaded hurricanes, but mostly as wind events. Even the Great Storm of 1915, whose straight-north track penetrated the West Bank with demonic incisiveness, mostly caused wind damage. The limited flooding that did occur was mostly on the East Bank; the only significant West Bank inundations were in the rural Myrtle Grove area in lower Plaquemines Parish, and much of it derived from overtopping of the backed-up river.[13]

By the mid- to late 1900s, however, federal levees had largely subdued the Mississippi flood threat, and few West Bankers questioned their might. The new threat now came from tropical storms pushing Gulf waters across the frayed Barataria Basin and up various canals leading into sunken neighborhoods. For years officials did not fully appreciate just how frayed the marshes had become, and failed to make the connection that unchecked development and soil subsidence had put ever-growing numbers of people in harm's way.

Sheer luck also encouraged the complacency. For fifty years, from 1915 to 1965, the West Bank managed to evade direct hits by major hurricanes, sparing it untold damages but also depriving it of lessons about risk. One major storm did strike New Orleans in that period, the Hurricane of 1947, but its southeast-to-northwest track over Lake Pontchartrain put the West Bank in a favorable position, as its northerly winds pushed waters southward, away from people. As in 1915, the East Bank suffered the brunt of the flooding. So unaffected was the area across the river that, while some East Bankers were still waist-deep in water, West Bank officials paraded to a ceremony inaugurating Peters Road along the Intracoastal Canal in Harvey.[14]

The West Bank's lucky streak nearly ran out in 1965. In late August, a tropical depression formed off Surinam and grew into a storm named Betsy. The system wobbled over to Puerto Rico, where it stalled, drifted toward Florida, stalled again—then darted to Miami and bolted at 20 knots across the Gulf of Mexico. Nearly a quarter-million denizens of coastal Louisiana headed inland, including to the West Bank, while locals either remained at home or took shelter in sturdy public buildings. Few if any evacuated; folks at the time viewed New Orleans as fortified from hurricanes, not imperiled by them.[15]

Late on September 9, Betsy made landfall directly over Grand Isle and moved inland on a northwestward path, paralleling the western side of the lower Mississippi. Winds swirling in from the north swept across the Barataria Basin and peaked in Port Sulphur at 100 mph before the recorder failed; gusts elsewhere reach 140 and even 160 mph.

Accompanying the winds was the surge. The waters of Barataria Bay swelled by seven to nine feet, while a seven-foot surge at the mouth of the Mississippi reversed flow and spilled river water over the banks. At the time, Betsy's surge was the highest ever recorded in the region, due in part to the sheer forward thrust of the storm.

Bad as this was for the West Bank, Betsy's energy sent the highest surge, over ten feet, into the eastern marshes of St. Bernard and Orleans Parish, where work was well underway on the Mississippi River–Gulf Outlet Canal—that same seaway for which West Bank officials had fought so hard to dig through the Barataria. The MR-GO allowed Betsy's surge into the Industrial Canal, where levees breached and seawater inundated four populated basins in the Seventh, Eighth, and Ninth wards.

At dawn on September 10, most of southeastern Louisiana—over 4,100 square miles from the Atchafalaya River to the Chandeleurs Islands and from Ponchatoula to South Pass—practically blended with the Gulf of Mexico. Only the natural levees of the Mississippi and Bayou Lafourche, plus the western half of levee-protected metro New Orleans, remained dry. Eastern regions were less fortunate: saltwater inundated Plaquemines, St. Bernard, and eastern Orleans parishes, plus large expanses of mostly uninhabited zones of eight other coastal parishes.[16]

Hurricane Betsy killed 81 Louisianians, injured thousands, and caused $372 million in damage, nearly $3 billion in today's dollars. The West Bank, though spared serious flooding, suffered wind damage and utility outages. It served heroically as a refuge for flood victims and as a base camp for rescue and relief operations at the Algiers Naval Station and Alvin Callender Field.[17] As for damages, news got worse as one went south, and at West Jefferson's southernmost point, where Betsy made landfall, "the Coast Guard . . . estimated that 98 per cent of Grand Isle's buildings had been destroyed."[18]

Betsy inaugurated a new era of risk perception. With an eroding coast and an encroaching sea, the sinking metropolis now needed to be rimmed circumferentially, not just along the river and lake. Betsy also ended the era in which people perceived New Orleans as a sanctuary from storms. Experts and officials instead increasingly viewed the metropolis as a place to be evacuated, not a destination for evacuees.

Betsy also instigated a new era of risk response. Six weeks after the disaster, Congress passed the Flood Control Act of 1965, which authorized $56,235,000 for "hurricane-flood protection on Lake Pontchartrain [including] the Seabrook Lock feature" at the lake end of the Industrial Canal. Among the efforts precipitated by the law was the Lake Pontchartrain and Vicinity Hurricane Protection Project (LPVHPP), whereby the federal government would partner with state and local entities to build hurricane-protection levees, flood walls, gates and other lateral surge blockages to what would later be called Category 3–level standards. As the project name implied, the targeted areas were almost entirely on the East Bank—where most of the population lived, where most of the Betsy flooding occurred, and where most of the political clout was. The only mention for protection across the river was for Grand Isle.[19] The West Bank per se got nothing.

Frankly, the East Bank didn't get nearly as much as promised. "The project, when designed, was expected to take about 13 years to complete and cost about $85 million," testified the General Accounting Office retrospectively. Instead, the Army Corps "encountered project delays and cost increases due to design changes caused by technical issues, environmental concerns, legal challenges, and local opposition to portions of the project[;] costs had grown to $757 million and the expected completion date had slipped to 2008."[20] Four decades after Betsy, the LPVHPP remained up to 40 percent incomplete, and some of what had been built turned out to be dangerously under-engineered.

Over those decades, life on the West Bank carried on in blissful or willful ignorance of the mounting danger. A fundamental debate raged about the region's future. "While most of the New Orleans area had begun construction of its hurricane protection levees following Hurricane Betsy in 1965," wrote the organization now in charge of the region's levees,

> the West Bank went without flood protection because of disputes between environ-mentalists and large land developers. *No one could decide where to put the levees.* Developers wanted to enclose large undeveloped tracts of land for future growth of western Jefferson Parish, but environmentalists wanted to limit the area of protection to save the wetland tracts and [create] Jean Lafitte National Park. [So] no levees were built, and west Jefferson remained exposed to hurricane flooding.[21]

In fact, there *were* levees along canals and backswamps; any artificially drained area must have a contained perimeter. But they were modest parish embankments erected by local drainage departments for the purposes of impounding internal water for pumped removal—that is, getting inside water out. Other such berms had been built by parish levee districts and were designed to keep outside water from coming in, but due to lack of funding they were not held to federal standards. Interagency discord and bureaucratic ineptitude worsened matters: private contractors working for various parish officials had built West Bank levees piecemeal over many years, and now "no levee district [found itself] in charge of past levee construction." Said one frustrated official of the resulting confusion, "You don't have any problems [about authority and responsibility] on the east bank. You got them all on the West Bank."[22]

Twenty years after Betsy, Hurricane Juan struck—and the West Bank's luck finally ran out. The late-October system followed an extraordinarily erratic path, forming only three hundred miles offshore and tracing two 360-degree loops over Vermilion Bay before shooting eastward on Halloween, its counter-clockwise rotation pushing Gulf water directly into Barataria Bay. Though Juan never gauged stronger than Category 1 and soon weakened to a tropical storm, its slow jaunt allowed persistent winds to produce a substantial surge, exceeding that of the much stronger Betsy. Highest-ever water stages of four to five feet were recorded by Lafitte, as well as at the locks of the Algiers and Harvey canals.[23] This surge would not have come so far inland had it not been for coastal erosion, canal excavation, and soil subsidence.

It got worse. On Tuesday, October 29, 1985, "a 250-foot section of a makeshift levee holding back flooded marshes washed away," reported Bruce Nolan of the

Times-Picayune. Two Marrero subdivisions had to be speedily evacuated. Another breach occurred in the rear of Westwego, and water crept northward of Lapalco Boulevard and up the Harvey Canal. Volunteers sandbagged frantically: citizens, in effect, building ad hoc levees within hours where government had failed them for years.[24] To make matters worse, the system dumped eight to twelve inches of rain, and drainage pumps could not eject it "uphill," into waterbodies already bloated by the surge. "Huge sections of West Bank subdivisions remained under water late Tuesday," wrote Nolan, "with no word on when the floodwaters might subside." Officials had plenty of words. Said Jefferson Parish President Joseph Yenni, "a hurricane protection levee would have prevented the two subdivisions from flooding. . . . The problem on the West Bank is not the pumping capacity. It's the lack of a hurricane protection levee."[25]

Juan caused nearly a billion dollars of damage in Louisiana, most of it on the West Bank and in the Barataria Basin. Worst hit were Marrero's Westminster Park and Lincolnshire subdivisions, where twelve hundred homes were flooded up to their kitchen countertops. Lawsuits flew in the aftermath, with everyone from levee districts to developers to engineers targeted for liability.[26] But ultimately what led to the deluge were decades of environmental hazard and human exposure creeping closer and closer to each other, and the agents behind them included nearly all of us, from the public and private sectors to elected officials, developers, homebuilders, banks, mortgage lenders, and homebuyers, to oil, gas, and shipping interests and the consumers behind them.

Juan was not the region's worst disaster; the nineteenth-century crevasse deluges were bigger, deeper, longer, more destructive, and more frequent. But that problem had been resolved, and those days were over. Juan rated as the West Bank's worst hurricane-induced flood to date, and everyone sensed more would come.

Like Betsy for the East Bank, Juan catalyzed the federalization of surge protection for the West Bank. A year after the storm, Louisiana's congressional delegation empowered West Bank levee districts to secure authorization and funding for the Army Corps of Engineers to build federal-quality hurricane protection levees from Westwego to the Harvey Canal. Ten years later, in 1996, new floodwalls and levees were extended eastward from the Harvey Canal to Harvey, Gretna, Algiers, and Belle Chasse, and westward from Westwego along Lake Cataouatche and over to Bridge City, Avondale, and Waggaman.[27] By the new century, the West Bank's rear flanks were certainly better than pre-Juan, but not nearly up to threat level. And the "system," if it may be called that, had holes galore: gaps in levees along State Highway 90 west of Avondale and along the Company and Harvey canals; insufficient levee height along the southern fringe; and, worst of all, a gigantic open spot in the form of the ungated Gulf Intracoastal Waterway, where Bayou Barataria forked into the Harvey and Algiers canals.[28]

On Tuesday, August 23, 2005, tropical air fueled by unusually warm seas spiraled upwardly over the Bahamas. The system became Tropical Storm Katrina, and late Thursday, the Category 1 hurricane struck North Miami with 75 m.p.h. winds and killed nine people before entering the Gulf of Mexico. There, a loop current of deep warm water from the Caribbean supercharged the vortex. Computer models at first forecasted Katrina's track as striking the Florida peninsula, then the panhandle, then Alabama and Mississippi. The farther west it crept, the more energy it gained.

With Katrina now a strengthening Category 3 storm and computer models concurring on a Louisiana landfall, officials on Saturday declared emergencies and called for evacuations of the entire metropolis. Troopers activated the contraflow evacuation plan, allowing motorists to utilize incoming interstate lanes to exit the metropolis. Many departed Saturday; more left Sunday, August 28, when winds reach Category 4 and 5 levels.

Katrina's low barometric pressure sucked up a dome of seawater and gales blew it landward. Under natural conditions, coastal wetlands would have absorbed or spurned most of the intruding tide. But massive land loss hampered that effect, and man-made canals increased penetrability, chief among them the MR-GO. Pressure mounted on the floodwalls of the adjoining Industrial Canal, as waters swelled fourteen feet above sea level.

Hurricane Katrina made landfall at 6:30 a.m. over Barataria Bay, between Grand Isle and the mouth of the Mississippi. Its straight-north track spelled bad news for East Plaquemines, St. Bernard Parish, and the eastern half of New Orleans, and terrible news for Hancock County, Mississippi. But it worked in the favor of the urbanized West Bank, because the Mississippi's banks acted as a shield against the easterly surge, while Katrina's northerly winds pushed water southward away from populated areas. As a result, water levels rose only around 2 to 5 feet in the mid-Barataria. East of the river, by contrast, they rose 14 feet in Lake Pontchartrain, 15–18 feet off Plaquemines and St. Bernard parishes, and nearly 30 feet off Biloxi.[29] To be sure, rain fell in torrents over the West Bank, wind gusts surpassed 100 mph, runoff accumulated in the streets, and buildings and utilities were damaged extensively. But within the West Bank conurbation of Orleans, Jefferson, and Plaquemines (Belle Chasse), it got no worse than that. Once again, sheer luck spared the West Bank from calamity.

Calamitous indeed were the effects of Hurricane Katrina on the East Bank. Federal floodwalls and levees breached in seven major spots and over forty others, leaving 169 of the 350 linear miles of the so-called protection system compromised in some fashion. Seawater inundated 80 percent of the urbanized footprint of Orleans Parish and 99 percent of St. Bernard Parish with saltwater up to ten feet deep, plus parts of Jefferson Parish and most of Plaquemines Parish.[30] The deluge, which would last weeks because New Orleans's bowl-shaped topography had trapped the floodwaters, ranked as the costliest disaster in American history, and among the deadliest, with more than 1,800 killed in Louisiana and Mississippi. The catastrophe brought worldwide media attention to the region, and more than a few pundits foresaw the death of a great American city. Their prediction got a boost three weeks later when another hurricane peaking at Category 5, named Rita, passed close enough to New Orleans to re-rupture some of the Katrina breaches and cause surge damage well up into the Barataria Basin.

The West Bank played a paradoxical role in Katrina and its aftermath, part victim, part witness, part bystander, part beneficiary, part casualty. For the first terrible days, the West Bank offered the only escape from the East Bank flood zone, for those few who could make it to the bridge, and for weeks, it was the only way to get back into New Orleans, all other ingresses and egresses having been inundated.

West Bankers both suffered and evaded the disaster. They were at first evacuees, then hosts of evacuees. They played a central role in the recovery, as a base camp, access corridor, and supply region, yet they figured into the recovery mostly as an afterthought. World media largely ignored the cross-river region, except for an incident on September 2 in which a group of mostly black flood victims, desperate after four days of heat and homelessness, began walking over the Crescent City Connection, only to be aggressively turned away by Gretna police, one of whom fired a shotgun to make his point. In much Katrina coverage and remembrance, the "Bridge to Gretna" incident marks the sole mention of the West Bank, and in some circles, the name "Gretna" has come to symbolize sinister reactionary forces. Then again, West Bankers are used to being ignored—having long been characterized as unenlightened—and know well what it means to live in the shadows of what goes on across the river.

For those who returned to Third World conditions on the East Bank, however, the West Bank in the autumn of 2005 practically dazzled the eye. The lights were on! Wal-Mart was open! Shelves were stocked! Restaurants, banks, gas stations, malls: you could run errands and begin rebuilding your life. Some flood victims moved to the West Bank, temporarily or otherwise; rents rose, and real estate boomed. East Bankers got to know the West Bank like never before, and West Bankers had never seen so much traffic and congestion. Some griped about the long lines, but most welcomed their neighbors and counted their blessings: but for a nudge in Katrina's path, *they* could have gone under. For once, it might be said, the East Bank envied the West Bank.

The Katrina fiasco revealed egregious errors in the geoengineering of New Orleans, and the responsible party was the Army Corps of Engineers, for the proximate cause (levee failures), if not the ultimate cause (a century of coastal deterioration vis-à-vis a powerful storm over rising seas). The Corps was also responsible for getting the water out and fixing the failures. First the department launched Task Force Unwatering, whereby truck-mounted pumps were brought in to remove a quarter of a trillion gallons of floodwater over fifty-three days, into late October 2005. Next, Task Force Guardian set about repairing the damaged floodwalls and levees in time for the (mercifully quiet) 2006 hurricane season. That same year, the Louisiana state legislature created the Southeastern Louisiana Flood Protection Authority–West (SLFPA-W) as the West Bank partner of the Army Corps of Engineers in its fast-tracked effort to create a true *system* of flood defenses, one that was holistically envisioned, held to the same standards, constructed integrally, and maintained and operated as a unified entity. All prior levees were piecemeal projects, "systems" in name only, and misleadingly described as "flood *protection.*"

The new system would be officially called the Hurricane and Storm Damage Risk Reduction System (HSDRRS), and it would comprise three parts: the Lake Pontchartrain and Vicinity Project on the East Bank, the West Bank and Vicinity (WBV) Project, and the New Orleans to Venice Project for lower-river communities. Engineered to protect against a storm magnitude calculated as having a 1 percent chance of occurring in any given year (Katrina was deemed to be a 0.25 percent storm, or 1 in 396 years), the WBV Project would protect the West Bank from River Mile 70, south of Belle Chasse, to River Mile 118.5, at the Davis Pond Diversion west of Waggaman. The project encompassed over 30 miles of interconnected earthen levees and/or floodwalls with 67 closeable devices, most of them sluice or sector floodgates designed to prevent brackish water from coming in from the south, and integrated with pumps to remove rainfall runoff accumulating in populated areas to the north. Main gates were installed at each of the extant man-made canals, namely the Company, Harvey, and Algiers canals, at or near where they connected with natural waterways, such as bayous Segnette, Barataria, and Fatma. New operators' stations, built like wartime bunkers and raised 25 feet above the grade, accompanied each pump.

The linchpin of the WBV Project was the West Closure Complex, positioned at the West Bank's hydrological vortex: where the Harvey and Algiers Canals branch off from Bayou Barataria, all three of which are also components of the federal Gulf Intracoastal Waterway. The West Closure Complex comprises a 225-foot-wide channel bordered by two sector gates, wedge-shaped steel devices that pivot to seal off the waterway and block the surge. To their side stands a 530-foot-long, rectangular concrete bunker-like building housing eleven 5,000-horsepower pumps capable of ejecting 19,000 cubic feet of stormwater runoff per second. They are powered by four generators fueled by capacious diesel tanks, fronted by debris-removing raking devices, and surrounded by pilings to prevent vessel collisions. The sector gates are the largest in North America, and the pumping station is the largest in the world, costing $1.1 billion, over a quarter of the budget of the WBV, which itself was over a quarter of the $14.5 billion price tag for the entire HSDRRS. Contractors began work in 2006 and ended in 2011, at which point the Corps turned over maintenance and operation to the SLFPA-W.[31]

With construction underway in 2008, another powerful hurricane made its way into the Gulf around the third anniversary of Katrina. Category 4 Gustav approached southeastern Louisiana at a 45-degree angle, making landfall possible along a 200-mile stretch. It triggered the largest peacetime evacuation in American history, nearly two million people heading inland from Venice to Lafayette. At one point the track looked especially threatening for the West Bank, a sort of powered-up reverse Juan track from 1985 or a "deadly Katrina-Rita hybrid" from 2005. "Large sections of the West Bank could see surge overtopping pieces of a still-incomplete levee system," reported Mark Schleifstein of the *Times-Picayune*, citing Ivor van Heerden, the coastal geologist who had gained renown during Katrina.[32] New Orleans Mayor Ray Nagin, who took his share of criticism for the 2005 fiasco, did not mince words for Gustav, calling it the "mother of all storms[,] worse than a Betsy, worse than a Katrina. . . . You need to be scared and you need to get your butts out of New Orleans right now." According to reporter Leslie Williams, Nagin expected "Gustav to 'punch holes in the Harvey Canal,' which could cause the West Bank to become a bathtub. The West Bank has 8-foot to 10-foot-high protection, he said. Gustav's storm surge may be 15 to 24 feet high."[33]

Gustav made landfall over Cocodrie early on September 1. A million New Orleans–area residents watched media reports tensely from their evacuated positions, sensing that a repeat of the Katrina deluge might well mean the end for their beleaguered metropolis.

Instead, to their great relief, levees and floodwalls withstood the pressure, though barely in some places. By mid-afternoon, the threat had passed. Most of Gustav's surge had gone to the East Bank, and that which pushed into the Barataria Bay got buffered by the marshes in the central basin, though at the expense of places like Grand Isle and Lafitte. Most of Gustav's wind damage went to Baton Rouge and points south and west. For New Orleans, the problem now was, how do you get a million people back home? Gustav left residents pondering whether a great metropolis could endure, much less progress, in the face of incessant threats and evacuations.

Four years later, and seven years to the day since Katrina (August 29, 2012), Category 1 Hurricane Isaac struck near New Orleans on a northwestern track. Though not enough of a threat to warrant an evacuation, Isaac's slow 45-hour-long linger made its wind, surge, and precipitation that much more damaging. Isaac was also the first major test of the HSDRRS, and the system worked well—maybe too well. Three areas—Braithwaite, LaPlace, and Lafitte—suffered more serious deluges during Isaac than they had during Katrina, and all three were suspiciously positioned just beyond the HSDRRS, suggesting that the surge reverberated off the concrete walls protecting city folks and ended up in their country neighbors' backyards. The Corps ran models comparing Isaac's surge to what would have happened without the HSDRRS and found no significant differences, with the minor exception of Lafitte, which had an additional foot of water.[34] Residents of that scenic bayou town protested that the incident ought to justify their decades-long call for federal levee protection. While that might not be forthcoming, state funds were allocated in 2019 to build a "jigsaw puzzle of ring levees" to encircle sections of the wending coastal town, which has recently garnered national attention for its front-line vulnerability to climate change.[35]

18

From Suburbia to Ethno-Urbia

New Orleans found itself in an unexpected renaissance in the early 2010s. After a three-year slog of a recovery following the 2005 deluge, rebuilding efforts finally gained momentum by decade's end, buoyed in no small part by the inspirational 2009 football season of the New Orleans Saints. Glowing media coverage accompanied the team's NFL Super Bowl victory in February 2010, and after a competent new mayoral administration arrived at City Hall three months later, billions of federal recovery dollars finally began flowing into urban improvement projects.

New Orleans turned out to be a good place to ride out the Great Recession. Its unemployment rate fell well below the national average, and in a housing economy replete with foreclosures, flood-damaged New Orleans was among the few places *building* new houses. As well, the city held out a special appeal to a generation of authenticity-starved millennials who, on a quest for personal meaning, found here a veritable university seminar of progressive causes. As early as 2006 but particularly around 2009–2010, substantial numbers of college graduates started moving into the city—they called it "NOLA"—and more often than not, they settled in the historic core, to avail themselves of its architectural splendors and cultural enchantments. New businesses opened to cater to the "brain gain"; rents and real estate prices rose; neighborhoods gentrified; tourists partook enthusiastically of the new attractions; and trendy hotels and bistros opened ad nauseam. With new parks, streetcar lines, bike lanes, and a festival practically every weekend, "NOLA" seemed to be one big boutique city, at least in the urban core, and it affected the zeitgeist. A poll of voters on quality of life satisfaction showed a rise from around 55 percent during 2005–2009 to around 70 percent during the 2010s, with the greatest jump (fifteen points) occurring in the Super Bowl season of 2009–2010.[1] Books, articles, dissertations, news stories, blogs, websites, documentaries, movies—New Orleans became one of the most studied, talked about, even fetishized places in the nation, a world city once again, though for different reasons. Post-recovery New Orleans became the Brooklyn or Portland of the South: cool, cocky, chic, and costly.

Except for everywhere that wasn't—and that included the West Bank. The cross-river region had dodged the disaster, but it also missed out on the reinvestment and the renaissance. So the West Bank just soldiered on in its quotidian decency, uncool, unassuming, unaffected, and inexpensive.

Those characteristics kept the NOLA-smitten cognoscenti away from the West Bank. They also made the West Bank everything that NOLA wasn't: an inexpensive home for locally born folks of the working to middle class, white and black—a place where local brogues are still common, where hipsters are rare, and where folks embody local traits with a minimum of self-awareness. The West Bank had urban agriculture before it was cool, affordable housing after it became scarce, and cultural authenticity before it became savored. Its unpretentious aura and reasonable real estate also attracted immigrants in large numbers, and they settled in surprisingly integrated residential patterns among the locals. Despite New Orleans's historical fame as a bastion of multiculturalism and deep-rooted localism, today it is the West Bank and other suburban areas where these cultural manifestations thrive in their most vital forms.

∽∽∽

Diversity had long found a home on the West Bank. In the 1890s, one could find in Gretna and Algiers people of Asian and African ancestry working at a Chinese market garden operating within a short distance of German, Irish, and Italian households, while in Westwego Cajun speakers processed seafood caught by Acadians, Houma, Croatians, Sicilians, and French Creoles working side-by-side with African Americans living in a subdivision created by a Spaniard—all within a polyglot American metropolis.

Although the West Bank was too rural to be a major immigration magnet historically, circumstances changed by the late 1900s. A new ethnic group had arrived in the late 1970s, and while they were attracted by the area's housing and jobs, what drove them here was war. Vietnamese Catholics, persecuted in North Vietnam, had sought refuge in the South, where some became a privileged class, more attuned to Western ways and favored by the Diem regime. In the war against the Viet Cong, they allied themselves with the Americans, and when Saigon fell in 1975 they, along with many other South Vietnamese, were deemed enemies of the reunified regime. Thousands fled, among them the pro-American urban South Vietnam establishment, for which the US government felt a protective responsibility. Under chaotic conditions, they boarded US planes and arrived at American military bases, including Fort Smith in Arkansas and Eglin Air Force Base in Pensacola, Florida.[2]

Now what? American Catholics worked on resettlement plans, and the largest Catholic region nearest to Eglin was in southern Louisiana, which, like Vietnam, was a deltaic environment with a French colonial heritage and a fisheries economy. Under the leadership of Archbishop Philip M. Hannan, the archdiocese of New Orleans and the Associated Catholic Charities (ACC) spearheaded the local aid effort.

In the spring of 1975, the New Orleans ACC met with refugees of Vung Tau and Phuc Tinh at Eglin, "telling them that the Crescent City had a warm climate and plenty of good fishing nearby," reported the *Times-Picayune*. "This information seemed very appealing to a great many refugees in the camp and . . . a large number of Vietnamese [applied] to go to New Orleans under the aegis of ACC."[3]

On May 26, 1975, nineteen refugees arrived at the Trailways bus station in downtown New Orleans, with hundreds more on their way. The ACC next surveyed the region "to locate adequate housing in advance of the arrival of the refugees,"[4] seeking contiguous unoccupied low-cost rental units. Staff members found the largest cluster in eastern New Orleans, in a development called Versailles, and in 1978 secured an additional seventy-one housing units in Woodland Estate in Algiers, plus eighty-nine units in the Normandy Apartments in Bridge City and other complexes in Marrero, Harvey, and Gretna.[5] "Our agency was looking for vacant housing," recalled Susan Weishar of ACC, "and that's why the Vietnamese ended up [in these locations]: available, affordable housing."[6] They didn't find it in the historic core; they found it in the suburban fringe. In this regard, the West Bank was in the vanguard of a new human geography in the United States, whereby immigrants and refugees no longer crowded into aged tenements in the inner city, as they had in the 1800s and early 1900s, but rather in the modern suburban subdivisions originally built for "white flight."

By May 1978, 7,141 Vietnamese had settled in Louisiana, of whom 80 percent, in 800 households, chose greater New Orleans. Communities formed in Versailles (2,063 people) on the East Bank, and in Woodland in Algiers (780), in Bridge City at the foot of the Huey P. Long Bridge (571), and in pockets elsewhere in West Jefferson (another 500).[7] Within two months of settlement, the refugees assumed responsibility for their own rent, and within a few years, "the majority of Vietnamese had jobs, many had automobiles . . . an increasing number owned their own homes, [and] approximately 200 of them were enrolled at the University of New Orleans."[8] They found employment in commercial fishing, welding at Avondale Shipyards, and food services in restaurants, seafood processing, and retailers such as Schwegmann's.[9] Each Vietnamese "village" maintained its own identity and sense of place. According to a 1990 study, Versailles was called Hung Vuong Village after the mythic dynasty of the mother country; Woodland was dubbed Hung Dao Village in honor of a military hero, and the West Jefferson community became Tu Du Village, meaning "freedom."[10] A Vietnamese commercial cluster formed around Stumpf Boulevard by the West Bank Expressway in Gretna, where the Pho Tau Bay Restaurant, opened in 1980 and named for a Ho Chi Minh City restaurant chain, became popular and attracted other Vietnamese businesses.[11]

Members of the community also reintroduced to the West Bank a land use that had predominated a century ago but had since disappeared: urban agriculture. The refugees created intensively cultivated multi-tier plots along the Algiers Canal as well as across the river in Versailles, where they raised tumeric, ginger, Vietnamese coriander, taro, water spinach, Malabar nightshade, and Oriental melon, as well as onions, tomato, squash, sweet potato, corn, tomato, mustard greens, collard greens, and sugarcane. After Katrina's saline floodwaters tainted the soil in Versailles, the agricultural action intensified in Hung Dao Village in lower Algiers, where it continues today.[12]

By 2010, there were 10,603 people of Asian ancestry living on the West Bank, or about 4.4 percent of the population; more than half were of Vietnamese ancestry, clustered in particular subdivisions from Algiers to Avondale.[13] Other Vietnamese-Americans, as well as Cambodians and Laotians, gravitated to the Gulf Coast during the 1980s and 1990s, and would come to own roughly half the region's offshore fishing vessels.[14] Said one shrimper about lower Louisiana, "It is like Vietnam, very much. You have the Mississippi—like the Mekong, big river.

And you have all the bayous—exactly like Vietnam. And you have thunderstorms in the afternoon, and mosquitoes. You have rice paddies and sugarcane."[15]

Many Vietnamese families rose into the middle class with remarkable speed, becoming homeowners rather than renters and entrepreneurs rather than employees. Their children excelled scholastically, en route to college and the professional class. Just how swiftly they succeeded astonished one former West Banker. "In 1987," wrote Judy Laborde, then the marketing director for Oakwood Mall, "I got the idea to stage a mall event that would publically honor all the valedictorians and salutatorians from [West Bank] high schools. . . . As I compiled the names, [I realized] 80 percent were Vietnamese. . . . In just 12 years, these immigrants who came to America under the worst of circumstances were now the highest achieving students. Here I am 31 years later still saying 'wow.'"[16]

The exigencies of their arrival, as a group of refugees, steered the Vietnamese into rather constelled settlement patterns, and while some would diffuse over time, the enclaves generally remain today. Other groups, who arrived individually as immigrants, tended to settle more dispersedly, wherever the cost of housing aligned with their means, where jobs could be attained, and where cultural spaces and social resources formed to meet their needs: churches, temples, mosques, community centers, schools, and businesses, particularly those catering to ethnic foodways.

A favored area for Arabic-speaking immigrants is the Gretna/Terrytown area, which in 2016 had the second largest Arab population in the region, estimated at 380 but probably much higher.[17] Most came to Louisiana from Lebanon (43 percent), others from Syria, Palestine, Egypt, Iraq, Jordan, and other Middle Eastern cultures. Together they gave the state "among the fastest growing Arab populations in the country," with East and West Jefferson having the most. Many heads of household are self-employed entrepreneurs running gas stations and convenience stores throughout the metro area.[18] Serving their religious needs is the Masjid Omar, a mosque with a qubba (dome) and minaret, and the Muslim Academy, a private elementary school founded in the year 2000 and now enrolling nearly 300 students. Both are on or near Lapalco Boulevard, convenient to where most West Bank Muslims reside.

Their neighbors in Gretna/Terrytown include around seven thousand people of Hispanic ethnicity, mostly from Mexico and Central America; over two thousand people of Asian ancestry, mostly Vietnamese; and a roughly even split of native-born whites and blacks who together total over thirty thousand. These demographics make Terrytown and unincorporated Gretna among the most diverse zip codes in the state, something quickly evidenced by a drive around its principal arteries. A Taste of Thailand restaurant sits across the street from Los Panchos; El Sabor Catracho (a nickname for Hondurans) is just down Stumpf from Antoine's Cakes; and Tan Dinh and Pho Bang draw local patrons, as well as effusive foodies from the NOLA crowd across the river.

The West Bank is also home to three of the most thoroughly international cultural spaces in the region. The Hong Kong Market is the area's only full-size Asian grocery store, and attracts restaurateurs and shoppers metro-wide. The food court at the West Bank Nawlins Flea Market on Scotsdale Drive in Harvey offers a variety of South and Central American dishes. The decades-old Algiers Market, wedged in an odd interstitial space in the shadows of the Crescent City Connection, is really three adjacent ethnic emporia, one more ad hoc than the other (wood-pallet walkways along muddy paths, hand-strung electrical cords, blue-tarp walls), and together they are a dead ringer for the *mercados* of Teguci-galpa and the *tianguis* of Mexico City. La Pulga, as Spanish speakers call the flea market, is today said to be "one of the best places in the city to find Mexican and Central American cuisine"[19]—if only East Bankers ventured out to find it. "I think that's the biggest barrier—crossing that river and crossing that bridge," said one entrepreneur in the Vietnamese market. "But it's a lovely world on the other side—and full of flavor. It's really metaphorical, that bridge: Sometimes we have to be willing to cross [it] to see what's on the other side."[20]

How poignant to contemplate that all this multiculturalism plays out on spaces that, barely two generations ago, were strictly segregated racially, and that, two lifetimes ago, were either slave plantations or swamplands. What has happened on the West Bank is happening across America. "Ah, suburbia, land of the bland," wrote urbanist Amanda Kolson Hurley in an article titled "2018 Was the Year of the Complicated Suburb." "White-picket-fenced realm of white-bread people and cookie-cutter housing[:] That's still the stereotype that persists. [But] in the past several years, a much more complex picture has emerged—one of Asian and Latino 'ethnoburbs,' rising suburban poverty, and Baby Boomers stuck in their split-levels."[21]

The early years of the West Bank's third century will likely prove to be a turn-ing point in its demographic future. The subregion entered the new millennium with a quarter million people—250,369 residents, the majority white (126,896 compared to 104,599 black, 9,280 of Asian ancestry, and 12,751 of Hispanic ethnicity, according to the 2000 census for the urbanized tri-parish area, from Waggaman to Belle Chasse, excluding rural fringes). Ten years later, in 2010, a white exodus plus natural decreases caused a decrease of 16,000 in the white population, while the black population flatlined and the Asian and Hispanic population increased by at least 1,400 and 9,000, not counting undocumented immigrants. For the first time since the 1800s, the West Bank is now majority-black, although it has been majority nonwhite since the 1990s. Despite the West Bank's population decline, it now comprises a larger segment of the metro population, because of Katrina-related losses on the East Bank. In 2000 the West Bank was home to 25 percent of greater New Orleans's population south of Lake Pontchartrain; in 2010 it was 30 percent.[22]

Jefferson Parish is Louisiana's premier example of "ethno-urbia." Sixteen percent of its 50,000 public school students are classified as English language learners, well above the national average and more than double the percentage of the second highest parish, East Baton Rouge. Eighty-six percent of those 7,700 youth speak Spanish, mostly from Central America and Mexico; 7 percent speak Arabic; 3 percent Vietnamese, and the rest speak any one of nearly fifty other languages. With the American-born black population on both banks of Jefferson Parish growing by over 10 percent during 2000–2014, the white population plummeting by 21 percent, and Hispanics and Asians growing by 85 and 29 percent respectively, the likely demographic future of the parish, and of the West Bank, is an ethno-racial plurality.[23]

The new West Bankers didn't choose "The Wank" for its cultural charm or architectural splendor. Nor did the aging Baby Boomers, for that matter, two generations earlier. They came for the affordability, the convenience, and the work, attributes found here for many years. What was written about Algiers a century ago rings true today for the West Bank generally, despite great changes in the landscape and economy: "Algiers . . . is one of the cheapest districts in which to live in the entire city, [yet] enjoys all the conveniences known to the city. . . . There is that feeling existing in small towns [where] people know each other and are interested in one another's welfare. . . . Along the river front the hum of the buzz saw and the clanking of the hammer at the shipyards may be heard early and late, [as] there are fewer idle men in Algiers than any town in Louisiana."[24]

19

Cross-Bank Relations

My dear neighbors . . . of New Orleans:

You come among us with your city manners cast around you like a cloak of grandeur, looking upon us, if perchance we emerge from our abodes, as [curiosities for] our customs and manners. . . . Ye fancy us a conglomeration of criminality, gazing unembarrassed within our doors . . . Ye make our fields and environs rendezvous for various pugilists[,] for drunken soldiery [and] gentlemanly duels, and ourselves the target at which you aim your editorial remarks, [yet] all originating from the refuse of your own community. . . .

Now, I pray you, if you would know us, come to our houses as brothers and friends . . . and cease those periodical visitations upon us of so much unappreciated interest.

—"Remonstrance from Algiers," *Daily Picayune,* July 15, 1855

Like so many water-straddling cities, metro New Orleans sees its share of infighting between its sibling banks. At issue are power, pride, and resources, and because the historical geography of their urban development is tilted, so too is the nature of the love-hate relationship. The East Bank tends to looks down at the West Bank, a disdain infused with classism and born of city-country condescension. Belittlement goes from East to West; resentment from West to East. "The bridge is free *to* the West Bank," East Bankers used to joke; "you have to *pay* to return." West Bankers retort with a hearty Bronx cheer—a cross-river sneer if ever there was one—and reappropriate the abuse, endearingly nicknaming their haven "The Wank," as if to say, *"Yeah so what. We like it here. The West Bank is the best bank!"* (To which pedants snicker, "That's 'the *better* bank.'") Life on the two banks seems to have further distanced in recent years, with so many flashpoints in the public discourse—disaster, recovery, federal aid, gentrification, displacement, short-term rentals, affordability, culture-versus-community, authenticity-versus-appropriation, over-tourism, streetcar expansion, the future of Charity Hospital, the outmigration of the working class, the in-migration of the NOLA transplants—being overwhelmingly East Bank phenomenon, in which the average West Banker is practically a spectator, close physically but far socially. Many East Bankers, especially among the NOLA set, know precious little about the West Bank except for Algiers Point, selected restaurants, and the Jean Lafitte Preserve. Everything else is drive-over suburbs—what you have to endure to get to Mosca's.

Some West Bankers go further and speak of divorce. Twice recently, a state representative sponsored legislation for Algiers to become its own parish, claiming residents of "the red-headed stepsister of New Orleans" were "tired of not being serviced" by city government."[1] His words echoed those of an "aggravated" Algerine in 1877, who wrote that the 1870 annexation had "doubled the taxes" for "nothing at all which she did not have before the union. . . . Algiers wants either that the city do something for her or consent to a separation."[2] A year later, the *Daily Picayune* reported, "Algerines threaten to secede if something is not done [for] improvements [to] drainage."[3] Jefferson Parish was not immune to secession talk; in 1950 its police jury spoke openly of "solv[ing] the complicated Jefferson governmental problems by setting up two parishes, one on each side of the river."[4] Exasperated Algerines speak of joining Jefferson Parish when they despair over relations with New Orleans. Those who joke about Algiers being the city's red-headed stepsister say Gretna is her "country cousin"; others recall East Bankers considering anything across the river to be "the woods"—a term previously used to describe the backswamp.

Bridges are built to interconnect, but that connection yields equalization only when conditions permit. The narrower the river, and the earlier and more frequently it has been bridged, the more likely each bank will develop generally comparable environments (built, economic, and social). Consider the many Old World cities that spanned their rivers long ago: London's Thames, Dublin's Liffey, Amsterdam's Amstel, Paris's Seine, Rome's Tiber, St. Petersburg's Neva. Today their paired banks exhibit cityscapes of generally equivalent stature, in terms of urban granularity and historicity, if not character and costs. So too American cities like Boston and Philadelphia, where may be found both prestigious and modest addresses, power and the lack thereof, on either side of their transecting rivers. The narrow and shallow rivers bisecting these cities, spanned many years ago, now tend to unify more than they divide. La Rive Droit no longer looks down on La Rive Gauche in Paris, just as Boston does not spurn Cambridge.

Manhattan Island, on the other hand, had deep and wide harbors separating it from its neighbors, such that Brooklyn and Queens across the East River, un-bridged until well into New York City's third century, developed more modest neighborhoods with more plebeian populations. Manhattan tends to sneer at its "outer boroughs" (and only stopped deriding Brooklyn when Brooklyn started to become, well, like Manhattan). Much of New Jersey, the butt of many New Yorkers' jokes, remained rural until tunnels and bridges connected it with Man-hattan Island across the Hudson River. Seattle tends to look down on Tacoma, and San Francisco on Oakland.

Similarly, cities on the lower Mississippi found themselves fronting one of the world's great rivers, and most remained unbridged into the twentieth century. Their cross-river counterparts are consistently less wealthy, more functional, less renowned, and culturally asymmetrical. Of course, other factors are at play, namely racial disparity and the geography of industry, yet the truism generally still holds: *the wider the water body, and the later its spanning in the course of the city's history, the greater the asymmetry of the two banks.* Consider the lopsided nature of St. Louis and East St. Louis, Memphis and West Memphis, Natchez and Vidalia, Baton Rouge and Port Allen, and the two banks of New Orleans. Fully 217 years had passed after the founding of New Orleans before a bridge linked the East and West banks, and not until the Space Age was the urban core bridged. That was long enough for the communities on either side of the Mis-sissippi to follow two very different developmental trajectories: an international port and world city on the East Bank, growing from bourg to faubourg, and a provincial service and industrial sector on the West Bank, growing from "subru-ral" to "intersuburban." When bridges finally came into place, the dissimilarities did not disappear, but rather came into relief. East Bankers and West Bankers had so much, and so little, in common.

≈≈≈

When community rifts form around water bodies, bridges can become flash-points. In 2012, a remarkable decoder of cross-bank relations came to public referendum: whether the tolls on the Crescent City Connection, those off-again, on-again commuter nuisances, should sunset or continue for another twenty years.

Supporters argued that the $1 toll (40 cents for those with tags) funded critical maintenance on one of the busiest bridges in the nation, underwritten by precisely those who used it, thus freeing up state funds for other needs. Their side organized as Bridging Progress, "a political action committee of business, civic and elected leaders [that] raised $250,000 to tout the need for the tolls in radio, television and direct mail ads."[5]

Opponents, with scant resources but determined leadership in Harvey resident Mike Teachworth, pointed to a state promise that the 1989 toll would end once the bridge was paid off in 2012. They also cited past mishandling of toll revenue as evidence that this "tax"—netting some $20 million a year—was not only unfair to West Bankers and a chokepoint on regional growth, but entrusted to the wrong hands.

On November 6, voters went to the polls for the tri-parish referendum. Turnout was substantial on account of the federal and presidential elections, and the results were amazingly close, with only eighteen votes spelling victory for tolls supporters, 154,393 to 154,375.

The near-tie implied a metropolis divided by a common river, and while both banks depend on that river, they don't necessarily depend equally on each other. West Bank voters opposed the toll by a commanding 60–40 margin, while those on the East Bank supported it 54-to-46. Had the vote been limited to West Bank residents, as many argued it should have, the toll would have been soundly defeated: West Jeff, West Orleans, and West Plaquemines precincts all opposed the tolls, by 61 percent, 53 percent, and 56 percent respectively. Likewise, toll opponents also would have prevailed if the vote had been limited to all of Jefferson (54 percent against) and/or Plaquemines (56 percent against), regardless of bank. What changed the calculus was the East Bank of Orleans Parish, which voted 57 percent in favor.[6]

A handful of West Bank precincts bucked the trend, and closer inspection explains why. Three pro-toll precincts were located in lower Plaquemines, home to folks so far from the metropolitan core that they infrequently use the bridge. The other pro-toll West Bankers lived in and near Algiers Point, where one precinct voted nearly 7-to-1 in favor, by far the highest on either bank. Their reasoning probably involved their passionate support of the Algiers Ferry, a financially stretched operation that, while not directly benefiting from toll revenue, would breathe easier if the bridge retained its own funding stream and ferry riders were not lured into driving over a free bridge. Fiercest opposition, meanwhile, came from precincts in Westwego, Marrero, and Teachworth's Harvey, where many residents endure long daily commutes and have no use for ferries. There was also a fair amount of toll opposition in poor areas on the East Bank and in the heavily Vietnamese precincts of eastern New Orleans, whose residents have brethren on the West Bank.

The November 2012 referendum showed that West Bankers have something of a "have to" relationship with the East Bank, and travel there mostly out of necessity—namely jobs. An economist would call it inelastic demand. Those on the East Bank, on the other hand, are more likely go West for "want to" reasons (inelastic demand, often to dine or recreate), and/or do so only occasionally. So it made perfect sense that West Bankers would seek to unburden themselves of tolls while East Bankers would be content to keep that revenue stream in place.

It was folks in Orleans Parish who spelled the difference in the referendum. Why? Most New Orleanians satisfy most of their needs on the East Bank and don't have to bear a daily toll cost, but this only partially explains their toll support. Most of the city's prosperous precincts, including Uptown, the Garden District, French Quarter, Marigny, Bywater, and Mid-City, voted strongly in favor of the toll, something that did *not* occur in wealthy parts of East Jefferson. Residents of these historic districts tend to be progressive in their political philosophies and supportive of public investment, while the more conservative sensibilities of the East Jeff suburbs contested the notion that government should collect fees for an asset already paid off. Whatever philosophical reasoning East Bankers might have brought to the polls, however, held little sway among the West Bankers who actually forked over the cash. In essence, pocketbook pragmatism drove the West Bank vote, while the East Bank, unburdened by the daily expenditure, indulged in a more philosophical rationale.[7]

Alas, the 2012 referendum ended up being little more than a fleeting sociological experiment. The suspiciously slim margin had riled anti-toll advocates, and the indomitable Mike Teachworth took legal action, "arguing that hundreds of legally registered voters were not allowed to vote [because] they were given provisional ballots restricting their participation to federal elections."[8] A judge ordered a recount, which affirmed the results, but he nonetheless agreed with Teachworth's point and nullified the November referendum. The tolls were temporarily suspended until a do-over could be held, scheduled for JazzFest weekend in May 2013. Turnout was (unsurprisingly) low, but those who did vote were passionate, and this time the anti-toll side won by 78 percent, 73,656 to 20,730. East Bank Orleans Parish voters seemed to have taken their philosophies to JazzFest, whereas West Bankers took their pragmatism to the polling booths. "All of these people came together [and] stood up and fought," beamed a jubilant Mike Teachworth. "It's a great day for the West Bank."[9]

≈≈≈

Has a toll-free Crescent City Connection helped equalize the two banks? Did new investment dollars and prospective homebuyers speed past the demolished toll plazas and into the West Bank promised land? Extraneous variables obfuscate causality, such that it's tough to say which changes are attributable to which policy. Certainly West Bank commuters delighted in the savings of money and time, and some probably perceived an improvement in their quality of life. But if it were anything like a (very different) change made to that *other* bridge, the sunset of the tolls hardly marked the dawn of a new era for the West Bank.

That *other* bridge, of course, was the Huey P. Long Bridge, and while it had no tollbooths, its notoriously narrow vehicular lanes—a consequence of the span's original intention as a railroad bridge—took a toll on the nerves of generations of motorists. Jefferson Parish advocates felt the slender passage throttled development in the western part of their West Bank, where lay 9,000 nearly contiguous acres of drained open land. Increasing the bridge's daily vehicular capacity from 50,000 to 100,000, they argued, would finally open up this "last frontier." The symbiotic transportation/development relationship was literally written into the program than would fund the widening: the Transportation Infrastructure Model for Economic Development (TIMED) Program, created in 1989 by state legislation.[10]

Seven decades after the 1935 inauguration, work began to widen the Huey P.'s four nine-foot-wide lanes to six eleven-foot lanes plus shoulders. The Louisiana Department of Transportation and Development would oversee the $1.2 billion project, requiring that contractors not interrupt train, vehicular, and river traffic while executing their obligations.

In 2007, work got underway with the strengthening of five concrete piers upon their caissons, each broadened into the shape of a "Y" to undergird the new road decks. Next, existing railroad supports were relocated to make room for the new approaches. Steel trusses were then built out from the widened piers, piece by piece like an erector set, using temporary support towers placed into the riverbed. Then came the heart-stopping "truss lift" phase in 2010, in which three massive preassembled truss span sections were floated in on multiple barges and hoisted into place, a ballet of cable and steel upon a swift current amid moving conveyances in every direction. With piers and trusses ready, the bridge could now bear the roadway weight. Approaches were constructed, the road deck built, the lanes laid out, and electrical and other systems installed.[11]

The herculean feat concluded within seven years, and the Huey P. officially reopened with a public celebration on June 16, 2013. "Now that the bridge is wider," wrote journalist Andrea Shaw, giving voice to consensus sentiment in West Jefferson, "the Huey P. can jump-start the area much in the same way the Crescent City Connection did for Algiers, Gretna and Terrytown in the late 1950s and 1980s." Parish President John Young used another analogy: "The Huey P. Long Bridge is going to be to Jefferson Parish what the Superdome was to Poydras Street. The fact is, all of our raw undeveloped land lies on the West Bank. *That's the future.*"[12] The future even had a name: "Fairfield," an envisioned development to be created south of Bridge City between Westwego and Avondale, with "a business park, school and recreational amenities [and] upscale residential, high-technology and light-industry [aimed] to retain residents and diversify Jefferson's economy."[13]

Aside from the heavy industry at Avondale, this area has long gotten an extemporized treatment by market forces and the government nudges that drive development. Partially ringed to the south with a parish levee and the Cataouatche (Marcello) Canal in the late 1960s, the former swamp dried out, allowing for roads and some small subdivisions to extend backward. But being on the wrong side of a bridge too far and too narrow for too long, in a metropolis whose population was hardly exploding, meant western West Jeff would mostly remain armadillo habitat. It didn't help that its rear flank, extending into St. Charles Parish, had no hurricane-protection levee built to federal standards, making it the last major gap in the metropolitan perimeter defenses. And like all drained swamplands in greater New Orleans, the land inside the parish levees had dropped below sea level, to six feet, making it the lowest substantially sized tract throughout the entire West Bank.

Generations had known this area as Churchill Farms, for the sprawling nurs-ery offering ornamentals to horticulturalists even before the Huey P. was built. "Orleanians wishing an objective for a very short Sunday drive should drive across the river [on the ferry] at Walnut street, and follow the Westwego canal on the west bank," read a 1929 ad for the operation.[14] The area later came under the ownership of crime boss Carlos Marcello, who controlled an illicit Gulf Coast empire from an East Jefferson motel and who sank the money into West Bank land—over four thousand acres of it, assessed at a suspiciously low $8,800.[15] After Jefferson Parish increased the taxable value thirtyfold, and as Louisiana Power and Light Company sued for the right to put transmission lines across it, the family considered other uses for the land. Marcello himself "claimed to have given [Louisiana Gov. John J. McKeithen] $168,000, hoping in exchange the state would build a road through Churchill Farms, Marcello's West Bank estate," reported the *Times-Picayune*. "The road was never built."[16] Not to be dissuaded, Marcello offered McKeithen a 250-acre tract on which to build, of all things, the Louisiana Superdome. "We had it all set up for the domed stadium," Marcello be-moaned in a secret recording. "Had everything straightened out, man. Here the train could bring the people right there. The planes could bring 'em right there. Water, everything. I got the plans." McKeithen, who denied receiving the money, did acknowledge meeting with someone about Churchill Farms, but retorted "'there was no way in the world' he would consider building the Superdome on land belonging to Marcello."[17] Later in the 1970s, Churchill Farms came to national notoriety as a reputed rendezvous site in the lurid conspiracy theories linking Marcello to the assassination of President John F. Kennedy. Marcello family descendants are still major landowners in the area, having recently sold over a thousand acres to the West Jefferson Levee District—this time for tree-planting and flood protection.[18]

Today western West Jeff is home to the sort of ad hoc mix of uses you might find in the back of your house, in that oddball room with more potential than need. Part playground, part workshop, part dream, and part dump, western West Jeff is aptly nameless, its moniker and character construed by whichever users find whatever uses there.

For weekend warriors, that might be racing at the NOLA Motor Sports Park (former Marcello land); horseback riding; swamp and air-boat tours; boating and fishing at Bayou Segnette; golf at the 18-hole TPC Louisiana course (home of the

PGA Zurich Classic); a wave pool; a campground and rentable floating cabins; baseball diamonds and sports facilities; or trade shows and events at the John A. Alario Sr. Center and Segnette Field, the West Bank's largest arena complex.

For students and workers, there's the Churchill Technology and Business Park (on Marcello-donated land), the Patrick F. Taylor Science & Technology Academy, the Delgado River City Site and Advanced Manufacturing Center. For industrialists, there are the Dyno Nobel ammonia plant and Cornerstone Chemical, which had been quietly producing hydrogen cyanide since the 1950s until neighbors caught wind in 2019 and protested, illustrating the flashpoints that can arise in a place like the West Bank, where residents and industry have long coexisted.[19] Nearby is the 206-acre former Avondale Shipyards, closed since 2013 and attempting to transform "from a place that used to build hulking thousand-ton ships into a modern, efficient cargo and logistics hub."[20]

For Jefferson Parish government, it's the headquarters of the Economic Development Commission (JEDCO), and only three miles away, the Jefferson Parish Landfill, destination for municipal garbage and demolition debris and reputedly the source of malodorous vapors.

The only missing ingredients for the impending boom, the theory went, were flood protection and transportation access. In 2011, contractors for the US Army Corps of Engineers completed the Western Tie-In, 4.5 miles of federal levees and floodwalls along the Davis Pond Diversion Canal and the Outer Cataouatche Canal, closing off that final gap in the post-Katrina Risk Reduction System. The improvements helped lower premiums on federal flood insurance, good news for real estate interests. Two years later, the widened Huey P. opened for traffic, greenlighting more potential homebuyers into the area. Hopes peaked that the future had finally arrived for the forests of western West Jeff.

Had it? "Five years later," wrote journalist Drew Broach in 2018, "that hasn't happened—but it might still." A shaky economy, diminishing parish populations, fluctuations in the price of petroleum, the shocking closure of Avondale, lingering flood concerns, and the specter of building new commuter suburbs at a time when young people increasingly want urban lifestyles, all conspired to thwart the conquest of the "last frontier."

Indeed, traffic counts on the widened Huey P. actually *declined* after the widening, suggesting that geo-economics outweighed transportation in the cross-bank development formula. By some accounts, traffic-flow dynamics shifted against the interests of the West Bank. "Parish Councilman Paul Johnston said some of his West Bank constituents now forsake the Copeland's restaurant in nearby Harvey for a drive over the bridge to the Copeland's in Elmwood," reported Broach. "The reason: They can get to South Clearview Parkway in seven minutes, compared with 20 to 30 minutes to make it down clogged Manhattan Boulevard in Harvey." While the West Bank had anticipated a boom, "it is actually the east end of the bridge, in Elmwood, that has seen a surge of activity since the bridge expansion."[21]

"But it might still," Broach was quick to add to his assessment, pointing out in early 2019 that a new subdivision—once common news, now unusual—had broken ground in Waggaman, spurred by the widened bridge and the Avondale redevelopment.[22] That same year, JEDCO released its proposed Churchill Technology & Business Park Master Plan for the Fairfield Planning Area, featuring futuristic renderings of a vast office and residential complex for one hundred thousand employees and fifty thousand residents.[23]

The last frontier may yet realize such ambitions, but history—and geography—are not on its side. The area is already four to six feet below sea level, and immediately to its south are eroding marshes and the rising tide of Lake Cataouatche. Populations of both Jefferson and Orleans parishes recently declined for the first time since Katrina, and millennial home-buyers as well as high-tech employers tend to eschew 1990-vintage office-park developments.[24] Where are these thousands going to come from? The last frontier could become the next mistake, a replay of New Orleans East fifty years ago, only now in an era of climate change and utter uncertainly in coastal areas. The best advice for the West Bank may be to increase density in and among its necklace of historic communities on the higher ground closer to the river, and use the undeveloped periphery as a natural buffer—to be enjoyed under normal conditions, and to absorb and store water during rainstorms and hurricanes.

Contrast western West Jeff with its eastern counterpart, the lower coast of Algiers. Whereas the former strives to develop and despairs at its forests, the latter does the opposite, embracing its status as the only rural riverfront land remaining in the City of New Orleans, where one can see deer, raise cattle, and run a farm. This was once the Stanton Plantation, last major sugarcane operation in New Orleans. Covering 1,600 acres, with 150 buildings, 400 workers, and its own harbor and rails, it felt more like a banana-republic commodity plantation than part of a major American city. Crevasse flooding and economic woes led to its demise in the 1920s, and in 1930, the Stanton Plantation Company sold off much of the land to a real estate agent who envisioned the area as a place for the "country home [with] trees and shrubbery."[25] Large lots were laid out, and the people who bought them pointedly desired bucolic lifestyles. Too, the excavation of the Algiers (Gulf Intracoastal) Canal in 1956 imposed a sort of geo-psychological limit on downriver expansion; the waterway technically made the lower coast an island, helping keep sprawl at bay.

As for the City of New Orleans and its real estate sector, their eyes mostly gazed eastward, along the Interstate-10 corridor, where would arise "a suburb within a city" named New Orleans East. They generally assumed a laissez-faire attitude in regard to the lower coast, in contrast to Jefferson Parish's aggressive developmental push on its forested fringe.

The one major exception was the exclusive English Turn gated community and golf course, but even here, the appeal derives from the subdivision's pastoral environs. Wealthy people buy mansions in English Turn because of its rural isolation, not in spite of it. Other lower coast residents embrace the area's country air. There are big houses set far back on long, open lots, neighboring the occasional disheveled shack, forest patch, cattle pasture—and Buddhist temple. There is also the Sugar Roots Farm, which raises and sells "eggs, honey, and produce . . . teaching [children] how to feed themselves using a sustainable, free-range working farm model."[26] Two miles downriver is A Studio in the Woods, "a nonprofit artist retreat . . . infused with art, love and a profound respect for nature[,] grown with the forest [and] built sustainably with salvaged goods."[27] Just further is the twelve-hundred-acre Audubon Wilderness Park and Species Survival Center, last large forest in the metro area, home to native species as well as rare animals nurtured toward reproduction by highly specialized scientists. And just over the parish line in Belle Chasse is a World War II–era munitions depot that is now home to the world's largest fish collection. Here the Tulane University Biodiversity Research Institute maintains over seven million specimens of fish, some of which last swam in the nineteenth century, floating in jars lined up on enormous shelves inside earthen-covered military bunkers—a surreal sight where once stood French colonial Fort St. Leon. Like its West Jeff counterpart upriver, the lower West Bank is "the city's country," a land of forests and fields and quirks, wherein one may discern, with a bit of squinting, the West Bank landscape of a long, long time ago.

20

The West Banks of the World

One of the longest journeys in the world is the journey from Brooklyn to Manhattan.
—Norman Podhoretz, *Making It* (1967)

The world abounds in West Banks. Just about every city has one—not literally or nominally, of course, but phenomenologically. They have to, because the working families and gritty industries that keep cities running have to be somewhere, and they've been pushed out of the historic center by bistros and boutiques. The West Banks of the world are separate yet near their urban cores, apart yet convenient, a spacious counterpart to inner-city crowding and costs. Historically, this made them attractive for land uses like truck farms and manufacturing, and for the folks who worked those jobs, a place in which to reside and raise their families.

Yet as ubiquitous as they are, the world's West Banks defy a perfect, pat term, probably because they draw so little scholarly attention. "Suburbs" doesn't quite do it, because, as we have seen for New Orleans's West Bank, some communities therein began as nucleated villages and are "cities" by any definition. "Inner suburb" or "trolley suburb" don't work either, because, unlike the faubourgs and *banlieues* of the East Bank, there was no primary bourg to which abutting neighborhoods could attach. Nor do the jargon terms "exurbs," "beta cities," or "edge cities," all of which miss the mark. Subrural? Subtopia? Interurban? Ethnoburbs? Inner-ring suburbs? Second-hand suburbs?[1] All true; none perfect.

The West Banks of the world, and our West Bank, are at once working-class and middle-class, mostly modern yet historically undergirded, suburban and interurban, dependent on the urban core yet increasingly autarkic. Their "hybrid quality . . . confounds the neat binaries of town and country, village and city, man-made and natural,"[2] such that their apparent exceptions—the West Bank's many affluent communities, for example—are not really exceptions but evidence of their variability.

West Banks are typically liminal, marginal, and ordinary to the eyes of those who don't live there. To those who do, they are home—decent, affordable, and pleasant. Maybe they defy a perfect term because those who know them best aren't in the business of coining academic cant. Urbanists, by their very nature, spend little time studying suburbs as legitimate environments, despite that most Americans live there, and more continue to move there than to the trendy inner cities that get all the attention. To be sure, the academy is investigating emerging suburban topics like diversity and inequity, and academic architects are increasingly making the case for "retrofitting suburbia" for livability and sustainability.[3] But in the meanwhile, too many urbanists still disdain and avoid suburbia, and urban studies programs outnumber suburban studies a hundred to one. The West Banks of the world, it seems, will likely persevere in their quotidian normalcy, unmolested by scholarly inquiry.

෴

> Here are . . . perhaps a larger number of saw mills [and] planing mills—some of them equal in extent and character to any in the United States. We have here some twenty-five foundries, engine and boiler manufacturers, and numerous machine shops. We have probably the largest and best-managed sugar refinery in the United States . . . foundries engaged on railroad works; one extensive locomotive works . . . railroad car works . . . oil manufacturing . . . extensive chemical works. . . . furniture . . . agricultural implements . . . brass founding. . . . [This] is the place where not only extensive mercantile, but most mechanical and manufacturing operations, may also successfully be prosecuted.[4]

That description came from John Hogan as he marveled in 1854 at the exploding industry of a former French outpost on the Mississippi River. It was St. Louis in Missouri, but his words could nearly fit the West Bank of New Orleans—despite that the Crescent City has long had a weak industrial sector, lagging behind its peer cities, including the Gateway City.

This points to another reason why the West Bank warrants attention from scholars of New Orleans. In this mostly mercantilist entrepôt, the West Bank was the great exception: it *had* industry; it *had* a diversified economy; it *added* value to raw materials rather than just handling them. Whereas the East Bank, home to the Port of New Orleans (and thousands of middlemen), over-relied on the Mississippi River for the relatively easy money of transshipment commerce, the West Bank had little choice but to develop value-added industry (lumber milling, cottonseed oil, foundries, sugar processing) and manufacturing (ships, metalworks, boilers, rail cars, locomotives). It dug canals and laid railroads and used them to deliver raw materials (timber, clay, shells, moss, finfish, shellfish, livestock, petrol) to West Bank sawmills, brick kilns, canneries, slaughterhouses, and refineries. It had a lattice of small farms and dairies interspersed among villages and towns—uncommon in a landscape of cash-crop plantations and swamps—which supported a society of independent farmers and creative entrepreneurs, each of whom could become savers, consumers, and investors within their own regional economy.

Of course, this was no idyllic free market with free people. Few things stifled industrialization more than the institution of slavery, with its commitment to an agrarian order and unholy degradation of labor. On the matters of innovation and entrepreneurship, bondage brought out the worst in the master and suppressed the best of the enslaved. Nevertheless, compared to the adjoining plantation country, the West Bank had an unusually substantial farm-and-village economic geography, and compared to New Orleans's much larger population across the river, West Bankers made for a relative industrial powerhouse. They also had a supportive government, as evidenced by the ahead-of-its-time 1887 Jefferson Parish police jury motion "to offer every inducement and encouragement [for] enterprises and manufactories . . . to [be] located in our midst."[5]

In these regards, the West Bank had elements of the midwestern or northern model of development—"based on 'small farms, free labor, and a rising industrialism,'" as well as the southern system, "based on 'the plantation, with staple crops and slave labor.'"[6] As John Hogan attested in the earlier quote, the midwestern/southern city of St. Louis surged in industry and manufacturing in the mid- to late 1800s, precisely when New Orleans saw its riverine monopoly slip away, with little to take its place. The main reason, argues historian Lawrence Powell, was St. Louis's extensive array of "aspirational towns" in its hinterland, which set the city within an ambit of "petty entrepreneurism," well connected by river, rail, and road. Abetted by good physical geography and abundant natural resources, the isolated frontier waystation was thus able to interact systemically with its region and develop into a diverse, value-added manufacturing center, producing what it consumed and consuming what it produced.

New Orleans proper, clinging to a narrow natural levee and overly dependent on river commerce and slave plantations, had little of this industry-friendly regional economic geography, *but for the West Bank.*[7] Had the ways of the West Bank flourished on the East Bank, the New Orleans metropolis might have developed a more diversified economy of value-added industry with a greater sense of regionalism.

To this day, it struggles in all three regards.

~~~

> Algiers stands out [as a] river town of an earlier epoch. [T]he habits and customs of its citizens [retain] consciousness of its separate existence. In almost every part of Algiers there are actual reminders [of] its former separate identity. The visitor is more apt to think of it as one of the smaller towns in the bayou or upriver [regions] than as the [city] of New Orleans.[8]

That small-town ambience thrives in Algiers Point, in Old Gretna and the older parts of Harvey and Marrero, and in Westwego's Salaville, where from the right perch one can glimpse both the skyscrapers of the Central Business District and the fishing fleet of Bayou Segnette. And the "habits and customs" of West Bank citizens still betray a sense of place that has largely dissipated from the historic districts of the East Bank, because the West Banks of the world have a remarkable capacity for retaining local culture traits, even as they incorporate new cultures.

The national assimilation that began after the Louisiana Purchase in 1803 mostly affected the East Bank in the century ahead. That's where most Anglo-Americans moved, that's where Anglos and Creoles competed for power, and that's where American dollars were invested and American ways eventually prevailed (mostly). The West Bank, separated by a wide and unbridged Mississippi, saw markedly less national assimilation, leaving it to persevere longer in its provincial ways. Ambitious merchants and northern businessmen spent their time and money in New Orleans proper, and built opulent mansions in

East Bank neighborhoods such as the Garden District. The West Bank was the country, and while there certainly were lucrative investment opportunities for out-of-state Anglo industrialists and railroad men, for the most part the region remained in the domain of the *ancienne* population. Those Anglos who did figure prominently in local society—for example, John McDonogh, Stephen Henderson, and Joseph Hale Harvey—generally "creolized" themselves. Geographical isolation fostered cultural continuity; into the mid-twentieth century, the French language could still be heard in Westwego, folks still hand-peeled shrimp and crabs, and the riches of the Barataria still made their way inland on canals dug by slaves.

While the French language is now mostly gone, many West Bankers are only a couple of generations removed from Francophone ancestors, and most themselves are locally born with deep local roots. The region has a higher nativity rate than New Orleans proper, measured by the US Census as the proportion of residents born in-state. Roughly 80 percent of residents of the urbanized West Bank were born in Louisiana, whereas that figure is only 55 percent in the famous historic neighborhoods of the East Bank. A 1978 historic-district report remarked on Algiers Point's unusually large number of "longtime resident families. It is not at all uncommon to find three generations of the same family living within the Point area, if not in the same house. [Many] have lived here since before 1860; several have continuously occupied their original family homes. . . . This strong tie with the past has greatly enriched the entire community."[9] Where local people live for many generations, of course, means treasure troves of local culture, in all its ramifications. One is more likely to hear New Orleans accents, for example, in Algiers, Harvey or Marrero than in just about any "quintessential" historic district in the heart of New Orleans. The French Quarter and Garden District are both majority-transplant, in places by wide margins.[10]

The reason is not a mystery: transplants to New Orleans, particularly educated professionals, tend to want to live in historic houses in walkable neighborhoods, and have little interest in the Westwegos and Gretnas of the region. Nor do they choose New Orleans East or Harahan, which have roughly the same high rates of nativity (that is, being locally born) as the West Bank. It's a common paradox: place-rooted people typically live in (apparently) "placeless" places, whereas mobile professionals gravitate to distinctive historical neighborhoods that have a strong sense of place. And to make matters all the more paradoxical, locally rooted people are increasingly likely to become neighbors with foreign immigrants, who savor the affordability and are more interested in the American Dream than the American past.

Relatedly, many old families who owned West Bank terrain and operated facilities here in the 1800s are still heavily invested here in the 2000s. The descendants of the Destréhans and the Harveys, for example, still oversee the wharves along the Harvey Canal, according to the bylaws stipulated by Louise Destréhan Harvey in 1898; their corporate logo is a sketch of the circa-1846 Harvey Castle in which Louise lived. The Marrero Land & Improvement Company, traceable to the investments of the Isleño-Anglo-American Confederate veteran Louis Herman Marrero, still owns much of the land in Marrero and around Bayou Segnette. The estate of "Drainage King" George A. Hero lives on in the Hero Lands Company, which controls properties in the very areas Hero had drained. Jack Stumpf & Associates, from an old German Gretna family, still owns commercial lots along and near Stumpf Boulevard. The Lockport-based Bollinger family continues to operate shipyards and repair facilities, including a prominent dry dock at Algiers Point, continuing this 185-year-old West Bank industry. Names like "Ames Farms," "Fazande Tract," "Destrehan Division," and "Cedar Grove Plantation" all remain on the official Jefferson Parish assessors' map. And compared to the East Bank, the West Bank's old French long-lots are much better preserved, as irregular "sections" in the otherwise checkerboard modern-day township-and-range survey system.[11]

Perhaps this enduring localism is the upside to being ignored. Living outside the limelight, in the shadows of the rambunctious, has made the West Bank a place where folks can live affordably, where old New Orleans perseveres, and where future New Orleans has found a home.

Appendix 1

West Bank/East Bank
EQUIVALENCIES AND DIFFERENCES

The historiography of greater New Orleans is East Bank-dominant, and for good reason. The city originated on the East Bank, and that side of the river has consistently been home to most of the metropolitan population, economy, and cultural production. Where that preponderance of attention becomes problematic is in its disproportionality: while the West Bank today is home to 30 percent of metro New Orleans residents, and roughly the same percentage of the urbanized footprint, it gets at most one-tenth that level of coverage in the historical and cultural literature.

This book addresses that imbalance by giving the West Bank the attention it deserves, and examining what distinguishes it from its cross-river counterpart. The following table pegs East Bank features or phenomena to their differentiating equivalents on the West Bank.

East Bank feature/phenomenon	West Bank equivalent
Brackish bays and marshes behind populated area (Lakes Pontchartrain, Maurepas, and Borgne) provide food, resources, and access to Gulf of Mexico.	Brackish bays behind populated area (Lakes Cataouatche and Salvador and adjoining Barataria marshes and bays) provide food, natural resources, and Gulf access.

East Bank feature/phenomenon	West Bank equivalent
Bayou St. John is main rivulet providing access from riverfront to back lakes, bays, and Gulf.	Bayou Barataria, Bayou Fatma, and Bayou Segnette connect West Bank to its back bays and Gulf.
Metaire, Gentilly, and Esplanade (Bayou Road) ridges are main interbasin topographic elevations left behind by former river distributaries, providing foot access through backswamp.	Elevated ridges of Bayou des Familles and Bayou Barataria distributaries allow for terrestrial movement southward through backswamp.
Predominantly shallow, slack current runs along East Bank riverfront, forming sandy battures; man-made levee is moved outwardly to reclaim accreted land.	Predominantly deep, swift current runs along West Bank riverfront, causing constant cave-ins and crevasses; revetments installed to protect bank from erosion.
Point bars predominate over cutbanks, meaning that sediment accretion historically prevailed over bankside erosion, thus giving East Bank wider natural levees.	Cutbanks predominate over point bars, meaning that bankside erosion prevailed over accretion, giving West Bank narrower natural levees.
East Bank mostly occupies inner side of river meander, such that French long-lot plantations converge in main uptown crescent.	West Bank mostly occupies outer side of river meander, such that long-lots diverge, widening with distance from Mississippi.
French Quarter	No true equivalent, although Algiers Point is often viewed as such.
East Bank urbanizes from *bourg* (French Quarter) to *faubourgs* (inner suburbs) to *banlieue* (outskirts, later streetcar suburbs), in a nucleated core-to-periphery pattern.	West Bank had no original *bourg* and therefore no *faubourgs*, but rather a necklace of dispersed riverfront "villages" among small farms, industry and plantations; geography is inter-urban rather than nucleated.

East Bank feature/phenomenon	West Bank equivalent
Port activity predominates along Mississippi, with round-the-clock loading and unloading of vessels	Industry predominates along Mississippi, including dry docks, ship building, foundries, and value-added industries
Carondelet (Old Basin) and New Basin Canal are two premier man-made waterways linking neighborhoods to resources of Lake Pontchartrain Basin.	Company Canal and Destrehan (Harvey) Canal are two premier man-made waterways linking villages to resources of Barataria Basin.
East Bank has high population density; large populations living in limited space heightens competition for living space, raising land values.	West Bank has low population living on ample space, making decent land reasonably cheap and influencing different residential and land-use patterns.
East Bank is home to elite residential areas such as Garden District, and most of region's aristocracy ("uptown blue-bloods").	West Bank has no equivalent of Garden District; elites here were typically landed gentry residing in plantation houses. Today, affluent tend to live in gated golf-course communities.
Enslavement is mostly urban; urban core is major slave trading center until Civil War.	Enslavement is mostly rural (field labor); West Bank is major depot for slaves in early 1700s and smuggling route in early 1800s, but is not a major antebellum slave-trading center.
Strong "front-of-town," "back-of-town" geography in residential settlements; whites predominate in "front" and African Americans in "back."	Plenty of space in "front of town" means whites and African Americans reside in lateral spaces, both occupying higher natural levee, rather than front/behind spaces.

East Bank feature/phenomenon	West Bank equivalent
Settlement patterns are mostly informed by geographies of power, convenience, nuisance, and risk.	Settlement patterns are mostly informed by transportation links (ferries, railroads, bridges) to East Bank, as well as other factors.
French-speaking Creole cultural pre-domination gives way to growing Anglo-American influences during mid-1800s.	Americanization is slower to take root; old Creole ways persist nearly into 1900s; Acadian French heard in the streets of Westwego into 1950s.
East Bank's commercial destiny is as maritime nexus of foreland and hinter-land; connectivity to markets comes courtesy Mississippi.	Connectivity to external markets comes courtesy railroads to points west; West Bank's destiny is in expanding western territories of the United States.
Original circa-1900 pump stations placed in center of hydrological basins to be drained, forcing outfall canals in Lakeview and Gentilly to be above-grade and prone to breaching.	Pump stations are placed on periphery of hydrological basins to be drained, allowing outfall canals to be below-grade and not in need of levees—a safer condition than on East Bank.
East Bank drains entire backswamp basin within its conurbation except Bayou Bienvenue.	West Bank drains all backswamp basins except Bayou Segnette, where fishing boats today still dock within sight of West Bank Expressway.
Centralized business district forms in urban core, with high commercial land values and high-rise buildings.	West Bank business districts are small and dispersed, with no centralized cluster of high-rises and zero true sky-scrapers.
East Bank is minimally interactive with Acadian (Cajun) region.	West Bank is significantly interactive with Acadian region, particularly in Marrero and Westwego.

East Bank feature/phenomenon	West Bank equivalent
Conurbation is mostly concretized in its land covers, except for eastern New Orleans.	Conurbation is interspersed with fields, forests, and subrural environments, including metro's largest wooded areas.
East Bank is home to 70 percent of metro area's population, and most of its wealthiest and poorest classes.	West Bank is home to 30 percent of metro population, and is disproportionately working-class and middle-class, with fewer very rich and very poor.
East Bank (urban core) is attractive to immigrants in 1800s and early 1900s; less so today.	West Bank is attractive for immigrants in late 1900s and early 2000s; less so historically.
East Bank within tri-parish conurbation is majority white, 302,500 to 213,228 black in 2010.	West Bank within tri-parish conurbation is majority black, 110,558 to 104,948 white in 2010; increasingly diverse.
Populations in historic districts are majority transplant; gentrification is controversial topic, and outsider influence exerts constant pressure on local culture and traditions, making preservation efforts highly conscientious.	West Bank populations are mostly locally born; gentrification is all but unknown except in Algiers Point and parts of McDonoghville and Gretna; local cultural traits are retained with little self-awareness.
Home to vast majority of tourism economy and visitor experiences.	Rarely visited by tourists except for Algiers Point and swamp tours.
Storm surge threat comes from Lake Pontchartrain to the north and GICWW/MR-GO "funnel" to the east, now blocked by Inner Harbor Navigation Canal Storm Surge Barrier.	Storm surge threat comes from Barataria Basin to the south, via GICWW (Bayou Barataria and Harvey and Algiers canals), now blocked by West Closure Complex.

Appendix 2

Timeline

HISTORICAL GEOGRAPHY OF THE WEST BANK

c. 1500 West Bank landscape is patchwork of cornfields and native villages interspersed among dense forest along Mississippi and distributaries, with transient encampments in coastal marsh.

1519–1543 Three Spanish expeditions explore Gulf Coast and interior South, leaving no settlements but spreading European diseases that decimate indigenous populations in subsequent centuries.

1682 French Canadian Robert La Salle sails down Mississippi and passes future New Orleans site; claims watershed for France and names it "Louisiana" for King Louis XIV.

1699 Le Moyne brothers Iberville and Bienville explore Gulf Coast and lower Mississippi; pass West Bank on March 6, recording detailed descriptions of place and people. Iberville establishes French colonial Louisiana.

1712 Disillusioned and distracted, French Crown cedes Louisiana as commercial monopoly to financier Antoine Crozat. Private effort strives to discover gold and silver mines, raise tobacco, and trade with Spanish Mexico.

1715 King Louis XIV dies; five-year-old great-grandson Louis XV ascends to throne, for whom Philippe II, duc d'Orléans acts as regent of France.

1716 Crown issues edict regulating land grants and establishing *arpent* system in Louisiana, whereby riverine land is surveyed into elongated parcels perpendicular to waterway. French "long lots" deeply influence morphology of future West Bank.

1717 Crozat's failure to develop Louisiana opens opportunity for Scottish financier John Law to propose elaborate land development scheme. Befriending Philippe, Law secures monopoly charter for Louisiana, establishes Company of the West, and launches marketing campaign to recruit investors and settlers.

1717 Directive to found New Orleans issued in Company of the West ledger, dated September 9.

1718 In late March or early April, Bienville's men starting clearing vegetation to found New Orleans.

1719 First large group of Africans arrives in chains, commencing fourteen decades of slavery in Louisiana.

1719 Company depot, workshop, slave prison, lumber mill, and farm are established at present-day Algiers Point. "Company Plantation" is earliest French development on West Bank.

1719 Bienville grants himself ownership of most of East Bank crescent plus West Bank in present-day Algiers, Behrman, and Aurora; self-aggrandizing move angers Company officials.

1719–1721 Law's Company recruits thousands of French citizens, as well as German and Swiss farmers, to sail for Louisiana; Germans settle Côte des Allemands mostly on West Bank upriver from New Orleans.

1720 John Law's "Mississippi Bubble" bursts; Company of the West undergoes frantic restructuring and reemerges as Company of the Indies.

1720s Indigenous population in Louisiana estimated at "well over 35,000," compared to "some 2,500 French, plus 1,500 slaves."[1]

1721 Company officials decide on December 23 to make New Orleans capital and headquarters of Louisiana.

1726   Company Plantation in present-day Algiers operates sixty arpents of croplands and pastures, worked by twenty-five slaves.

1727   West Bank has 111 land parcels, up to German Coast, on which live 297 members of white master families, 29 white servants, 460 black slaves, and 5 Indian slaves. Most reside within today's urbanized West Bank.

1731   Company Plantation spans 250 arpents throughout today's Algiers and Gretna, of which 60 percent is cleared for rice, tobacco, and indigo production.

1731   Company of the Indies goes bankrupt, ending private venture in Louisiana and shifting colony to Crown control.

1732   One of earliest free black owners of West Bank land, named Scipion, is recorded as having sold his parcel to "Simon, a mullatto."[2]

1736–1740   Slaves of Claude Joseph Villars Dubreuil excavate canal to access backswamp timber, which Dubreuil uses to construct twenty small vessels, marking beginning of West Bank's shipbuilding industry.

1730s   Term "Barataria," implying barratry (maritime lawlessness), first appears on Louisiana maps for marshes and bays south of West Bank.

1746–1749   French engineers construct *Batterie de l'ance* on West Bank and *Batterie de la point* on East Bank of English Turn Bend. Known as Fort St. Leon after 1757, bastions are abandoned in late 1760s, rebuilt by Americans in 1807–1809, and abandoned by 1817. Site later becomes Villere Plantation and Fort St. Leon Plantation; some ruins remain into early twentieth century.[3]

1750   Alexandre de Batz builds chateau named Mon Plaisir for Jean-Charles de Pradel; one of first grand estates on West Bank, Monsplaisir later becomes home of John McDonogh and is subsequently swept away by river in 1870s.

1752   Man-made levees are in place along West Bank as far down as Fort St. Leon.[4]

1754–1785   French and Indian War pits France against England over Ohio Valley claims. As war rages, British troops exile French settlers from Acadie in present-day Nova Scotia, Canada; thousands of displaced Acadians eventually settle in lower Louisiana during 1764–1785, drawn by Spanish land grants and French culture. "Cajuns" of the Côte des Acadiens interact economically and socially with West Bank; some settle in Westwego starting in 1890s.

1762–1769   To prevent lands from falling into hands of victorious British at end of French and Indian War, France transfers to Spain all of Louisiana west of Mississippi, plus "Isle of Orleans." West Bank is now Spanish, though population remains largely Francophone. Spain views Louisiana as *barrera* between British colonies and Spanish Main, and aims to increase population. Targeted groups include *Málagueños, Granadinos,* and *Isleños,* some of whom settle in or near West Bank.

1785   Intermarried Harang and Zeringue families come into possession of Petit Desert Plantation on Nine Mile Point; operation grows in 1800s under direction of Camille Zeringue, who becomes influential figure in future Westwego area.

1791   Caste war breaks out in Saint-Domingue and explodes into full-scale slave insurrection.

1795   Protocols for growing Louisiana sugarcane and granulating juice are perfected, leading to large-scale shift in West Bank plantation agriculture, from rice and indigo to sugarcane.

1800   Apprehensive about American interest in Louisiana, Spain, under duress from Napoleon, secretly retrocedes Louisiana to militarily powerful France, but continues to administer colony.

1802   Napoleon sends 20,000 troops to control situation in Saint-Domingue. Yellow fever decimates many; slave revolt intensifies and eventually expels French regime, leading to independence of Haiti in 1804. Loss of extremely valuable sugar colony quells Napoleon's interest in Louisiana.

1802   Spain rescinds American right of deposit at New Orleans, exacerbating tensions; President Thomas Jefferson launches effort to purchase New Orleans from France. Threat of war emerges, with England casting eyes on Louisiana as well.

1803   Wary of overextending his empire, in need of money, and in light of impending war, Napoleon sells entire Louisiana colony to United States; treaty signed April 30 and commemorated December 20. West Bank is now American.

Early 1800s   Ever-shifting channel of Mississippi scours West Bank, eroding up to one thousand feet of valuable riverfront land by century's end, particularly in McDonoghville.

1804–1820   Heyday of Barataria smuggling, overseen by Lafitte brothers and using Grande Terre Island for transshipment into West Bank and New Orleans.

1805   Barthélémy Duverjé runs three small abattoirs at foot of Lavergne Street, first livestock usage of this area that will earn Pointe St. Antoine (now Algiers Point) the nickname "Slaughterhouse Point."

1805   Orleans County is created by American territorial government, including today's West Bank; City of New Orleans gains charter as incorporated entity on East Bank.

1807   Orleans Parish is created as coterminous jurisdiction with Orleans County (District), the former serving judicial and civic purposes, the latter for elections and taxation.

1807 to 1825   What is now the urbanized area of the West Bank is administered in this era by legislative acts set out in 1805 under territorial government, and under the state starting in 1812. Governance later takes form of police jury overseeing unincorporated Orleans Parish lands on both sides of river.

1808   Act Prohibiting Importation of Slaves is passed, ending international slave trade into United States but creating illicit market for slave smuggling through Barataria region.

1809   New Orleans City Council acts to clear East Bank of ship repair activity, making room for loading and unloading; opens opportunity for West Bank.

1811   Major slave revolt erupts on German Coast upriver from New Orleans, followed by ruthless suppression. While most bloodshed occurs on East Bank, tensions between white and black, free and enslaved, are heightened, and institution of slavery entails constant policing and threat of violence.

1812   Barthélémy Duverjé builds archetypal French Creole Louisiana country manse at present-day Algiers Point; later becomes Algiers Courthouse until destroyed by 1895 blaze.

1814   John McDonogh has riverside portion of his plantation subdivided as McDonoghville, first street grid and urbanization on West Bank.

1814   US Master Commandant Daniel Todd Patterson raids Baratarians at Grande Terre Island to prevent their siding with British in impending attack; Jean Lafitte arranges for Baratarians to support American side in exchange for amnesty.

1815   British attack on New Orleans ends in epic defeat by American forces at Chalmette, even as smaller invading units achieve brief victories on West Bank.

1815   Nearly fifty West Bank long-lot plantations are in operation along forty river-fronting miles between present-day English Turn and Avondale.

1819   Frenchman André Séguin opens state's first marine ways, allowing for vessel construction and repair, at foot of present-day Seguin Street in Algiers.

1821   Duverjé Plantation is subdivided as Duverjéville, creating street grid of today's Algiers Point more than a century after settlement is first established as a depot.

1822   Andry family builds large Creole house to oversee sugarcane plantation in lower Algiers. Sold by 1841 to Jean Baptiste Le-Pretre and to Thomas P. Stanton in 1869, plantation becomes last major sugarcane operation in New Orleans, lasting into 1920s.

1821–1823   Guy Noël Destréhan purchases Derbigny and LeBreton (Robin) plantations, beginning Destréhan family's highly influential presence on West Bank, ongoing to this day.

1820s   "Freetown," first free black settlement on West Bank, forms in John McDonogh's subdivision.

1825   State legislature creates new parish, named Jefferson, out of Orleans Parish; jurisdiction spans both banks and runs from Lake Pontchartrain to Grand Isle. New parish is subdivided into twelve districts, each governed by a commissioner.

1826   Engineer Jean Jerome petitions State Legislature to build a European-style stone segmental arch bridge across Mississippi River at New Orleans, first such plan.

1827   State Legislature grants Bazile Gosselin and Auguste Coycault exclusive right to open steam ferry for cross-river service, accommodating twenty passengers. By 1834, two ferries connect New Orleans and Algiers with regular service; by 1858, three.[5]

1829–1841   Barataria and Lafourche Canal forms; acquires land from Zeringue Plantation and secures state support to excavate navigation channel to southwest. By 1834, Company Canal is in operation; by 1841, workers complete second stretch to Bayou Lafourche, giving rise to Lockport.

1830s   Names "Algiers" and "Tunisburg" (Tunis) become associated with subdivisions in former Duverjé and Cazalard plantations, in allusion to North African cities associated with American military actions during the Second Barbary War (1815) and France's 1830 colonization of Algeria.

1830s   Regular ferry service begins operation in Faubourg St. Mary and Lafayette to Algiers and Gretna, seeding West Bank with new pool of residents, investors, and commuters.

1833   City surveyor Joseph Pilié subdivides Toussaint Mossy's plantation, abandoning angled orientation of Duverjéville and conflating new Mossyville grid with McDonoghville.

1834   State legislature creates "Police Jury of the Parish of Jefferson," where jurors represent eight to twelve districts, or wards.

1834   Work begins on US Marine Hospital in McDonoghville, based on designs by architect Robert Mills. Funding shortfall caused by Panic of 1837 delays work and introduces moisture problems; when completed in 1849, hospital spans 160 feet and rises nearly as high, featuring Gothic fenestration and crenelated towers. But problems with dampness persist, and it is largely abandoned a decade later.[6]

1834–1839   Cazalard plantation subdivided as Tunisburg (Tunis), later known as McLellanville, now around Odeon Avenue and Horace streets.

1836   Nicolas Noël Destréhan hires Pierre Benjamin Buisson to subdivide Mechanickham, now Old Town Gretna. Destréhan also designs Cosmopolite City (today's Harvey) with a type of "Oglethorpe Plan," though it is never executed.

1837   Region's first dry dock opens on Algiers riverfront for ship repair, operated by New Orleans Floating Dry Dock Company.

1839   Destréhan hires contract laborers to excavate navigation canal to link with Bayou Barataria; becomes Harvey Canal and later a key segment of Gulf Intracoastal Waterway.

1840   State creates "Police Jury of the Parish of Orleans on the Right Bank of the River Mississippi" to govern Algiers, distinguishing between administration of Left (East) and Right (West) banks of areas inside Orleans Parish but outside City of New Orleans.

1840   Camille Zeringue builds Seven Oaks Plantation House, largest plantation mansion in vicinity and a major West Bank landmark.

1842   Crevasse in Algiers sweeps structures into Mississippi.

1842   City directory lists twelve ship carpenters in Algiers, plus eight regular carpenters, "three ship captains, two painters, two engineers, a joiner, a ship's blacksmith, a mechanic, a caulker, a blockmaker and two shipbuilders."[7]

1844   Gretna Fire Engine Company incorporates three years after initial organization; later becomes David Crocket Fire Company, said to be oldest continually active volunteer fire company in region.

1845   Nicolas Noël Destréhan arranges marriage of daughter Louise to Captain Joseph Hale Harvey; couple soon becomes among most powerful on West Bank. Next year they build "Harvey's Castle" along family's canal in Harvey; later becomes Jefferson Parish Courthouse and a well-known landmark of West Bank.

1846   John P. Whitney establishes Belleville Iron Works in Algiers; covering 150,000 square feet and employing 300 men, Belleville becomes area's largest foundry and name of neighborhood.

1846   State legislature does away with counties as state sub-jurisdictional units, for their confusion and redundancy with parishes. West Bank now comprises parts of Orleans, Jefferson, Plaquemines parishes.

1847   Cave-in of bank by Eliza Street leads to breach of levee and subsequent flooding. Levee is later realigned inland to avoid erosive river currents in upper Algiers/McDonoghville area.[8]

1848   St. Bartholomew Church founded in Algiers Point, named for patriarch of family of Barthélémy Duverjé that donated original land parcel; later renamed Holy Name of Mary Parish. Affiliated cemetery is established 1866; extant Gothic-style church built in 1929.

1849   City directory lists thirty-four ship carpenters, joiners, and painters, two ship smiths and three ship builders in Algiers.

1849   United States government purchases riverfront land near Le-Beuf Plantation House (1840, still standing) in Algiers to be used as dry dock and supply depot; ends up leasing it out for agriculture until 1901, when naval station is established upon additional land acquired in 1894 from Trepagnier and Oliver families.[9]

1849   High water levels in the Mississippi rupture Fortier Plantation levee in present-day Waggaman on West Bank; later causes Sauvé's Crevasse on East Bank, which results in New Orleans's worst nineteenth-century deluge.

1840s–1860s   Movement to incorporate Algiers as separate municipal entity from New Orleans gains support; in 1855 state broadens police jury's power, making Algiers a *de facto* city, yet still without a municipal incorporation charter.

1850   Crevasse at Lacoste Plantation's levee floods plantations six miles below Algiers Point.

1850   McDonoghville Cemetery established by John McDonogh for his slaves as well as his own entombment; remains later removed to Baltimore.

1851   "Railroad fever" comes to West Bank. Delegates at New Orleans, Algiers, Attakapas and Opelousas Railroad Convention in June resolve to build line connecting Algiers with Washington on Bayou Courtableau in St. Landry Parish.

1851   Two crevasses on Lacoste and Gardere properties flood Gretna-Harvey area.[10]

1851   Algiers organizes its first fire engine company, replacing informal bucket brigades with what would become Pelican No. 1, Brooklyn No. 2, Morgan No. 3, and Washington No. 1 stations. Professionalization of fire protection reflects and furthers community growth, as insurance companies start issuing fire policies to local homeowners.[11]

1852–1857   Investors obtain state charter to build New Orleans, Opelousas and Great Western Railroad "to a point on the Sabine River . . . through the State of Texas to El Paso [and] thence to the Pacific Ocean." By fall 1854, line spans 52 miles to Bayou Lafourche; by spring 1857, 80 miles to Berwick Bay.

1856–1858   Jefferson Parish police jury revamped to give each village three elected commissioners to oversee public works; new policy gives some authority and spatial form to West Bank's organic population clusters.

1857–1859   St. Joseph Church is established on Lavoisier and Sixth Street in Gretna, its German, Irish, and French congregants having been previously served by Redemptorists who ferried over from New Orleans. Later expanded to include a rectory, school, and convent, this "Mother Church of West Jefferson" now occupies a circa-1927 Spanish Baroque structure with adjoining loggia and plaza.

1858   Each bank of Jefferson Parish gets its own governance, that on West being the "Police Jury of Jefferson, Right Bank."

1858   Algiers is home to twelve dry docks, making it vital to the entire region's maritime economy. Ship smiths, carpenters (joiners), painters, and other specialized nautical craftsmen live nearby.

1850s   Laurent Millaudon presides over 3,700 acres of Jefferson Parish, of which 1,800 acres sit between Harvey and Company canals, used to raise sugarcane with over 400 slaves. Millaudon sells estate to son H. C. Millaudon in 1859 for equivalent of over $30 million in today's dollars, making family one of Louisiana's richest.

1858   Bell Crevasse forms in levee at present-day Avenue B in Marrero/Harvey; by mid-June, floodwaters extend nearly to Gulf. Breach finally sealed in December using ring levees, ending one of West Bank's worst disasters.

1858   William Tell Hook and Ladder Company Cemetery established in Gretna.

1859   Company Canal comes into possession of Robert R. Barrow, who reorganizes company and recommits to completing western terminus. For decades to come, Company Canal competes with Harvey Canal for Barataria trade.

Late 1850s–1860s   Most tumultuous era in West Bank history—hydrologically, politically, militarily, and socially.

1860   Manuel Abascal (1842–1909), born in Spain and arrived to New Orleans via Havana, opens grocery in Algiers. Store becomes a West Bank favorite for imported delicacies; uses West Bank's excellent rail connections to distribute regionally. Abascal becomes major local investor and civil leader, serving on levee board and donating money to various Algiers community projects. Family operates grocery at 500 Pelican Avenue until 1969.

1861   Louisiana secedes from Union on January 26 and later joins Confederate States of America. Federal blockade quiets activity at Port of New Orleans; West Bank shipbuilding industry is commandeered for war effort.

1861   In late December, old US Marine Hospital in Gretna, used by Confederates to store gunpowder, explodes, weakening levee and flooding McDonoghville riverfront, including John McDonogh's old plantation house.

1862   In late April, Flag Officer Farragut's Union fleet, following naval battle at mouth of the Mississippi, proceeds upriver to take New Orleans, as Confederates scuttle West Bank dry docks and destroy shipyards. On May 1 federal authorities occupy New Orleans and seize railroads on West Bank; Union troops camp by Company Canal to guard New Orleans, Opelousas, and Great Western Railroad.

1864   New Louisiana Constitution passed by biracial legislature officially abolishes slavery in Louisiana; thousands of emancipated West Bankers begin struggle to arrange for work and housing, establishing residential settlement patterns still visible today.

1865   April high water triggers cave-in at Algiers Point riverfront and crevasse at McGee's Plantation, four miles downriver.

1869   State legislature centralizes livestock slaughtering under one operator; makeshift landing and processing facilities are hastily erected in Algiers, later moved to Arabi. Legal case goes to United States Supreme Court, which in 1873 rules on controversial *Slaughter-house Cases*.

1869–1871   New Orleans, Mobile and Texas Railroad lays track to connect Gulf Coast with northern Texas through West Bank. Company locates terminal near Company Canal and names facility "West-We-Go" to advertise western access. Later known as Texas & Pacific Railroad.

1869–1870   Over 1,200 Chinese arrive to Louisiana as laborers; largest single cohort on West Bank comes from San Francisco via St. Louis and arrives at Merrill plantation, future Marrero, in June 1870.

1870   Harvey family attempts to build proper lock for Harvey Canal, but quicksand puts chamber out of plumb, forcing return to mule-drawn circa-1840s "submarine railway."

1870   On March 16, state law annexes Algiers, previously of unincorporated Orleans Parish, into City of New Orleans; parish and city limits have been coterminous ever since.

1870s–1950s   Many old plantations formerly devoted to cash-crop commodities using slave labor are subdivided into small-parcel truck farms and leased to farmers, many of them former slaves or recent immigrants. Checkerboard of intensive gardens and small farms dominates rural fringes of West Bank into era of suburbanization, when many are subdivided again, this time with street grids and house lots.

1870s   Forty years after Mechanickham and Gretna are laid out, both subdivisions are expanded with New Mechanickham and New Gretna annexes, today all part of City of Gretna.

1870s   Shipping magnate Charles Morgan, having acquired Great Western (Morgan's Louisiana & Texas Railroad), expands Algiers rail yards to accommodate Texas cotton. Company later goes intermodal, building scores of vessels; Morgan's Louisiana and Texas Railroad and Steamship Company connects Algiers with both coasts and Caribbean.

1870s   With federal authority growing after Civil War, United States government commits to Mississippi River control for navigation and flood control. Federal expenditures on waterway improvements grow twelvefold since 1850s.

1873   A. B. Merrill sells his West Bank plantation to Oak A. Ames, who along with brothers Oliver and Frank and their hired black workforce, soon yield five million pounds of sugar annually. Brothers subdivide lands to lease to small farmers, which become known as the Southside, Front Place, and Estelle farms. Area is called Amesville, now Marrero.

1874–1879   Captain James Eads gets permission to install jetties at mouth of Mississippi, constraining flow of river and letting current flush out bedload sediment; resolves shoaling impediment and rejuvenates shipping activity at Port of New Orleans.

1874   After annexation of Jefferson Parish City of Carrollton into New Orleans, police jury relocates parish courthouse to West Bank, leasing Harvey's Castle from Louise Harvey. Loss of Carrollton and Jefferson City (in 1870) on East Bank makes West Bank home to most Jefferson Parish residents, which lasts into 1930s.

1877   P. S. Dolhonde donates square in New Mechanickham, on what is now Dolhonde Street in Gretna "on which to build a courthouse & jail."[12] Donation plants seed for today's Jefferson Parish Correctional Facility and Thomas F. Donelon Courthouse.

1870s–1880s   Ferryman Thomas Pickles secures leases for ferries connecting Algiers to various parts of New Orleans; by 1889 Pickles controls five ferries and local streetcar lines.[13]

1878   Congress authorizes Barataria Ship Canal Company to dig deep-draft seaway from West Bank to Gulf to circumvent shoaling problems at river's mouth. But Eads's Jetties are presently resolving that problem, and seaway idea is shelved—only to revive sixty years later.

1879   Congress creates Mississippi River Commission to work with Corps of Engineers in advising and funding state and local governments in controlling Mississippi with levees.

1880–1883   Railroad tycoon Jay Gould, having gained control of Texas & Pacific Railroad, buys out New Orleans Pacific Railroad's track charter to Shreveport and Charles Morgan's line to Donaldson, aiming to unite T&P's eastern and western track networks. T&P builds terminal in Gretna and installs rail ferry *Gouldsboro* in 1881. Lower Gretna, McDonoghville, and Freetown become known as Gouldsboro, and adjacent river as Gouldsboro Bend.[14]

1880s–1960s   Algiers Yard, long occupied by Southern Pacific tracks, runs 22 blocks in length, lined by massive industrial buildings containing blacksmith shops, machine shops, foundries, wood mills, paint sheds and other spaces for assembly of locomotives, rolling stock, and vessels.

1881   Crevasse floods streets of Gretna.

1882   Inaugural run of Algiers, Gretna & Tunisburg Railroad for local passenger service.

1884   Right and left bank police juries of Jefferson Parish are reconsolidated into single parish-wide body, which uses William Tell Hall in Gretna as its courthouse.

1884   Davis Crevasse in St. Charles Parish sends river water into lowlands and floods rear of Gretna, Algiers, and much of West Bank, "submerg[ing] the entire rear portion of town and compell[ing] the building of a protection levee."[15]

1884–1890   Four spur dikes are installed on Gouldsboro Bend (Gretna/Algiers) and two at Greenville Bend (Westwego/Marrero), to slow current and decrease risk of cave-ins and crevasses.

1887   Jefferson Parish police jury adopts policy of actively recruiting industry to come to West Bank.

1887–1906   Corps of Engineers installs revetments on river bank from Anson Street to Seguin Street, to absorb energy of current and reduce abrasion to levee.

1889   Civil engineer Elmer Lawrence Corthell proposes belt road and bridge across Mississippi at Nine-Mile Point, initial conception of span that would become Huey P. Long Bridge in 1935.

1890   Gazetteer describes Gretna (population 4,000) as "chiefly a manufacturing town, [with] three large oil mills, one cooperage manufactory, the Union Stone company, the Louisiana Cypress Lumber company, two moss factories, a large brick manufactory, and other concerns."[16]

1890   Algiers has 3.3 miles of streetcar lines for local passenger service.

1890   McDonoghville population is 2,235.[17]

1890s   Tiny Chinese hamlet operates market garden by Southern Pacific Railway track near Gretna and exports produce regionally.

1891   Crevasse develops from pipe cut in levee on Ames (formerly Millaudon) Plantation in present-day Westwego/Marrero; widens to over one thousand feet in June. Floodwaters spread to Vacherie and Bayou Lafourche; worst West Bank disaster since Bell Crevasse of 1858.

1892   August cave-in destroys Algiers train depot; motivates Orleans Levee Board in 1893 to spend $100,000 on levee upgrades.

1892   Spanish-born Pablo Sala acquires part of former Zeringue Plantation and lays out lots adjacent to Company Canal. Within a year, up to two hundred people live in "Salaville" section of Westwego.

1893   October 1 hurricane devastates Cajun fishing community of Chênière Caminada near Grand Isle; survivors sail up Company Canal and Harvey Canal for refuge on West Bank, and many settle permanently in Westwego.

1893   Pablo Sala converts circa-1840 Seven Oaks Plantation House near Westwego into Columbia Gardens resort, offering entertainment, ornamental gardens, sports, and access to mansion. Entrepreneurial venture is ahead of its time and very popular, but declines after Sala's death in 1894.

1890s   "Cannery Row" forms on Sala Avenue at 2nd Street in Westwego, becoming region's premier seafood processing and canning district, employing hundreds of women, white and black.

1895   Ten blocks in Algiers Point burn in October 21 blaze. Nearly two hundred houses are destroyed and dozens more damaged, leaving twelve hundred residents homeless; community rebuilds within a year, now the heart of today's Algiers Point.

1896   Large sugar house burns at peak of milling season on Aurora Plantation below Algiers; main house is spared, but fifty-thousand-dollar loss accelerates decline of sugarcane plantation landscape on West Bank of Orleans Parish.[18]

1898   Matriarch Louise Destréhan Harvey professionalizes operation of family canal by incorporating the Harvey Canal Land and Improvement Company, keeping control among kin. It remains today, as the Harvey Canal Limited Partnership.

1898   State legislature passes Lawrason Act, which defines a city as an incorporated area with population more than five thousand, a town between one thousand and five thousand residents, and a village fewer than one thousand. Law affects status and governing bodies of West Bank communities as they begin to incorporate in early twentieth century.

1900   Drainage work, overseen by New Orleans Sewerage and Water Board, begins in Algiers. Streets are torn up, drains and pipes laid, pump station installed, and, in 1907, work commences on three-mile-long Algiers Outfall Canal to connect with Bayou Barataria.

1901   Using riverfront land originally purchased in 1849 and augmented in 1894, United States Navy installs Dry Dock YFD-2 as central facility of new Naval Station New Orleans. Over next three years, Navy expropriates adjacent properties and Marine Corps opens barracks at naval base. Facility becomes, by 1919, "a place of deposit for supplies, a coaling station, and a repair plant" as well as "an important base for general military and industrial supplies, a training camp for sailors, and a Marine Barracks. [The] dry dock at the Naval Station is capable of raising out of the water a vessel of 18,000 tons of displacement."[19]

1901   Front (First) Street opened to connect McDonoghville and Gretna, marking beginning of modern continuous highway system.[20]

1902   One year after Louisiana's first successful oil well near Jennings, well is drilled in Algiers near Fifth District pumping station, "in the hope of striking a flow of crude petroleum in paying quality." Sixty-five-foot-high derrick is placed where "a flow of natural gas was encountered by Mr. Ernst nearly fifteen years ago, and ever since . . . has flowed uninterruptedly [and] has been used for illuminating Mr. Ernst's residence, yard, and both dairies."[21] Oil and gas handling, processing, and support services would become West Bank's most lucrative industry.

1902   Millions of buffalo fish die in Harvey Canal; stench forces Horace Harvey to cut levee and let river water flush out carrion—thus fast-tracking plans to build modern lock at juncture with Mississippi. Work commences 1903; lock opens 1907.

1903   Bayou Lafourche is mostly sealed off from Mississippi; water in bayou drops to near sea level, allowing lock to be removed at Lockport and enabling Company Canal to finally connect to Attakapas County.

1905   Algiers Railway and Lighting Company electrifies streetcar service.

1905   Businessmen in Victoria, Texas, form Interstate Inland Waterway League, aiming to create eighteen-thousand-mile network of interconnected waterways from Great Lakes through Mississippi Valley to Gulf Coast. Group becomes today's Gulf Intracoastal Canal Association, coordinating with federal authorities on management of waterway, which transects West Bank.

1907   President Theodore Roosevelt forms Inland Waterways Commission, to challenge railroad monopolies by aiding navigation sector. Commission gives rise to Gulf Intracoastal Waterway, which comes through West Bank in 1920s–1950s.

1907   Lock at Harvey Canal passes engineering tests and is officially opened with ceremony on March 30, bringing antebellum waterway into twentieth century.

1907   Before dawn on April 14, fire of unknown origin ignites at Durac Terrebonne Fishermen's Exchange in Westwego. Northeasterly winds spread flames along Sala Avenue; neighbors form bucket brigade until horse-drawn fire engines arrive from East Bank. By noon, forty-two buildings are destroyed, including town hall, post office, two schools, Presbyterian Church, bakery, and two stores, leaving up to six hundred homeless. Blaze is West Bank's worst since Algiers in 1895; charitable donations help victims rebuild four blocks along Sala Avenue.[22]

1907   New Jefferson Parish Courthouse is built in Gretna in eclectic Neoclassical-Beaux Arts style; now serves as Gretna City Hall.

1907   Rise of automobile leads to construction of Newton Street Viaduct to get traffic over Southern Pacific Rail Yards and onto what is now Gen. Meyer Avenue. Decline of rail yards leads to removal of overpass in 1960, replaced by grade-level pavement at 1000–1200 Newton.

1909–1915   Modern mechanized drainage begins on West Bank with formation of tax-funded drainage districts in upper Harvey and Marrero (1909), and in lower Harvey, Gretna, McDonoghville, plus portions of Orleans and Plaquemines Parish (1912). Fast-tracked by efforts of "Drainage King" George A. Hero, projects are hugely successful, resulting in rapid removal of standing water in 1915. But landscape subsequently subsides below sea level, creating flood risk.

1912   Missouri Pacific Railroad Company purchases Seven Oaks Plantation House on former Zeringue Plantation; area becomes train yard, tank farm, and terminal for Walnut Street Train Ferry. Mansion's eighteen rooms are rented out to tenants.

1913   Gretna is incorporated, putting original Gretna and Mechanickham subdivisions, plus 1870s annexes, in official limits of Town of Gretna (City of Gretna after 1916).

1913   Immigration and Naturalization Service establishes immigration station by the naval station two miles below Algiers Point, "largest south of Philadelphia. Its purpose is to exclude from the country undesirable aliens . . . who would probably become a burden to the community." Until its closure in 1934, station processes thousands of immigrants and guest workers, primarily from Latin America and Caribbean.[23]

1914-1918   War in Europe, and United States involvement in 1917–1918, demonstrates inadequacy of nation's rail system to handle matériel heading to front, and advances calls for more inland waterways. Government builds fleet of modern tow barges; Corps of Engineers commits to interior and intracoastal waterways.

1915   Algiers boasts 9.3 miles of streetcar lines for local passenger service.

1915   Southern Shell Fish Company opens along Harvey Canal; later said to be "largest shrimp canning operation in the world."[24]

1916   State legislature passes constitutional amendment for City of New Orleans to build bridge over Mississippi at Nine Mile in Jefferson Parish, through its Public Belt Railroad Commission.

1917   Corps of Engineers begins negotiations with Barrows and Harveys to acquire either family's canal, the Company or the Harvey, to become federal Gulf Intracoastal Waterway.

1918   New Orleans City Council passes ordinance for creation of Board of Advisory Engineers within Public Belt Railroad Commission, to research all angles of bridge project.

1918   About five hundred African Americans live in Cutoff in lower Algiers, for whom philanthropically funded Rosenwald School opens; institution is now Rosenwald Middle School and Collegiate Academies.

1919   Board of Advisory Engineers of Public Belt Railroad Commission releases report recommending bridge to Nine Mile Point, fixing site for future Huey P. Long Bridge.

1919   Corps decides to purchase Harvey Canal to connect Intracoastal Waterway with Mississippi; agreement reached in 1921 and finalized in 1924.

1919   Westwego incorporates as a town; redesignated a city in 1951.

1920s West Bank electrified streetcar system peaks with service from lower Algiers and Algiers Point through Monroe Street in Freetown and McDonoghville to Gretna, and along Fourth Street through Harvey, terminating at Barataria Boulevard in Amesville (Marrero).

1921   Corrine Degree Walker purchases land in Amesville, now called Marrero; enclave leads to formation of African American community on Walkertown Road, now Ames Boulevard.

1921   Celotex establishes major manufacturing plant in Marrero to convert sugarcane bagasse into rigid insulation boards and ceiling tiles; by late 1930s, facility spans 150 acres, employs 1600 workers, and exports 400 million square board feet to worldwide market.

1922   Cave-in at Stanton Plantation on lower coast of Algiers is contained by crib levee, preventing major crevasse, but damage leads to demise of circa-1822 plantation house and sugarcane operation, last one in New Orleans proper.[25]

1922–1923   Concrete sidewalks laid throughout Gretna; Jefferson Memorial Arch erected in front of courthouse.[26]

1924   Harvey Canal officially becomes part of Intracoastal Waterway, while wharves remain in family control. Government demolishes old Harvey Castle, widens and dredges channel, and begins work on larger lock, completed in 1934.

1925   Bridge builder Ralph Modjeski wins War Department permit for high cantilever bridge at Nine Mile Point, future Huey P. Long Bridge.

1925   Behrman Highway is cut through now-drained swamp, opening up development between Algiers and Belle Chasse. Land donated by Julius Bodenger's Elmwood Land Development to become Algiers Park (1933), today's Brechtel Park, later spurs new subdivision here.[27]

1925   Proposed "Hero-Hackett Bridge," envisioned by George Hero and Allen Hackett to connect Race Street in New Orleans to Perry Street in Gretna, wins support from Jefferson Parish police jury. But delay in securing War Department permission pushes project into Depression, costing it financing and losing ground to pending Huey P. Long Bridge construction.

1925   Bayou Barataria (Barataria Basin) Waterway, authorized in 1919, is dredged across 37 miles of marshes to connect Bayou Villars with Grand Isle.[28]

Mid-1920s   George Hero tries growing maidencane grass on his Belle Chasse holding; when that fails, he parlays his son's wartime aviation service into creation of Alvin Callender Field, today's Belle Chasse Naval Air Station.

1925–1940s Catholic Church builds Hope Haven Institute and Madonna Manor on either side of Barataria Boulevard in Marrero; orphanage, school, and church feature striking Spanish Baroque architecture.

1926   Concrete sidewalks laid throughout Westwego.[29]

1927   Louisiana Power & Light Company (LaPaLCo) forms as subsidiary of regional electrical corporation. Predecessor of Entergy Louisiana becomes major influencer of West Bank development patterns and land use; name lives in Lapalco Boulevard, where company held right-of-way for transmission corridor.

1927   Louisiana Land and Exploration Company and The Texas Company begin exploring Lafitte Oil Field using derricks erected on foundations, but later switch to patented drilling barges floated in on canals. Hundreds of miles of oil and gas extraction canals are later cut through Barataria wetlands, creating economic wealth but also coastal deterioration.[30]

1927   United States Supreme Court in 1927 rules against New Orleans's 1924 racial zoning ordinance in *Harmon v. Tyler*, after which segregationist efforts in real estate shift to contractual strategies, namely racist deed covenants.

1927–1929   Gretna-born novelist Robert Emmet Kennedy publishes *Gritny People* and *Red Bean Row*, about life in West Bank's poor black communities.

1929–1931   Streetcars on Naval Station, Marrero-Gretna, Algiers, Algiers-Gretna, and Gretna and Belt lines are replaced by rubber-tire buses.

1930   Main road from Algiers to Westwego is paved, West Bank's first modern auto highway (now Highway 18, plus 4th and 5th Street in Gretna and Franklin Avenue in McDonoghville and Algiers). Section from Gretna to Westwego becomes known as "one of the worst traffic bottlenecks in the State" and eventuates calls for West Bank Expressway.[31]

1932   Federal government opens quarantine station in lower Algiers; remains in service into 1960s.[32]

1932   Gretna-Belle Chasse Highway (today's State Highway 23) is paved; road to Grand Isle is built (today's State Highway 1),

paved in 1948, and elevated in 2009 with new Leeville Bridge
due to extreme coastal land loss.[33]

1932 Agreement reached to fund bridge at Nine Mile Point, in
which Public Belt Railroad Commission will issue bonds,
federal government would underwrite them, city and state
would build bridge, and Southern Pacific would pay annual
rent to offset expenses. Work commences shortly thereafter.

1932 Barataria Basin contains 1,480 square miles of land; by 2016,
only 1,047 square miles remain, the rest having been dredged,
eroded, or inundated.

1930s–1950s Hundreds of linear miles are dredged through marshes of Barataria Basin to access oil and gas wells. Most are later abandoned,
allowing salt water to intrude inland; for rest of century, land
disappears at rate of two to five square miles per year throughout basin.

1930s Algiers Water Pageant held during carnival, featuring Krewe
of Alla. "On the Monday afternoon before Mardi Gras, Algiers
. . . gives its Carnival parade[,] an unusual procession of water
floats ascending the Mississippi River. Countless small craft
ply the water carrying the King's loyal subjects, [amid] shrill
and guttural boat whistles proclaiming the royal presence."[34]

1933 City-run Touro-Shakespeare Home, an uptown New Orleans
alms house founded in 1895 by funds from Judah Touro's
will, moves to 2650 Gen. Meyer Avenue in Algiers. Becomes
Touro-Shakespeare Nursing Home; currently empty and falling into decay.

1935 Ceremonies on December 16 inaugurate Huey P. Long Bridge,
first span across lower Mississippi. West Bank, from Algiers
to Avondale, is home to fifty-five thousand people, in which
"Gretna is the parish seat and an industrial center; Harvey
is the terminus for the Intracoastal Canal; Marrero is a dairy
center and an industrial center [with five thousand jobs];
Westwego has many large industries established there . . .

and Grand Isle a recreational and health resort of the first magnitude."[35]

1935   The Texas Company drills deepest well in nation in Barataria Bay's Lafitte Oil Field, which produces over a thousand barrels a day for years. Pipeline is laid through swamp in 1936 to bring crude to Marrero and Harvey facilities. Lafitte Oil Field has 42 producing wells by 1938; by 1955, there are 87 producing wells and 15 million cubic feet of natural gas extracted daily.[36]

1938   With new Huey P. Long Bridge accessing West Jefferson, investors establish Avondale Marine Ways at former train ferry terminal. Shipyard later becomes largest private employer in Louisiana, and gives rise to subdivisions in Avondale, Waggaman, and Bridge City.

1939   Fifty-five percent of locally made products shipped out of Port of New Orleans are manufactured on West Bank, despite being home to only 15 percent of metro population.

1940   Aurora neighborhood subdivided out of old Aurora (Jourdan) Plantation by Ernest B. Norman Sr., aiming to house thousands of workers expected at Algiers's Todd Shipyards and naval station.

1941–1945   World War II brings major industrial investments and plant workforces to greater New Orleans; West Bank ship repair and shipbuilding industry booms. More than four thousand workers are employed at naval station in Algiers; further downriver along Belle Chasse riverfront, military creates extensive array of earth-covered concrete depots to store torpedo warheads, black powder, and other munitions for naval combat in Pacific.

1941   United States government covertly works to arrest suspected Nazis in Latin America and bring them stateside, including to Camp Algiers, at former Immigrant and Naturalization Station. Instead, many German Jewish refugees get caught up in operation, and Camp Algiers is instead is used to house anti-Nazis throughout war. Site later becomes headquarters for US Customs and Border Protection.

1942   Five major seafood processors—Ed Martin Seafood, Robinson's
        Shrimp, Louisiana Blue Crab, Hudson Seafood, and Cutcher
        Seafood—employ 567 people in Westwego's Sala Avenue "Can-
        nery Row."

1943   Local officials and shipping magnates meet with Army Corps
        and agree that a tidewater seaway would put New Orleans and
        inland waterway system back in competition with traffic in
        Panama Canal. Initially envisioned in 1870s, idea comes back
        to life as "West Bank Seaway."

1943   West Bank is home to 53,315 people residing in 15,200 dwell-
        ings; total number of West Bank jobs is at least 39,000, al-
        though many are held by commuting East Bankers.[37]

1946   New York City planning czar Robert Moses submits report,
        Arterial Plan for New Orleans, to Louisiana Highway Depart-
        ment, envisioning region's future transportation system. "The
        natural area of residential expansion at New Orleans," Moses
        declares, "is in the direction of Algiers and Gretna."

1946–1954   West Bank business leaders unite to form Westbank Business
        & Industry Association; organization becomes private-sector
        voice advocating for transportation improvements, flood con-
        trol, and better commercial and civic environments.

1947   Norman family of Aurora Plantation donates forty acres to
        Marianites for operation of normal school; later renamed Our
        Lady of Holy Cross College, now University of Holy Cross,
        West Bank's only four-year residential institution of higher
        learning.

1948   West Bank, from Algiers to Avondale, is home to over eighty-
        five thousand people, up from fifty-five thousand in 1935.

1949   Sixty percent of locally made products shipped out of Port of
        New Orleans are manufactured on West Bank—despite being
        home to only 15 percent of metro population.

1949   Louisiana Power & Light Company and New Orleans Public
        Service, Inc. become part of Middle South Utilities, Inc., which

spearheads research and construction of new electrical plants on West Bank.

1950   Marrero, whose population grew from two thousand to thirteen thousand since 1936, counts among its riverfront industries Continental Can Company, producing 175 million cans annually with a million-dollar payroll; Celotex Corporation, whose twenty-seven hundred workers convert bagasse sugarcane fiber into various products; Penick & Ford, with its million-gallon tanks of cane syrup and molasses; Stauffer Chemical Company and its sulphur-grinding operation; and numerous crude terminals and oil storage firms.[38]

1950–1955   Gretna's Huey P. Long Avenue is widened and improved, with hopes of becoming "Great White Way of the West Bank." New subdivisions Gretna Gardens, Gretna Green, Garden Park, Oakdale, Belleview, and Rose Park open, as Gretna's population approaches twenty thousand.[39]

1951   Westwego, "seafood center of Jefferson Parish," boasts seven plants processing "hundreds of tons of tasty oysters, succulent shrimp and crabs, both hard and soft. Three of these, the Ed Martin Seafood Co., Robinson Canning Co. and the Cutcher Canning Co., operate all through the year" and distribute nationwide. Westwego's population grows from under five thousand to over eight thousand during 1940s, fueled by wartime ship-building contracts at nearby Avondale.[40]

1951   Nine Mile Point electrical power plant goes online, "Middle South's highest-output generating facility at that time," producing electricity from natural gas–fired steam generators. Facility adds to Westwego's riverfront skyline of towering grain elevators and sprawling oil tanks interspersed with fields, farms, and forests.[41]

1952   State legislature passes Bridges and Ferries Authority Act, empowering public-private commissions to build, operate, and repair bridges, highways, and ferries. Law produces Mississippi River Bridge Authority, with charge of building new

Mississippi River bridge downtown. After much debate, route is finalized at Thalia-Bringier Street crossing.

1952   Orange Grove Plantation is sold to American Cyanamid Company, which establishes cyanide plant for use in plastics and petroleum products. After decades of operating legally and quietly in rural area west of Waggaman, new owner Cornerstone Chemical (2011) files for expansion permit in 2018—bringing cyanide to public attention and resulting in alarm. Change in perception is indicative of West Bank's shift from industrial to residential in era of rising environmental concerns.

1953–1958   Metropolis gets new causeway across Lake Pontchartrain, two expressways, two tunnels, bridges small and large, widened arteries, new civic centers, track consolidation into new Union Passenger Terminal, expansion at Moisant Airport, Algiers Canal, and plans for new seaway, as well as scores of road-rail grade separations and intersection redesigns.

1954   Work begins on grade-level "West Bank Four-Lane Expressway" from Algiers to Huey P. Long Bridge, to be connected to new Mississippi River Bridge, whose construction gets under way in June.

1954   United States Supreme Court rules in *Brown v. Board of Education of Topeka* that state laws racially segregating public schools are unconstitutional. Nervous about mounting civil rights movement, local governments on West Bank invest in improvements in black-only facilities, hoping to placate calls for full-scale integration.

1954   Gretna, with close to twenty thousand inhabitants, bills itself as "largest city on the West Bank of the Mississippi below St. Louis." With expectation of new bridge, parish seat grows by one new building per day, embarks on ambitious street-paving program, and opens Magnolia Park for harness racing and "a baseball park for the colored people at Huey P. Long Avenue and Gretna Boulevard."[42]

1955   West Bank is home to 91,100 people living in 26,500 dwell-
       ings; up from 53,315 people and 15,200 dwellings in 1943.
       Number of households with telephones increases from 3,580
       in 1940 to 20,485 in 1955.[43]

1955   Belle Chasse Tunnel, beneath new Gulf Intracoastal Waterway
       alternative route (Algiers Canal), is completed for traffic to
       Plaquemines Parish.[44]

1955   Jefferson Parish ranks as fifth largest oil producer among state's
       sixty-four parishes; Louisiana ranks third in nation. Harvey
       is dubbed "Little Houston of Louisiana" by one industry ad-
       vocate, "with nearly two hundred concerns serving the oil
       industry lining both banks of the [Harvey] Canal."[45]

1956   Bill to fund excavation of seaway to Port of New Orleans be-
       comes law, but West Bank loses on siting decision. Seaway will
       instead cut through eastern Orleans and St. Bernard parishes,
       to be named Mississippi River–Gulf Outlet (MR-GO).

1956   Algiers Canal is opened as Gulf Intracoastal Waterway alter-
       native route, having been authorized in 1948 to relieve bot-
       tleneck on main GIWW channel through Harvey Canal. New
       roadways are built over and under canal: $1.8 million bridge
       (today's "Green Bridge" on Gen. DeGaulle Drive–Woodland
       Highway 407), and for $3.6 million, a railroad bridge, auto
       bridge, and auto tunnel to access Belle Chasse in Plaquemines
       Parish.

1957   "Of the estimated 180,000 persons living in Jefferson Parish,
       some 115,000 live on the East Bank . . . while the remaining
       65,000 live on the West Bank. Three decades ago, however,
       the bulk of the population lived in the latter area."[46]

1957   Jefferson Parish creates Zoning and Planning Board to oversee
       future development and land use, aided by Palmer and Baker
       engineering consultants.[47]

1957   West Side Shopping Center, billed as "city within a city," opens
       on 5th Street Highway at Franklin, abutting new West Bank

Expressway. Designed for thirty stores unified by covered pedestrian mall, with parking for two thousand cars and twenty-two acres for future expansion, shopping center later straddles Expressway and remains one of West Bank's largest commercial areas today.[48]

1957   Bayou Segnette Waterway, 12.2 miles long, is dredged through swamp "to afford the larger modern fishing and shrimping boats a shorter and direct route to the packing and canning industries on Bayou Segnette." Thirty years later, most waterway traffic by tonnage is crude petroleum.[49]

1957–1958   Jefferson Parish voters adopt a parish council form of government, with a president and seven-member council. New government goes into effect on March 10, 1958, ending old police jury system with its seventeen ward-based jurors.[50]

1958   At 12:01 a.m. on April 15, Greater New Orleans Mississippi River Bridge opens to traffic; dedication ceremonies held on October 18. After 240 years of watery separation, East and West banks of New Orleans proper are now linked.

1958   Plaquemines Parish dedicates Allen Callender Field to become nation's first joint operating field for Air National Guard, Air Force Reserve, Marine Air Reserve, Naval Aircraft, and Coast Guard; later becomes today's Belle Chasse Naval Air Station.

1959–1962   Original bed of Company Canal, dug in 1830, is filled, becoming Louisiana Street in Westwego.

1960   West Bank's population approaches one hundred thousand; Jefferson Parish's population reaches two hundred thousand, having doubled in ten years and quadrupled in twenty years.

1960   Belle Chasse Plantation House, largest antebellum mansion in West Plaquemines and once home of Confederate Secretary of State Judah P. Benjamin, is demolished.

1960   Developer Paul Kapelow opens new subdivision in former Oakwood tract near bridge and names it for his daughter Terry. By 1970, Terrytown is home to 13,643 people.

1960   West Jefferson Hospital, funded by $1.5 million bond issue passed in 1956, opens in Marrero with 30 doctors and 160 beds. By 1983, it has 209 physicians and 528 beds.

1960   Newton Street viaduct is removed for grade-level passage through former railyards and onto Gen. Meyer Avenue.

1960   On November 14, four black kindergarteners arrive to two previously white-only public elementary schools in Ninth Ward. As grade-by-grade process of de jure integration begins, so does de facto segregation, via "white flight" to suburbs like West Bank.

1960s   Salt water intrusion changes salinity in Little Lake, halfway between West Bank and Grand Isle, from nearly 0 parts per thousand in 1900 to 7 ppt. Lafitte, once a freshwater community, becomes brackish.

1963   Chamber of Commerce's *Directory of Manufacturers* lists twenty-one West Bank firms employing fifty or more people across seven manufacturing sectors: shipbuilding (approximately 5,000 workers), paper and allied products (1,250 workers), food processing (1,220), chemicals and allied products (1,100), petrochemical refining (875), fabricated metal products (775), and building materials (625).[51]

1963   Zatarain's, famed Louisiana spice company founded in 1886, is bought by Avondale Shipyards founder James Viviant and moved to Gretna, where it operates today in recently upgraded facility.

1963   Timberlane Country Club is adjoined by exclusive residential area Timberlane Estates.

1960s–1980s   Golf course communities, rising in popularity throughout the Sun Belt, are built throughout West Bank, where developers find plenty of space and an incoming upper middle class desiring country-club lifestyles.

1964   Jefferson Council presents plans for proposed I-29 to split from I-10 (under construction) to form part of New Orleans Outer

Belt to cross Mississippi from Chalmette to Algiers, run along "Dixie Freeway" south of West Bank Expressway, and recross river at Luling to Destrehan.

1964   Tolls on Mississippi River Bridge lifted in May. Daily usage soon exceeds design capacity, making commuters "fight a daily 'battle of the bridge.'"[52]

1964–1965   Civil Rights Act and Voting Rights Act bring end to de jure racial segregation, but most neighborhoods, schools, and other aspects of West Bank life remain segregated de facto.

1964–1966   Fischer Housing Development constructed and opened in part of Oakdale Tract previously made up of truck farm and houses; "the Projects" have over a thousand subsidized rental units, two schools, library, health center, and other facilities.

1965   Hurricane Betsy strikes in September. West Bank evades serious flooding but endures wind damage and utility outages; serves as refuge and base camp for rescue and relief operations. Afterwards, Congress passes Flood Control Act of 1965, authorizing $56 million for hurricane-flood protection, mostly on East Bank, and much of it never actualized.

1967   Last explicitly segregationist pronouncement appears in *Jefferson Parish Yearly Review.*

1968   Congressman Hale Boggs wins federal approval for Outer Belt and Dixie Freeway through West Bank.

1969   Fiery collision of *SS Union Faith* with three oil barges threatens Mississippi River Bridge and communities on both banks. Easter morning incident, latest in long line of shipping collisions, leads to regulatory reforms in vessel lighting, ship-to-ship communications, and centralized river traffic control.

1970   West Bank's total population surpasses 170,000.

1970   Middle South Utilities, Inc., predecessor of Entergy Louisiana, begins permit process to build area's first nuclear power plant, Waterford 3, on West Bank of St. Charles Parish.

Early 1970s   Plans to elevate West Bank Expressway gain traction, in part because Dixie Freeway is cancelled.

1970s   Under management of Ogden Corporation, Avondale Ship-yards, Inc., ranks as state's largest private employer and nation's most productive shipbuilder, winning steady stream of military and commercial contracts, including gargantuan oil drilling barges. Payroll of $100 million employs over ten thousand working day and night, and spins off additional twenty thousand service-related jobs, mostly on West Bank.[53]

1972   Legislation enables Louisiana Offshore Oil Port (LOOP) in 1972, resulting in construction of Port Fourchon in 1981.

1970–1972   Bridge on Lapalco Boulevard costs $4.6 million; built above Harvey Canal, with 45-foot clearance.

1974   Evidencing that West Bank had become its own subregion, study finds that only 7.7 percent of West Bankers commute daily to downtown New Orleans; nearly 60 percent of those who live on West Bank also work there.

1975   Woodmere subdivision opens in Harvey south of Lapalco Boulevard along western flanks of Harvey Canal.

1975   West Bank population of Jefferson and Orleans parishes estimated at one hundred ninety-three thousand, roughly double from fifteen years prior.

1975   First Vietnamese refugees arrive to New Orleans, by invitation of Archbishop Philip M. Hannan; Associated Catholic Charities finds housing to settle families in Algiers's Woodland Estate, Bridge City, Marrero, Harvey, and Gretna. By 2010, there are 10,550 people of Asian ancestry on West Bank, constituting 4.5 percent of population; more than half are of Vietnamese ancestry.

Mid-1970s   Barataria Boulevard, Belle Chasse Highway, Behrman Highway, and Lapalco Boulevard all widened to four lanes.

1970s–1980s   Barataria Basin land-loss rates peak at eight to nine square miles per year.

1976   Legislation arranges financing for Greater New Orleans Mississippi River Bridge No. 2.

1977   Work begins on $200 million raising of West Bank Expressway, toward connecting it with upcoming second span of bridge.

1977   Texas Pacific-Missouri Pacific Railroad Company bulldozes what remains of circa-1840 Seven Oaks Plantation House, costing Westwego what could have been major tourist destination.

1977   Grain dust at Westwego's Continental Grain Company Elevator ignites from spark of static electricity and explodes in retort heard ten miles away. Blast destroys sequence of silos and kills thirty-six people gathered for Christmas party; leads to new national safety standards in grain elevator industry.

1978   May 3 downpours inundate parts of West Bank.

1978   Following local advocacy, US Department of the Interior designates Algiers Point as a National Register Historic District. Movement is paralleled by effort to distinguish "Algiers Point" from subdivisions further back and downriver.

1979   President Jimmy Carter signs bill creating Barataria Preserve as part of Jean Lafitte National Historical Park, after years of advocacy by local resident Frank Ehret, State Senator Elwyn Nicholson, and others. Designation reflects gradual change in public sentiment about wetlands, from "wastelands" to valued resources.

1980   Torrential downpours on April 13 dump 14.5 inches of rain in Westwego and Harvey; water overtops Harvey Canal and Lake Cataouatche levee and accumulates in low-lying subdivisions faster than pumps can remove it. Parts of Avondale, Westwego, Marrero, Gretna, Terrytown, and Algiers flood.[54]

1981   Construction work begins on Mississippi River Bridge No. 2, to be built parallel to 1958 span and downriver by four hundred feet.

1981   Port Fourchon opens at mouth of Bayou Lafourche.

1983   Petroleum prices plummet, stilling extraction worldwide; market slightly rebounds in 1986 only to slip again in 1988. Gulf Coast in general and New Orleans in particular are gravely affected, as roughly fifty thousand well-paying O&G jobs disappear statewide. West Bank petrol employment shrinks, and sheen comes off new shopping malls and subdivisions.

1983   Algiers Landing Restaurant, built in a rustic rambling cannery style, opens on Bermuda Street Wharf. Becomes prominent landmark on West Bank skyline viewable from French Quarter, but an eyesore after closing in 1995; demolished 1999.

1984   New bridge over Harvey Canal is opened for traffic; elevation of West Bank Expressway is mostly complete.

1985   "Green Bridge" on Woodland Highway/Gen. DeGaulle Drive opened over Algiers (Intracoastal) Canal, providing convenient access to English Turn promontory.[55]

1985   Entergy Louisiana's Waterford 3 Nuclear Power Plant goes on-line in Killona, on West Bank of St. Charles Parish.

1985   US Department of the Interior designates Mechanikham-Gretna National Register Historic District; becomes local historic district (with demolition restrictions and architectural guidelines) in 1997.

1985   Late October Hurricane Juan strikes West Bank and pushes Gulf water into Barataria Bay; surge ruptures parish levees, leading to substantial flooding in Marrero and Westwego subdivisions, worsened by heavy rainfall. Juan causes nearly a billion dollars of damage in Louisiana, most of it on and near West Bank.

1986   Last year's Hurricane Juan flooding catalyses federalization of surge protection: West Bank levee districts secure authorization and funding for Army Corps of Engineers to build federal-quality hurricane protection levees from Westwego to Harvey Canal.

1986   Exclusive golf course community named English Turn is launched by Jack Nicklaus Development Corporation in lower coast of Algiers.

1988   Dedication ceremony of Greater New Orleans Mississippi River Bridge No. 2 held on September 30; together with first bridge, spans are officially named Crescent City Connection in 1989.

1989   Unpopular tolls are collected on new bridge; remain in place until controversial 2012–2013 referendums.

1989   Middle South Utilities, Inc., having moved from New York to New Orleans in 1975, is renamed Entergy Corporation. Entergy New Orleans provides electrical service to both banks of Orleans Parish, whereas Entergy Louisiana serves rest of West Bank and most of state.

1989   Community advocates launch "Terrytown, Not Gretna" campaign to clarify identity of subdivision in unincorporated Jefferson Parish, a common problem throughout West Bank suburbs.

1980s–1990s   Oil slump of 1980s followed by end of Cold War in 1990s leads to slackening of vessel-building contracts at Avondale Shipyards, setting stage for later sales of shipyards and eventual closure in 2013.

1990   Oil bust takes its toll: West Bank, home to 42 percent of Jefferson Parish population, accounts for only 20 percent of occupational license taxes; has double the unemployment rate (17 percent) of East Jefferson.

1993   Orleans Parish Historic District Landmarks Commission designates Algiers Point Historic District, for the first time putting demolition restrictions and architectural guidelines on the neighborhood.

1993   Freeport-McMoRan and Audubon Institute establish Endangered Species Survival Center on twelve hundred acres owned by City of New Orleans and US Coast Guard in lower coast of Algiers. Combined with neighboring Tulane University Biodiversity Research Institute and F. Edward Hebert Research Center (former Navy munitions depot) in Belle Chasse, area constitutes last expansive forest on natural levee in or near metro area.

1994   First Gretna Heritage Festival held in spring; later moves to early fall and becomes largest festival on West Bank, featuring area's ethnic groups with food, music, and amusements.

1996   New floodwalls and levees are extended eastward from Harvey Canal through Harvey, Gretna, Algiers, and Belle Chasse, and westward from Westwego along Lake Cataouatche to Bridge City, Avondale, and Waggaman.

1999–2000   Avondale Shipyards sold to Litton Industries and then Northrop Grumman.

2000   West Bank population hits quarter-million mark, home to one-quarter of metro New Orleans residents. Within tri-parish conurbation, from Waggaman to Belle Chasse and excluding rural outskirts, West Bank has 250,369 residents, among them 126,896 whites and 104,599 African Americans. East Bank conurbation, from Kenner to Meraux, is home to 740,045, including 373,357 whites and 327,619 African Americans.[56]

2002   Century-old Plaquemines Parish Courthouse in Point à la Hache burns in bizarre arson plot; nucleus of Plaquemines Parish government subsequently shifts to Belle Chasse on West Bank, also home to parish's main population cluster.

2004   Army Corps repair work on section of Westwego riverfront unearths remains of 1864 ironclad *USS Chickasaw*, scuttled in 1944 after years of service as train ferry and coal barge.

2005   City of Gretna designates McDonoghville Historic District, its second after Mechanikham-Gretna District was created in 1997, toward preserving Jefferson Parish's largest extent of nineteenth-century neighborhoods.

2005   Hurricane Katrina's surge on August 29 breaches federal levees
        and floodwalls on East Bank navigation and drainage canals;
        catastrophic flooding ensues, causing over fifteen hundred
        deaths and bringing metropolis to its knees. West Bank is
        spared flooding and plays paradoxical roles in recovery, part
        victim, part witness, part refuge, part beneficiary, part casualty.
        "Bridge to Gretna" incident on September 2 becomes most-
        remembered West Bank-related news story of Katrina era.

2006   State legislature creates Southeastern Louisiana Flood Protec-
        tion Authority-West (SLFPA-W) as state partner to US. Army
        Corps of Engineers' new fast-tracked effort to create Hurri-
        cane and Storm Damage Risk Reduction System. West Bank
        and Vicinity Project encompasses over 30 miles of earthen
        levees and/or floodwalls with 67 closeable devices, most of
        them sluice or sector floodgates. Project is complete by 2012,
        but local and federal authorities dispute responsibilities and
        costs for future operations and maintenance.

2008   Jefferson Parish Courthouse, built in 1958 as seventh court-
        house in parish's history and tallest building on West Bank, is
        demolished and replaced by Jefferson Parish General Govern-
        ment Building. New complex, designed by Sizeler Thompson
        Brown Architects, centralizes various offices of parish govern-
        ment, including legislative, executive, and judicial branches,
        at 200 Derbigny Street in Gretna.

2008   On September 1, Hurricane Gustav threatens region and trig-
        gers full-scale regional evacuation. But levees and floodwalls
        withstand the surge, and West Bank sees only wind damage
        and disruption.

2009   Celotex plant at 7500 Fourth Street on Marrero riverfront,
        founded in 1920 and home to nearly two thousand jobs mak-
        ing insulation boards from bagasse (bought out by Knight-
        Celotex in 2001) closes permanently after heavy wind damage
        by Hurricane Katrina followed by Great Recession. In addition
        to loss of jobs, Marrero is stuck with environmental concerns
        over asbestos and major eyesore after 2017 fire.[57]

2009 Beechgrove (Claiborne) subdivision opens on outskirts of Westwego, first of its size built here since Katrina; in response to new understanding of risk, every house is raised eight feet above grade. Priced affordably, homes are overseen by multi-agency partnership aimed at helping working-class renters become home owners.

2010 West Bank population drops by ten thousand since 2000, to 240,590, and becomes majority-black for first time since 1800s, with African Americans outnumbering whites 110,558 to 104,948. Those of Asian ancestry rise to 10,603; those of Hispanic ethnicity to 21,382. Main drivers of change are exodus and natural decline of white population, which drops by over 16,000 in ten years, and rise of immigrant populations, while black population remains steady. Because of even greater Katrina-related population losses on East Bank, however, West Bank now comprises 30 percent of metro population, up from 25 percent in 2000.[58]

2010 "Renaissance" gets underway in New Orleans proper, as recovery gains steam, Saints win Super Bowl, and gentrification of historic neighborhoods intensifies. But West Bank sees little spillover effects.

2010s Overbuilding of golf courses and country-club subdivisions in 1970s–1980s, coupled with storm damages and decline in popularity of golf, lead to closures of a number of West Bank courses. Property values in golf course subdivisions are affected, as gated communities fall out of fashion with young home-buyers seeking more urban lifestyles.

2010s Churchill Technology and Business Park, Patrick F. Taylor Science & Technology Academy, Delgado River City Site, Advanced Manufacturing Center, and Dyno Nobel ammonia plant set up in western West Jeff, parish's "last frontier."

2010s As West Bank industrial landscape wanes in favor of residential and commercial uses, citizens become increasingly resistant to living with industry. Decade sees mounting protests against land uses once welcomed, including cyanide manufacturer near Waggaman, barge-mooring along Westwego riverfront, freight railroad connector through Gretna, crude-oil tank cars rolling through Gouldsboro, and coal terminal at Myrtle Grove in Plaquemines Parish.

2010s West Bank sees precipitous decline in Mardi Gras parades, from over a dozen krewes to only two (NOMTOC and Adonis) by mid-2010s, as krewes opt for larger crowds on prestigious St. Charles Avenue and revelers follow them, leaving suburban parades lightly attended region-wide.

2011 After 110 years, Naval Support Facility New Orleans closes; Algiers complex becomes Marine Corps Support Facility New Orleans, having moved to West Bank after closing facility on Poland Avenue. With leadership of New Orleans City Council member Jackie Clarkson, Algiers complex becomes mixed-use development known as Federal City, with residential, commercial, educational, and health-care components in addition to military and police personnel.

2011 Contractors for Army Corps of Engineers complete Western Tie-In, 4.5 miles of federal levees and floodwalls along Davis Pond Diversion Canal and Outer Cataouatche Canal, closing off final gap in post-Katrina Hurricane and Storm Damage Risk Reduction System (HSDRRS).

2012 On seventh anniversary of Hurricane Katrina, Category-1 Hurricane Isaac strikes New Orleans area, dumping enormous amounts of precipitation as system slows to a crawl; surge flooding occurs in outlying areas including Lafitte, where water levels are slightly exacerbated by reverberations of surge off the HSDRRS "wall" south of Marrero.

2012–2013 Fate of tolls on Crescent City Connection comes to public referendum. Despite strident opposition on West Bank, initial tally gives razor-thin victory to pro-toll side. But judge finds flaw in ballots; do-over is held in May 2013, and this time anti-toll side wins handily.

2013   Louisiana Department of Transportation and Development and contractors complete seven-year, $1.2 billion project to broaden Huey P. Long Bridge. Widened lanes are welcomed by motorists, but expected boom in West Bank investment does not materialize.

2013–2014   Northrop Grumman consolidates shipbuilding activity in Pascagoula, Mississippi, and closes Avondale Shipyards, costing West Bank five thousand skilled jobs and dealing western West Jefferson severe economic blow.

2014   Jefferson Parish Economic Development Commission (JEDCO) Conference Center and Patrick F. Taylor Science and Technology Academy open in Churchill Park; become foundation of larger effort to catalyze development in western West Jefferson (Fairfield) area.

2015   Entergy opens Nine Mile Point 6 with combined-cycle gas turbine technology, using 30 percent less fuel than earlier plant. West Bank continues to be main exporter of electricity to region.

2016   Barataria Basin has 1,047 square miles of land, down from 1,480 square miles in 1932.

2018   Plaquemines Parish government fights Louisiana Coastal Protection and Restoration Authority over permitting of proposed Mid-Barataria Sediment Diversion at Myrtle Grove, which would inject up to 50,000 cubic feet per second of Mississippi River water into Barataria to push back saltwater and deposit new sediment. Fishing interests fear freshening of estuarine waters will drive away valuable finfish and affect oyster beds.

2018   Avondale Marine purchases 254-acre Avondale Shipyards, dormant since 2013 except for University of New Orleans's Maritime Center of Excellence, with plans to create value-added manufacturing center and intermodal logistics hub.

2018   Jefferson Parish becomes Louisiana's premier example of "ethnoburbia." With parish's American-born black population growing by 10 percent during 2000–2014, white population plummeting by 21 percent, and Hispanics and Asians growing by 85 and 29 percent respectively, future of West Bank is ethno-racial diversity.

2019   Jefferson Parish Economic Development Commission releases master plan envisioning fifty thousand residents and one hundred thousand employees living and working in "last frontier" of metropolis, Churchill Park area of Fairfield in western West Jefferson.

2019   Algiers marks three-hundredth anniversary of initial French settlement on West Bank, one year after official commemoration of tricentennial of founding of New Orleans.

Notes

Preface

1. Mariners on the Mississippi today refer to the western side of the channel as the Right De-scending Bank (RDB) or Left Ascending Bank (LAB), and the eastern side as the Right Ascending Bank (RAB) or Left Descending Bank (LDB), regardless of cardinal directions. "West Bank" is synonymous with RDB and LAB, and "East Bank" with RAB and LDB. The terms are not unique to New Orleans.

2. I borrow this phrase from A. J. Liebling in *The Earl of Louisiana* (New York: Ballantine Books, 1960), p. 69.

3. In this volume, I use "metropolitan area" and "metropolis" to mean greater New Orleans south of Lake Pontchartrain, namely the contiguous urbanized portion of Orleans, Jefferson, St. Bernard, and Plaquemines parishes. While the City of New Orleans itself is majority-black and has been since the late 1970s (and prior to the 1830s), the metropolis is majority white, as is its East Bank. The West Bank, on the other hand, recently became majority-black. Figures and percentages vary depending on which areas are considered to be contiguously urbanized.

1. Sediment upon the Sea, People upon the Land

1. Various scientific studies date the St. Bernard Delta Complex, the first to build land in what is now greater New Orleans, to anywhere from 1900 years ago to 4600 years ago, with the most likely window 3500 to 4500 years ago. For more information, see W. J. Autin, Torbjorn E. Tornqvist, Tristram R. Kidder, Whitney J. Autin, Klaas van der Borg, Arie F. M. de Jong, Cornelis J. W. Klerks, Els M. A. Snijders, Joep E. A. Storms, Remke L. van Dam, and Michael C. Wiemann, "A Revised Chronology for Mississippi River Subdeltas," *Science* 273 (1996): 1693–96. See also Marc P. Hijma, Zhixiong Shen, Torbjorn E. Tornqvist, and Barbara Mauz, "Late Holocene Evolution of a Coupled, Mud-Dominated Delta Plain-Chenier Plain System, Coastal Louisiana, USA," *Earth Surface Dynamics* 5, no. 4 (November 2017): 689–710.

2. *Balbancha* was a Choctaw word also used to describe the New Orleans area, meaning land of many languages. Daniele Coxe, *A Description of the English Province of Carolina, by the Spaniards Call'd Florida, and by the French La Louisiane* (1727; repr., San Francisco: California State Library, 1940), p. 21; Marc-Antoine Caillot, *A Company Man: The Remarkable French-Atlantic Voyage of a Clerk for the Company of the Indies*, ed. Erin M. Greenwald and trans. Teri F. Chalmers (New Orleans: The Historic New Orleans Collection, 2013), p. 78.

3. This was the observation of Iberville on March 2, 1699, as he entered the mouth of the Mississippi. Pierre Le Moyne, sieur d'Iberville, *A Comparative View of French Louisiana, 1699 and 1762: The Journals of Pierre Le Moyne d'Iberville and Jean-Jacques-Blaise d'Abbadie*, ed. Carl A. Brasseaux (Lafayette: Center for Louisiana Studies, University of Southwestern Louisiana, 1979), p. 40.

4. Anonymous Crew Member, "Historical Journal: or, Narrative of the Expedition Made by Order of Louis XIV, King of France, under Command of M. D'Iberville to Explore the Colbert (Mississippi) River and Establish a Colony in Louisiana," in *Historical Collections of Louisiana and Florida*, vol. 7, ed. B. F. French (1699; repr., New York, NY, 1875), p. 70.

5. Robert T. Saucier, *Geomorphology and Quaternary Geologic History of the Lower Mississippi Valley*, 2 vols. (Vicksburg, MS: US Army Corps of Engineers, 1994), vol. 1, p. 276; H. N. Fisk, *Geological Investigations of the Alluvial Valley of the Lower Mississippi River* (Vicksburg, MS: US Army Corps of Engineers, Mississippi River Commission, 1944); and D. E. Frazier, "Recent Deltaic Deposits of the Mississippi River: Their Development and Chronology," *Transactions of the Gulf Coast Association of Geological Societies* 17 (1967): 287–315.

6. The two cutbanks are (1) from Westwego to Algiers Point and (2) from Aurora to the Lower Coast of Algiers. The three point bars (promontories) are Nine Mile Point, Algiers Point, and English Turn Bend.

7. David Fritz and Sally K. Reeves, *Algiers Point: Historical Ambience and Property Analysis of Squares Ten, Thirteen, and Twenty, with a View toward Their Archaeological Potential* (New Orleans: Department of the Army, Corps of Engineers, June 1984), pp. 3–4.

8. Pierre Clément de Laussat, *Memoirs of My Life* (1831; Baton Rouge: Louisiana State University Press for The Historic New Orleans Collection, 1978), p. 68.

9. Iberville, *A Comparative View of French Louisiana*, pp. 40–42.

10. This is *Arundinaria gigantean*, a bamboo native to North America. Christopher G. Brantley and Steven G. Platt, "Canebrake Conservation in the Southeastern United States," *Wildlife Society Bulletin* 29, no. 4 (Winter 2001): 1175–77.

11. Sally Kittredge Evans, Frederick Stielow, and Betsy Swanson, *Grand Isle on the Gulf—An Early History* (Metairie, LA: Jefferson Parish Historical Commission, 1979), pp. 11–19.

12. Bennet Dowler, MD, reporting on findings of Dr. Daniel Drake and Dr. Rogers, in *Tableaux, Geographical, Commercial, Geological, and Sanitary, of New Orleans* (New Orleans: Daily Delta, 1853), pp. 8–9.

13. Fred B. Kniffen, Hiram F. Gregory, and George A. Stokes, *The Historic Indian Tribes of Louisiana, from 1542 to the Present* (Baton Rouge: Louisiana State University Press, 1987), p. 20. See also "Indian Economies," map and analysis in Fred B. Kniffen and Sam Bowers Hilliard, *Louisiana: Its Land and People* (Baton Rouge: Louisiana State University Press, 1988), p. 107.

14. Spanish surveyor Carlos Trudeau, 1803, as quoted in Betsy Swanson, *Terre Haute de Barataria: An Historic Upland on an Old River Distributary Overtaken by Forest in the Barataria Unit of the Jean Lafitte National Historic Park and Preserve* (Harahan, LA: Jefferson Parish Historical Commission Monograph XI, 1991), p. 17.

15. Presentations and personal communications at "Indigenous Spaces, French Expectations: Exploring Exchanges Between Native and Non-Native Peoples in Louisiana," New Orleans Center for the Gulf South Symposium, March 14, 2018.

16. William M. Denevan, "The Pristine Myth: The Landscape of the Americas in 1492," *Annals of the Association of American Geographers* 82, no. 3 (September 1992): 369.

17. This river may have been the Mississippi or the Mobile. Francisco de Garay, as quoted by Frederic Austin Ogg, *The Opening of the Mississippi: A Struggle for Supremacy in the American Interior* (New York: Macmillan, 1904), p. 16.

18. Carl Ortwin Sauer, *Sixteenth Century North America: The Land and the People as Seen by the Europeans* (Berkeley: University of California Press, 1971), pp. 36–46.

19. Charles Hudson, *Knights of Spain, Warriors of the Sun: Hernando de Soto and South's Ancient Chiefdoms* (Athens: University of Georgia Press, 1997), pp. 387–97. Ogg, *The Opening of the Mississippi*, puts the number of surviving crewmembers at 372.

20. Pierre Le Moyne, Sieur d'Iberville, *Iberville's Gulf Journals*, ed. Richebourg Gaillard McWilliams (1700; trans. University of Alabama, 1991), p. 63.

21. "Toward 1725: Continuation of the Memoir of Bienville," *Mississippi Provincial Archives, 1704–1743: French Dominion*, vol. 3, ed. Dunbar Rowland and Albert Godfrey Sanders (Jackson, MS, 1932), pp. 526–27.

22. Chevalier Guy de Soniat du Fossat, *Synopsis of the History of Louisiana from the Founding of the Colony to End of the Year 1791*, ed. and trans. Charles T. Soniat (New Orleans, 1903), p. 8.

23. William M. Denevan, "The Pristine Myth: The Landscape of the Americas in 1492," *Annals of the Association of American Geographers* 82, no. 3 (September 1992): 370.

24. Father Zenobius Membré, "Narrative of La Salle's Voyage Down the Mississippi, By Father Zenobius Membré," in *The Journeys of René-Robert Cavelier Sieur de La Salle*, vol. 1, ed. Isaac Joslin Cox (1905; repr., Austin, TX, 1968), pp. 131–59 (quote on p. 143).

25. Iberville, *A Comparative View of French Louisiana*, pp. 19–20, and Iberville, *Iberville's Gulf Journals*, p. 56.

26. Anonymous Crew Member, "Historical Journal," p. 61.

27. Iberville, *Iberville's Gulf Journals*, pp. 63–64.

28. Anonymous Crew Member, "Historical Journal," p. 74.

29. Iberville, *Iberville's Gulf Journals*, p. 69; Kniffen et al., *The Historic Indian Tribes of Louisiana*, p. 49.

30. According to historian Marc de Villiers du Terrage, on March 31 to April 2, 1682, La Salle and his men came upon a recently destroyed Tangibaho [sic] village in Quinipissas territory, probably along the portage to Bayou St. John in present-day New Orleans. Marc de Villiers du Terrage, "A History of the Foundation of New Orleans, 1717–1722," *Louisiana Historical Quarterly* 3, no. 2 (April 1920): 161.

31. For this reason, Lake Salvador was historically known as Lake Washa, a name still used for a small water body southwest of Houma. "Toward 1725: Continuation of the Memoir of Bienville," ed. Roland and Sanders, p. 527.

32. Kniffen et al., *The Historic Indian Tribes of Louisiana*, pp. 52–57, 123.

33. Daniel H. Usner, "American Indians in New Orleans: Native Communities Were Integral to the City's Foundation," in *New Orleans and the World: The Tricentennial Anthology*, ed. Nancy Dixon (New Orleans: Louisiana Endowment for the Humanities, 2017), pp. 13–16.

34. Kathleen DuVal, "Interconnectedness and Diversity in 'French Louisiana,'" in *Powhatan's Mantle: Indians in the Colonial Southeast*, ed. Gregory A. Waselkov, Peter H. Wood, and Tom Hatley (Lincoln: University of Nebraska Press, 2006), p. 138.

35. *The Journal of Sauvole: Historical Journal of the Establishment of the French in Louisiana by M. de Sauvole, 1699–1701*, trans. and ed. Jay Higginbotham (Mobile, AL: Colonial Books, 1969), p. 40.

2. The Colonial Imperative

1. Edward M. Coleman, "The Concession of Louisiana 1719–1763" (Master's thesis, Graduate College of the State University of Iowa, 1927), p. 26.

2. Carl J. Ekberg, *French Roots in the Illinois Country* (Urbana and Chicago: University of Illinois Press, 1998), p. 54, and "The Illinois Country: The Veritable New France," lecture presented at the France and Louisiana: Journée D'Étude Symposium, The Historical New Orleans Collection, New Orleans, Louisiana, January 23, 2000, attended by author.

3. Milton B. Newton Jr., *Louisiana: A Geographical Portrait* (Baton Rouge: Geoforensics, 1987), pp. 210–12, and John Whitling Hall, "Louisiana Survey Systems: Their Antecedents, Distribution, and Characteristics" (PhD diss., Louisiana State University Department of Geography and Anthropology, 1970), p. 33.

4. The Edict of October 12, 1716, trans. Henry P. Dart, "The First Law Regulating Land Grants in French Colonial Louisiana," *Louisiana Historical Quarterly* 14, no. 3 (July 1931): 346.

5. Ibid., 347.

6. Marcel Giraud, *A History of French Louisiana, Volume Two: Years of Transition, 1715–1717* (1958; Baton Rouge: Louisiana State University Press, 1993), p. 136. This quote is from the historian Giraud regarding the Edict of 1716, not from the edict itself.

7. As quoted by Marc de Villiers du Terrage, "A History of the Foundation of New Orleans (1717–1722)," *Louisiana Historical Quarterly* 3, no. 2 (April 1920): 174 (emphasis in original). The date for September of 1717 is obscured in the register, but ancillary information indicates it was September 9, 1717.

8. Ibid., pp. 173–75. The name *Nouvelle Orléans* probably came from a May 1717 report by Bienville and Jean Michelle Seigneur de L'Epinet which suggested founding a new post and naming it after Philippe, Duc d'Orléans.

9. Le Page du Pratz, *The History of Louisiana* (1758; trans. J. S. W. Harmanson, 1774; repr., New Orleans: Pelican Press, 1947), p. 17.

10. For details on the controversy over siting New Orleans, see Richard Campanella, *Time and Place in New Orleans* (Gretna, LA: Pelican Publishing Company, 2002).

11. Heloise H. Cruzat and Henry P. Dart, "Documents Concerning Bienville's Lands in Louisiana, 1719–1737: First Installment." *Louisiana Historical Quarterly* 10, no. 1 (January 1927): 8–17.

12. René Le Conte, "The Germans in Louisiana in the Eighteenth Century" (1924) trans. Glenn R. Conrad, *Louisiana History* 8, no. 1 (Winter 1967): 70–72.

13. Philomena Hauck, *Bienville: Father of Louisiana* (Lafayette: The Center for Louisiana Studies, University of Southwestern Louisiana, 1998), pp. 82–83, 144.

14. René Le Conte, "The Germans in Louisiana in the Eighteenth Century" (1924), trans. Glenn R. Conrad, *Louisiana History* 8, no. 1 (Winter 1967): 77.

15. Charles R. Maduell Jr., *The Census Tables for the French Colony of Louisiana from 1699 to 1732* (Baltimore, Maryland: Genealogical Publishing Company, 1972), pp. vii, 39.

16. Marcel Giraud, *A History of French Louisiana, Volume Five: The Company of the Indies, 1723–1731* (Baton Rouge: Louisiana State University Press, 1987), p. xi.

17. Letter, Bienville to the Council, February 1, 1723, *Mississippi Provincial Archives, 1704–1743: French Dominion,* vol. 3, ed. Dunbar Rowland and Albert Godfrey Sanders (Jackson, MS, 1932), pp. 343–44.

18. Heloise Hulse Cruzat, "Sidelights of Louisiana History," *Louisiana Historical Quarterly* 1, no. 3 (1918): 76.

19. Samuel Wilson Jr., "The Plantation of the Company of the Indies," *Louisiana History* 31, no. 2 (Spring 1990): 161–63; Cruzat, "Sidelights of Louisiana History," 76, 141.

20. Wilson, "The Plantation of the Company of the Indies," 162.

21. Betsy Swanson, *Historic Jefferson Parish, From Shore to Shore* (1975; repr., Gretna, LA: Pelican Publishing Company, 2004), p. 85.

22. Letter, Father Raphael to the Abbe Raguet, December 28, 1726, *Mississippi Provincial Archives, 1701–1729: French Dominion,* vol. 2, ed. Dunbar Rowland and Albert Godfrey Sanders (Jackson, MS, 1929), p. 521.

23. Erin M. Greenwald, "Arriving Africans and a Changing New Orleans," in *New Orleans in the Founding Era,* ed. Erin Greenwald and trans. Henry Colomer (New Orleans: The Historic New Orleans Collection, 2018), p. 104.

24. Marc-Antoine Caillot, *A Company Man: The Remarkable French-Atlantic Voyage of a Clerk for the Company of the Indies,* ed. Erin M. Greenwald and trans. Teri F. Chalmers (New Orleans: The Historic New Orleans Collection, 2013), p. 101; Erin Michelle Greenwald, :Company Towns and Tropical Baptisms: From Lorient to Louisiana on a French Atlantic Circuit" (PhD diss., Ohio State University, 2011), pp. 154–55.

25. Greenwald, "Arriving Africans and a Changing New Orleans," pp. 95–99.

26. Wilson, "The Plantation of the Company of the Indies," 164. "Ordinance of Our Lords, the Commissioners of the Council . . . of the Company of the Indies, September 2, 1721." The phrase *pièce d'Inde* (literally, "coin of India") meant the book value of a healthy male slave in his prime, and implied that anyone who deviated from this description, by age, capacity, or gender, would be worth less.

27. Ibid., 165–67.

28. Computed from Left Bank Ascending section of the "Census of New Orleans as Reported by M. Perier, Commandant General of Louisiana, July 1, 1727," as transcribed by Maduell, pp. 100–103.

NOTES TO PAGES 22-28

29. "Survey of the Plantation of the Company of the Indies, Made by the Sieur Lassus, February 8, 1728," and a subsequent 1731 inventory, reproduced by Wilson in "The Plantation of the Company of the Indies," 170–74; see also 179.

30. Le Page du Pratz, *The History of Louisiana*, p. 361.

31. Ibid., pp. 71–73; Gordon M. Sayre, *The Indian Chief as Tragic Hero: Native Resistance and the Literatures of America, from Moctezuma to Tecumseh* (Chapel Hill: University of North Carolina Press, 2006), p. 231.

32. Scipion appears in documents again in 1736, when he signed an agreement to hire himself out to help row a keelboat up to Illinois, followed by other jobs, for a period of one year. For this Scipion would be paid two hundred livres. "Notes on the Census of New Orleans for January 1732" and supplement "List of Landowners," as transcribed by Maduell, p. 147; Donald E. Everett, "Free Persons of Color in Colonial Louisiana," *Louisiana History* 7, no. 1 (Winter 1966): 21–50.

33. Le Page du Pratz, as quoted by Wilson, "The Plantation of the Company of the Indies," 174–75.

34. Wilson, "The Plantation of the Company of the Indies," 176–77.

35. Maduell, *The Census Tables for the French Colony of Louisiana*, p. 149.

36. Computed from "List of Landowners" (1732 Census), as transcribed by Maduell, pp. 147–49.

37. Lawrence N. Powell, *The Accidental City: Improvising New Orleans* (Cambridge: Harvard University Press, 2012), p. 82.

38. Henrietta H. Cruzat and Henry P. Dart, "Documents Concerning Bienville's Lands in Louisiana, 1719–1737: Fourth Installment," *Louisiana Historical Quarterly* 10, no. 4 (October 1927): 538–39.

39. From "Map of Bienville's Concessions," Cruzat and Dart, "Documents Concerning Bienville's Lands: First Installment," 8–9. See also Copies of Certificates of Survey of the Bienville Land in 1737, trans. Cruzat and Dart, "Documents Concerning Bienville's Lands: Fourth Installment," 540.

40. Henry P. Dart, "Documents Concerning Bienville's Lands in Louisiana, 1719–1737: Third Installment," *Louisiana Historical Quarterly* 10, no. 4 (October 1927): 368; Census of New Orleans as Reported by M. Perier, Commandant General of Louisiana, July 1, 1727," as transcribed by Charles R. Maduell Jr., *The Census Tables for the French Colony of Louisiana from 1699 to 1732* (Baltimore, MD: Genealogical Publishing Company, 1972), p. 100; Sally K. Reeves and William D. Reeves, "Cultural History," in *Archeological Testing of Quarters A (16OR137) at the Naval Support Activity, West Bank Facility, Algiers, Orleans Parish, Louisiana,* by Melissa M. Green, Sally K. Reeves, William D. Reeves, and Stephen P. Austin, for the US Army Corps of Engineers, Fort Worth District. Miscellaneous Report of Investigations, no. 78, November 1996: 9–11, 34.

41. Gwendolyn Midlo Hall, *Africans in Colonial Louisiana: The Development of Afro-Creole Culture in the Eighteenth Century* (Baton Rouge: Louisiana State University Press, 1992), pp. 135–36.

42. Reeves and Reeves, "Cultural History," 9–10, 34–35.

43. Wilson, "The Plantation of the Company of the Indies," 179.

44. John H. B. Latrobe, *Southern Travels: Journal of John H. B. Latrobe, 1834,* ed. Samuel Wilson Jr. (New Orleans: The Historic New Orleans Collection, 1986), p. 38.

45. Report from 1764 cited by Wilson in "The Plantation of the Company of the Indies," 178–179.

46. Gilbert C. Din and John E. Harkins, *The New Orleans Cabildo: Colonial Louisiana's First City Government, 1769–1803* (Baton Rouge: Louisiana State University Press, 1996), pp. 11–12. The population of free people of color in New Orleans grew from 97 to 1,566 over the course of the Spanish

regime. Exhibit, "Recovered Memories: Spain, New Orleans, and the Support for the American Revolution," Cabildo, New Orleans, Louisiana State Museum, 2018.

47. Gilbert C. Din, *Populating the Barrera: Spanish Immigration Efforts in Colonial Louisiana* (Lafayette: University of Louisiana Press, 2014), pp. 1–22.

48. This ownership sequence comes from the multi-author *Historical Sketch Book and Guide to New Orleans and Environs* (New York: Will H. Coleman, 1885), p. 287.

49. This term referred to the entire Barataria Basin, including the West Bank. "Map of Western Louisiana," 1763, Ministry of Defense, Archivo General Militar de Madrid. Exhibit, "Recovered Memories: Spain, New Orleans, and the Support for the American Revolution."

50. Din and Harkins, *The New Orleans Cabildo*, pp. 31–32.

51. Din, *Populating the Barrera*, pp. 153–59.

52. Plan No. 1593: Bartolome Duverges; Punta San Antonio, 1803. Pintado Papers, mss. 890, Box 1223, Louisiana and Lower Mississippi Valley Collections, LSU Libraries, Baton Rouge. http://www.louisianadigitallibrary.org/islandora/object/lsu-sc-pintado%3A589

53. Gilbert C. Din, *Francisco Bouligny: A Bourbon Soldier in Spanish Louisiana* (Baton Rouge: Louisiana State University Press, 1993), pp. 51–53.

54. Samuel Wilson Jr. "Seven Oaks Plantation (Petit Desert), Westwego, Jefferson Parish, Louisiana" (Washington, DC: National Park Service, Historic American Building Survey, 1953), HABS No. LA-1158, pp. 2–3; Map, *A Plan of the Coast of Part of West Florida & Louisiana: Including the River Yazous*, by George Gauld and Julius Erasmus (1778), Library of Congress, online https://www.loc.gov/resource/g4012c.ct000670/

55. James Pitot, *Observations on the Colony of Louisiana from 1796 to 1802* (New Orleans: The Historic New Orleans Collection, and Baton Rouge: Louisiana State University Press, 1979), pp. 68–69.

56. Thomas A. Becnel, *The Barrow Family and the Barataria and Lafourche Canal: The Transportation Revolution in Louisiana, 1829–1925* (Baton Rouge: Louisiana State University Press, 1989), p. 28; Swanson, *Historic Jefferson Parish*, pp. 87–88.

3. Entrepôt for Contraband

1. Lawrence N. Powell, *The Accidental City: Improvising New Orleans* (Cambridge: Harvard University Press, 2012), p. 101.

2. William D. Reeves, *Harvey: The Canal, The Family, The Community, Written in Honor of the 100th Anniversary of the Harvey Canal Limited Partnership* (The Harvey Land and Improvement Company, 1998), p. 2.

3. M. Perrin Du Lac, *Travels through the Two Louisianas . . . in 1801, 1802, & 1803* (London, 1807), pp. 91–92.

4. "How Swampy Barataria Got Its Name: A Letter to the Editor," by Betsy Swanson, NOLA.com/*Times-Picayune*, July 19, 2011.

5. Robert C. Vogel, "The Patterson and Ross Raid on Barataria, September 1814," *Louisiana History* 33, no. 2 (Spring 1992): 159.

6. Pierre Clément de Laussat, *Memoirs of My Life* (1831; Baton Rouge: Louisiana State University Press for The Historic New Orleans Collection, 1978), p. 89.

7. Joe G. Taylor, "The Foreign Slave Trade in Louisiana After 1808," *Louisiana History* 1, no. 1 (Winter 1960): 37.

8. David Head, "Slave Smuggling by Foreign Privateers: The Illegal Slave Trade and the Geopolitics of the Early Republic," *Journal of the Early Republic* 33, no. 3 (Fall 2013): 446.

9. William C. Davis, *The Pirates Laffite: The Treacherous World of the Corsairs of the Gulf* (New York: Harcourt, Inc., 2005), pp. 56–57; Vogel, "The Patterson and Ross Raid on Barataria," 160; William D. Reeves and Daniel Alario Sr., *Westwego: From Cheniere to Canal* (Harahan, LA: Jefferson Parish Historical Series, Monograph XIV, 1996), p. 5; Thomas A. Becnel, *The Barrow Family and the Barataria and Lafourche Canal: The Transportation Revolution in Louisiana, 1829–1925* (Baton Rouge: Louisiana State University Press, 1989), p. 28.

10. Arsène Lacarrière Latour, *Historical Memoir of the War in West Florida and Louisiana in 1814–15* (Philadelphia, PA: John Conrad and Co., 1816), pp. 14–15.

11. Head, "Slave Smuggling by Foreign Privateers," 433–62; Taylor, "The Foreign Slave Trade in Louisiana After 1808"; and other sources.

12. Vogel, "The Patterson and Ross Raid on Barataria," 168.

13. Alexander Walker, *Jackson and New Orleans. An Authentic Narrative of the Achievements of the American Army Under Andrew Jackson, Before New Orleans, in the Winter of 1814, '15* (New York and Cincinnati: J.C. Derby, Publishers, 1856), p. 242.

14. Le Chevalier de Tousard, writing before the battle, as quoted by Norman B. Wilkinson, "The Assaults on New Orleans, 1814–1815," *Louisiana History* 3, no. 1 (Winter 1962): 46.

15. Walker, *Jackson and New Orleans*, p. 242.

16. Ibid., p. 358.

17. For a review of the shifting interpretations, see Robert C. Vogel, "Jean Laffite, the Baratarians, and the Battle of New Orleans: A Reappraisal," *Louisiana History* 41, no. 3 (Summer 2000): 261–76.

4. The Formation of Villages

1. Pierre Clément de Laussat, *Memoirs of My Life* (1831; Baton Rouge: Louisiana State University Press for The Historic New Orleans Collection, 1978), pp. 16, 24, 66.

2. Ibid., p. 67.

3. Ibid., p. 70.

4. Orleans Territorial Acts 1807, First Legislature, Second Session, ch. 1, sec. 9, p. 10, as reported in *Louisiana Atlas of Historical County Boundaries*, ed. John H. Long and Peggy Tuck Sinko (Chicago: William M. Scholl Center for American History and Culture, The Newberry Library, 2010), p. 191. See also Richard Campanella, "A Mysterious Switch: Louisiana's Change from Counties to Parishes," *Louisiana Cultural Vistas*, Spring 2017.

5. Arsène Lacarrière Latour, "Map Showing the Landing of the British Army" (US Army, 7th Military District, 1815), The Historic New Orleans Collection.

6. James L. Furman, *Reminiscences of an Octogenarian or the Auto-Biography of a School Teacher* (New Orleans: Office Baptist Visitor, 1904), as transcribed by William D. Reeves in *Destrehan/Harvey History Manuscript-Binder 1* (unpublished manuscript, Farnet Family Collection), Green Section, "History of the Destrehan-Harvey Family" (1997), p. 3.4.

7. An 1815 map labeled the parcel as "Propriété de la Ville." J. Tanesse, *Plan of the City and Suburbs of New Orleans: From an Actual Survey Made in 1815,* Library of Congress.

8. William Garrett Piston, "Maritime Shipbuilding and Related Activities in Louisiana, 1542–1986," *Louisiana History* 29, no. 2 (Spring 1988): 166.

9. "Sad Scenes and Other Incidents—The Old Courthouse—A Stately Mansion with a Romantic History," *Daily Picayune,* October 21, 1895, p. 9.

10. "An Act for the Relief of Bartholomew Duverge" [*sic*], *Courrier de la Louisiane,* April 16, 1821, p. 2.

11. David Fritz and Sally K. Reeves, *Algiers Point: Historical Ambience and Property Analysis of Squares Ten, Thirteen, and Twenty, with a View toward Their Archaeological Potential* (New Orleans, Louisiana: Department of the Army, Corps of Engineers, June 1984), p. 101.

12. *Louisiana Courier,* January 29, 1821, as cited by Samuel Wilson Jr. in "The Plantation of the Company of the Indies," *Louisiana History,* Volume 31, no. 2 (Spring 1990): 182.

13. "Sad Scenes and Other Incidents," *Daily Picayune,* p. 9.

14. Piston, "Maritime Shipbuilding and Related Activities in Louisiana," p. 166.

15. Betsy Swanson, *Historic Jefferson Parish, From Shore to Shore* (1975; repr., Gretna, Louisiana: Pelican Publishing Company, 2004), p. 110.

16. See, for example, Charles F. Zimpel's *Topographic Map of New-Orleans and Its Vicinity* (New Orleans, 1834).

17. "Tomorrow By F. Dutillet," *Louisiana Courier,* February 26, 1833, as reproduced in Wilson, "The Plantation of the Company of the Indies," 183–85.

18. "Sale by the Sheriff of the Parish of Orleans—Succession of Touissaint Mossy, Senior, and Marie Aimée St. Amand, his Wife," *Daily Picayune,* May 15, 1849, p. 3.

19. Lewis E. Atherton, "John McDonogh—New Orleans Mercantile Capitalist," *Journal of Southern History* 7, no. 4 (November 1941): 451–81. The newspaper description of McDonogh's appearance comes from the *Daily Picayune,* October 27, 1850.

20. Laussat, *Memoirs of My Life,* p. 25.

21. Swanson, *Historic Jefferson Parish,* pp. 109–11; see also the watercolor, *Mon Plaisir Le Chateau et Jardin du Chevalier de Pradel* (2001) painted by Jim Blanchard, The Historic New Orleans Collection, 2001.39.3.

22. R. Christopher Goodwin & Associates, *Cultural Resources Survey of Gretna Phase II Levee Enlargement Item M-99.4 to 95.5-R, Jefferson Parish, Louisiana* (New Orleans: US Army Corps of Engineers, 1990), pp. 28–29.

23. Zimpel, *Topographic Map of New-Orleans and Its Vicinity.*

24. Betsy Swanson, *Historic Jefferson Parish,* p. 110.

25. Frank J. Borne Jr. *Jefferson Parish's Modern Government on Its Golden Anniversary, 1958–2008* (Jefferson Parish Historical Series/Jefferson Parish Historical Commission, 2008), pp. 1–4.

26. Louisiana Acts 1825, 7th Legislature, First Session, pp. 108–12, as reported in Long and Sinko, *Louisiana Atlas of Historical County Boundaries,* p. 136, 192.

27. Marc R. Matrana, *Lost Plantation: The Rise and Fall of Seven Oaks* (Jackson: University of Mississippi Press, 2005), pp. 20–21.

28. Richard Remy Dixon, "Many Stories Told of How Algiers Got Its Name," *Times-Picayune,* March 16, 1970, sec. 2, p. 3.

29. "A Duel Near Algiers, *The Picayune,* July 25, 1837, p. 2.

30. Sally K. Reeves and William D. Reeves, "Cultural History," in *Archeological Testing of Quarters A (16OR137) at the Naval Support Activity, West Bank Facility, Algiers, Orleans Parish, Louisiana,* by Melissa M. Green, Sally K. Reeves, William D. Reeves, and Stephen P. Austin, for the US Army Corps of Engineers, Fort Worth District, Miscellaneous Report of Investigations, no. 78, November 1996: 9–15, 34–51.

31. Zimpel, *Topographic Map of New-Orleans and Its Vicinity; Historical Sketch Book and Guide to New Orleans and Environs* (New York: Will H. Coleman, 1885), p. 288.

32. Reeves and Reeves, "Cultural History," *Archeological Testing of Quarters A,* p. 50; Ann Masson, "Benjamin Buisson," in *Encyclopedia of Louisiana* in knowlouisiana.org, ed. David Johnson (Louisiana Endowment for the Humanities, 2010), published September 28, 2012. http://www.knowlouisiana .org/entry/benjamin-buisson.

33. Springbett and Pilié, *Topographical Map of the City and Environs of New Orleans (1839),* reproduced in *Archeological Testing of Quarters A (16OR137) at the Naval Support Activity, West Bank Facility, Algiers, Orleans Parish, Louisiana,* by Melissa M. Green, Sally K. Reeves, William D. Reeves, and Stephen P. Austin, for the US Army Corps of Engineers, Fort Worth District, Miscellaneous Report of Investigations, no. 78, November 1996, p. 17.

34. "McLellanville: There's a New Town on the Map of Louisiana, Tunisburg Being Found Too Old," undated circa-1890 article reproduced in Richard Remy Dixon, *Old Algiers: A Story of Algiers, Yesterday and Today* (New Orleans: Algiers Annexation Centennial Committee, 1980), p. 57; William H. Seymour, *The Story of Algiers 1718–1896* (1896; repr., Gretna, Louisiana: Pelican Publishing Company, 1971), p. 18–19.

35. Reeves and Reeves, "Cultural History," in *Archeological Testing of Quarters A,* p. 20.

36. *Historical Sketch Book and Guide to New Orleans and Environs* (New York: Will H. Coleman, 1885), p. 289.

37. Fritz and Reeves, *Algiers Point: Historical Ambience,* p. 60.

38. Swanson, *Historic Jefferson Parish,* p. 116.

39. Masson, "Benjamin Buisson," in *Encyclopedia of Louisiana,* http://www.knowlouisiana.org/ entry/benjamin-buisson.

40. This explanation comes from "Mechanics' Home," *Portland Weekly Advertiser* (Portland, ME), May 2, 1843, p. 2.

41. Horace H. Harvey, Katherine Harvey Rogér, and Louise Destrehan Rogér D'Oliveira, *To Reach Afar: Memoirs and Biography of the Destrehan and Harvey Families of Louisiana* (Clearwater, FL: Hercules Publishing Company, 1974), p. 61; William D. Reeves, *Harvey: The Canal, The Family, The Community, Written in Honor of the 100th Anniversary of the Harvey Canal Limited Partnership* (The Harvey Land and Improvement Company, 1998), p. 4; Judy H. Pinter, "Louise Destrehan Harvey: A Pioneer Business Woman in Nineteenth-Century New Orleans, Louisiana" (Master's thesis, University of New Orleans, 2016), p. 14.

42. Reeves, *Destrehan/Harvey History Manuscript-Binder 1,* chap. 2, "Nicholas Noel Destrehan: From Destrehan to Harvey," pp. 1–6.

43. Ellen C. Merrill, *The Germans of Louisiana* (Gretna, LA: Pelican Publishing Company, 2005), page 86; Swanson, *Historic Jefferson Parish,* p. 116.

44. Goodwin & Associates, *Cultural Resources Survey of Gretna Phase II*, p. 28.

45. Leslie George Whitbread, *Place Names of Jefferson Parish: An Introductory Account* (Metairie, LA: Jefferson Parish Historical Commission, 1977), p. 5. See Mary Grace Curry's *Gretna—A Sesquicentennial Salute* (Jefferson Parish Historical Commission, 1986), pp. 1–3, for a review of the various name-origin theories, including the possible identity of the romantic magistrate.

46. "A Gretna Green Marriage," *Daily Picayune*, December 20, 1840, p. 2.

47. "The St. Mary's Ferry," advertisement in *The Daily Picayune*, March 13, 1842, p. 2.

48. Benjamin Norman, *Norman's New Orleans and Environs* (New York: D. Appleton & Co. and B. M. Norman, 1845), p. 195.

49. Hans C. Rasmussen, "The Culture of Bullfighting in Antebellum New Orleans," *Louisiana History* 55, no. 2 (Spring 2014): 140, 167.

50. Furman, *Reminiscences of an Octogenarian*, pp. 3.1–3.3.

51. Original Public Land Survey System map of Township 13 South, Range 24 East, Section 1, and Township 14 South, Range 24 East, Sections 43, 44, and 56, plus adjoining sections pertaining to Antoine Foucher. Louisiana Office of State Lands, Division of Administration, SONRIS Interactive State Lands GIS, online *http://sonris*-www.dnr.state.la.us/gis/agsweb/IE/JSViewer/index .html?TemplateID=381

52. Reeves, *Destrehan/Harvey History Manuscript-Binder 1*, chap. 1, "First Settlers of Harvey and Gretna," pp. 1–4.

53. Reeves, *Harvey: The Canal, The Family, The Community*, pp. 1–3.

54. John Kendall, "The City's Charities," in *History of New Orleans* (Chicago and New York: The Lewis Publishing Company, 1922).

55. Reeves, *Harvey: The Canal, The Family, The Community*, pp. 1–5; Original Public Land Survey System maps of the Louisiana Office of State Lands, Division of Administration; Swanson, *Historic Jefferson Parish*, p. 89.

56. This early plan for Milneburgh (Milneburg) appears on Zimpel's *Topographic Map of New-Orleans and Its Vicinity*. Parts of this plan were eventually laid out and may be seen in Gentilly today.

57. Reeves, *Destrehan/Harvey History Manuscript-Binder 1*, chap. 2, p. 15.

58. "Brick—Brick," *Daily Picayune*, June 28, 1849, ad on page 3.

59. Cosmopolite Brick Manufactory at Harvey's Canal, *Weekly Picayune*, February 19, 1881, p. 5. The operator was Joseph Hale Harvey.

5. Canals, Railroads, Ships, and Industry

1. William D. Reeves, *Harvey: The Canal, The Family, The Community, Written in Honor of the 100th Anniversary of the Harvey Canal Limited Partnership* (The Harvey Land and Improvement Company, 1998), pp. 4–5.

2. Furman, *Reminiscences of an Octogenarian*, as transcribed by William D. Reeves in *Destrehan/Harvey History Manuscript-Binder 1* (unpublished manuscript, Farnet Family Collection), Green Section, "History of the Destrehan-Harvey Family" (1997), p. 3.3; Reeves, *Harvey: The Canal, The Family, The Community*, p. 5; Alice Rightor, "When Statues Were Gowned in Mother Hubbards: Destrehan, Famed Canal Building, Was Eccentric," *Times-Picayune*, April 29, 1923, p. 1 of magazine section.

3. *John McAuliffe and Another v. Nicholas Noel Destrehan,* Appeal from the District Court of the First District, New Orleans, January 1845, in Merritt M. Robinson, *Reports of Cases Argued and Determined in the Supreme Court of Louisiana,* vol. 9 (New Orleans: Samuel M. Steward, Publisher, 1845), pp. 466–67.

4. Horace H. Harvey et al., *To Reach Afar: Memoirs and Biography of the Destrehan and Harvey Families of Louisiana* (Hercules Publishing, 1974), p. 61.

5. Furman, *Reminiscences of an Octogenarian,* pp. 3.1–3.3. See also pages 1.1–1.2.

6. Reeves, *Harvey: The Canal, The Family, The Community,* p. 8.

7. As quoted from *Stachlin v. Destrehan* in Reeves, *Destrehan/Harvey History Manuscript-Binder 1,* chap. ?, pp. 14–15.

8. Judy H. Pinter, "Louise Destrehan Harvey: A Pioneer Business Woman in Nineteenth-Century New Orleans, Louisiana" (master's thesis, University of New Orleans, 2016), pp. 14–18.

9. Katherine Harvey Roger, "Picture from the Past," *Jefferson Parish Yearly Review* (Kenner, LA, 1945), p. 89; Pinter, "Louise Destrehan Harvey," p. 19.

10. Harnett T. Kane, *The Bayous of Louisiana* (New York: Bonanza Books, 1963), p. 38.

11. Rightor, "When Statues Were Gowned in Mother Hubbards," p. 1 of magazine section.

12. Reeves, *Destrehan Manuscript Binder 2* (Spiral Bound), chap. 2, pp. 7–8.

13. Reeves, *Harvey: The Canal, The Family, The Community,* p. 10; Reeves, *Destrehan/Harvey History Manuscript-Binder 1,* chap. 3, pp. 4–5.

14. Furman, *Reminiscences of an Octogenarian,* p. 3.3.

15. This local fad reflected a philosophical transformation in which European artists and philosophers reacted against lofty Enlightenment ideals and the expanding influence of Logos by celebrating beauty and embracing *pathos.* The movement came to be known as Romanticism, and it particularly influenced architects, who abandoned staid classical Greek and Roman idioms and found inspiration instead in picturesque ruins from the Middle Ages and the Renaissance. The Romantics revived Italianate and Gothic styles, among others, and had a special penchant for old castles, which they restored or rebuilt along rivers such as the Rhine. Featured on the "grand tour" taken by aspiring architects, the style spread, and crenelated Gothic "castles" became a popular look, especially along urban riverfronts. New Orleans and Louisiana had their share, particularly on the West Bank. The best surviving example of this fashion, which ran from the 1830s through 1860s, is the Old State Capitol Building in Baton Rouge.

16. Sally K. Reeves and Willian D. Reeves, "Cultural History," in *Archeological Testing of Quarters A (160R137) at the Naval Support Activity, West Bank Facility, Algiers, Orleans Parish, Louisiana,* by Melissa M. Green, Sally K. Reeves, Willian D. Reeves, and Stephen P. Austin, for the US Army Corps of Engineers, Fort Worth District. Miscellaneous Report of Investigations, no. 78, November 1996: 20.

17. Reeves, *Harvey: The Canal, The Family, The Community,* pp. 6–7; Reeves, *Destrehan/Harvey History Manuscript-Binder 1,* chap. 3, p. 6.

18. David Fritz and Sally K. Reeves, *Algiers Point: Historical Ambience and Property Analysis of Squares Ten, Thirteen, and Twenty, with a View toward Their Archaeological Potential* (New Orleans, LA: Department of the Army, Corps of Engineers, June 1984), p. 101.

19. Reeves, *Destrehan/Harvey History Manuscript-Binder 1,* chap. 3, p. 6.

20. Merl E. Reed, *New Orleans and the Railroads: The Struggle for Commercial Empire, 1830–1860* (Baton Rouge: Louisiana State University Press), p. 84.

21. Ibid., pp. 33–67.

22. Bennet Dowler, MD, *Tableaux, Geographical, Commercial, Geological, and Sanitary, of New Orleans* (New Orleans: Daily Delta, 1853), p. 24.

23. Reed, *New Orleans and the Railroads*, p. 68.

24. "Southwestern Railroad Convention," *Daily Picayune*, January 4, 1852, p. 2.

25. A. G. Blanchard, "Report of the Preliminary Survey of the Algiers & Opelousas Railroad," *Louisiana Acts* (Baton Rouge, 1853), pp. 115–23, as quoted by Mark Reutter and J. Parker Lamb in "Crescent City Bound," *Railroad History*, no. 193 (Fall–Winter 2005–2006): 12.

26. "The Courts—Third District Court—Judge Kennedy—Test of the Railroad Tax," *Daily Picayune*, February 1, 1853.

27. A. G. Blanchard, "New-Orleans and Opelousas Rail-Road—Survey of the Route of the Rail-Road to Opelousas," in *Debow's Review of the Southern and Southwestern States*, vol. 12, New Series Volume 5, 1852, p. 439.

28. Blanchard, "New-Orleans and Opelousas Rail-Road," p. 441.

29. "New Orleans, Opelousas and Great Western Railroad Company vs. succession of John McDonogh," *Daily Picayune*, January 11, 1853, p. 6.

30. Reed, *New Orleans and the Railroads*, p. 115.

31. Augustus S. Phelps, "New-Orleans and Opelousas Rail-Road Engineer's Report," December 29, 1851, in *Debow's Review of the Southern and Southwestern States*, vol. 12, New Series Volume 5, 1852, p. 435.

32. Edward H. Barton, "Report Upon the Sanitary Condition of New Orleans," in *Report of the Sanitary Commission on the Epidemic Yellow Fever of 1853* (New Orleans: City Council, 1854), pp. 318, 395.

33. "Opelousas Railroad," *The New Orleans Bee*, December 5, 1853, p. 1.

34. Reed, *New Orleans and the Railroads*, pp. 115–16.

35. "Railroads," *A. Mygatt & Co.'s New Orleans Business Directory for 1858* (New Orleans: A. Mygatt & Co., 1858), p. L.

36. Reed, *New Orleans and the Railroads*, p. 119.

37. Fritz and Reeves, *Algiers Point: Historical Ambience*, pp. 77, 101.

38. David G. Surdam, "The Antebellum Texas Cattle Trade Across the Gulf of Mexico," *Southwestern Historical Quarterly* 100, no. 4 (April 1997): 477–92; Edward Everett Dale, as quoted by Mitchell Franklin in "The Foundations and Meaning of the Slaughterhouse Cases," *Tulane Law Review* 38, no. 1 (October 1943): 7.

39. Franklin, "The Foundations and Meaning of the Slaughterhouse Cases," pp. 1–3.

40. Ibid., p. 4.

41. Edward McPherson, "Judicial Decisions and Opinions: The Louisiana Slaughter-House Cases." *Hand-Book of Politics for 1874: Being a Record of Important Political Action, National and State, from July 15, 1872, to July 15, 1874* (Washington, DC, 1874), p. 41.

42. *The Times*, July 27, 1869, as quoted by Mitchell Franklin in "The Foundations and Meaning of the Slaughterhouse Cases," p. 3n; Ronald M. Labbé and Jonathan Lurie, *The Slaughterhouse Cases: Regulation, Reconstruction, and the Fourteenth Amendment* (Lawrence, KS, 2003), pp. 109–10.

43. Labbé and Lurie, *The Slaughterhouse Cases*, pp. 120–22; 163.

44. Michael A. Ross, "Justice Miller's Reconstruction: The *Slaughter-House Cases*, Health Codes, and Civil Rights in New Orleans, 1861–1873," *Journal of Southern History* 64, no. 4 (November 1998): 649–76; Labbé and Lurie, *The Slaughterhouse Cases*, p. 243.

45. Katherine Harvey Roger, "Picture from the Past," *Jefferson Parish Yearly Review* (Kenner, LA, 1945), pp. 98–99.

46. *The Navigator* (Pittsburgh, PA: Cramer, Spear, and Eichbaum, 1814), p. 225; S. A. Ferrall, *A Ramble of Six Thousand Miles through the United States of America* (London: Effingham Wilson, Royal Exchange, 1832), p. 190.

47. John H. B. Latrobe, *Southern Travels: Journal of John H. B. Latrobe, 1834,* ed. Samuel Wilson Jr. (New Orleans: The Historic New Orleans Collection, 1986), p. 40. The watercraft nomenclature is gleaned from the records of vessels officially registered or enrolled at the Port of New Orleans from 1804 to 1870. Survey of Federal Archives in Louisiana, Division of Community Service Programs–Works Projects Administration, *Ship Registers and Enrollments of New Orleans, Louisiana,* vol. 1–2 (Baton Rouge: Louisiana State University, 1941).

48. James E. Winston, "Notes on the Economic History of New Orleans," *Mississippi Valley Historical Review* 11, no. 2 (September 1924): 203; Frank Haigh Dixon, "A Traffic History of the Mississippi River System," Document no. 11, National Waterways Commission (Washington, DC: Government Printing Office, December 1909), 15.

49. William Garrett Piston, "Maritime Shipbuilding and Related Activities in Louisiana, 1542–1986," *Louisiana History* 29, no. 2 (Spring 1988): 166.

50. Fritz and Reeves, *Algiers Point*, pp. 11, 102.

51. *General Digest of the Ordinances and Resolutions of the Corporation of New-Orleans,* "An Ordinance concerning the Port and Levee of New-Orleans," Article 8, approved February 29, 1829 (New Orleans: Jerome Bayon, 1831), p. 319.

52. *François Vallette and Another v. John Patten and Others,* Appeal from the District Court of the First District, December 1844, in Merritt M. Robinson, *Reports of Cases Argued and Determined in the Supreme Court of Louisiana,* vol. 9 (New Orleans: Samuel M. Steward, Publisher, 1845), p. 369.

53. Gary A. Van Zante, *New Orleans 1867: Photographs by Theodore Lilienthal* (London, New York: Merrell Publishers, 2008), p. 230.

54. "A Visit to the Floating Dock," *Daily Picayune,* June 17, 1838, p. 2.

55. Benjamin Norman, *Norman's New Orleans and Environs* (New York: D. Appleton and B. M. Norman, 1845), pp. 194–95; Piston, "Maritime Shipbuilding and Related Activities in Louisiana," p. 166; Richard Remy Dixon, *Algiers: The Heart of New Orleans* (New Orleans: First National Bank of Commerce/Upton Printing Company, 1973), p. 5

56. Fritz and Reeves, *Algiers Point: Historical Ambience,* p. 11.

57. Piston, "Maritime Shipbuilding and Related Activities in Louisiana," p. 166.

58. "Algiers Business Directory," *A. Mygatt & Co.'s New Orleans Business Directory for 1858* (New Orleans: A. Mygatt, 1858), p. 241–43; William H. Seymour, *The Story of Algiers, Now the Fifth District of New Orleans* (Algiers Democrat Publishing Company, 1896), p. 57.

59. "New Orleans Dry Dock Association," *Daily Picayune,* September 11, 1860, p. 7.

60. *Historical Sketch Book and Guide to New Orleans and Environs* (New York: Will H. Coleman, 1885), p. 290.

61. *Ship Registers and Enrollments of New Orleans, Louisiana, Volume 5, 1851–1860,* The Survey of Federal Archives in Louisiana, Service Division (Work Projects Administration, 1942), p. XV. See also listings of all ship commissions in volumes 1–5 for those built in Algiers.

62. Ibid., p. 25.

63. *Historical Sketch Book and Guide to New Orleans,* p. 288.

64. "The Late J. P. Whitney," *Daily Picayune,* February 1, 1848, p. 2; "The Belleville Iron Works," *American and Commercial Daily Advertiser* (Baltimore), February 6, 1847, p. 2.

65. Quoted from an undated antebellum advertisement for Belleville Iron Works reproduced in *Old Algiers: A Story of Algiers, Yesterday and Today,* by Richard Remy Dixon (Gretna, LA: Algiers Annexation to New Orleans Centennial Committee, 1980), p. 39.

66. Seymour, *The Story of Algiers,* p. 19.

67. "Southern Cotton Manufacturers," *Daily Picayune,* July 9, 1849, p. 2.

68. "Algiers Business Directory," p. 241.

69. Dixon, *Old Algiers,* p. 39; Seymour, *The Story of Algiers,* p. 57.

70. *François Vallette and Another v. John Patten and Others,* pp. 367–72.

71. Harvey et al., *To Reach Afar,* pp. 59, 72.

72. These are 1863 prices, cited by Betsy Swanson in *Historic Jefferson Parish, From Shore to Shore* (1975; repr., Gretna, LA: Pelican Publishing Company, 2004), p. 90.

73. *Historical Sketch Book and Guide to New Orleans,* p. 250.

74. Ibid., p. 188.

75. Harvey et al., *To Reach Afar,* pp. 59, 72.

76. Rightor, "When Statues Were Gowned in Mother Hubbards," p. 1 of magazine section.

77. Thomas A. Becnel, *The Barrow Family and the Barataria and Lafourche Canal: The Transportation Revolution in Louisiana, 1829–1925* (Baton Rouge: Louisiana State University Press, 1989), pp. 29–30; Edwin Ney Bruce, "The Growth and Development of Westwego, 1827–1942" (1942, forerunner of master's thesis, "Louisiana: A Community Study," Tulane University, 1947), pp. 1–3, manuscript stored at Westwego Historical Society.

78. Becnel, *The Barrow Family and the Barataria and Lafourche Canal,* pp. 1–3.

79. Ibid., pp. 59, 63.

80. Reeves, *Destrehan/Harvey History Manuscript-Binder 1,* chap. 3, p. 10.

81. R. R. Barrow, *A Miscellaneous Essay on the Political Parties of the Country, The Rise of Abolitionism and the Impolicy of Secession* (New Orleans: L. Marchand, 1861), p. 13.

82. Martha Reinhard Smallwood Field, *Louisiana Voyages: The Travel Writings of Catharine Cole* (Jackson: University Press of Mississippi, 2006), p. 22.

83. "Oyster Men," *New Orleans Item,* October 23, 1894, p. 3.

84. Richard Campanella, "Lugger Culture: Distinctive Sailboats Once Defined Coastal Louisiana's Oyster Trade," *Louisiana Cultural Vistas,* Autumn 2016.

85. "No. 152: An Act, to authorize Joseph H. Harvey, of the Parish of Jefferson, to construct a Lock, to connect the Destréhan Canal with the Mississippi River," March 16, 1854, in *Acts Passed*

by the *Second Legislature of the State of Louisiana* (New Orleans: Emile La Sere, State Printer, 1854), p. 116.

86. Harvey et al., *To Reach Afar*, pp. 92–93.

6. Crescendo and Calamity

1. "Ferries," *A. Mygatt & Co.'s New Orleans Business Directory for 1858* (New Orleans: A. Mygatt, 1858), p. xxxix.

2. *Historical Sketch Book and Guide to New Orleans and Environs* (New York: Will H. Coleman, 1885), p. 148.

3. "Some Large Landholders of Jefferson Parish, 1850, Compiled from the 1850 Census of Agriculture for Louisiana," *Louisiana History* 27, no. 3 (Summer 1986): 238; Marc R. Matrana, "On Cane and Coolies: Chinese Laborers on Post-Antebellum Louisiana Sugar Plantations As Exemplified on the Millaudon Plantation of Jefferson Parish," *Jefferson History Notebook* 7, no. 1 (February 2003): 1–8; "Valuable Plantation," *Daily Confederation* (Montgomery, AL), March 16, 1859, p. 2.

4. "The Puritan and the Cavalier; or, The Elements of American Colonial Society," *De Bow's Review*, September 1861, vol. 31, p. 210, as analyzed by Jan C. Dawson, "The Puritan and the Cavalier: The South's Perception of Contrasting Traditions," *Journal of Southern History* 44, no. 4 (November 1978): 597–614.

5. Abraham Lincoln, "First Inaugural Address—Final Text," March 4, 1861, *The Collected Works of Abraham Lincoln*, vol. 4, ed. Roy P. Basler (New Brunswick, NJ: Rutgers University Press, 1953), page 271 (emphasis in original).

6. Abraham Lincoln, "Proclamation of a Blockade," April 19, 1861, *The Collected Works of Abraham Lincoln*, pp. 338–39.

7. As recollected by Benjamin F. Butler, in *Reminiscences of Abraham Lincoln by Distinguished Men of His Time*, ed. Allen Thorndike Rice (New York: North American Review, 1889), p. 142. Lincoln later added to the above directive, "but don't interfere with the slavery question."

8. R. R. Barrow, *A Miscellaneous Essay on the Political Parties of the Country, The Rise of Abolitionism and the Impolicy of Secession* (New Orleans: L. Marchand, 1861), p. 11; Thomas A. Becnel, *The Barrow Family and the Barataria and Lafourche Canal: The Transportation Revolution in Louisiana, 1829–1925* (Baton Rouge: Louisiana State University Press, 1989), pp. 70–75.

9. Map, "Approaches to New Orleans, Prepared by the Order of Maj. Gen. N. P. Banks [by] Henry L. Abbott," Department of the Gulf, Map No. 5, February 14, 1863, The Historic New Orleans Collection, Accession No. 1974.25.18.122.

10. "The City—Great Conflagration on the River," *Daily Picayune*, May 6, 1861, p. 4. Damages that night foretold much greater losses one year later, as the Union fleet broke past Confederate defenses at the mouth of the Mississippi to take New Orleans. On both sides of the river, Confederates torched wharves, warehouses, and vessels to deprive the enemy of spoils, shrouding the metropolis in smoke. By the time it cleared, the South's greatest city was under Union control.

11. "Terrible Explosion; Powder Mill Blown," *The Daily True Delta*, December 29, 1861, p. 2.

12. "The Explosion," *The Daily True Delta*, December 31, 1861, p. 3.

13. *Historical Sketch Book and Guide to New Orleans*, p. 289.

14. Thomas K. Wharton, *Queen of the South—New Orleans, 1853–1862: The Journal of Thomas K. Wharton*, ed. Samuel Wilson Jr., Patricia Brady, and Lynn D. Adams (New Orleans: The Historic New Orleans Collection and New York Public Library, 1999), p. 266.

15. War Department, Confederate States of America, *Proceedings of the Court of Inquiry Relative to the Fall of New Orleans* (Richmond, VA: R. M. Smith, 1864), pp. 10–12, 20–22.

16. James M. Merrill, "Confederate Shipbuilding at New Orleans," *Journal of Southern History* 28, no. 1 (February 1962): 87–93; Federal Writers' Project of the Works Progress Administration, *New Orleans City Guide* (Boston: Houghton Mifflin Company, 1938), p. 360.

17. *Historical Sketch Book and Guide to New Orleans*, p. 291.

18. Letter, Benjamin F. Butler to Abraham Lincoln, May 8, 1862, The Abraham Lincoln Papers at the Library of Congress.

19. "Scenes in Louisiana," *Frank Leslie's Illustrated Newspaper*, March 7, 1863, p. 1; Richard Biddle Irwin, *History of the Nineteenth Army Corps* (New York: G. P. Putnam's Sons, 1892), pp. 16, 48; Thomas A. Becnel, *The Barrow Family and the Barataria and Lafourche Canal*, p. 75.

20. As quoted in the *New Orleans Times* by William D. Reeves in *Destrehan/Harvey History Manuscript-Binder 1* (unpublished manuscript, Farnet Family Collection), chap. 3, p. 10.

7. The Political Chessboard

1. "Division of the City of New-Orleans into Three Municipalities," March 8, 1836, *A New Digest of the Statute Laws of the State of Louisiana*, compiled by Henry A. Bullard and Thomas Curry (New Orleans: E. Johns & Co., 1842), vol. 1, p. 15. In this era, the state controlled all questions of municipal identity, including incorporation, governance, delineation, annexation, separation, and consolidation. They were not matters of public referendum.

2. "New Orleans—Constitutional Provision," Section 43, in *The Revised Statutes of Louisiana*, compiled by U. B. Phillips (New Orleans: John Claiborne, State Printer, 1856), p. 366; Collin B. Hamer Jr., "Records of the City of Lafayette (1833–1852) in the City Archives Department of the New Orleans Public Library," *Louisiana History* 13, no. 4 (Autumn 1972): 413–31.

3. The Historical Records Survey, "A Brief History of Jefferson Parish," *Inventory of the Parish Archives of Louisiana—No. 26, Jefferson Parish* (Baton Rouge: Department of Archives, Louisiana State University, April 1940), p. 10.

4. Overlapping jurisdictions of both counties and parishes would coexist in Louisiana until 1846, when the state finally abandoned unpopular counties in favor of parishes, for their ecclesiastic familiarity to Louisiana's largely Catholic population.

5. Orleans Territorial Acts 1807, First Legislature, Second Session, ch. 1, sec. 9, p. 10, as reported in *Louisiana Atlas of Historical County Boundaries*, ed. John H. Long and Peggy Tuck Sinko (Chicago: William M. Scholl Center for American History and Culture, The Newberry Library, 2010), p. 191; Richard Remy Dixon, *Old Algiers: A Story of Algiers, Yesterday and Today* (Gretna, LA: Algiers Annexation to New Orleans Centennial Committee, 1980), p. 9; Richard Campanella, "A Mysterious Switch: Louisiana's Change from Counties to Parishes," *Louisiana Cultural Vistas*, Spring 2017.

6. Police Jury of the Parish of Jefferson, Meeting of the 13th of January and 7th of February, 1834, Article 25, in *Transcriptions of Parish Records of Louisiana—No. 26, Jefferson Parish, Series I, Police Jury Minutes, Volume 1, 1834–1843* (The Historical Records Survey, Works Progress Administration, 1940), pp. 17–21.

7. Meinrad Greiner, *The Louisiana Digest, Embracing the Laws of the Legislature of a General Nature Enacted From the Year 1804 to 1841*, vol. 1 (New Orleans: Benjamin Levy, Publisher, 1841), p. 392; *Jefferson Parish Events 1825–2000*, ed. Mary G. Curry and Charmaine Currault Rini (Jefferson, LA: Jefferson Parish Historical Commission, 2000), pp. 1–2.

8. The boundaries of the First District ran from the parish line "to the upper boundary of Mrs. Joseph Verloin Dugruy's plantation," which, according to the 1834 Charles Zimpel map, aligns with today's Barataria Boulevard in Marrero. Mary Grace Curry, *Gretna—A Sesquicentennial Salute* (Jefferson Parish Historical Commission, 1986), p. 5.

9. Based on author's analysis of WPA transcriptions of Jefferson Parish Police Jury minutes from 1834 onward, in all volumes of The Historical Records Survey, *Inventory of the Parish Archives of Louisiana—No. 26, Jefferson Parish* (Baton Rouge: Department of Archives, Louisiana State University, April 1940).

10. *Overview*, Lawrason Act, Louisiana Revised Statutes, January 2019, online https://app.lla .state.la.us/llala.nsf/ . . . /$FILE/Lawrason%20Act%20FAQ.pdf.

11. "Shall Algiers Be A City," *Daily Picayune*, November 23, 1866.

12. Dixon, *Old Algiers*, p. 9.

13. Edward McPherson, "Judicial Decisions and Opinions: The Louisiana Slaughter-House Cases," *Hand-Book of Politics for 1874: Being a Record of Important Political Action, National and State, from July 15, 1872 to July 15, 1874* (Washington, DC, 1874), 41; Ronald M. Labbé and Jonathan Lurie, *The Slaughterhouse Cases: Regulation, Reconstruction, and the Fourteenth Amendment* (Lawrence: University Press of Kansas, 2003), pp. 109–10.

14. "Algiers as Part of this Port," *Daily Picayune*, April 1, 1866.

15. Richard Campanella, "The Annexation of Carrollton," *New Orleans Times-Picayune*, September 8, 2017, InsideOut section; "The Annexation of Algiers," *New Orleans Times-Picayune*, August 11, 2017, InsideOut section; "How New Orleans Took Uptown from Jefferson Parish," *New Orleans Times-Picayune*, July 14, 2017, InsideOut section; "When Lafayette City Became New Orleans," *New Orleans Times-Picayune*, June 9, 2017, InsideOut section.

16. "Local Intelligence: Present Condition and Appearance of the Fifth District," *New Orleans Times*, March 27, 1870, p. 10.

17. *Algiers Independent*, March 31, 1870, as quoted by Dixon, *Old Algiers*, p. 11.

18. "Aggravated Algiers—Why She is Unhappy in her Union with New Orleans," *New Orleans Times*, October 2, 1877; Richard Campanella, "Great Fire of 1895 Transformed Algiers," *New Orleans Times-Picayune*, November 13, 2015.

19. Mark Ballard, "Bills Would Allow Algiers to Secede from City of New Orleans; Here's What's Next," *Baton Rouge Advocate*, May 15, 2015, http://www.theadvocate.com/baton_rouge/news/politics/ legislature/article_aa9ddc81-1442-56f9-a9ae-4dcc171811ae.html.

20. "Alexander's Bill," *Daily Picayune*, March 2, 1870; "Amended Charter," *New Orleans Times*, March 15, 1870.

21. "Barber's Bill," *Daily Picayune*, February 28, 1874.

22. Meloncy C. Soniat, "The Faubourgs Forming the Upper Section of the City of New Orleans," *The Louisiana Historical Quarterly* 20 (January–October 1937), pp. 192–211.

23. LeRoy L. Hall, "Final Report of the Jefferson Parish Police Jury," *Jefferson Parish Yearly Review* (Kenner, LA, 1954), p. 20.

24. The Historical Records Survey, "A Brief History of Jefferson Parish," p. 7.

25. William D. Reeves, *Destrehan/Harvey History Manuscript-Binder 1* (unpublished manuscript, Farnet Family Collection), chap. 4, "Origins of the Town of Harvey," pt. 1, pp. 1–2.

26. The Historical Records Survey, *Inventory of the Parish Archives of Louisiana—No. 26*, p. 35.

27. Based on author's analysis of Jefferson Parish Police Jury meeting minutes, 1834 to 1940, as transcribed by the Works Progress Administration and made digitally available by the Jefferson Parish Historical Society.

28. The Historical Records Survey, "A Brief History of Jefferson Parish," pp. 15–17; Curry and Rini, *Jefferson Parish Events 1825–2000*, pp. 8, 11.

29. The Historical Records Survey, "A Brief History of Jefferson Parish," Police Jury of Jefferson Parish, *Jefferson Parish Year Book*, 1939, p. 145.

30. Judy Dobbins Mills, "Terrytown: A New Residential Concept for Jefferson Parish Approaches Its 50th Year," Jefferson History Notebook (Jefferson Historical Society of Louisiana) 12, no. 1, April 2009, p. 9.

8. A Modern Economy Emerges

1. Meeting Minutes, Office of the Police Jury, Parish of Jefferson, April 7, 1887. The Historical Records Survey, *Transcription of Parish Records of Louisiana: No. 26, Jefferson Parish (Gretna): Series 1 Police Jury Minutes Vol. 5. 1879–1888* (Division of Professional and Service Projects, Work Projects Administration, April 1940), p. 331; Mary Grace Curry, *Gretna—A Sesquicentennial Salute* (Jefferson Parish Historical Commission, 1986), p. 10.

2. Curry, *Gretna—A Sesquicentennial Salute*, p. 10; LeRoy L. Hall, "Final Report of the Jefferson Parish Police Jury," *Jefferson Parish Yearly Review* (Kenner, LA, 1954), p. 23.

3. *Biographical and Historical Memoirs of Louisiana*, vol. 1 (Chicago: The Goodspeed Publishing Company, 1892), p. 239; Curry, *Gretna—A Sesquicentennial Salute*, p. 11. Regarding Gretna's population, the 1890 Census reported either 3,332 or 5,425 residents, depending on the area enumerated (*Biographical and Historical Memoirs of Louisiana*, vol. 1, pp. 14, 239). The Sanborn Fire Insurance Map of 1895 estimated Gretna's population at 4,000.

4. This was the Southern Pacific line. Sanborn Fire Insurance Maps for Gretna, Jefferson Parish, 1895–1896.

5. "Morgan's Louisiana and Texas Railroad," *Galveston Weekly News*, November 18, 1880, p. 4.

6. Ernst von Hesse-Wartegg, *Travels on the Lower Mississippi, 1879–1880*, ed. and trans. Frederic Trautmann (Columbia: University of Missouri Press, 1990), p. 144.

7. "Morgan's Louisiana and Texas Railroad and Steamship Company," *Daily Picayune*, April 16, 1884, p. 2.

8. William D. Reeves, *Historic Louisiana: An Illustrated History* (New Orleans: Louisiana Historical Society/Historical Publishing Network, 2003), pp. 56–58.

9. "Hon. Carleton Hunt's Campaign Speech," *Daily Picayune,* November 5, 1882, p. 3.

10. Sanborn Fire Insurance Maps for Algiers/Fifth Municipal District of New Orleans, 1885–1886.

11. Richard Remy Dixon, *Old Algiers: A Story of Algiers, Yesterday and Today* (New Orleans: Algiers Annexation Centennial Committee, 1980), pp. 133, 138.

12. Sanborn Fire Insurance Maps for Algiers/Fifth Municipal District of New Orleans, 1895–1896.

13. Louis C. Hennick and E. Harper Charlton, *Street Railways of Louisiana* (Gretna, LA: A Firebird Press Book–Pelican Publishing Company, 1998), p. 12.

14. Hermann Zagel, trans. and Richard A. Weiss, ed., in "The Gretna-Algiers Railroad," *Louisiana History* 17, no. 4 (Autumn 1976): 458–63; two quotes from pp. 460 and 46.

15. Hennick and Charlton, *Street Railways of Louisiana,* p. 13.

16. "Map of the City of New Orleans and Vicinity July 1925," Louisiana State Museum Historical Map Collection; Louis C. Hennick and E. Harper Charlton, *The Streetcars of New Orleans* (Gretna: A Firebird Press Book–Pelican Publishing Company, 2000), pp. 20, 223-24; Dixon, *Old Algiers,* p. 146.

17. Hennick and Charlton, *Street Railways of Louisiana,* p. 20.

18. "An Act, to Amend an Act . . . and to Authorize Said Charles Morgan to Incorporate . . . Morgan's Louisiana and Texas Railroad, Formerly Known as the New Orleans, Opelousas, and Great Western Railroad," *Acts Passed by the General Assembly of the State of Louisiana,* New Orleans, January 1, 1872, pp. 37–39; Walter Pritchard, "A Forgotten Louisiana Engineer: G. W. R. Bayley and His 'History of the Railroads of Louisiana,'" *Louisiana Historical Quarterly* 30, no. 4 (October 1947): 1262–71.

19. Pritchard, "A Forgotten Louisiana Engineer," 1307; William D. Reeves and Daniel Alario Sr., *Westwego: From Cheniere to Canal* (Harahan, LA: Jefferson Parish Historical Series, Monograph 14, 1996), pp. 28–31.

20. Marc R. Matrana, *Lost Plantation: The Rise and Fall of Seven Oaks* (Jackson: University of Mississippi Press, 2005), pp. 75–77.

21. Pritchard, "A Forgotten Louisiana Engineer," pp. 1262–71.

22. Mark Reutter and J. Parker Lamb in "Crescent City Bound," *Railroad History,* No. 193 (Fall–Winter 2005–2006): 14; "'The Gouldsboro'—Arrival of the New Rail Ferryboat for the New Orleans Pacific Railroad," *Daily Picayune,* December 31, 1881, p. 8.

23. "Longer than Any City Block: Cares and Responsibilities of the Man Who Directs Great Transfer Barge at Harahan," *New Orleans Times-Picayune,* May 14, 1916, p. 52; Federal Writers' Project of the Works Progress Administration, *New Orleans City Guide* (Boston: Houghton Mifflin, 1938); Department of the Interior, US Geological Survey, *Louisiana—New Orleans Quadrangle, N.W. Quarter* and *N.E. Quarter,* 1932.

24. "Harvey, A Brief History of the Thriving Town Opposite Louisiana Avenue," *The Daily Item,* December 1, 1894, p. 3.

25. Ibid.

26. Scipion appears in documents again in 1736, when he signed an agreement to hire himself out to help row a keelboat to Illinois, followed by other jobs, for a period of one year. For this Scipion would be paid 200 livres. "Notes on the Census of New Orleans for January 1732" and

supplement "List of Landowners," as transcribed by Charles R. Maduell Jr., *The Census Tables for the French Colony of Louisiana from 1699 to 1732* (Baltimore: Genealogical Publishing Company, 1972), p. 147; Donald E. Everett, "Free Persons of Color in Colonial Louisiana," *Louisiana History* 7, no. 1 (Winter 1966): 21–50.

27. *Donaldsonville Chief,* March 14, 1874, as quoted by Lucy M. Cohen, *Chinese in the Post–Civil War South: A People without a History* (Baton Rouge: Louisiana State University Press, 1984), p. 143.

28. "Chinese Plantation Hands—Arrival on the Great Republic—Something About Them," *New Orleans Republican,* July 3, 1870, p. 1.

29. "How the Chinese Work—Visit to a Plantation," *New Orleans Republican,* July 24, 1870, p. 1.

30. "The Chinese Laborers—A Ripple on the Surface—Brief Trouble, Soon Ended—The Cabbage Revolt," *New Orleans Republican,* July 26, 1870, p. 1.

31. "Chinese Market Garden—Curious Profitable Farm Above Gretna," *New Orleans Times-Democrat,* August 20, 1897.

32. Personal email communication with Sheriff Harry Lee, June 16, 2004, and June 14, 2005; Betsy Peterson, "Inside the Chinese Community," *The Courier,* November 8–14, 1973.

33. Reeves and Alario Sr., *Westwego: From Cheniere to Canal,* pp. 28–30.

34. "Chinese Plantation Hands," *New Orleans Republican,* July 3, 1870; "The Chinese Laborers," *New Orleans Republican,* July 26, 1870, and Wesley Jackson, "Letter Helped Open Door to Christianity for Chinese," *Times-Picayune,* December 23, 1973, sec. 3, p. 2; Betsy Swanson, *Historic Jefferson Parish, From Shore to Shore* (1975; repr. Gretna, Louisiana: Pelican Publishing Company, 2004), pp. 96–97.

35. "Harvey, A Brief History of the Thriving Town," p. 3.

36. Alcée Fortier, *Louisiana, Comprising Sketches of Parishes, Towns, Events, Institutions, and Persons, Arranged in Cyclopedic Form,* vol. 3 (Century Historical Association, 1914), pp. 282–83.

37. Numa Hero, "Jefferson and Plaquemines Drainage District," *Jefferson Parish Yearbook* (Police Jury of Jefferson Parish, 1935), p. 121.

38. Allen Powell II, "Marrero Street Renamed for Historic Settler Corrine Degree Walker," *New Orleans Times-Picayune,* https://www.nola.com/news/index.ssf/2009/03/marrero_street_renamed_for_his.html.

39. C. G. Muench, "Why We Are in Jefferson Parish," *Jefferson Parish Yearly Review* (Jefferson Parish, 1938), p. 37–45; Emily Ann Thompson, *The Soundscape of Modernity: Architectural Acoustics and the Culture of Listening in America, 1900–1933* (Cambridge, MA: The MIT Press, 2002), pp. 218–19.

40. Muench, "Why We Are in Jefferson Parish," pp. 47–49.

41. Weaver Toledano, "Jefferson Parish Is Ready Now," *Jefferson Parish Yearly Review* (Kenner, LA, 1951), p. 7.

42. Allen Powell II, "Celotex Park Facility on Fourth Street in Marrero to Be Redeveloped," *Times-Picayune,* August 25, 2010, https://www.nola.com/business/2010/08/celotex_park_facility_on_fourt.html.

43. Edwin Ney Bruce, "The Growth and Development of Westwego, 1827–1942" (1942, forerunner of master's thesis, "Louisiana: A Community Study," Tulane University, 1947), p. 4, manuscript stored at Westwego Historical Society.

44. Ibid.

45. Matrana, *Lost Plantation*, p. 84.

46. "Westwego Cannery," *Daily Picayune*, December 18, 1913, p. 5.

47. Sanborn Fire Insurance Map, Westwego Sheet 1129, updated for 1937.

48. Milton J. Linder, "Shrimp," *Jefferson Parish Yearbook* (Official Publication of the Police Jury, 1936), pp. 36–37.

49. Bruce, "The Growth and Development of Westwego," p. 33.

50. Gleaned from photographs at the Westwego Historical Museum.

51. "Town of Westwego," *Jefferson Parish Yearbook* (Official Publication of the Police Jury, 1936), p. 73.

9. The Battle for the Intracoastal Waterway

1. "An Act to Authorize the Barataria Ship Canal Company," June 15, 1878, *Annual Report of the Chief of Engineers to the Secretary of War for the Year 1878*, pt. 1 (Washington, DC: Government Printing Office, 1878), p. 168; "Harvey's Canal—It is Purchased by the Barataria Ship Canal Company for $100,000," *Daily Picayune*, May 6, 1880, p. 2.

2. "Excursion To Grand Pass—The Barataria Ship Canal," *Daily Picayune*, November 11, 1877, p. 6.

3. William D. Reeves, *Harvey: The Canal, The Family, The Community, Written in Honor of the 100th Anniversary of the Harvey Canal Limited Partnership* (The Harvey Land and Improvement Company, 1998), pp. 14–25.

4. Thomas A. Becnel, *The Barrow Family and the Barataria and Lafourche Canal: The Transportation Revolution in Louisiana, 1829–1925* (Baton Rouge: Louisiana State University Press, 1989), pp. 101–32.

5. "A Waterway for Fuel Oil," *Daily Picayune*, April 24, 1902, p. 3; "Gretna Gossip," *Daily Picayune*, January 8, 1902, p. 12; "Four Miles of Dead Fish an Unprecedented Plague Threatening . . . the Busy Harvey Canal," *Daily Picayune*, July 7, 1902, p. 3.

6. "The River May Be Turned into Harvey's Canal To-Day," *Daily Picayune*, July 9, 1902, p. 9; "Dies from Shock: Mrs. Horace Harvey of Harvey Canal Passes Away," *New Orleans Item*, May 26, 1902, p. 3; "Mrs. Joseph H. Harvey, Founder of the Town and Canal Bearing Her Name, Passes Away," *Daily Picayune*, November 17, 1903, p. 8.

7. "The River Gives Relief At Harvey's Canal," *Daily Picayune*, July 12, 1902, p. 13; "Harvey Canal Clean, And Residents Are Returning to Their Threatened Homes," *Daily Picayune*, July 20, 1902, p. 21.

8. "Harvey Canal's Locks Open within Two Weeks," *Daily Picayune*, July 23, 1905, p. 4; "Harvey Canal Locks," *Daily Picayune*, August 16, 1905, p. 7.

9. "Harvey Canal Locks: Grand Isle Will Be the First Vessel Through," *Daily Picayune*, March 29, 1907, p. 7.

10. "Harvey Canal Locks Fully Tested and Now Complete," *Daily Picayune*, January 13, 1907, p. 5.

11. Lynn M. Alperin, *History of the Gulf Intracoastal Waterway* (National Waterways Study, US Army Engineer Water Resources Support Center/Institute for Water Resources, January 1983), pp. 1–2.

12. Erik Friso Haites, "Ohio and Mississippi River Transportation 1810–1860" (PhD diss., Purdue University, 1969), pp. 11–16; Thomas A. Becnel, *The Barrow Family and the Barataria and Lafourche Canal*, p. 38.

13. Ronald M. Labbé and Jonathan Lurie, *The Slaughterhouse Cases: Regulation, Reconstruction, and the Fourteenth Amendment* (Lawrence: University Press of Kansas, 2003), pp. 19–20.

14. Alperin, *History of the Gulf Intracoastal Waterway*, p. 23.

15. Ibid., pp. 4–10.

16. Letter from the Secretary of War, *Intracoastal Waterway: St. Georges Sound to the Rio Grande Section* (Washington, DC, War Department, Office of the Chief of Engineers, January 15, 1914), p. 36.

17. Ibid., pp. 33–34.

18. Ibid.

19. "City's Wartime Appetite Forces Approximate Gain of 300 Per Cent in Foodstuffs Freighted through Waterways from Marsh and Bayou," *New Orleans Item*, January 26, 1919, p. 1.

20. John Barrow Jr., as quoted by Becnel, *The Barrow Family and the Barataria and Lafourche Canal*, pp. 148, 151.

21. William D. Reeves, *Harvey: The Canal, The Family, The Community*, pp. 36–39.

22. *Jefferson Parish Events 1825–2000*, ed. Mary G. Curry and Charmaine Currault Rini (Jefferson, LA: Jefferson Parish Historical Commission, 2000), p. 9.

23. Becnel, *The Barrow Family and the Barataria and Lafourche Canal*, pp. 158–179.

24. Daniel Hubbell, "Westwego, Harvey Canals Predated GIWW," *The Waterways Journal Weekly*, July 30, 2018, visited online August 6, 2018. https://www.waterwaysjournal.net/2018/07/30/westwego-harvey-canals-predated-giww/

25. Data computed by author based on 2008 State of Louisiana employment data produced in collaboration with the United States Census Bureau and provided by Greater New Orleans Community Data Center.

26. "End of an Era: Canal Stretch Being Filled In," *Times-Picayune*, December 17, 1961, sec. 5, p. 1.

27. Becnel, *The Barrow Family and the Barataria and Lafourche Canal*, p. 187.

28. Harnett T. Kane, *The Bayous of Louisiana* (New York: Bonanza Books, 1963), p. 41.

10. Landscape Change in Three Acts

1. Katherine Harvey Roger, "Picture from the Past," *Jefferson Parish Yearly Review* (Kenner, LA: 1945), p. 99.

2. Samuel Wilson Jr. "Seven Oaks Plantation (Petit Desert), Westwego, Jefferson Parish, Louisiana" (Washington, DC: National Park Service, Historic American Building Survey, 1953), HABS No. LA-1158, pp. 1–4; Marc R. Matrana, *Lost Plantation: The Rise and Fall of Seven Oaks* (Jackson: University of Mississippi Press, 2005), pp. 75–77; Charles F. Zimpel, *Topographic Map of New-Orleans and Its Vicinity*, New Orleans, March 1834.

3. Wilson, "Seven Oaks Plantation (Petit Desert)," p. 5.

4. Matrana, *Lost Plantation*, p. 75.

5. Ibid., p. 77.

6. New Orleans West quadrangle map sheet, United States Department of the Interior, 1932, 1938, and 1958; Matrana, *Lost Plantation*.

7. Recollection communicated to author by docent at Westwego Historical Museum, June 7, 2018.

8. Matrana, *Lost Plantation*.

9. Kenneth R. Aslakson, *Making Race in the Courtroom: The Legal Construction of Three Races in Early New Orleans* (New York: NYU Press, 2014), p. 225; Kathleen Gilmore and Vergil E. Noble, *Archeological Testing at Fort St. Leon (16PL35), Plaquemines Parish, Louisiana* (New Orleans: US Army Corps of Engineers, 1983), p. 43.

10. Iroquois Research Institute, *Cultural Resources Survey of Fourteen Mississippi Levee and Revetment Items* (New Orleans: Department of the Army, New Orleans District, Corps of Engineers, 1982), pp. 50–53.

11. Pierre Clément de Laussat, *Memoirs of My Life* (1831; Baton Rouge: Louisiana State University Press for The Historic New Orleans Collection, 1978), p. 20.

12. Charles P. Roland, *Louisiana Sugar Plantations during the American Civil War* (Leiden, Netherlands: E. J. Brill, 1957), p. 137 (Epilogue).

13. Iroquois Research Institute, *Cultural Resources Survey*, p. 54.

14. "From Local No. 155, Algiers, La.," *The Blacksmith's Journal* 9, no. 7 (July 1908): 25–28; "Samples Grown Only a Few Miles Below the City," *Daily Picayune*, July 10, 1901, p. 7; Richard Remy Dixon, *Old Algiers: A Story of Algiers, Yesterday and Today* (New Orleans: Algiers Annexation Centennial Committee, 1980), p. 56; "Richard Milliken Dies Yesterday Morning as a Result of His Accident," *Daily Picayune*, May 29, 1896, p. 11.

15. "N.O. Men Open Sugar Mill in Honduras," *New Orleans Item*, August 3, 1915, p. 27.

16. Richard Campanella, *Time and Place in New Orleans: Past Geographies in the Present Day* (Gretna, LA: Pelican Publishing Company, 2002), p. 142.

17. "Completed Crib Backs Up Levee at Danger Point; Work at Stanton Plantation Proves Satisfactory," *Times-Picayune*, May 25, 1922, p. 3.

18. "Stanton Tract Figures in Deal: Part of Famous Plantation Will be Subdivided by Firm," *New Orleans States*, March 13, 1926, p. 3.

19. "Russel Clarke Buys Plantation as Country Home," *Times-Picayune*, April 19, 1930, p. 37.

20. "Plans Country Home on Plantation in City," *New Orleans States*, April 19, 1930, p. 5; Iroquois Research Institute, *Cultural Resources Survey*, p. 55.

21. A major exception would come in the 1980s, when developers created the affluent English Turn gated golf course community in what had been Stanton's backswamp.

11. Flood, Wind, and Fire

1. Ernst von Hesse-Wartegg, *Travels on the Lower Mississippi, 1879–1880*, ed. and trans. Frederic Trautmann (Columbia: University of Missouri Press, 1990), p. 139.

2. Pierre Clément de Laussat, *Memoirs of My Life* (1831; Baton Rouge: Louisiana State University Press for The Historic New Orleans Collection, 1978), p. 71.

3. Based on digital bathymetric and bankline data of the lower Mississippi River during the 1990s and 2000s, mapped and distributed by the US Army Corps of Engineers–New Orleans District and analyzed by the author.

4. Laussat, *Memoirs of My Life*, p. 124, editorial endnote.

5. John Adems Paxton, *The New-Orleans Directory and Register* (New Orleans, 1823), p. 138.

6. Laussat, *Memoirs of My Life*, p. 63.

7. As quoted by Adam Hodgson, *Remarks during a Journey through North America in the Years 1819, 1820, and 1821* (New York: Samuel Whiting, 1823), 164.

8. Ari Kelman, "A River and its City: Critical Episodes in the Environmental History of New Orleans" (PhD diss., Brown University Department of History, 1998); Richard Campanella, *Time and Place in New Orleans: Past Geographies in the Present Day* (Gretna, LA: Pelican Publishing Company, 2002); Richard Campanella, "A River Ran through It: How the Watery St. Mary Batture Evolved into Convention Center Boulevard," *New Orleans Times-Picayune*, July 22, 2018, p. 1.

9. Paxton, *The New-Orleans Directory and Register*, pp. 32–33.

10. Charles Laveau Trudeau, *Plan of the City of New Orleans and Adjacent Plantations*, 1798 map updated in 1875 by Alexander Debrunner (New Orleans: H. Wehrmann, 1875), Library of Congress.

11. Comparison by author of modern satellite imagery with *Norman's Plan of New Orleans & Environs*, by Henry Moellhausen, published by Benjamin Moore Norman, 1845, Library of Congress.

12. Bennet Dowler, MD, *Tableaux, Geographical, Commercial, Geological, and Sanitary, of New Orleans* (New Orleans: Daily Delta, 1853), p. 10.

13. Laussat, *Memoirs of My Life*, p. 25.

14. Based on a meta-analysis of various primary and secondary sources by the author. See also David Fritz and Sally K. Reeves, *Algiers Point: Historical Ambience and Property Analysis of Squares Ten, Thirteen, and Twenty, with a View toward Their Archaeological Potential* (New Orleans: Department of the Army, Corps of Engineers, June 1984), pp. 1–11.

15. Police Jury of the Parish of Jefferson Minute Book, 1834–1843, Police Regulations of the Parish of Jefferson Adopted on the Seventh [of] February 1834, Articles 17–20, in *Transcriptions of Parish Records of Louisiana, No. 26 Jefferson Parish, Series I, Police Jury Minutes, Volume 1, 1834–1843* (The Historical Records Survey, Works Progress Administration, 1940), pp. 15–16.

16. "The Crevasse at Algiers," *Daily Picayune*, February 25, 1842, p. 2; "Land Slide at Algiers," *Lafayette City Advertiser*, February 26, 1842, p. 2, as cited in David Fritz and Sally K. Reeves, *Algiers Point: Historical Ambience and Property Analysis of Squares Ten, Thirteen, and Twenty, with a View toward Their Archaeological Potential* (New Orleans, Louisiana: Department of the Army, Corps of Engineers, June 1984), pp. 4–5.

17. "A Crevasse," *Daily Picayune*, May 9, 1847, p. 2.

18. As quoted by Richard Campanella in "The Katrina of the 1800s Was Called Sauve's Crevasse," *New Orleans Times-Picayune*, June 11, 2014.

19. "The Crevasse at Tunisburg," *Daily Picayune*, May 20, 1849, p. 2.

20. "The Lacoste Crevasse," *Daily Picayune*, February 13, 1850, p. 2.

21. "The Bell Crevasse," *Daily Picayune*, May 17, 1858, p. 5.

22. "The Bell Crevasse," *Daily Picayune*, May 17, 1858, p. 5.

23. Louisiana Board of Swamp Land Commissioners, *Annual Report of the Board of Swamp Land Commissioners to the Legislature of the State of Louisiana* (Baton Rouge: J. M. Taylor, State Printer, 1860), p. 89.

24. "Extent of the Bell Crevasse," *Jefferson Journal,* June 16, 1858, as quoted in *The Daily Advocate,* June 19, 1858, p. 2; "The Bell Crevasse—Extent of the Inundation—List of the Principal Sufferers, *Daily Picayune,* April 24, 1858, p. 1.

25. "The Bell Crevasse," *Georgia Telegraph* (Macon, Georgia), May 11, 1858, p. 1.

26. "Extent of the Bell Crevasse," *Jefferson Journal,* June 16, 1858, as quoted in *The Daily Advocate,* June 19, 1858, p. 2.

27. Thomas K. Wharton, *Queen of the South—New Orleans, 1853–1862: The Journal of Thomas K. Wharton,* ed. Samuel Wilson Jr., Patricia Brady, and Lynn D. Adams (New Orleans: The Historic New Orleans Collection and New York Public Library, 1999), p. 163; "The Bell Crevasse," *Daily Picayune,* May 17, 1858, p. 5.

28. "The Bell Crevasse," *Daily Picayune,* May 17, 1858, p. 5.

29. "Special Meeting Thursday 12th January 1860," in *Transcriptions of Parish Records of Louisiana, No. 26 Jefferson Parish, Series I,* Police Jury of the Parish of Jefferson Minute Book, 1858–1864, vol. 3 (The Historical Records Survey, Works Progress Administration, 1940), pp. 189–90.

30. "The Great Bell Crevasse," *Alexandria Gazette,* October 5, 1858, p. 2; "Effects of the Bell Crevasse," *Augusta Chronicle, December* 23, 1858, p. 2; Map, "Approaches to New Orleans, Prepared by the Order of Maj. Gen. N.P. Banks [by] Henry L. Abbott," Department of the Gulf, Map No. 5, February 14, 1863, The Historic New Orleans Collection, Accession No. 1974.25.18.122.

31. "The Explosion," *The Daily True Delta,* December 31, 1861, p. 3.

32. "The Crevasse at McGee's Plantation," *The New-Orleans Times,* April 29, 1865, p. 1.

33. Albert E. Cowdrey, *Land's End: A History of the New Orleans District* (New Orleans: US Army Corps of Engineers, 1977), p. 21.

34. Kelman, "A River and its City," p. 311.

35. Letter, E. B. Wheelock to Maj. Amos Stickney, November 17, 1883, in C. B. Comstock, *Annual Report of the Mississippi River Commission for 1883* (Washington, DC: Government Printing Office, 1884), pp. 474–77.

36. "More Light: Facts About the Ames Crevasse," *New Orleans Item,* May 5, 1891, p. 1; "The Ames Crevasse," *New Orleans Item,* March 19, 1891, p. 1; "The River and Levees—The Ames Crevasse 250 Feet Wide," *Daily Picayune,* March 20, 1891, p. 1; "Another Crevasse," *New Orleans Item,* March 21, 1891, p. 1; "Fleeing for Safety," *Boston Daily Advertiser,* March 25, 1891, p. 1; "Crevasse and Water, "*New Orleans Item,* March 28, 1891, p. 1; Thomas A. Becnel, *The Barrow Family and the Barataria and Lafourche Canal: The Transportation Revolution in Louisiana, 1829-1925* (Baton Rouge: Louisiana State University Press, 1989), p. 105.

37. "Floating Prairies in Louisiana," *Evening News* (San Jose, CA), June 2, 1891, p. 2.

38. "Ho, for the Ames Crevasse," *New Orleans Item,* April 11, 1891, p. 4.

39. "The Levees—The Work at Ames Crevasse," *Daily Picayune,* August 20, 1891, p. 8. See the Mississippi River Commission map "Works of Improvement in New Orleans Harbor, LA." (1892) in Cowdrey, *Land's End,* p. 67.

40. "The Flood—The Belmont Crayfish Hole Develops into a Crevasse," *Daily Picayune*, June 13, 1892, p. 2; "An Algiers Cave—The Fort Jackson Depot Tumbling into the River," *New Orleans Item*, August 14, 1892, p. 1.

41. Map, Mississippi River Commission "Works of Improvement in New Orleans Harbor, LA" (June 30, 1892), in Cowdrey, *Land's End*, p. 67.

42. Letter, W. G. Price, US Assistant Engineer, to Maj. Amos Stickney, Corps of Engineers, November 19, 1883, in Comstock, *Annual Report of the Mississippi River Commission for 1883*, pp. 475–76.

43. Survey of the Mississippi River, Chart No. 76 (Mississippi River Commission, 1874, annotated in 1911).

44. R. Christopher Goodwin & Associates, *Cultural Resources Survey of Gretna Phase II Levee Enlargement Item M-99.4 to 95.5-R, Jefferson Parish, Louisiana* (New Orleans: US Army Corps of Engineers, 1990), p. 12.

45. "Completed Crib Backs Up Levee at Danger Point; Work at Stanton Plantation Proves Satisfactory," *Times-Picayune*, May 25, 1922, p. 3.

46. "Concrete Mats," US Army Corps of Engineers—New Orleans District, https://www.mvn .usace.army.mil/Missions/Engineering/Channel-Improvement-and-Stabilization-Program/ Revetment-Types/Concrete/, visited August 11, 2018.

47. Mark Schleifstein, "Watery Graveyard: A Collapsed Riverbank Exposes a Host of Sunken Vessels—and Reveals a Slice of History, NOLA.com/*Times-Picayune*, March 13, 2005.

48. Researcher Klaus J. Meyer-arendt reports the first beach recreation on Grand Isle to have been documented in 1811, the first beachfront homes around 1855, and the first hotel in 1866. Klaus J. Meyer-arendt, "Resort Evolution along the Gulf of Mexico Littoral: Historical, Morphological, and Environmental Aspects" (PhD diss., Louisiana State University, 1987), pp. 57–59.

49. Sally Kittredge Evans, Frederick Stielow, and Betsy Swanson, *Grand Isle on the Gulf—An Early History* (Metairie, LA: Jefferson Parish Historical Commission, 1979), p. 82.

50. National Oceanic and Atmospheric Center-Tropical Prediction Center/National Hurricane Center, *Historical North Atlantic Tropical Cyclone Tracks 1851–2005*, National Oceanic and Atmospheric Administration Coastal Services Center, Charleston, SC.

51. Rose C. Falls, *Cheniere Caminada, or, The Wind of Death: The Story of the Storm in Louisiana* (New Orleans: Hopkins Printing Office, 1893), pp. 24–32.

52. "The Storm's Wake," *New Orleans Item*, October 3, 1893, p. 1; Falls, *Cheniere Caminada*, pp. 41–43.

53. Falls, *Cheniere Caminada*, pp. 8, 11, 17, 57; "The State Engineers Make a Full Report," *Daily Picayune*, April 30, 1894, p. 8.

54. "The Disaster—Details from Cheniere are Simply Fearful," *New Orleans Item*, October 6, 1893, p. 4.

55. Falls, *Cheniere Caminada*, pp. 8, 11, 17; "The State Engineers Make a Full Report," *Daily Picayune*, April 30, 1894, p. 8.

56. "Bayou Cook—Grand Bayou—Another Section Adds to the Fearful Total," *Daily Picayune*, October 5, 1893, p. 1.

57. United States Bureau of Fisheries, *Report of the Commissioner of Fisheries to the Secretary of the Department of Commerce and Labor,* "Fisheries of the Gulf States," (Washington, DC: US Government Printing Office, 1899), p. 146.

58. "At Harvey's Canal—The Little Colony of Refugees Grown Larger Daily," *Daily Picayune,* October 11, 1893, p. 2.

59. "Storm Echoes—The Scattering of the Colony at Harvey's Canal," *Daily Picayune,* April 4, 1894, p. 10.

60. "Harvey, A Brief History of the Thriving Town Opposite Louisiana Avenue," *The Daily Item,* December 1, 1894, p. 3.

61. These surnames are drawn from the list of victims and survivors from Chênière Caminada; not all were among those who settled permanently in Westwego. Falls, *Cheniere Caminada,* pp. 59–61.

62. Edwin Ney Bruce, "The Growth and Development of Westwego, 1827–1942" (1942, forerunner of master's thesis, "Louisiana: A Community Study," Tulane University, 1947), pp. 8, 40, manuscript stored at Westwego Historical Society.

63. At the time, the Census Bureau defined "mother tongue" as the first language of the respondent's childhood household. This question was asked in the censuses of 1910–1940 and 1960–1970. Based on an analysis by the author of the 1970 US Census, at the census-tract level.

64. Based on the 2013–2017 estimates of the responses to the "Ancestry" question of the US Census Bureau's American Community Survey, as analyzed and mapped by www.thecinyc.com, visited December 11, 2018, online https://www.thecinyc.com/2013–17-ahr-multimap

65. Katherine Harvey Roger, "Picture from the Past," *Jefferson Parish Yearly Review* (Kenner, LA, 1945), p. 95.

66. Meyer-arendt, "Resort Evolution along the Gulf of Mexico Littoral," pp. 58–68.

67. This section on the Great Algiers Fire of 1895 is adapted from the author's Cityscapes column, "Great Fire of 1895 Transformed Algiers," *New Orleans Times-Picayune,* November 13, 2015, InsideOut section. Sources include "The Algiers Fire Proves a Calamity, Spreading over an Area Exceeding Nine Squares and Rendering," *Daily Picayune,* October 21, 1895, pp. 1, 9; "Destitution in Destruction's Wake," *Daily Picayune,* October 22, 1895; "Paul Bouffia Charged with Arson," *Daily Picayune,* October 21, 1895; "Bridge Falls at a Fire," *Daily Inter Ocean* (Chicago), October 22, 1895; "Getting Relief Down to a System," *Daily Picayune,* October 24, 1895; "City Hall—The Official Report of the Algiers Fire," *Daily Picayune,* November 8, 1895; and "Bouffa Not Guilty of Arson," *Charlotte Observer,* November 15, 1895, as well as Sanborn Fire Insurance Maps of 1885 and 1896, and William H. Seymour, *The Story of Algiers, Now the Fifth District of New Orleans* (Algiers Democrat Publishing Company, 1896).

68. Seymour, *The Story of Algiers,* p. 111.

69. Ibid., p. 113.

70. Ibid., p. 117.

71. *History of the Fire Department of New Orleans, From the Earliest Days to the Present Time,* ed. Thomas O'Connor (New Orleans, 1895), pp. 266, 435–36; "Twenty-Five Years A Fire Fighter, Chief Engineer Thomas O'Connor Celebrates His Silver Anniversary, *Daily Picayune,* January 5, 1894, p. 12.

72. "Paul Bouffia Charged with Arson."

73. "Bridge Falls at a Fire."

74. "Getting Relief Down to a System."

75. Seymour, *The Story of Algiers*, p. 127.

76. "Towns over the River Share in Prosperity," *Sunday Daily States*, August 31, 1902, as transcribed by Kevin Herridge in *The Algerine*, no. 29 (December 2007): 10–12.

12. Bridging the Banks, Draining the Swamps

1. Daniel Hubbell, "Fanciful Ideas Were Proposed For New Orleans' First Bridge," *Waterways Journal*, June 22, 2018, https://www.waterwaysjournal.net.

2. City Hall—Mayor Shakspeare Makes a Bold Move in the Water Works Matter," *Daily Picayune*, January 17, 1889, p. 8.

3. *Daily News* (Charlotte, North Carolina), March 8, 1889, p. 2; "Railroads—The New Orleans Bridge to be the Longest in the World," *Daily Picayune*, February 9, 1893, p. 12.

4. "Washington—An Act Authorising the Construction of the New Orleans Bridge Introduced," *Daily Picayune*, February 5, 1889, p. 1.

5. Hubbell, "Fanciful Ideas Were Proposed For New Orleans' First Bridge."

6. "Bridge of Great Size—It is to Span the Mississippi Above New Orleans," *Idaho Avalanche* (Silver City, Idaho), August 6, 1897, p. 3.

7. "Elmer L. Corthell, Director of Jetty Work Here, Dies; Great Engineer Also Planned Bridge over Mississippi at Nine-Mile Point," *Times-Picayune*, May 18, 1916, p. 4.

8. Ordinance No. 5149, "Commission Council Series Creating the Board of Advisory Engineers," July 3, 1918, as quoted in Board of Advisory Engineers, Public Belt Railroad Commission, *Report: Mississippi River Railroad Crossing at New Orleans and Plan of Terminal Development* (New Orleans: Public Belt Railroad Commission, 1919), pp. 24–26.

9. Board of Advisory Engineers, *Report: Mississippi River Railroad Crossing*, pp. 30–32.

10. Ibid., pp. 119, 292–93.

11. Ibid., pp. 35–36, 104–5.

12. Modjeski and Masters, "Greater New Orleans Bridge over the Mississippi River: Final Report to the Mississippi River Bridge Authority (New Orleans: Modjeski and Masters/ Mississippi River Bridge Authority, 1960), pp. 7–8.

13. "Dedicating the Huey P. Long–Public Belt Bridge—The Longest Railroad Span in the World," *Times-Picayune*, December 16, 1935, p. 15.

14. Tonja Koob Marking and Jennifer Snape, *Images of America: Huey P. Long Bridge* (Charleston, SC: Arcadia Publishing, 2013).

15. "Dedicating the Huey P. Long-Public Belt Bridge," p. 15.

16. Julius Dupont of Houma, president of the Old Spanish Trail Association, quoted in "Mississippi River Bridge Formally Open for Traffic," *Times-Picayune*, December 17, 1935, p. 6.

17. Police Jury of Jefferson Parish, *Jefferson Parish Year Book*, 1935, pp. 18–27.

18. "Today and Tomorrow," Police Jury of Jefferson Parish, *Jefferson Parish Year Book*, 1935, p. 27.

19. René Pierre Meric Jr. and Philip J. Meric, *Avondale, A Model for Success: The Story of a Great American Shipyard* (New Orleans: Philip J. Meric Consulting, 2015), pp. xi–3.

20. "Buy Bridge-Head Lots at Belt City," *New Orleans States,* March 14, 1926, p. 20.

21. Area Description—Security Map of Metropolitan New Orleans, La., Area No. D42, Westwego, Jefferson Parish, Louisiana, as mapped in "Home Owners Loan Corporation—Map of Greater New Orleans," by Wm. E. Boesch (1939), accessed through Robert K. Nelson, LaDale Winling, Richard Marciano, Nathan Connolly et al., *"Mapping Inequality," American Panorama,* ed. Robert K. Nelson and Edward L. Ayers, https://dsl.richmond.edu/, accessed October 8, 2018.

22. Modjeski and Masters, "Greater New Orleans Bridge," p. 8.

23. These are 1945 figures supplied by the State Highway Department. As cited by Robert Moses and Andrews & Clark in *Arterial Plan for New Orleans* (Baton Rouge: Department of Highways, 1946), p. 21.

24. Federal Writers' Project of the Works Progress Administration, *New Orleans City Guide* (Boston: Houghton Mifflin Company, 1938), p. xxv; George Hero III, "Compiled Memories—Early Memories (Before 1935) of Planters Road," self-published document provided to author by George Hero III, April 25, 2019.

25. George Washington Cable, "New Orleans Revisited," *The Book News Monthly* (April 1909), pp. 564, 560.

26. Drainage Advisory Board, *Report on the Drainage of the City of New Orleans* (New Orleans: T. Fitzwilliam & Co. Printers, pp. 28, 38, 43. For the sake of clarity, irregular capitalization in the original document has been standardized in the quoted material.

27. "Algiers Canal Next Drainage Work, Sewerage Board Opening Bids for the Contract," *Daily Picayune,* March 28, 1907, p. 5; "Algiers Drainage Is Now Assured"; *Daily Picayune,* September 13, 1907, p. 4.

28. "Algiers System of Water and Sewerage to Begin Operation on the First of August," *Daily Picayune* June 27, 1909, p. 32.

29. "Over the River—Items along the Line from Gretna to Algiers; Drainage and Other Improvements," *Daily Picayune,* December 11, 1910, p. 5; "Gretna Gossip," *Daily Picayune,* March 17, 1909, p. 5; "Drainage Scheme for Reclaiming 36,000 Acres of Land in Three Parishes," *Daily Picayune,* October 11, 1911, p. 5.

30. "Large Refinery for Louisiana," *Sugar: An English Spanish Technical Journal Devoted to Sugar Production* 22, no. 1 (January 1920): 195.

31. "Monumental Task—Mayor Says George A. Hero Carrying Heaviest Burden of All—Drainage in Jefferson-Plaquemines District Will Work Wonders for All," *Daily Picayune,* October 19, 1913.

32. "George A. Hero," *The South: The Nation's Greatest Asset—Manufacturers Record* LXIII, no. 12 (March 27, 1913) part 2, p. 194.

33. Numa Hero, "Jefferson and Plaquemines Drainage District," *Jefferson Parish Yearbook* (Police Jury of Jefferson Parish, 1935), p. 121.

34. "Greatest Drainage Pumps in Operation in Louisiana," *Municipal Engineering* 63, no. 1 (January 1915): 216.

35. "Large Refinery for Louisiana," *Sugar: An English Spanish Technical Journal devoted to Sugar Production* 22, no. 1 (January 1920): 195; "New Orleans, La," *Western Contractor* 25, no. 666 (October 15, 1913): 30.

36. "Greatest Drainage Pumps in Operation in Louisiana," *Municipal Engineering* 48, no. 1 (January 1915): 216.

37. "Great Pumping Station at Work Across the River," *Times-Picayune*, February 14, 1915, p. 1.

38. Ibid.

39. "'I'll Drain a Million Acres More!,' George A. Hero to Celebration Dinner," *New Orleans Item*, February 14, 1915, p. 1.

40. "Hero, George A." *National Cyclopædia of American Biography,* vol. 15 (New York: James T. White & Co, 1916), p. 196; "Wilson Greets City as Giant Pumps Reclaim West Section," *New Orleans Item*, February 13, 1915 (afternoon edition), p. 1.

41. "Wilson Greets City," p. 1.

42. Modjeski and Masters, "Greater New Orleans Bridge," p. 7.

43. Transcript of interview of George Harry Hero III by Peggy Scott Laborde, conducted 2016, provided to author by interviewer.

44. "George A. Hero, Capitalist, Span Advocate, Dead," *Times-Picayune*, December 20, 1932, pp. 1–2.

13. Booming Times, Bombastic Visions

1. Jerry E. Strahan, *Andrew Jackson Higgins and the Boats That Won World War II* (Baton Rouge: Louisiana State University Press, 1994); Jerry Purvis Sanson, *Louisiana during World War II: Politics and Society, 1939–1945* (Baton Rouge: Louisiana State University Press, 1999).

2. "545,041 New Population of New Orleans," *Old French Quarter News*, July 16, 1943, p. 1; "City Growing; Population [of Metro Area] is now 630,000," *Old French Quarter News*, November 30, 1945, p. 1.

3. Ray M. Thompson, "Industry!," *Jefferson Parish Yearly Review* (Kenner, LA: Police Jury of Jefferson Parish, 1943), p. 9; Thomas Ewing Dabney, "Go West-Side, New Orleans, to Your New Frontier," *Jefferson Parish Yearly Review* (Kenner, LA: Police Jury of Jefferson Parish, 1948), p. 47. Historical West Bank population figures are difficult to ascertain because the area's semirural nature and unincorporated structure meant the United States Census Bureau typically lumped its enumerations with the rest of Orleans or Jefferson Parish. Not until the mid-1900s did data aggregation at the census-tract level become regularly available. The 1935 and 1948 figures used here are gleaned from editions of the *Jefferson Parish Yearly Review*.

4. The 55 percent figure comes from The Historical Records Survey, "A Brief History of Jefferson Parish," Inventory of the Parish Archives of Louisiana—No. 26, Jefferson Parish (Baton Rouge: Department of Archives, Louisiana State University, April, 1940), p. 12. The 60 percent figure comes from Dabney, "Go West-Side, New Orleans," p. 43.

5. Dabney, "Go West-Side, New Orleans," pp. 43, 47 (emphasis added).

6. Gary A. Bolding, "The New Orleans Seaway Movement," *Louisiana History* 10, no. 1 (Winter 1969): 49.

7. LeRoy L. Hall, "Final Report of the Jefferson Parish Police Jury," *Jefferson Parish Yearly Review* (Kenner, LA: 1954), p. 29.

8. "Lehde Is Elected Dock Board Head," *Times-Picayune,* June 24, 1943, p. 10; Arthur A. Grant, "The West . . . and Best Seaway to the Gulf," *Jefferson Parish Yearly Review* (Kenner, LA: Police Jury of Jefferson Parish, 1945), p. 27.

9. "Parade and Program to Dedicate New Canal Link," *New Orleans States,* July 27, 1943, p. 3.

10. Dabney, "Go West-Side, New Orleans," pp. 38, 41.

11. Ibid., p. 53 (emphasis added).

12. Grant, "The West . . . and Best Seaway to the Gulf," p. 26.

13. Captain Harry G. Koch, "Alternative Connection of the Intracoastal Canal with the Mississippi to Relieve Harvey Canal," *Jefferson Parish Yearly Review* (Kenner, LA: Police Jury of Jefferson Parish, 1946), pp. 29–31.

14. Robert Moses and Andrews & Clark, *Arterial Plan for New Orleans* (Baton Rouge: Department of Highways, 1946), map on pp. 18–19.

15. Bolding, "The New Orleans Seaway Movement," 56–57; Richard Campanella, *Time and Place in New Orleans: Past Geographies in the Present Day* (Gretna, LA: Pelican Publishing Company, 2002).

16. "$61,000,000 for Flood Control Work Assured," *New Orleans States,* June 11, 1948, p. 32; Daniel J. Hubbell, *The Lower Mississippi River from Baton Rouge to Head of Passes: A Mariner's Handbook,* unpublished manuscript provided to author by Daniel J. Hubbell, p. 13.

17. Hubbell, *The Lower Mississippi River,* p. 13.

18. "New Canal May Open This Year," *Times-Picayune,* January 2, 1955, p. 137; "Canal Job Given to Orleans Firm," *Times-Picayune,* December 11, 1955, p. 21; "Algiers Lock Opens," *New Orleans States,* April 30, 1956, p. 10.

19. US Army Corps of Engineers, New Orleans District, *Water Resources Development in Louisiana* (New Orleans, 1995), p. 90, and *Waterborne Commerce of the United States, Part 2, Waterways and Harbors, Gulf Coast, Mississippi River System and Antilles* (Washington, DC, 1998), pp. 165, 170, 207.

20. Dabney, "Go West-Side, New Orleans," pp. 41–42.

21. William J. White, "Gretna Prepares for the Bridge," *Jefferson Parish Yearly Review* (Kenner, LA: 1955), p. 177.

22. Modjeski and Masters, "Greater New Orleans Bridge," p. 8.

23. Moses and Andrews & Clark, *Arterial Plan for New Orleans,* p. 8.

24. "The Logical Location for a Mississippi River Bridge," *Jefferson Parish Yearly Review* (Kenner, LA: 1945), pp. 113–17; Ad, Hero-Hackett Bridge, *Jefferson Parish Year Book,* 1935, p. 105; W. R. Toledano, "Jefferson—A Parish with a Future," *Jefferson Parish Year Book,* 1938, p. 11.

25. Thomas Ewing Dabney, "Jefferson's Surging Growth Demands This Bridge," *Jefferson Parish Yearly Review,* 1943, pp. 82–92.

26. Modjeski and Masters, "Greater New Orleans Bridge," p. 8.

27. Moses and Andrews & Clark, *Arterial Plan for New Orleans,* p. 9.

28. "Silver Span for a Golden Future," *Jefferson Parish Yearly Review* (Kenner, LA: 1950), p. 85; William J. White, "Gretna Greets the Future," *Jefferson Parish Yearly Review* (Kenner, LA: 1952), p. 170.

29. Louisiana State Legislature, Act No. 8, 1952, as cited by Louisiana Department of Transportation and Development / Mead & Hunt in *Historic Context for Louisiana Bridges Louisiana Statewide Historic Bridge Inventory* (Baton Rouge: Louisiana Department of Transportation and Development / Mead & Hunt, 2013), p. 36.

30. "Ferry Disruption," *New Orleans States,* July 2, 1952, p. 16.

31. Moses and Andrews & Clark, *Arterial Plan for New Orleans,* p. 8.

32. Modjeski and Masters, "Greater New Orleans Bridge," pp. 10–14.

33. Area No. B-14, deemed "Still Desirable" (second out of four rankings, with the lowest deemed "Hazardous" and the highest described as "Best"), as indicated on the Home Owners Loan Corporation—Map of Greater New Orleans, by Wm. E. Boesch (1939), by Robert K. Nelson, LaDale Winling, Richard Marciano, Nathan Connolly, et al., *"Mapping Inequality,"* American Panorama, ed. Robert K. Nelson and Edward L. Ayers, accessed October 8, 2018. For block level numerical evidence from 1939, see Sam R. Carter, *A Report on Survey of Metropolitan New Orleans Land Use, Real Property, and Low Income Housing Area* (New Orleans: Works Projects Administration, Louisiana State Department of Public Welfare, and Housing Authority of New Orleans, 1941), insert map on residency by race.

34. Modjeski and Masters, "Greater New Orleans Bridge," p. 9.

35. Ibid., pp. 7, 33–107; quote on pages 7 and 33–34.

36. "Provisions of River Span Authority Bill Disclosed," *New Orleans Times-Picayune,* May 12, 1952, pp. 1, 6.

37. Moses and Andrews & Clark, *Arterial Plan for New Orleans,* p. 8.

38. Ibid., p. 29 (emphasis added).

39. "Pattern for Expansion," *Jefferson Parish Yearly Review* (Kenner, LA: 1954), p. 29; "Part II, Progress Report," *Jefferson Parish Yearly Review* (Kenner, LA: 1956), p. 23.

40. Frank J. Clancy, "Progress Report of the Parish," *Jefferson Parish Yearly Review* (Kenner, LA: 1955), p. 43–49.

41. William J. White, "Gretna Prepares for the Bridge," *Jefferson Parish Yearly Review* (Kenner, LA: 1955), p. 175.

42. Modjeski and Masters, "Greater New Orleans Bridge; "Auto Smashes New Span Rail; Book Driver," *New Orleans States,* April 16, 1958, p. 1.

43. Frank J. Borne Jr., *Jefferson Parish's Modern Government on Its Golden Anniversary, 1958–2008* (Jefferson Parish Historical Series/Jefferson Parish Historical Commission, 2008), p. 12.

44. "Dedication Set for Air Center," *New Orleans Times-Picayune,* April 2, 1958, p. 28.

14. From Subrural to Suburban

1. "Upcoming Society Meetings," *The Algerine,* no. 62 (June 2016): 3.

2. "New Sewerage Lines Favored; Extensions to Three Outlying Section of City Backed," *New Orleans Times-Picayune,* June 6, 1951, p. 1.

3. "Woman Designer of Homes Features Show Nearing End; Plans Among Many Attractions at Exhibit," *New Orleans Times-Picayune,* May 27, 1951, p. 8.

4. "Aurora Gardens—the National Award-Winning Community," circa-1956 marketing brochure, from author's personal collection.

5. Sam R. Carter, *A Report on Survey of Metropolitan New Orleans Land Use, Real Property, and Low Income Housing Area* (New Orleans: Works Projects Administration, Louisiana State Department of Public Welfare, and Housing Authority of New Orleans, 1941), insert map on residency by race.

6. Ursula Manetta Lewis, interviewed by Kevin Herridge on December 12, 2001, and transcribed by Herridge in "The Ursula Manetta Lewis Interview," *The Algerine,* no. 33 (December 2008): 20 (emphasis added).

7. Analysis of 1960 census tract 6-D and 1970 census tracts 606, 607, and 608 (Orleans Parish, LA) by author using US Census Bureau data files, Washington, DC.

8. Frank Laro, "Orleans Boasts of 100 Farms, and 'It's a Good Life,'" *New Orleans States,* November 17, 1951, p. 3.

9. Julius F. Hotard and Lem W. Higgins, "A Report on Jefferson's Schools," *Jefferson Parish Yearly Review* (Kenner, LA, 1960), p. 115.

10. Frank Schneider, "New 4000-Home Project Begun, Store Areas, Schools, Churches Included," *New Orleans Times-Picayune,* September 20, 1959, p. 1.

11. "Choose the House that Suits You Best in TERRYTOWN," *Jefferson Parish Yearly Review* (Kenner, LA, 1963), p. 84.

12. "Home Building in Jefferson," *Jefferson Parish Yearly Review* (Kenner, LA, 1962), p. 81.

13. Judy Dobbins Mills, "Terrytown: A New Residential Concept for Jefferson Parish Approaches Its 50th Year," *Jefferson History Notebook* (Jefferson Historical Society of Louisiana) 12, no. 1 (April 2009): 3.

14. Analysis of 1970 census tracts 250 and 252 (Jefferson Parish, LA) by author using US Census Bureau data files, Washington, D.C.

15. Mills, "Terrytown: A New Residential Concept," 9.

16. "West Bank's Population Rise Cited by Sears' V-P," *New Orleans Times-Picayune,* September 6, 1963, sec. 2, p. 12.

17. "Country Club Site Is Leased; Timberlane to Have Big Golf Course," *New Orleans Times-Picayune,* June 9, 1958, p. 26; "Investor Buys Timberlane Lots, Acreage," *New Orleans Times-Picayune,* February 3, 1963, sec. 5, p. 1.

18. Allen Powell II, "Timberlane Estates Gates Cost Gretna $65,000," NOLA.com/ *Times-Picayune,* March 11, 2010; analysis of 1970 census tract 251 (Jefferson Parish, LA) by author using US Census Bureau data files, Washington, DC.

19. 1980 Census data and maps, as presented in Allen Rosenzweig & Associates, *Jefferson Parish Neighborhood Communication System: Volume 3: 1983 Summary Report* (Metairie, LA: Rosenzweig & Associates, 1983), pp. 9–15.

20. Sandra Barbier, "Algiers Project Needs Permit," *New Orleans Times-Picayune,* December 18, 1985, p. A-28.

21. "Dixie Freeway Route Proposed," *New Orleans Times-Picayune,* October 24, 1964, p. 8; Regional Planning Commission, *History of Regional Growth* (Regional Planning Commission of Jefferson, Orleans, and St. Bernard Parishes, LA, November 1969), pp. 78–83.

22. "Transportation: Parish Prepared for Interurbia," *Jefferson Parish Yearly Review* (Jefferson Parish: Parish Publications, Inc. 1969–1970 edition), p. 69.

23. Modjeski and Masters, *Greater New Orleans Bridge No. 2 over the Mississippi River: Final Report, Main Bridge Design and Construction-Substructure State Project No. 283-08-47; Superstructure State Project No. 283-08-48 (New Orleans, Louisiana:* Modjeski and Masters, June 15, 1988), p. 2.

24. William J. White, "Gretna," *Jefferson Parish Yearly Review* (Kenner, LA, 1974–1975 issue), p. 24; William J. White, "Jefferson's Capital City—Gretna," *Jefferson Parish Yearly Review* (Kenner, LA, 1964), p. 171; "Transportation: Parish Prepared for Interurbia," p. 69.

25. These figures include only urbanized West Jefferson and Orleans, not West Plaquemines or south of Marrero. Analysis of 1960 and 1970s US Census Bureau census tracts by author.

26. Regional Planning Commission, *History of Regional Growth*, pp. 82–83.

15. Geographies of Ethnicity, Race, and Class

1. Thomas K. Wharton, *Queen of the South—New Orleans, 1853–1862: The Journal of Thomas K. Wharton*, ed. Samuel Wilson Jr., Patricia Brady, and Lynn D. Adams (New Orleans: The Historic New Orleans Collection and New York Public Library, 1999), p. 105.

2. Samuel Wilson Jr., "Louisiana Drawings by Alexandre De Batz," *Journal of the Society of Architectural Historians* 22, no. 2 (May 1963): 79–80; Erin M. Greenwald, "Arriving Africans and a Changing New Orleans," in *New Orleans in the Founding Era*, ed. Erin Greenwald and trans. Henry Colomer (New Orleans: The Historic New Orleans Collection, 2018), p. 104.

3. Gilbert C. Din, "'Cimarrones' and the San Malo Band in Spanish Louisiana," *Louisiana History* 21, no. 3 (Summer 1980): 237–62.

4. Research by Kevin Herridge, "Freetown: Where Was It?," *The Algerine* 26 (March 2007): 21–22.

5. "U.S. Coffee-House Ball Room, 'Mrs. P.J. Auth respectfully informs her friends of Algiers and Free Town of Gretna . . . ,'" *Daily Picayune*, February 4, 1841, p. 2.

6. Research by Tom Yates, as cited in Herridge, "Freetown: Where Was It?," 16.

7. Dominique Rouquette, "The Choctaws" (1850), as quoted by Daniel N. Usner, *American Indians of Early New Orleans: From Calumet to Raquette* (Baton Rouge: Louisiana State University Press, 2018), p. 73.

8. Lines quoted from "Emancipation Jubilee" leaflet, New Orleans, 1864, The Historic New Orleans Collection, Accession No. 91–720-RL.

9. William D. Reeves and Daniel Alario Sr., *Westwego: From Cheniere to Canal* (Harahan, LA: Jefferson Parish Historical Series, Monograph XIV, 1996), pp. 168–70.

10. R. Emmet Kennedy, *Red Bean Row* (New York: Dodd, Mead, 1929) and *Gritny People* (New York: Dodd, Mead, 1927); Bryan Giemza, *Irish Catholic Writers and the Invention of the American South* (Baton Rouge: Louisiana State University Press, 2013), pp. 151–52.

11. Reeves and Alario, *Westwego: From Cheniere to Canal*, pp. 49, 168–70.

12. Dora Pitts, interviewed by Gina Rivere in "True Vine Baptist Church in Westwego turns 150," NOLA.com/*Times-Picayune—West Bank Community News*, October 18, 2015, http://blog.nola.com/westbank/2015/10/true_vine_baptist_church_turns.html.

13. Allen Powell II, "Marrero Street Renamed for Historic Settler Corrine Degree Walker," *New Orleans Times-Picayune*, March 3, 2009, https://www.nola.com/news/index.ssf/2009/03/marrero_street_renamed_for_his.html.

14. "U.S. Coffee-House Ball Room," p. 2.

15. *New Orleans Republican*, July 7, 1871, as quoted in Herridge, "Freetown: Where Was It?," 19.

16. Kennedy, *Gritny People*, p. 114.

17. "[T]he colored people at their 'Come Clean' and 'Big Easy' Dance Halls at East Green and West Green never missed a Saturday Night Session." John J. Holtgreve, "Just Around the Corner of Time," *Jefferson Parish Yearly Review* (Kenner, LA, 1954), p. 13.

18. *New Orleans Times-Democrat*, August 14, 1911, p. 5.

19. Pops Foster, *Pops Foster: The Autobiography of a New Orleans Jazzman*, ed. Tom Stoddard (Berkeley, 1971), pp. 26, 79.

20. Letter from Algiers Citizens Protesting New Ferry Discriminations, December 7, 1925, printed in the *Algiers Herald* and reprinted in *The Algerine*, no. 24 (September 2006): 12.

21. Historical Records Survey, "A Brief History of Jefferson Parish," Police Jury of Jefferson Parish, *Jefferson Parish Year Book*, 1939, p. 173; William J. White, "Gretna" The First Mile West," *Jefferson Parish Yearly Review* (Kenner, LA, 1953), p. 155.

22. Martha B. Mallory, interviewed by Allyson Ward Neal in *Algiers—The Untold Story: The African American Experiences, 1929–1955* (New Orleans: Beautiful Zion Baptist Church, 2001), p. 35.

23. Sam R. Carter, *A Report on Survey of Metropolitan New Orleans Land Use, Real Property, and Low Income Housing Area* (New Orleans: Works Projects Administration, Louisiana State Department of Public Welfare, and Housing Authority of New Orleans, 1941), inset map on residency by race.

24. Lillian Alveris Williams, as interviewed in Neal, *Algiers—The Untold Story*, pp. 15, 83.

25. Transcriptions of Parish Records of Louisiana, No. 26 Jefferson Parish (Gretna) Series I Police Jury Minutes, vol. 11, 1924–1929 (The Historical Records Survey Projects, 1940), entry in Police Jury notes of July 12, 1926, p. 149.

26. Richard Campanella, "'Two Centuries of Paradox:' The Geography of New Orleans' African-American Population, from Antebellum to Postdiluvian Times," in *Hurricane Katrina in Transatlantic Perspective*, ed. Romain Huret and Randy J. Sparks (Baton Rouge: Louisiana State University Press, 2014); "Segregation by Co-operation of Civ[i]c Bodies," *Times-Picayune*, November 23, 1924, sec. 2, p. 1; Joel A. Devalcourt, "Streets of Justice?: Civil Rights Commemorative Boulevards and the Struggle for Revitalization in African American Communities—A Case Study of Central City, New Orleans" (master's thesis, University of New Orleans, Department of Urban and Regional Planning, 2011).

27. M. A. Baccich, E. E. Lafaye, and R. E. E. DeMontluzin-Gentilly Terrace Company, "Gentilly Terrace: Here's Your Opportunity" (1909), pp. 20–21, pamphlet archived at the Williams Research Center, The Historic New Orleans Collection.

28. "Segregation by Co-operation of Civ[i]c Bodies," sec. 2, p. 1.

29. "Plats of Belt Bridge Subdivision," May 13, 1936, The Historical Records Survey, "A Brief History of Jefferson Parish," *Inventory of the Parish Archives of Louisiana—No. 26, Jefferson Parish* (Baton Rouge: Department of Archives, Louisiana State University, April, 1940), p. 128.

30. "Resolution," signed by President W. R. Toledano and Secretary William Hepting, January 13, 1937, No. 13 Minute Book, transcriptions of Parish Records of Louisiana, No. 26. Jefferson Parish (Gretna), Series I Police Jury Minutes, vol. 13, 1935–1938, prepared by the Historical Records Survey Community Services Programs, Works Progress Administration, pp. 113–14, 119.

31. Home Owners Loan Corporation—Map of Greater New Orleans, by Wm. E. Boesch (1939), as stored by Robert K. Nelson, LaDale Winling, Richard Marciano, Nathan Connolly, et al., "*Mapping*

Inequality," American Panorama, ed. Robert K. Nelson and Edward L. Ayers, accessed October 8, 2018.

32. Areas No. D-26, D-28, D-32, and D-42 (assessed 1939), Home Owners Loan Corporation—Map of Greater New Orleans, by Wm. E. Boesch (1939), as stored by Nelson et al., "*Mapping Inequality.*"

33. Amy E. Hillier, "Redlining and the Homeowners' Loan Corporation," *Scholarly Commons: Departmental Papers—City and Regional Planning* (2003), http://repository.upenn.edu/cplan_papers/3.

34. Todd M. Michney and LaDale Winling, "New Perspectives on New Deal Housing Policy: Explicating and Mapping HOLC Loans to African Americans," *Journal of Urban History* 2 (January 2019): online https://journals.sagepub.com/doi/full/10.1177/0096144218819429.

35. William D. Reeves, *Historic Louisiana: An Illustrated History* (New Orleans: Louisiana Historical Society/Historical Publishing Network, 2003) pp. 56–58.

36. Carter, *Survey of Metropolitan New Orleans Land Use,* inset map on residency by race.

37. "Cut Off Site Inspected; Negro Settlement in Algiers May Get Pubic School," *New Orleans Times-Picayune,* April 4, 1918, p. 14.

38. Extracts from various articles and photo captions in the *Jefferson Parish Yearly Review* (Kenner, LA), 1952 to 1967.

39. "Tract Near City Cut into Farms to Aid Workers," *New Orleans Times-Picayune,* June 8, 1932, p. 24.

40. "Home Building to Start Today," *New Orleans Times-Picayune,* October 2, 1963, sec. 1, p. 9.

41. "3350 Housing Units Sought: Low-Income Homes Aim in NOHA Project," *New Orleans Times-Picayune,* December 16, 1967, p. 1; Fred Barry, "Algiers Growth Is Spectacular," *New Orleans Times-Picayune,* January 26, 1965, sec. 8, p. 5; "Work Completion Noted by Council," *New Orleans Times-Picayune,* February 13, 1965, sec. 1, p. 2; "HANO Will Aid in Uplifting Lower 9th Ward," *New Orleans Times-Picayune,* January 29, 1967, sec. 7, p. 38.

42. "Algiers Residents Oppose Public Housing Proposals," *New Orleans Times-Picayune,* April 24, 1968, sec. 2, p. 6.

43. United Press International, "New Orleans Police Kill 3 Blacks," *Dallas Morning News,* November, 14, 1980, p. 8.

16. Connecting the Crescent City

1. Department of Transportation/United States Coast Guard, *Draft Environmental Impact Statement—West Bank Expressway, Jefferson Parish, Louisiana* (New Orleans: Eighth Coast Guard District, July 1976), pp. 2.1–2.2.

2. "Clear the Expressway," *New Orleans Times-Picayune,* June 6, 1977, p. 14.

3. DOT/USCG, *Draft Environmental Impact Statement,* pp. 1.1–1.5, 1.9.

4. Ibid., pp. v–vi.

5. "Clear the Expressway," p. 14.

6. Department of Transportation/United States Coast Guard, *Final Environmental Impact Statement for the Mississippi River Bridge No. 2, Orleans Parish-Jefferson Parish, Louisiana, Volume 3 of 4* (New Orleans: Eighth Coast Guard District, 1978), p. 7.1.

7. "Super Transportation," *New Orleans Times-Picayune,* January 30, 1977, sec. 7, p. 6.

8. Mary Judice, "Start on Super Port This Year," *New Orleans Times-Picayune,* January 29, 1978, sec. 7, p. 16; Bruce Nolan, "Redesign of West Bank Expressway Under Way," *New Orleans Times-Picayune,* June 15, 1979, sec. 1, p. 3.

9. Modjeski and Masters, *Greater New Orleans Bridge No. 2 over the Mississippi River: Final Report, Main Bridge Design and Construction-Substructure State Project No. 283-08-47; Superstructure State Project No. 283-08-48* (New Orleans: Modjeski and Masters, June 15, 1988), p. 9.

10. Robert Moses and Andrews & Clark, *Arterial Plan for New Orleans* (Baton Rouge: Department of Highways, 1946), p. 8; DOT/USCG, *Final Environmental Impact Statement,* pp. 9.11–9.15.

11. Modjeski and Masters, *Greater New Orleans Bridge No. 2,* pp. 3–4.

12. Joan Treadway, "New Span for River: Bridge Recommendation Due in 12–14 Months," *New Orleans Times-Picayune,* January 5, 1973, p. 6.

13. Modjeski and Masters, *Greater New Orleans Bridge No. 2,* p. 10.

14. DOT/USCG, *Final Environmental Impact Statement,* pp. 7.1–7.2.

15. Modjeski and Masters, *Greater New Orleans Bridge No. 2,* p. 7.9.

16. Bruce Nolan, "Redesign of West Bank Expressway Under Way," *New Orleans Times-Picayune,* June 15, 1979, sec. 1, p. 3.

17. Paul Atkinson, "Elevated Roadway Gets Another Look," *New Orleans Times-Picayune/ States-Item,* August 13, 1981, sec. 1, p. 15.

18. West Bank Bureau, "Expressway Work to Expand," *New Orleans Times-Picayune/ States-Item,* July 30, 1983, sec. 1, p. 15; Paul Atkinson, "West Bank Expressway to Open," *New Orleans Times-Picayune/ States-Item,* January 12, 1985, p. A-27.

19. Modjeski and Masters, *Greater New Orleans Bridge No. 2,* p. 2; R. J. Bennett, "Analysis of Crescent City Connection (Greater New Orleans Bridge No. 2), Bridge Engineering 2 Conference 2007, University of Bath, Bath, United Kingdom, April 27, 2007.

20. Pier 3 on the Algiers cutbank, a place historically vulnerable to cave-ins and erosion, had to be wrapped in a blanket of riprap four to thirteen feet thick.

21. Modjeski and Masters, *Greater New Orleans Bridge No. 2,* pp. 7–33.

22. Ibid., p. 30.

23. See, for example, the October 1983 photograph on page 48 of Modjeski and Masters, *Greater New Orleans Bridge No. 2.*

24. Modjeski and Masters, *Greater New Orleans Bridge No. 2,* p. 65.

25. Paul Atkinson, "New Bridge a Cushy Ride on First Day," *New Orleans Times-Picayune,* October 1, 1988, pp. 1–4; Sandra Barbier, "For Bridge Buffs, It's a Natural High," *New Orleans Times-Picayune,* October 1, 1988, pp. 1–4.

26. Atkinson, "New Bridge a Cushy Ride on First Day," pp. 1–4; Barbier, "For Bridge Buffs, It's a Natural High," pp. 1–4.

17. Troubles Wash Ashore

1. John Hall, "Oil Prices Plunge, Threaten Louisiana's Recovery," *New Orleans Times-Picayune,* October 1, 1988, p. 1.

2. Joe Darby, "Economic Data Show Contrasts in Jefferson Parish," *New Orleans Times-Picayune*, July 3, 1991, Sec. B, pp. 1–2

3. William Conner and John W. Day, *The Ecology of Barataria Basin, Louisiana: An Estuarine Profile* (US Department of the Interior—Fish and Wildlife Service, Biological Report 87(7.13), 1987), graphs on page 135.

4. Thomas A. Becnel, *The Barrow Family and the Barataria and Lafourche Canal: The Transportation Revolution in Louisiana, 1829–1925* (Baton Rouge: Louisiana State University Press, 1989), p. 27.

5. Jason Theriot, "Building America's First Offshore Oil Port: LOOP," *The Journal of American History* 99 no. 1 (May 2012): 188–96.

6. A. J. Liebling, *The Earl of Louisiana* (New York: Ballantine Books, 1960), pp. 59–60.

7. Ray M. Thompson, "Oil: The Biggest Little Word in the World," *Jefferson Parish Yearly Review* (Kenner, LA, 1955), pp. 62–95; quote on page 87.

8. Theriot, "Building America's First Offshore Oil Port: LOOP," p. 190.

9. For more on sedimentary faults and coastal land loss, see the research of New Orleans–area scientists Nancye Dawers, Mark Kulp, Krista Jankowski, and David Culpepper, among others. For more on the role of the oil and gas industry, see the work of LSU coastal scientist Gene Turner.

10. B. R. Couvillion, Holly Beck, Donald Schoolmaster, and Michelle Fischer, *Land Area Change in Coastal Louisiana, 1932 to 2016: U.S. Geological Survey Scientific Investigations Map 3381* (2017), pp. 4, 11, https://doi.org/10.3133/sim3381.

11. Jefferson Parish Economic Development Commission, *Churchill Technology & Business Park Master Plan* (Jefferson Parish, February 2019), online www.jedco.org, visited April 7, 2019.

12. Isaac Cline, as quoted in "New Orleans is Getting Hotter—Increases in Temperature in Summer Attributed to the Drainage System," *Columbus Ledger-Enquirer* (Columbus, GA), June 13, 1918, p. 1, column 3.

13. "Many Lives Taken in Great Storm on Lower Coast; Twenty-Three Known Dead in Towns on the Lower River," *New Orleans Times-Picayune*, October 1, 1915, p. 2; Richard Campanella, *Bienville's Dilemma: A Historical Geography of New Orleans* (Lafayette: University of Louisiana Press, 2008), pp. 315–18.

14. "New Peters Road Opened with Official Ceremonies," *New Orleans Times-Picayune*, September 22, 1947, p. 31.

15. US Army Engineer District, New Orleans. *Hurricane Betsy, September 8–11, 1965, Serial No. 1880* (New Orleans, November 1965), p. 13.

16. US Army Engineer District, New Orleans. *Hurricane Betsy*, p. 24.

17. Gene Bourg, "Johnson Calls, Renews Aid Vow," *New Orleans Times-Picayune*, September 12, 1965, pp. 1–2.

18. Fred Barry, "Grand Isle But Wasteland Now," *New Orleans Times-Picayune*, September 12, 1965, pp. 1, 20.

19. Public Law 89–298, 89th Congress, S. 2300, Flood Control Act, General Projects, October 27, 1965.

20. US Government Accountability Office, "Army Corps of Engineers Lake Pontchartrain and Vicinity Hurricane Protection Project," Statement of Anu Mittal, Director, Natural Resources and

Environment, Testimony Before the Subcommittee on Energy and Water Development, Committee on Appropriations, House of Representatives, September 28, 2005, p. 1.

21. Southeast Louisiana Flood Protection Authority—West / West Jefferson Levee District / Algiers Levee District, "History," https://slfpaw.org/home/about-us/history/, visited November 8, 2018 (emphasis added).

22. Frank Renaudin, as quoted by Robert Rhoden, "Levee Takeover Debated," *Times-Picayune/ States-Item,* July 9, 1986, p. B-3.

23. US Army Corps of Engineers New Orleans District, *West Bank of the Mississippi River in the Vicinity of New Orleans, La. (East of the Harvey Canal) Feasibility Report and Environmental Impact Statement, Volume 1* (Department of the Army, Office of the Chief of Engineers, Washington, DC, 1994), pp. 15–16.

24. Bruce Nolan, "Residents Evacuate as Levees Fail," *New Orleans Times-Picayune/States-Item,* October 30, 1985, p. 1.

25. Ibid., p. 6.

26. Bruce Nolan, "On Those Man-Made Flood Losses," *New Orleans Times-Picayune/States-Item,* October 25, 1986, p. A-21.

27. Southeast Louisiana Flood Protection Authority, "History."

28. Southeast Louisiana Flood Protection Authority—West / West Jefferson Levee District / Algiers Levee District, "West Bank Hurricane Protection: Before and After," September 14, 2015, https://slfpaw.org/west-bank-hurricane-protection-before-and-after/, visited November 10, 2018.

29. National Oceanographic and Atmospheric Administration, Slosh Windfield-Envelope of High Water Graph for Katrina 2005, featured in "Katrina's Storm Surge: A Weather Underground 16-Part Series About Hurricane Katrina," by Margie Kieper, Weather Underground, https://www .wunderground.com/hurricane/Katrinas_surge_contents.asp, visited November 10, 2018.

30. US Army Corps of Engineers, New Orleans District, "Risk Reduction Plan: Background Information," https://www.mvn.usace.army.mil/Missions/HSDRRS/Risk-Reduction-Plan/, visited November 14, 2018.

31. US Army Corps of Engineers, New Orleans District, *Elevations for Design of Hurricane Protection Levees and Structures, Lake Pontchartrain and Vicinity, West Bank and Vicinity, and New Orleans to Venice, Louisiana Projects,* Report Version 2.0, December 2014, p. 10; Southeast Louisiana Flood Protection Authority, "West Bank Hurricane Protection: Before and After"; "The West Closure Complex: How It Works," NOLA.com/*Times-Picayune,* October 19, 2015, https://www.nola.com/ environment/index.ssf/2015/10/the_west_closure_complex_how_i.html, visited November 16, 2018.

32. Mark Schleifstein, "Gustav could be deadly Katrina-Rita hybrid," NOLA.com/*Times-Picayune,* August 30, 2008, https://www.nola.com/hurricane/index.ssf/2008/08/gustav_could_be_deadly_ katrina.html, visited November 16, 2018.

33. Leslie Williams, "Nagin Orders Evacuation in Face of 'Mother of All Storms,'" NOLA.com/ *Times-Picayune,* August 30, 2008, https://www.nola.com/hurricane/index.ssf/2008/08/new_orleans _evacuation_ordered.html.

34. US Army Corps of Engineers, "Hurricane Isaac with and without 2012 100-Year HSDRRS Evaluation," October 2012, public report, https://www.hsdl.org/?abstract&did=725551.

35. *The New York Times* featured Lafitte's story on the front page of its coverage of Louisiana's coastal crisis on February 25, 2018. Quote from Chad Calder, "Lafitte Area Gets $23 Million for Flood Protection Projects," *New Orleans Advocate,* January 30, 2019, https://www.theadvocate.com/new_orleans/news/article_9a4c69d0–24c0–11e9–8583–ff2750090fa8.html .

18. From Suburbia to Ethno-Urbia

1. Jessica Williams, "N.O. Voters More Content Than in Decades," *New Orleans Advocate,* November 29, 2018, pp. 1–4.

2. Christopher A. Airriess, "Creating Vietnamese Landscapes and Place in New Orleans," *Geographical Identities of Ethnic America: Race, Space, and Place,* ed. Kate A. Berry and Martha L. Henderson (Reno and Las Vegas: University of Nevada Press, 2002), pp. 230–34, and other sources.

3. Joan Treadway, "Resettlement Begins Here for Nineteen Vietnamese," *New Orleans Times-Picayune,* May 27, 1975, sec. A, p. 1.

4. Indo-Chinese Refugee Resettlement Task Force, *Impact Analysis of Indo-Chinese Resettlement in the New Orleans Metropolitan Area: A Task Force Study* (New Orleans: Study prepared for Mayor Ernest N. Morial, 1979), Appendix A: Indo-Chinese Refugee Program.

5. Airriess, "Creating Vietnamese Landscapes and Place in New Orleans," p. 233.

6. As quoted by Marc Leepson, "Delta to Delta," *Preservation* 52, no. 1 (January–February 2000): 46.

7. Wade R. Ragas and Vincent Maruggi, *Vietnamese Refugee Living Conditions in the New Orleans Metro Area: Working Paper No. 111* (New Orleans: University of New Orleans Division of Business and Economic Research, 1978), p. 6.

8. Alma H. Young, "Vietnamese-Black Interaction in New Orleans: A Preliminary Assessment," in *Perspectives on Ethnicity in New Orleans,* ed. John Cooke (New Orleans: Committee on Ethnicity in New Orleans, 1980), p. 55; Indo-Chinese Refugee Resettlement Task Force, *Impact Analysis of Indo-Chinese Resettlement in the New Orleans Metropolitan Area: A Task Force Study* (New Orleans: Study prepared for Mayor Ernest N. Morial, 1979), pp. 12–14.

9. Martha C. Ward and Zachary Gussow, "The Vietnamese in New Orleans: A Preliminary Report," in *Perspectives on Ethnicity in New Orleans,* ed. John Cooke (New Orleans: Committee on Ethnicity in New Orleans, 1979), pp. 39–40.

10. Center for the Pacific Rim, University of New Orleans, *The Asian Peoples of Southern Louisiana: An Ethnohistory* (US Department of the Interior, Jean Lafitte National Historical Park, 1990), pp. 247–48.

11. Joan Treadway and Coleman Warner, "East Meets West," *Times-Picayune,* August 6, 2001, sec. A, p. 1–7

12. Airriess, "Creating Vietnamese Landscapes and Place in New Orleans," pp. 20–21.

13. US Census Bureau, 2010 Census, digital files of block-level data analyzed by author, of urbanized West Bank across three parishes from Waggaman to Belle Chasse.

14. Coleman Warner, "Many Asians Drawn to Bounty of Seafood in Waters of Lower Plaquemines Parish," *Times-Picayune,* August 6, 2001, sec. A, p. 1.

15. Reena Shah, "A Touch of Vietnam on the Mississippi: Refugees Push to Succeed in Louisiana," *St. Petersburg Times,* December 25, 1988, p. 1A.

16. Judy Laborde, "Vietnamese Immigrants Define What U.S. Means," Readers' Views, *New Orleans Advocate,* December 18, 2018, p. 4B.

17. This is based on the US Census survey-based American Community Survey five-year estimates ending in 2016, which found that 0.94 percent of the 40,264 people living in the 70056 zip code identified as an Arab ethnic group. The largest Arab population was in Metairie.

18. Arab American Institute Foundation, "Louisiana Fact Sheet" (Arab American Institute Foundation, 2011), http://www.aaiusa.org/state-profiles.

19. Helen Freund, "Market Share: West Bank Mercados Offer International Flavors, Opportunities for Immigrants," *Gambit,* August 7–13, 2018, p. 14.

20. Tri Cung, as quoted by Freund, "Market Share: West Bank Mercados Offer International Flavors," pp. 14–16.

21. Amanda Kolson Hurley, "2018 Was the Year of the Complicated Suburb," *Citylab,* December 21, 2018, https://www.citylab.com/equity/2018/12/suburbs-urban-density-politics-demographics/578779/, visited December 21, 2018.

22. GIS analysis by author using 2000 and 2010 US Census data at the block level; all figures exclude the North Shore, the river parishes, and rural outskirts.

23. Faimon A. Roberts III, "Language Barrier: In Jefferson Schools, Growing Diversity Brings Challenges," *New Orleans Advocate,* December 22, 2018, pp. 1–7; Jeff Adelson, "Black Share of Population Growing in Suburbs, Shrinking in Orleans Parish, Census Bureau Reports," *New Orleans Advocate,* June 25, 2015, p. 1.

24. "Algiers, a City with a History—Fifth District Has as Much Romance as the Metropolis It Flanks—Good Place to Live," *Daily Picayune,* December 30, 1913, p. 32.

19. Cross-Bank Relations

1. Mark Ballard, "Bills Would Allow Algiers to Secede from City of New Orleans; Here's What's Next," *Baton Rouge Advocate,* May 15, 2015, http://www.theadvocate.com/baton_rouge/news/politics/legislature/article_aa9ddc81–1442–56f9-a9ae-4dcc171811ae.html.

2. "Aggravated Algiers—Why She is Unhappy in her Union with New Orleans," *New Orleans Times,* October 2, 1877, p. 3.

3. "City Matters," *Daily Picayune,* March 19, 1878, p. 2.

4. "Two-Parish Move," *New Orleans Times-Picayune,* May 4, 1950, p. 10.

5. Andrea Shaw, "Crescent City Connection tolls eliminated for good after referendum fails," NOLA.com/*Times-Picayune,* May 4, 2013, https://www.nola.com/politics/index.ssf/2013/05/crescent_city_connection_tolls_9.html visited December 19, 2018.

6. Analysis by author. These figures do not include early voters, whose precincts and banks could not be ascertained.

7. GIS analysis by author, originally published in a guest editorial titled "Democracy and Geography: Reflections on the Crescent City Connection Toll Referendum," by Richard Campanella, *New Orleans Times-Picayune,* November 25, 2012.

8. Shaw, "Crescent City Connection tolls eliminated."

9. Ibid.

10. Andrea Shaw, "Huey P. Long Bridge Widening to End Steering-Wheel Death Grip," NOLA .com/*Times-Picayune*, June 13, 2013.

11. "Major Bridge Widening Project Going to Plan," *World Highways*, October 2011, http://www. worldhighways.com/sections/key-projects/features/major-bridge-widening-project-going-to-plan/, visited December 19, 2018, and other sources.

12. Andrea Shaw, "Huey P. Long Bridge Expansion Opens 9,000 Acres to New Development, New Name," NOLA.com/*Times-Picayune*, June 15, 2013, https://www.nola.com/business/index .ssf/2013/06/huey_p_long_bridge_expansion_o.html, visited December 20, 2018 (italics added).

13. Shaw, "Huey P. Long Bridge Expansion Opens 9,000 Acres."

14. "Churchill Farm Nurseries Offer Written Guarantee to Protect Customer from Any Possible Loss," *New Orleans Times-Picayune*, July 14, 1929, sec. 2, p. 6.

15. "Churchill Farm Rule Stands," *New Orleans Times-Picayune*, June 15, 1971, p. 6.

16. Dean Baquet and Jim Amoss, "Marcello Tape Recalls La. Politics in Good 'Ol Days," *New Orleans Times-Picayune*, June 6, 1981, pp. 1–4.

17. Ibid.

18. Ramon Antonio Vargas, "Prominent Jefferson Parish Landowner Sells $13.5 Million Tract to Levee Board for Tree-Planting Project," *New Orleans Advocate*, September 14, 2016; George Lardner Jr., "Investigator Detailed Mafia Leaders' Threat Against Kennedy," *Washington Post*, July 21, 1979.

19. Chad Calder, "Council Defers Vote on Cyanide Plant Permit," *New Orleans Advocate*, March 21, 2019, p. 1B.

20. Faimon A. Roberts III, "Avondale Shipyard Purchased: Partnership to Bring Site into 'New Era,' Gov. Edwards Says," *New Orleans Advocate*, October 4, 2018, https://www.theadvocate.com/ new_orleans/news/business/article_07386d62-c776–11e8–8482-b78ac0798227.html, visited December 20, 2018.

21. Drew Broach, "5 years later, West Jefferson Awaits Boom from Huey P. Long Bridge Expansion," NOLA.com/*Times-Picayune*, June 21, 2018, https://www.nola.com/expo/news/erry-2018/ 06/1cb797e49c2984/huey_p_long_bridge_expansion_u.html, visited December 21, 2018.

22. Drew Broach, "New Subdivision at Waggaman Proposed 3 Months after Avondale Shipyard Sale," NOLA.com/*Times-Picayune*, January 10, 2019, https://www.nola.com/business/2019/01/new-subdivision-at-waggaman-proposed-3-months-after-avondale-shipyard-sale.html, visited January 10, 2019.

23. Jefferson Parish Economic Development Commission, *Churchill Technology & Business Park Master Plan* (Jefferson Parish, Louisiana, February 2019), www.jedco.org, visited April 7, 2019.

24. Jeff Adelson, "Census Estimates Show N.O. Shrinking; Numbers Dip for First Time Since Katrina," *New Orleans Advocate*, April 18, 2019, p. 1.

25. "Plans Country Home on Plantation in City," *New Orleans States*, April 19, 1930, p. 5; Iroquois Research Institute, *Cultural Resources Survey of Fourteen Mississippi Levee and Revetment Items* (New Orleans: Department of the Army, Corps of Engineers, 1982), p. 55.

26. "Sugar Roots Farm—What We Do," https://www.sugarrootsfarm.org/about-us/, visited December 25, 2018.

27. "About A Studio in the Woods," https://www.astudiointhewoods.org/about_asitw.html, visited December 25, 2018.

20. The West Banks of the World

1. Historian Thomas J. Sugrue uses the term "second-hand suburbs" to mean developments originally intended for white middle-class homeowners fleeing the inner city that were later largely abandoned by that demographic and are now increasingly home to working-class people of color, many of them renters. Thomas J. Sugrue, "The Origins of the Suburban Crisis," lecture at Tulane University School of Architecture, April 17, 2019, attended by author.

2. Amanda Holson Hurley, *Radical Suburbs: Experimental Living on the Fringes of the American City* (Cleveland: Belt Publishing, 2019), p. 26.

3. Ellen Dunham-Jones and June Williamson, *Retrofitting Suburbia: Urban Design Solutions for Redesigning Suburbs* (Hoboken, NJ: John Wiley & Sons, 2011).

4. John Hogan, *Thoughts About the City of St. Louis, Her Commerce and Manufacturers, Railroads, Etc.* (St. Louis: Republican Steam Press, 1854), p. 13. I thank Lawrence N. Powell for bringing this document to my attention.

5. Meeting Minutes, Office of the Police Jury, Parish of Jefferson, April 7, 1887. The Historical Records Survey, *Transcription of Parish Records of Louisiana: No. 26, Jefferson Parish (Gretna): Series 1 Police Jury Minutes Vol. V. 1879–1888* (Division of Professional and Service Projects, Work Projects Administration, April 1940), p. 331; Mary Grace Curry, *Gretna—A Sesquicentennial Salute* (Jefferson Parish Historical Commission, 1986), p. 10.

6. Walter Prescott Webb, *The Great Plains* (Lincoln: University of Nebraska Press, 1981), pp. 140–41, 184–85, and 201, as quoted by Robert D. Kaplan, *Earning the Rockies: How Geography Shapes America's Role in the World* (New York: Random House, 2017), p. 93.

7. Based on author's conversations with Lawrence N. Powell as well as his 2017 paper, "You Are Who You Trade With: Why Antebellum St. Louis Industrialized but New Orleans Didn't," scheduled to appear in *A French City in Colonial North America: Essays on Early St. Louis,* ed. Jay Gitlin and Peter Kantor (University of Nebraska Press), forthcoming 2020.

8. Federal Writers' Project of the Works Progress Administration, *New Orleans City Guide* (Boston: Houghton Mifflin Company, 1938), p. 358.

9. National Register of Historic Places Database, US Department of the Interior, *Algiers Point Historic District* (August 1, 1978), unpaginated report, https://www.crt.state.la.us/dataprojects/hp/nhl/view.asp.

10. GIS analysis by author, using US Census American Community Survey estimates of nativity by state, 2005–2009, aggregated at the census tract level.

11. Jefferson Parish Tax Assessors geospatial portal, http://geoportal.jeffparish.net/public.

Appendix 2. Timeline: Historical Geography of the West Bank

1. Kathleen DuVal, "Interconnectedness and Diversity in 'French Louisiana,'" in *Powhatan's Mantle: Indians in the Colonial Southeast,* ed. Gregory A. Waselkov, Peter H. Wood, and Tom Hatley (Lincoln: University of Nebraska Press, 2006), p. 138.

2. "Notes on the Census of New Orleans for January 1732" and supplement "List of Landowners," as transcribed by Charles R. Maduell Jr. in *The Census Tables for the French Colony of Louisiana from 1699 to 1732* (Baltimore: Genealogical Publishing Company, 1972), p. 147.

3. Kathleen Gilmore and Vergil E. Noble, *Archeological Testing at Fort St. Leon (16PL35), Plaquemines Parish, Louisiana* (New Orleans: US Army Corps of Engineers, 1983), pp. i–48.

4. Ibid., p. 10.

5. David Fritz and Sally K. Reeves, *Algiers Point: Historical Ambience and Property Analysis of Squares Ten, Thirteen, and Twenty, with a View toward Their Archaeological Potential* (New Orleans: Department of the Army, Corps of Engineers, June 1984), pp. 52–53.

6. Arthur Scully Jr., *James Dakin, Architect: His Career in New York and the South* (Baton Rouge: Louisiana State University Press, 1973), p. 63; William H. Seymour, *The Story of Algiers, Now the Fifth District of New Orleans* (Algiers Democrat Publishing Company, 1896), p. 33; *Historical Sketch Book and Guide to New Orleans and Environs* (New York: Will H. Coleman, 1885), p. 289.

7. Fritz and Reeves, *Algiers Point: Historical Ambience,* p. 11.

8. "Land Slide at Algiers," *Lafayette City Advertiser,* February 26, 1842, p. 2, as cited in Fritz and Reeves, *Algiers Point: Historical Ambience,* pp. 4–5.

9. Maj. David W. Kummer, *The Historic LeBeuf Plantation House and the Marine Corps in New Orleans: A Shared History* (Quantico, VA: History Division, United States Marine Corps, 2013), Appendix A.

10. William D. Reeves in *Destrehan/Harvey History Manuscript-Binder 1* (unpublished manuscript, Farnet Family Collection), chap. 3, p. 4.

11. *History of the Fire Department of New Orleans, From the Earliest Days to the Present Time,* ed. Thomas O'Connor (New Orleans, 1895), p. 142.

12. Police Jury of the Parish of Jefferson Minute Book, Meeting of July 2, 1877, in *Transcriptions of Parish Records of Louisiana, No. 26 Jefferson Parish,* (The Historical Records Survey, Works Progress Administration, 1940), p. 402.

13. Fritz and Reeves, *Algiers Point: Historical Ambience,* p. 55.

14. Mark Reutter and J. Parker Lamb in "Crescent City Bound," *Railroad History* 193, Fall–Winter 2005–2006, p. 14; "'The Gouldsboro'—Arrival of the New Rail Ferryboat for the New Orleans Pacific Railroad," *Daily Picayune,* December 31, 1881, p. 8.

15. *Historical Sketch Book and Guide to New Orleans and Environs* (New York: Will H. Coleman, 1885), pp. 279, 289.

16. *Biographical and Historical Memoirs of Louisiana, Volume I* (Chicago: The Goodspeed Publishing Company, 1892), p. 239; Mary Grace Curry, *Gretna—A Sesquicentennial Salute* (Jefferson Parish Historical Commission, 1986), p. 11.

17. Ibid., p. 14.

18. "A Large Fire on the Aurora Plantation," *Daily Picayune,* November 25, 1896, p. 9.

19. Orleans Parish School Board, *The New Orleans Book* (New Orleans: Searcy & Pfaff, Ltd, 1919), pp. 66–67; Kummer, *The Historic LeBeuf Plantation House,* Appendix A.

20. LeRoy L. Hall, "Final Report of the Jefferson Parish Police Jury," *Jefferson Parish Yearly Review* (Kenner, LA, 1954), p. 23.

21. "'Over the River': Work Formally Begun on the Algiers Oil Well," *Daily Picayune,* June 21, 1902, p. 7.

22. "Westwego Village Swept by a Disastrous Fire," *Daily Picayune,* April 15, 1907, p. 13; *New Orleans Item,* "Provisions Needed for the Fire Victims," April 15, 1907, p. 1.

23. Orleans Parish School Board, *The New Orleans Book* (New Orleans: Searcy & Pfaff, Ltd, 1919), pp. 66–67; Fritz and Reeves, *Algiers Point,* p. 48.

24. Hall, "Final Report of the Jefferson Parish Police Jury," p. 24.

25. "Completed Crib Backs Up Levee at Danger Point; Work at Stanton Plantation Proves Satisfactory," *Times-Picayune,* May 25, 1922, p. 3.

26. Weaver R. Toledano, "We Wanted Progress," *Jefferson Parish Yearly Review* (Kenner, LA, 1952), p. 13.

27. "Bodenger to Give Land for Bog Algiers Park," *New Orleans States,* August 27, 1925, p. 4; Richard Remy Dixon, *Old Algiers: A Story of Algiers, Yesterday and Today* (New Orleans: Algiers Annexation Centennial Committee, 1980), p. 80.

28. US Army Corps of Engineers, New Orleans District, *Water Resources Development in Louisiana* (US Army Corps of Engineers, New Orleans District, 1995), p. 97.

29. Toledano, "We Wanted Progress," p. 13.

30. Ray M. Thompson, "Oil: The Biggest Little Word in the World," *Jefferson Parish Yearly Review* (Kenner, LA, 1955), pp. 62–95.

31. "Silver Span for a Golden Future," *Jefferson Parish Yearly Review* (Kenner, LA, 1950), p. 85; Toledano, "We Wanted Progress," p. 15.

32. Fritz and Reeves, *Algiers Point: Historical Ambience,* p. 48.

33. Toledano, "We Wanted Progress," p. 15.

34. Federal Writers' Project of the Works Progress Administration, *New Orleans City Guide* (Boston: Houghton Mifflin Company, 1938), pp. 175, 180.

35. George Schneider, "Industry's Opportunity," *Jefferson Parish Year Book* (Police Jury of Jefferson Parish, 1935), p. 25

36. Thompson, "Oil: The Biggest Little Word in the World," pp. 62–95.

37. "West Bank Population, Housing Jump Reported," *New Orleans Times-Picayune,* June 25, 1956, p. 18.

38. Arthur Charbonnet, "Marrero: The Arc of Achievement," *Jefferson Parish Yearly Review* (Kenner, LA, 1951), pp. 49–57.

39. William J. White, "A Report on Gretna," *Jefferson Parish Yearly Review* (Kenner, LA, 1951), p. 153; William J. White, "Gretna Prepares for the Bridge," *Jefferson Parish Yearly Review* (Kenner, LA, 1955), p. 181.

40. R. J. Duplantis, "Go Ahead with Westwego," *Jefferson Parish Yearly Review* (Kenner, LA, 1951), p. 175.

41. Heidi Tyline King, *We Power Life: Entergy's First Century* (St. Louis, MO: Essex Publishing Group, 2013), p. 59.

42. William J. White, "Gretna: The Pulse of the Parish," *Jefferson Parish Yearly Review* (Kenner, LA, 1954), pp. 173–181.

43. "West Bank Population, Housing Jump Reported," *New Orleans Times-Picayune,* June 25, 1956, p. 18.

44. Lender Perez, "The Land of the Blue Goose," *Jefferson Parish Yearly Review* (Kenner, LA, 1956), p. 244.

45. Thompson, "Oil: The Biggest Little Word in the World," pp. 62–95; quote on page 87.

46. "Jefferson: The Fastest Growing Parish in Booming Louisiana," *Jefferson Parish Yearly Review* (Kenner, LA, 1957), p. 53.

47. Hall, "Final Report of the Jefferson Parish Police Jury," p. 28.

48. "Part II, Progress Report," *Jefferson Parish Yearly Review* (Kenner, LA, 1956), p. 26.

49. US Army Corps of Engineers, *Water Resources Development in Louisiana*, p. 98.

50. Hall, "Final Report of the Jefferson Parish Police Jury," p. 22.

51. Computed by author from listings in Chamber of Commerce of the New Orleans Area, *Directory of Manufacturers Employing Fifty or More People* (New Orleans: Chamber of Commerce, Research and Statistics Department, 1963).

52. William J. White, "Gretna," *Jefferson Parish Yearly Review* (Kenner, LA, 1974–1975 issue), p. 24; William J. White, "Jefferson's Capital City—Gretna," *Jefferson Parish Yearly Review* (Kenner, LA, 1964), p. 171; "Transportation: Parish Prepared for Interurbia," *Jefferson Parish Yearly Review* (Jefferson Parish: Parish Publications, Inc. 1969–1970 edition), p. 69.

53. René Pierre Meric Jr. and Philip J. Meric, *Avondale, A Model for Success: The Story of a Great American Shipyard* (New Orleans: Philip J. Meric Consulting, 2015), pp. 106–107.

54. Joe Darby, "May 3 Yardstick in Jeff Replaced by April 13, 1980," *New Orleans Times-Picayune*, April 14, 1980, p. 1.

55. West Bank Bureau, "Expressway Work to Expand," *New Orleans Times-Picayune*, July 30, 1983, sec. 1, p. 15.

56. GIS analysis by author using 2000 US Census data at the block level. All figures exclude North Shore, river parishes, and rural outskirts.

57. Allen Powell II, "Celotex Park facility on Fourth Street in Marrero To Be Redeveloped," *Times-Picayune*, August 25, 2010, https://www.nola.com/business/2010/08/celotex_park_facility _on_fourt.html.

58. GIS analysis by author using 2010 US Census data at the block level. Area studied includes tri-parish conurbation on each bank (Waggaman to Belle Chasse on West Bank; Kenner to Mereaux on East Bank), and excludes North Shore, river parishes, and rural outskirts.

Index